CONSTRUCTION SCHEDULING
PRINCIPLES AND PRACTICES

Jay S. Newitt

Brigham Young University

Upper Saddle River, New Jersey
Columbus, Ohio

Library of Congress Cataloging in Publication Data

Newitt, Jay S.

    Construction scheduling : principles and practices / Jay S. Newitt.— 1st ed.

      p. cm.

    Includes index.

    ISBN 0–13–113337–3 (casebound)

    1. Building industry—Management. 2. Building—Superintendence. 3. Production scheduling. I. Title.

TH438.4.N48 2005

690'.068'5—dc22

2004042071

Executive Editor: Ed Francis
Editorial Assistant: Jennifer Day
Project Coordination: Carlisle Publishers Services
Production Editor: Holly Shufeldt
Design Coordinator: Diane Ernsberger
Cover Designer: Jeff Vanik
Cover art: Index Stock
Production Manager: Deidra Schwartz
Marketing Manager: Mark Marsden

This book was set in Janson Text by Carlisle Communications, Ltd. It was printed and bound by R. R. Donnelley & Sons Company. The cover was printed by The Lehigh Press, Inc.

Primavera Project Planner® and SureTrak® are registered trademarks of Primavera Systems, Inc.
P3e/c™ is a trademark of Primavera Systems, Inc.
Microsoft Project® is a registered trademark of Microsoft Corporation in the United States and/or other countries.

Pearson Education Ltd.
Pearson Education Singapore Pte. Ltd.
Pearson Education Canada, Ltd.
Pearson Education—Japan

Pearson Education Australia Pty. Limited
Pearson Education North Asia Ltd.
Pearson Education de Mexico, S.A. de C.V.
Pearson Education Malaysia Pte. Ltd.

10 9 8 7 6 5 4 3 2 1
ISBN 0-13-113337-3

PREFACE

Anyone involved in the management of projects will find this text useful; however, it is written specifically for managers in the construction industry and students preparing for management positions. Therefore, the examples are construction related. However, this text would be extremely helpful to anyone in a project management position in manufacturing, engineering, computer and software design, technology, military or business management.

The text contains comprehensive and practical information on the subject of scheduling, everything from checklists to the practical uses of CPM, including instructions on the four most popular project management software programs (Primavera Project Planner, SureTrak, P3e/c, and Microsoft Project). The text focuses on the basics of using the Critical Path Method (CPM) to plan and schedule projects and explains the use of CPM the way project managers use it. It is based on practical experience rather than research and theory. The emphasis is on managing a project rather than focusing on the details of CPM, getting lost in those details, and forgetting that the purpose of the schedule is to help manage and control a project.

The techniques discussed have been used by project managers in a variety of projects, from throughout the nation and from students the author has taught for over 25 years in a four-year construction management curriculum at a major university. The author has consulted with and provided in-house training to over 150 construction companies and trained literally thousands of managers on these principles and techniques.

The last four chapters in the book contain practical instructions on how to use Primavera Project Planner (P3), P3e/c, SureTrak, and Microsoft Project. The software instructions are project driven, rather than software driven. The instructions are based on how managers use the software, rather than explaining every detail on every screen, in the order the screens appear. These chapters contain examples and assignments that teach how to use the software to communicate and manage the project.

There is a CD included with the text that has example schedules for each of the software packages discussed. The CD also contains an automated checklist created with Microsoft Excel that some managers may find useful. In addition, the CD also contains an example bar chart created with Microsoft Excel.

It is the author's sincere hope that the ideas and information contained in this book will be able to help project managers gain better control of their projects and thus their life. It is the author's desire that through the application of these ideas and techniques the manager will have more time to spend with family and loved ones rather than living at the project site. As managers of major projects we must learn and apply methods to improve the management of our projects without spending excessive hours each week doing so. It is time we learn to manage and control the project rather than allowing it to manage and control us. This book contains ideas to help us to work *smarter* so that we can play *harder*.

Appreciation is expressed to my wife Sylvia and our six children: Jayson, Alisa, Jennifer (who edited the entire original manuscript), Chris, Jalyn, and Jarica for their support and patience during the writing of the text.

Particular thanks are due to Dr. Neil Eldin, Texas A & M University, Charles R. Glagola, University of Florida, and James Stein, Eastern Michigan University, for their assistance with the text review.

As you read this text book and have any comments or suggestions, the author would be pleased to hear from you. For professors using the text, the sharing of a course syllabus would also be appreciated.

Jay S. Newitt
jay_newitt@byu.edu

CONTENTS

CHAPTER 3

CHECKLISTS, DAILY TO-DO LISTS, AND MAGNETIC SCHEDULING BOARDS   19

CHAPTER 4

BAR CHART SCHEDULES   31

CHAPTER 5

INTRODUCTION TO CPM SCHEDULING 43

CHAPTER 6

CREATING THE NETWORK LOGIC DIAGRAM 53

CHAPTER

DETERMINING DURATIONS   67

CHAPTER

CALCULATING START AND FINISH DATES   75

CHAPTER 9

CALCULATING TOTAL, SHARED, FREE, INDEPENDENT, AND NEGATIVE FLOAT   91

CHAPTER 10

USING LAGS IN NETWORK LOGIC DIAGRAMS   **107**

CHAPTER 11

REVIEWING AND ANALYZING THE SCHEDULE   **119**

CHAPTER 12

CREATING BAR CHARTS AND TABULAR REPORTS FROM NETWORK LOGIC DIAGRAMS   129

CHAPTER 13

LINEAR OR LINE-OF-BALANCE SCHEDULES   149

CHAPTER 16

COST SCHEDULE CONTROL SYSTEM CRITERIA (C/SCSC)   187

CHAPTER 17

CREATING TEAMWORK AND GETTING SUBCONTRACTORS TO
CONFORM TO THE SCHEDULE   195

CHAPTER 18

OTHER SCHEDULING TECHNIQUES 205

CHAPTER 19

INTRODUCTION TO COMPUTERIZED CPM SCHEDULING 217

CHAPTER **20**

MANAGING PROJECTS USING PRIMAVERA PROJECT PLANNER (P3)   225

CHAPTER 21

MANAGING PROJECTS USING SURETRAK   273

CHAPTER 22

MANAGING PROJECTS USING MICROSOFT PROJECT 319

CHAPTER **23**

MANAGING PROJECTS USING P3E/C   355

CHAPTER 1

Overview of Project Management Basics

INTRODUCTION

It is commonly assumed that the process of scheduling a construction project focuses predominately on time. However, focusing on time alone often excludes other important project objectives. Whereas this textbook covers the various principles and practices of construction scheduling, this chapter addresses the overall objectives of project management—some more important than time for certain projects. This chapter also discusses the importance of balance in meeting all the major project objectives, not just the time element.

FOUR PRIMARY OBJECTIVES OF PROJECT MANAGEMENT

Before discussing why and how to schedule, it is important to review the primary objectives of project management to ensure the schedule will meet those objectives. The best schedule is not the schedule showing the project completed in the shortest time period, it is the schedule that meets the primary objectives of the total project. Those primary objectives are to create a **quality** project, completed on **time,** within **budget,** and in a **safe** work environment. All four of these objectives must be considered in planning and scheduling a project (see Figure 1.1).

Quality

It is essential to meet or exceed the customers' expectations relating to the quality of the project. If a company wants continued work in the future, quality cannot be sacrificed in order to meet time, safety, or budget constraints. If quality is the driving force

FIGURE 1.1 The best schedule balances time, cost, quality, and safety

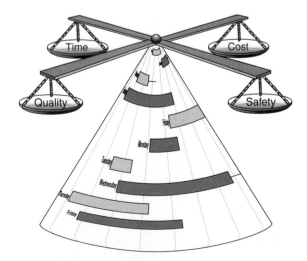

of a project, it will take longer than normal to complete and costs will increase. The quality expectations must be managed with realistic goals if time and cost objectives must also be met. Many managers can complete a "perfect" project if given an unlimited budget and an unlimited amount of time, but that is simply not realistic.

Time

If time is the driving force of the project, it must be done very quickly, quality cannot be maintained at the same level, quality decreases. Costs increase due to the need for working overtime or for excessive numbers of people, which decreases productivity. Safety is also compromised because there is not time to use proper safety equipment or restraints. When tradespeople are pressured to work rapidly, they work carelessly and take unnecessary chances.

Budget or Costs

If costs become the driving force of a project, work must be done at the lowest cost possible and quality goes down. The project is built with inferior products using the least expensive workforce, which may not be sufficiently trained to do quality work. This creates a savings on the initial project even though it may increase the costs of the completed project over time because maintenance costs may be higher. Safety is also compromised because the company may not invest in the proper safety equipment or provide training to incorporate safe work habits.

Safety

If safety becomes the driving force, the project must be done in an extremely safe environment, and consequently, there are time increases due to the extra safe work conditions. Costs also increase because productivity drops in order to remove all potential risks. Safety is an extremely important project objective and safety must be considered in the development of the schedule. Make sure trades and activities are not creating a safety conflict with each other. Look particularly close at activities that are scheduled concurrent with each other.

CHALLENGE OF BALANCING THE MAJOR OBJECTIVES

One of the major challenges of project management is to balance time, cost, quality, and safety while ensuring a safe work environment. The manager must keep all of these in mind and not let the pressure of one decrease the effectiveness of the others. Some projects inevitably demand that more emphasis be placed on one of these objectives. The experienced manager nonetheless will keep them as closely balanced as possible. It is important for the manager who wants to satisfy all stakeholders to underpromise and overdeliver. If, at the outset, it is sensed that quality must be above the norm, the added costs and time must be determined and included in the estimate and the schedule to ensure the project's success. Moreover, if initially it is realized that the project must be completed in an unrealistic time frame the additional costs and safety precautions must also be planned for in advance, along with steps taken to ensure that the project's quality standards are met.

An architect and engineer may desire to create a one-of-a-kind, monumental type of project, without much concern for the costs or time it takes to build the project. The owner may want a quality project completed tomorrow at low costs. This is a tough balancing act for the project manager. Specifications alone will not guarantee the total quality of the completed project. The final quality standards are set by the entire team involved in the process, depending on the costs and time allowed. It is extremely difficult, if not impossible, to complete an exceptionally high-quality project unusually fast, at a low cost, and in a very safe work environment. The proper amount of compromising of these major objectives creates a delicate situation that the project manager must consider and handle carefully. The project time schedule must represent a realistic attempt at meeting all four of these primary objectives. Again, the best schedule is not the shortest; it is the schedule that meets the project's time, cost, quality, and safety objectives.

A fifth objective, which some managers state as an additional possible primary objective, is to complete the project without any litigation. Typically, if the four primary objectives are met, the possibility of litigation is greatly diminished. However, if the project is overbudget, not completed on time, does not meet the quality standards, or if there is a major accident on-site, there is an increased chance of litigation. The manager that meets the four primary objectives will largely be free of litigation without it becoming an additional concern.

HOW TO ACHIEVE THE PRIMARY OBJECTIVES

In order to meet the primary objectives, the management team should consider the following acronym: **PODC.** The "P" stands for **plan.** The team must have a plan for how they are going to accomplish each of the objectives. Some managers claim they don't have time to plan. Others realize that they don't have time *not* to plan. Proper planning is what gives them time to successfully manage projects. The "O" stands for **organize**. The team must organize everything to do with the project in order to meet the primary objectives. They must organize the job site for efficiency in receiving materials and staging equipment. They must be personally organized so they are not crisis driven.

The "D" stands for **direct.** The managers must give directions to all the participants so that the planning and organizing will be communicated to everyone. If there is a great plan and the team members are organized but no direction is given, the result will be failure. Stand up and give directions.

Take command and make decisions. There must be a leader with the vision of the entire project to direct the workforce. Finally, the "C" stands for **control.** The main objective of management is to control time, cost, and quality, while providing a safe work environment. If the management team is not planning, organizing, directing, and controlling, why are they there? This is the purpose of management, to do these critical things. To achieve control is very challenging, but successful managers find rewards and excitement in accomplishing this enormous challenge.

When a project is in trouble, it is important to take a close look at the PODC. A common comparison can be seen in the world of sports. When a football coach is being interviewed by the media right after a surprising and difficult loss, the coach is typically asked what he or she is going to do to recover from the loss and what will be the focus to prepare for next week's game. The coach may say, "This week we are going back to the basics and focus on those basics and we will be ready for the next game." In football the basics are blocking, tackling, passing, running, kicking, and knowing and following the play. In project management, the basics are time, cost, quality, and safety by planning, organizing, directing, and controlling. If a project is in trouble, look at these basics and see where the team is failing in their plan, their method of organizing the project and the workforce, the way they are directing the work to be done, and the controls they have put in place to monitor time, costs, quality, and safety.

As discussed at the beginning of this chapter, the schedule is a key piece of the puzzle because it interfaces with all of the project management basics. The schedule shows the plan of how the project is going to be built, helps the management team organize the workforce to build the project in an orderly manner, gives direction to all team members on how the team is going to accomplish the primary objectives, and helps managers control the time, cost, and quality of the project while providing a safe work environment.

BEING A MANAGER—ASSUMING THE RESPONSIBILITY

The construction industry, along with about every other type of business, is looking for leaders who are also managers. One principle of management that needs to be discussed is that the leader should not use the schedule to place blame on everyone else. The schedule should be used to motivate and communicate to the work team who is doing what, when, and where. It should not be used as a legal "club" to force others into compliance. This book stresses the point that the schedule is primarily to be a management tool.

In order for the manager to be a leader, it is essential that he or she be proactive. Poor managers blame problems on everyone but themselves. This stifles personal improvement and change. The manager will be more successful if he or she realizes that any problem on the job site is the manager's responsibility. If the subcontractor shows up late or does inferior work, it is the manager's fault. The manager must consider possible solutions: What could be done to eliminate that problem in the future? Was sufficient notice given? Was the job explained in sufficient detail? Was the schedule accurate and available to the subcontractor?

If a change is not communicated to the proper workers, it is the manager's fault. If materials are not delivered on time or are the incorrect materials, it is the manager's fault. If the plans are full of errors and omissions, it is the manager's fault. We all know the manager isn't directly at fault, but this approach will lead to solving problems, rather than blaming others and ensuring that the same problems will not occur on future jobs.

Proactive managers who realize that problems on the job site are their responsibility find techniques, methods, or systems to correct those problems in the future. They look more critically at the construction drawings in order to eliminats problems prior to the construction of that detail. They find ways to better communicate with subcontractors, suppliers, owners, inspectors, and so on to solve problems in advance. If they simply blame others, no progress will be made on future jobs. Many times the well-planned and executed schedule is a key to solving several of these problems.

CONCLUSION

This chapter emphasized the critical importance of scheduling to manage time, cost, and quality while maintaining a safe work environment. It also discussed the challenges that project managers face in meeting these four objectives. The acronym *PODC* represents the major tasks that managers must take responsibility for: plan, organize, direct, and control. All of these are accomplished through the schedule. Remember, the best schedule is the one that meets the primary objectives of the project, not the one with the quickest time line. Be proactive, assume the responsibility, and schedule to solve and avoid problems.

APPLICATION

If you are an experienced project manager, think about past projects you have been involved with that have overlooked the concepts covered in this chapter. Consider the impact the application of these concepts would have had if they had been employed. Take seriously the idea that you, as a member of the management team, are responsible for the problems encountered during the project life cycle and take a proactive approach to eliminate similar problems on future projects. Would an accurate and detailed schedule that considered these concepts have eliminated some of the problems of past projects?

If you are a student and have not yet had the opportunity to be involved with project management, think about other projects you have been involved with in school or the community. Are these same concepts still valid? What about homework problems, projects, or papers you have done in school? Is there a compromise with quality if you put off the project to the point where you are tight on time? Is there even a cost value, maybe not in money, but in relationships or personal health if you put off major assignments to the point that time, rather than quality, is the driving force?

CHAPTER 2

WHY SCHEDULE?

▮▮▮▮I N T R O D U C T I O N▮▮▮▮

It is easier to be motivated to read a textbook or take a class on scheduling if the student realizes the benefits of the content. How can the course and text help someone personally to be more successful and to achieve his or her personal life and employment goals? This chapter attempts to answer this important question. We will examine the reasons for and benefits of creating a formal yet realistic schedule. It is hoped that reading this chapter will eliminate the attitude, "I don't have time to create a realistic and effective schedule," or, "I have built so many projects similar to this that I can do it in my sleep. I don't need a schedule." Quality schedules are vitally important to the success of a project.

A manager schedules to achieve control of not only time, but also cost, quality, and safety as discussed in Chapter 1. The schedule helps managers plan methods and procedures that will ensure that the project objectives are met. The management team schedules in order to accomplish activities in the most productive manner possible so that time is not wasted on the project. Then, the schedule becomes the primary tool to communicate that thinking and planning by the management team to all the shareholders in the project.

TIME MANAGEMENT MATRIX

Something that may help managers better use their time in the future is to understand how they are currently using their time. Stephen R. Covey's book *The Seven Habits of Highly Effective People* (New York: Simon & Schuster, 1989, pp. 150–154), in the chapter titled "The Time Management Matrix," helps managers to understand on what tasks they are currently spending their time (see Figure 2.1).

Covey categorizes work-related activities into four "quadrants." **Quadrant 1,** the crisis quadrant, is where many project managers spend the majority of their time taking care of the urgent and important activities dealing with crises, pressing problems, and deadline-driven projects. In spite of daily to-do lists, they go from crisis to crisis with the project managing them, rather than them managing the project. It is tough to break out of this quadrant. Most managers tend to live and die in Quadrant 1. If they just had a little more time to plan and get organized, they could eliminate some of these problems. Most managers realize, however, that many of these crises are self-made because the managers were too busy handling other crises.

Quadrant 2 is where the effective manager should be spending the majority of his or her time, handling the not urgent, but important activities such as relationship building and recognizing new opportunities. Quadrant 2 is where planning, organizing, directing, and controlling should take place. Scheduling is a Quadrant 2 activity as well. Yet, as discussed above, the typical manager doesn't have time for these tasks be-

FIGURE 2.1   The time management matrix

Quadrant 1 Urgent & Important	Quadrant 2 Not Urgent & Important
Crises Pressing problems Deadline-driven projects	Relationship building Recognizing new opportunities Planning, recreation
Quadrant 3 Urgent & Not Important	Quadrant 4 Not Urgent & Not Important
Interruptions, some calls Some mail, some reports Some meetings Popular activities	Trivia, busy work Some mail Some phone calls Time wasters Pleasant activities

cause of all the crises he or she is handling on a minute-to-minute basis. "If I only had time to get organized" is the wishful thought of many managers, but they don't have time because they are constantly putting out fires in the crisis quadrant.

Quadrant 3, the urgent, but not important quadrant is the area where many managers find they can steal time from. To control this quadrant, which entails interruptions, mail and reports, meetings, and social activities, managers must learn to be firm. People constantly rushing into your office to discuss the ball game, current affairs, or the latest office rumors consume large amounts of time with some managers. It's not that these conversations are unimportant. If they build relationships, they belong in Quadrant 2; but, if these activities are just time wasters and cause interruptions during critical thinking time when a manager is planning and scheduling, they should be eliminated. You must learn to say "No."

For example, a simple wrong-number phone call that takes only 10 seconds interrupts the train of thought, causing mistakes and many minutes of wasted time, both during and after the telephone conversation. A few minutes of undisturbed deep thinking and planning such as required for tasks such as estimating and scheduling, can save untold hours later in the day or week.

Control of the office space is the key to limiting the amount of time spent in Quadrant 3. It is essential for managers to have someone else take their phone calls during these minutes or hours of critical thinking. Other office workers must be trained to recognize signals such as a closed office door, which means do not interrupt unless it is an emergency. An almost closed door means please respect my privacy, but if it is important, go ahead and interrupt. A wide-open door means come on in and chat a moment. A system needs to be developed that allows the manager to control Quadrant 3 in order to have more time to spend on Quadrant 2 activities, and so you don't live and die in the crisis quadrant. Simply, time must be managed in order to manage other responsibilities. Managers cannot continue to work excessive hours because others are stealing their time.

Quadrant 4 is the time-wasting quadrant that consists of the neither urgent nor important activities such as busy work, some mail, some phone calls, time wasters, and some social activities. Most of the readers of this text are probably not spending excessive amounts of time in this quadrant. If you are, move that time into Quadrant 2 so that you are not forced to spend so much time in Quadrant 1.

USING THE SCHEDULE TO CONTROL YOUR PROJECTS AND YOUR LIFE

One of the major concerns with construction managers is the total control that projects seem to take over the manager's life. It is not uncommon for project managers to find themselves consumed by a project. Many work 60 to 80 hours per week, with 65 to 70 hours the standard. These long hours, in addition to the associated pressures of meeting the project objectives, tend to take their toll on managers. This type of lifestyle, if it continues over several years, threatens not only the personal health of the manager but also the manager's relationship with his or her family. "Burnout" is a problem in the management circles of many construction companies. As stated earlier, the key is to learn to control your projects so they do not control you. You must have balance not only in your construction projects but also in your real life, outside of the job site.

As a construction manager, you need to increase your level of professionalism to the point where you can learn to work smart as well as hard, enabling you to have time to do other things that are important to you. Managing major construction projects has a tendency to consume every thought, action, minute, and hour. As a manager, you must become better at planning and scheduling to allow you to spend time with those you love and cherish.

It is the author's experience, having worked and consulted with hundreds of project managers, that those who are consistently more successful on the job have a life outside the job as well. Managers have to manage their entire lives, not just projects. They cannot continue to work excessive hours on projects, going from crisis to crisis at the expense of other people and other things life has to offer. Managers must learn that by prior planning they can create a schedule that controls and communicates the construction process in sufficient detail that everyone knows who is to be doing what, when, and where. Thus, the manager can, on occasion, be gone from the jobsite and still have things running efficiently and effectively in his or her absence. To repeat, *managers must learn to control the project, rather than having it control them.* Proper scheduling can be a great aid in helping to achieve this.

Reduce Total Construction Time

Any schedule is better than no schedule. It is common to hear managers state, "because projects are always changing, schedules are impossible to keep." An excellent reply to this is, "that is why they must be scheduled!" Somehow managers must learn how to wrap their arms around a project and get control of the time element. It may be difficult, but it must be done. Through advanced planning and scheduling, the total proj-

Time Is Money
Based on a 9% Annual Interest Rate

Amount	Work Minute	Work Hour	Work Day	Week	Month	Year
$50,000,000	$36.06	$2,163.46	$17,308	$86,538	$375,000	$4,500,000
30,000,000	21.63	1,298.08	10,385	51,923	225,000	2,700,000
20,000,000	14.42	865.38	6,923	34,615	150,000	1,800,000
10,000,000	7.21	432.69	3,462	17,308	75,000	900,000
6,000,000	4.33	259.62	2,077	10,385	45,000	540,000
5,000,000	3.61	216.35	1,731	8,654	37,500	450,000
4,000,000	2.88	173.08	1,385	6,923	30,000	360,000
2,000,000	1.44	86.54	692	3,462	15,000	180,000
1,000,000	0.72	43.27	346	1,731	7,500	90,000
800,000	0.58	34.62	277	1,385	6,000	72,000
600,000	0.43	25.96	208	1,038	4,500	54,000
500,000	0.36	21.63	173	865	3,750	45,000
300,000	0.22	12.98	104	519	2,250	27,000
150,000	0.11	6.49	52	260	1,125	13,500
100,000	0.07	4.33	35	173	750	9,000
75,000	0.05	3.25	26	130	563	6,750

FIGURE 2.2   Interest costs per period of time

ect duration can be determined, and construction time can be reduced. Overall time reductions are possible through the detailed thinking that a formal schedule requires. Planning the project, well in advance, reduces the mistakes of doing activities out of order and the rework necessary because of inadequate advanced planning and scheduling. Some rework is always necessary because mistakes will be made, but excessive rework causes major delays and disruptions.

Reduce the Costs of Labor, Overhead, Interest on Loans, and Capital

Generally, if the project can be completed early, the overhead costs connected to that project are lower. Organizing labor so that productivity is at a maximum results in cost savings as well. A well-organized project helps decrease additional costs of overtime expended on the project. Interest costs can also be decreased if the project finishes early. Most people agree that time is money. The chart shown in Figure 2.2 illustrates the effect of time on projects:

To illustrate the effects of the chart in Figure 2.2, consider this scenario: The project just started, the job trailer is on the site, the security fence up, and the layout and excavation just started. Total cost to this point amounts to only $75,000. At the current time, the interest cost of one work minute is five cents and one work hour $3.25, or $26.00 per work day. That's with only $75,000 tied up in the project. Now notice what happens when there is $5 million into the project. The interest cost per work minute increases to $3.61, a work hour is $216.35, and a day is worth $1,731.00. That is a lot of money that someone is paying just on the interest of the construction costs. Even if the owner is wealthy enough to be working on a cash basis and that money is not being borrowed, there is still value in the money and time expended. If it could be invested at a 9 percent interest rate in a secure investment, there is still a cost based on the time the money is tied up in concrete, steel, drywall, and so on until the project becomes complete and starts to return on its own investment. The chart in Figure 2.2 is based on a five-day work week, so the daily interest is based on 1/5 the interest accrued weekly, not 1/7. The hourly rate is based on a 40-hour work week; therefore, it is 1/40 of the weekly amount.

If the project manager is crisis oriented and disorganized causing a one-week delay on a $10 million commercial or industrial job, that accounts for a huge $17,307.69 loss. Time really is money, and it is a lot of money! The above is true in residential construction as well. It is not uncommon for a manager to be responsible for 10 to 15 homes at once for a total in excess of $10 million.

On the other hand, consider a dynamic manager who has planned, organized, directed, and controlled the project that accounts for a time saving of one week on a $10 million job. That manager just saved $17,307.69. As stated, time really is money—it is either lost or saved by the way a project is planned and scheduled. This is just the savings on the interest being charged to the project. It does not include the dollars saved as a result of a manufacturing enterprise being put into operation earlier than anticipated, or an apartment building being completed early and collecting additional months or even weeks of rent, and the list goes on and on.

Some argue that it is too costly to furnish computers and provide the training necessary to empower construction site workers, project managers, and especially superintendents to schedule the work on-site. If doing this would save one week on a $5 million project, that would generate more than enough money to provide the computer, software, and training.

This savings resulting from scheduling holds true not only for commercial and industrial or heavy highway contractors but also for residential builders. If they could save just one week on each house they build annually, consider what the savings would amount to on homes with an average cost of $200,000 per home. If each manager is responsible for the construction of 20 homes per year, the interest cost savings would be enormous, to say nothing of the other cost savings by completing the projects quicker. What would that do to a home builder's reputation if the company consistently finished projects on time and underbudget?

The cost of delays can be enormous on large projects. The February 10, 1993, edition of *USA Today* announced that the MGM Grand hotel, being built in Las Vegas, was 45 days ahead of the projected schedule, which would increase the first year's revenue by about $70 million. The slot machines alone were forecast to take in about "$385,000 more per day than they would spit back to gamblers." Time really is money, and many negotiated contracts are awarded as much on the schedule as the estimate.

Provide a More Continuous Work Flow

A well-thought-out schedule will provide for a continuous work flow. Based on past experience, what is the flow of work at the beginning of the typical construction job? What is the work flow during the middle of the project? Is it different as the project approaches the completion date? Generally, the start and middle time periods of a project are more easy going and less hurried compared to the end. In residential construction it seems the typical house will go days during the middle phase without a truck parked in front, whereas, during the last week or two there is not a parking place within blocks because all the tradespeople are trying to get the project finished on time. The Home Builders Association's home shows across the country are particularly fun to watch the week or two prior to the opening of the show.

Commercial and industrial construction is not much different—the crunch comes at the end. This is a sign of poor management. The well-scheduled and planned project should see uniform activity during the entire project, with no big crisis at the end. Yes, that is a little unrealistic to imagine, but in theory it should work that way.

Increase Productivity

A well-planned and well-thought-out schedule will produce an improvement in productivity, especially when the prime tradespeople are consulted in the development of the schedule and have had input into the way the project is sequenced. Tradespeople will not be working on top of each other. There will be a uniform and orderly process happening and people will know what to do, when to do it, and where to do it.

You typically wouldn't consider building a project without a set of plans. The architectural plans tell what is being built and the schedule tells how it is going to be done. Yet, it is not uncommon for a management team to try to construct a project without a schedule.

Give Employees and Subcontractors a Goal to Work Toward

A schedule sets the goals and milestone objectives for the project and its workers. It is the plan of how the work is to be done. Without a schedule, employees and subcontractors don't have intermediate goals to work toward or a detailed plan of when activities are to be completed. The expectation is that everyone will work hard and the project will finish on time. It is surprising how often this happens in the construction industry, without a specific plan of construction methods or a formal schedule. But, many times the price paid is high in overtime, quality problems, safety violations, and years of litigation. A well-thought-out schedule that has been prepared with input from the project's prime stakeholders will eliminate many potential crises and create a higher level of support and teamwork. Owners sometimes poke fun at contractors with statements like, "a carefully prepared and well-thought-out project typically takes twice as long to construct as originally planned, whereas a poorly planned project will take three to four times as long." Owners of custom homes frequently joke about how long it took to build their home with comments such as "the contractor said he would have my house completed by July; he just didn't tell me which year."

Improve Your Company Image—Makes You Look Professional

A formal schedule, if used for no other purpose, will pay for the time it takes to develop it because it improves the company image and sets the company apart as a professional organization.

> *A Case Study on How a Schedule Improved a Company's Image:*   The project was a National Basketball Association (NBA) arena and the construction company had no experience in building projects of that size or magnitude. The management team had no experience with scheduling such a project and was at a loss as to how to proceed. The plans were very preliminary and without details. The roof system was undetermined: fabric maybe, trussed maybe, open maybe—that would be determined later. The schedule was needed for a proposal in a negotiated bid. So, the project manager and superintendent did their best. They admitted to a major amount of guesswork on how the project should be constructed. They admitted they felt incompetent to schedule this project. This was the company's first attempt at a critical path method (CPM) logic diagram (to be discussed in Chapter 6). They developed the logic diagram by hand, and then entered it into the computer. They located a color pen plotter and plotted the logic diagram and the overall bar chart in red, black, green, blue, and yellow on 2×3-foot sheets of paper. The schedules were mounted on a high-quality presentation board. To the surprise of the project manager and superintendent, the resulting schedules looked great!
>
> The schedules were delivered to the president and the development officer of the construction firm. Everyone commented on how great the schedules looked and what a great job had been done to create them. The schedules were used in the presentation to the owners and the firm was eventually awarded the project. The owners stated, "One of the major reasons the job was awarded to this company was their impressive schedule. The schedule gave us confidence in the contractor's ability to do the work." The schedule indeed was impressive looking, but how much better it would have been if the schedule were technically accurate as well.

That project turned out to be very successful, in part due to the general contractor's admission of his lack of experience with a project of this nature and, therefore, his dependence on the subcontractors to provide input into the final working schedule.

Owners are looking for professionals to partner with in building quality projects, on time, within budget, and in a safe work environment. The schedule has a major impact in this area. If you want to work for professionals, you need to *be* a professional. Managing by the seat of the pants won't do it anymore. The competition is getting organized and so must you if you are going to compete for the best and most profitable projects.

Meet Owners' Requirements

Owners are tired of their projects finishing late with loose controls. It is normal for current contract documents to require a detailed CPM schedule (Chapter 5 will cover CPM scheduling). The contract frequently specifies even the software to be used to develop and update the schedule. Owners are trying to force the contractors to become more professional, to do the job right, and to do it on time. Many contractors are find-

FIGURE 2.3 Scheduling creates critical thinking

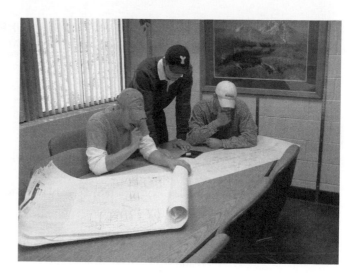

ing this as their edge in the marketplace. They are developing a reputation of integrity, finishing projects on time, and meeting the owners' requirements. These contractors are developing a realistic, workable schedule as they plan the project because they find it increases their chances to meet or exceed owners' expectations.

Force Detailed Thinking and Planning

If used for no other purpose, a formal schedule will pay for itself for this one reason alone: As a manager develops a schedule, he or she is forced to think out the process of how the project is to be built. *The management team has to mentally build the project in order to create the schedule* (Figure 2.3). As the processes are thought through in detail, many potential problems are eliminated that would not have been considered without formally scheduling the project. Some managers realize that developing the schedule was worth the time even if they had not continued to look at it during the construction process, because it forced them to think through the entire process. As a schedule is developed, the management team must think in detail about how they are going to build the project, including the equipment, people, processes, techniques, and tools needed. This detailed thinking, especially that required to create a CPM logic diagram, is of crucial importance.

Improve Communication

If a group of construction managers are asked "What is it that frustrates you the most about your job?", the list frequently includes the following:

❏ architects
❏ owners and owners' representatives

- ❑ subs (subcontractors, as stated by general contractors)
- ❑ general contractors (as stated by the subcontractors)
- ❑ suppliers
- ❑ engineers
- ❑ unskilled tradespeople
- ❑ changes
- ❑ inspectors
- ❑ having the wrong materials shipped to the jobsite
- ❑ materials always arriving late
- ❑ plans with so many errors and omissions
- ❑ upper management

A careful examination of the causes of frustration shows a common thread: *lack of communication*. Architects sometimes frustrate the project managers because the plans do not clearly communicate the details needed to build the project. The project managers frustrate the architects because they do not understand the plans and specifications. The owners are frustrated by the project managers because they constantly say one thing but do another. The project managers are frustrated by the owners because they are always changing their mind and never tell them about it. Subcontractors frustrate the project managers because they never show up at the right place at the right time because the project managers never give them proper directions and sufficient notification of when to proceed. The materials don't arrive on time because no one ordered them in time for delivery prior to the date they are to be installed. It is an enormous challenge to communicate all the details and changes required to construct a massive project with all the people and entities involved. One of the biggest, if not *the* biggest challenge in any organization, business, or group of people is effective communication.

A formal schedule not only reflects the manager's critical thinking but it also gives the manager the ability to communicate that thinking to everyone involved in the project. Everyone can share the same vision of how the work is to be accomplished. Everyone knows who is responsible for what, where, and when. As problems are encountered and solved, the schedule communicates to everyone how the project is going to be adjusted in order to meet the primary objectives of a quality project, finished on time, within budget, and in a safe work environment. That is the fallacy of a manager who says, "I don't need a schedule because I have built so many projects similar to this I can do it in my sleep." It is not a matter of his or her ability to know how to construct the project. It is a matter of being able to communicate that plan, those thoughts in the manager's head, to everyone involved in the project so that all share the same vision to construct a successful project.

The schedule in Figure 2.4 lists the activities to be completed by the electrician (who). Also, notice the schedule shows the electrician which floor level (where) to work on, what is to be done (in block, rough, or finish electrical), and when the activ-

Description	Dur	2004				2005	
		OCT	NOV	DEC	JAN	FEB	MAR	APR	MAY

Description	Dur																													

(Gantt chart data)

Hotel Project SLC Utah
Electrician
  1st floor

Description	Dur	
Electrical UG Rough	10d	Electrical UG Rough 01DEC04 ▬ 14DEC04
Electrical Rough in Block	7d	Electrical Rough in Block 17DEC04 ▬ 28DEC04
Site Electrical	20d	Site Electrical 29DEC04 ▬ 26JAN05
Elec Rough	9d	Elec Rough 27JAN05 ▬ 08FEB05
Elect Finish	6d	Elect Finish 30MAR05 ▬ 06APR05

  2nd Floor

Description	Dur	
Elec Rough	9d	Elec Rough 09FEB05 ▬ 21FEB05
Elect Finish	6d	Elect Finish 07APR05 ▬ 14APR05

  3rd Floor

Description	Dur	
Elec Rough	9d	Elec Rough 22FEB05 ▬ 04MAR05
Elect Finish	6d	Elect Finish 15APR05 ▬ 22APR05

  4th Floor

Description	Dur	
Elec Rough	10d	Elec Rough 04MAR05 ▬ 17MAR05
Elect Finish	7d	Elect Finish 25APR05 ▬ 03MAY05

FIGURE 2.4   A schedule that communicates *who* is doing *what, when,* and *where*

ity is scheduled to be done. This level of detail shows that the schedule has been thought through well and that it communicates the necessary information to everyone involved.

The last two reasons to formally schedule a project—forcing detailed thinking and then communicating that thinking—will be key time and again in determining the level of detail in which to schedule and in selecting the ideal scheduling method to use.

CONCLUSION

There are many benefits to formally scheduling projects. Not only does a well thought-out schedule help projects be built more efficiently but it also helps managers improve the quality of their own lives. As a manager you must also learn to manage projects, rather than having projects manage you. You cannot continue to live and die in the crisis quadrant. It is too hard on your health, personal welfare, families, and people you work with. Other benefits of scheduling include reducing total construction time; reducing the costs of labor, overhead, interest on loans, and capital; providing a more continuous work flow; increasing productivity; and giving employees and subcontractors a goal to work toward. The construction industry must become more professional in order to attract and keep the best and brightest people. Better scheduling is one of the keys to improving the professionalism of this industry. A formal schedule also helps make projects and businesses more professional and profitable. A well-developed and well-thought-out schedule communicates the construction process to everyone involved in the project.

APPLICATION

1. Select one of the concepts discussed in this chapter that you feel could improve your work performance. Consider why this is a challenge to you and what you are going to do about it. Then write down a personal commitment to improve in this area.

2. Interview a project manager or superintendent and ask questions about concepts covered in this chapter. For example, ask why the manager or superintendent does or does not schedule. How did projects that were carefully scheduled compare to projects that lacked a formal schedule? Was there a difference in the way the projects progressed?

3. Interview a subcontractor and ask how projects that are carefully scheduled compare to projects without a formal schedule. Would the subcontractor give a better price to a company that schedules and manages well versus a company that does not schedule or manage well? How much of an impact does a formal schedule have on the subcontractor's ability to make a profit?

CHAPTER 3

CHECKLISTS, DAILY TO-DO LISTS, AND MAGNETIC SCHEDULING BOARDS

▰▰▰▰▰▰▰I N T R O D U C T I O N▰▰▰▰▰▰▰

This chapter introduces the simpler methods of scheduling—methods that typically are not included in a textbook on construction scheduling because they are so basic. In reality, managers use these methods so effectively and so frequently that there is need for a discussion about them. Some of these techniques may be used more effectively than other more sophisticated, complicated scheduling methods (to be discussed later in the book) and should not be overlooked.

SELECTING A SCHEDULING SYSTEM

There are several items to consider when selecting which scheduling system to use. Keep in mind that the purpose of the schedule is to force detailed thinking and planning and then communicate that thinking and planning to everyone involved in the project, so that everyone knows where they should be, what they should be doing, and when they should be doing it. If two systems would do the job sufficiently, choose the simpler system.

Which scheduling technique to use depends on the size and complexity of the project. A more sophisticated project usually requires a more sophisticated schedule. Many times the contract specifies the type of scheduling system to be used and the details of specific reporting requirements. It is important to remember that the schedule is made for the person receiving it, not the person preparing it. If the skilled workers or the superintendent cannot comfortably read a CPM logic diagram, give them a bar chart. If a bar chart is difficult for them, provide a daily to-do list. The level of detail in the schedule also changes with the level of experience of the management team. A less experienced management team may need a more detailed schedule than an experienced team. The scheduling method must also be flexible because there will likely be changes made during the construction process.

CHECKLISTS

A checklist is probably the most rudimentary type of schedule. Whether used alone or combined with other scheduling systems, checklists can become valuable tools to help manage projects. Checklists simply consist of a list of steps to be taken in order to accomplish a desired outcome. Checklists help the manager remember and execute the details of a project. The purpose of a checklist is similar to a shopping list—to make sure nothing is forgotten. For some types of projects or for some managers, a checklist or series of checklists may be all that is needed in the way of planning and scheduling.

Figure 3.1 shows a checklist designed to remind an inexperienced concrete finisher the steps to be followed in finishing a concrete slab.

FIGURE 3.1 Concrete
finishing checklist

Checklist for Finishing Concrete Slabs	
1	Place Concrete
2	Strike off with Vibrating Screed
3	Bull Float
4	Hand Float as Needed
5	Wait for Bleed Water to Evaporate
6	Edge
7	1st Hand Trowel (5" X 24" Trowel)
8	Edge
9	2nd Hand Trowel (3" X 12" Trowel)
10	Broom Surface
11	Cure
12	Remove Forms

FIGURE 3.2 Interior
finishing checklist

Office Building—Interior Finishes	
1	Install Metal Stud Partitions
2	Rough Mech., Elect., & Plumb.
3	Inspection
4	Insulate
5	Install Drywall
6	Finish Drywall
7	Paint Drywall
8	Carpentry Trim (prefinished)
9	Wallpaper
10	Carpet
11	Hang Doors
12	Install Hardware

Figure 3.2 is an example of a checklist created to remind an inexperienced superintendent the correct activity order for finishing the interior of an office building. The superintendent could put a check mark in the left column as the activities are completed. Or, better yet, he or she could write the date on which they are finished. An additional column could be used to show the planned start date. The checklist could become more of an actual schedule if columns were added for the duration of each activity, the planned start and finish dates, and the actual start and finish dates. A simple checklist like this reminds the superintendent to schedule the rough inspections, which may have been overlooked.

A checklist is particularly helpful in situations such as remembering what tools, equipment, and materials need to be loaded on the truck for specific work to be done.

FIGURE 3.3 Concrete finishing equipment checklist

Tools & Equip. for Finishing Concrete Slabs	
	Shovels, Square Mouth & Round Nose
	Concrete Rakes
	Vibratory Screed
	Bull Float
	Hand Floats, Magnesium & Wooden
	Steel Trowels 5 X 24 & 3 X 12
	Margin Trowel
	Edgers, Hand
	Edger, Walking
	Knee Pads
	Kneeling Boards
	Brooms
	Curing Compound
	Sprayer, Curing

The importance of a checklist should not be overlooked just because of its simplicity. How many times do workers show up without the proper tools or materials and end up causing delays and additional costs? A simple checklist may avoid many of these delays and losses in productivity. Some managers use separate checklists for each job to be performed; for example, a plumbing checklist, a painting checklist, an insulation checklist, and so on. These specific checklists help laborers or other workers remember the items needed to successfully complete their assigned tasks in the proper order. Whenever a tool or item needed to do a job is forgotten, revise the checklist so that it is remembered next time.

Figure 3.3 shows a checklist used to make sure the concrete finishing crew loads the truck with the necessary tools and equipment. A check mark could be placed in the left column as the items are accounted for. This helps ensure the workers will have the proper tools and equipment when they get to the jobsite.

Figure 3.4 illustrates a checklist schedule for land development of a small community. Some managers call this type of schedule a *tabular schedule*.

Automating Checklist Schedules with Microsoft Excel

Consider the checklist or tabular schedule illustrated in Figure 3.5.

The checklist shown in Figure 3.5 is an example of an automated checklist developed for a superintendent responsible for the construction of homes from the framing point to the finished project. The bolded activities represent milestones. The activity dates between the milestones may vary some, but the company wants to make sure the milestone dates are met. The start date of each home is entered in the cell under the address. From that point on all the activity dates are *automatically* calculated, skipping weekends and holidays. As the project is updated, the actual dates are entered and the remaining schedule is again automatically calculated showing the

Land Development Process			
Community			
Activity Description	Planned Date	Actual Date	Notes
Preconstruction			
Prel. Design/Units, Lots, Streets			
Prel. Approval/Local Gov'ts			
Engineering—Hydrology			
Survey, Topo, Aerial Control			
Planning Process/Rezoning			
Lot, Street Alignment			
Final Plat, Submit for Approval			
Grading Plans			
Street, Drainage Design			
Sewer, Water Design			
Soil Percolation Tests			
As Stake Plans			
Legal Documents			
Sanitation Approval			
Survey and Stake-out			
Bidding/Contracts Let			
Construction			
Site Grading Completed			
Sewers Constructed			
Inspection			
Water System Constructed			
Inspection			
Drainage Culverts In			
Underground Electric Done			
Street Lighting Rough-in			
Street Grading			
Curbing Done			
Street Paving Done			
Lot Corners/Restake			
Street Lighting Finished			
Finish Grade			
Clean-up			

FIGURE 3.4 Checklist for land development

	A	B	C	D	E	F	G
1	OWNER	CARLSON	CORFIELD	VARLEY	PETERSON	MCLOUD	LUKE
2	PROJECT #	C05-6	C05-9	T05-1	C05-10	T05-2	T05-3
3	ADDRESS	446 E 3225 N	285 E 3250 N	326 Riverway	1326 Ivy	2825 Mountain	3290 Ridgeway
4	FRAME START DATE	Tue 2/15	Tue 2/22	Tue 3/1	Mon 3/7	Tue 3/15	Mon 3/21
5	FRAME 2	Wed 2/16	Wed 2/23	Wed 3/2	Tue 3/8	Wed 3/16	Tue 3/22
6	FRAME 3	Thu 2/17	Thu 2/24	Thu 3/3	Wed 3/9	Thu 3/17	Wed 3/23
7	FRAME 4	Fri 2/18	Fri 2/25	Fri 3/4	Thu 3/10	Fri 3/18	Thu 3/24
8	FRAME 5	Mon 2/21	Mon 2/28	Mon 3/7	Fri 3/11	Mon 3/21	Fri 3/25
9	FRAME 6	Tue 2/22	Tue 3/1	Tue 3/8	Mon 3/14	Tue 3/22	Mon 3/28
10	FRAME 7	Wed 2/23	Wed 3/2	Wed 3/9	Tue 3/15	Wed 3/23	Tue 3/29
11	FRAME 8	Thu 2/24	Thu 3/3	Thu 3/10	Wed 3/16	Thu 3/24	Wed 3/30
12	FRAME 9	Fri 2/25	Fri 3/4	Fri 3/11	Thu 3/17	Fri 3/25	Thu 3/31
13	FRAME 10	Mon 2/28	Mon 3/7	Mon 3/14	Fri 3/18	Mon 3/28	Fri 4/1
14	FRAME 11	Tue 3/1	Tue 3/8	Tue 3/15	Mon 3/21	Tue 3/29	Mon 4/4
15	FRAME 12	Wed 3/2	Wed 3/9	Wed 3/16	Tue 3/22	Wed 3/30	Tue 4/5
16	RGH PLUMBING & HVAC 1	Thu 3/3	Thu 3/10	Thu 3/17	Wed 3/23	Thu 3/31	Wed 4/6
17	RGH PLUMBING & HVAC 2	Fri 3/4	Fri 3/11	Fri 3/18	Thu 3/24	Fri 4/1	Thu 4/7
18	RGH ELECTRICAL 1	Mon 3/7	Mon 3/14	Mon 3/21	Fri 3/25	Mon 4/4	Fri 4/8
19	RGH ELECTRICAL2	Tue 3/8	Tue 3/15	Tue 3/22	Mon 3/28	Tue 4/5	Mon 4/11
20	FOUR-WAY A.M. /INSULATE P.M.	Wed 3/9	Wed 3/16	Wed 3/23	Tue 3/29	Wed 4/6	Tue 4/12
21	STOCK DW A.M. /HANG DW 1 P.M.	Thu 3/10	Thu 3/17	Thu 3/24	Wed 3/30	Thu 4/7	Wed 4/13
22	HANG DW 2	Fri 3/11	Fri 3/18	Fri 3/25	Thu 3/31	Fri 4/8	Thu 4/14
23	TAPE 1	Mon 3/14	Mon 3/21	Mon 3/28	Fri 4/1	Mon 4/11	Fri 4/15
24	TAPE 2	Tue 3/15	Tue 3/22	Tue 3/29	Mon 4/4	Tue 4/12	Mon 4/18
25	TAPE 3	Wed 3/16	Wed 3/23	Wed 3/30	Tue 4/5	Thu 4/13	Tue 4/19
26	TEXTURE	Thu 3/17	Thu 3/24	Thu 3/31	Wed 4/6	Thu 4/14	Wed 4/20
27	FINISH CARPENTRY 1	Fri 3/18	Fri 3/25	Fri 4/1	Thu 4/7	Fri 4/15	Thu 4/21
28	FINISH CARPENTRY 2	Mon 3/21	Mon 3/28	Mon 4/4	Fri 4/8	Mon 4/18	Fri 4/22
29	PAINT 1	Tue 3/22	Tue 3/29	Tue 4/5	Mon 4/11	Tue 4/19	Mon 4/25
30	PAINT2	Wed 3/23	Wed 3/30	Wed 4/6	Tue 4/12	Wed 4/20	Tue 4/26
31	PAINT 3 /DECK/ GARAGE STAIRS	Thu 3/24	Thu 3/31	Thu 4/7	Wed 4/13	Thu 4/21	Wed 4/27
32	CABINETS	Fri 3/25	Fri 4/1	Fri 4/8	Thu 4/14	Fri 4/22	Thu 4/28
33	CAB TOPS / GARAGE DOOR	Mon 3/28	Mon 4/4	Mon 4/11	Fri 4/15	Mon 4/25	Fri 4/29
34	APPLIANCES/ C.TILE / HDWR	Tue 3/29	Tue 4/5	Tue 4/12	Mon 4/18	Tue 4/26	Mon 5/2
35	FIN PLMB & ELECT	Wed 3/30	Wed 4/6	Wed 4/13	Tue 4/19	Wed 4/27	Tue 5/3
36	FIN HVAC	Thu 3/31	Thu 4/7	Thu 4/14	Wed 4/20	Thu 4/28	Wed 5/4
37	FINAL INSECTION	Fri 4/1	Fri 4/8	Fri 4/15	Thu 4/21	Fri 4/29	Thu 5/5
38	CARPET	Mon 4/4	Mon 4/11	Mon 4/18	Fri 4/22	Mon 5/2	Fri 5/6
39	FINAL CLEAN /SCREENS	Tue 4/5	Tue 4/12	Tue 4/19	Mon 4/25	Tue 5/3	Mon 5/9
40	TOUCH UP	Wed 4/6	Wed 4/13	Wed 4/20	Tue 4/26	Wed 5/4	Tue 5/10
41	PUNCH LIST	Thu 4/7	Thu 4/14	Thu 4/21	Wed 4/27	Thu 5/5	Wed 5/11
42	WALK-THRU	Fri 4/8	Fri 4/15	Fri 4/22	Thu 4/28	Fri 5/6	Thu 5/12

FIGURE 3.5 Automated checklist for home construction

adjusted schedule based on delays or accelerations. This automation is done using the WORKDAY function of Microsoft Excel. This example schedule is included on the CD accompanying this text (file name Checklist Automated.xls). The formula is =WORKDAY(B4,1,Holiday!$A$1:$A$9). "B4" is the cell that "1" day is added to. The "Holiday" is on the second sheet of the Excel file and contains a list of the holidays in cells A1 through A9. Using this function makes the simple checklist an extremely effective and powerful management tool. This example schedule is worth taking a closer look at on the disk included with this text. It could develop into a fairly sophisticated scheduling system. For those familiar with the critical path method (CPM), using the automated checklist or tabular schedule is similar to throwing a forward pass (discussed in detail in Chapter 8) with CPM to establish the start dates. There is no backward pass, float, or critical path; however, this type of schedule may be all that is needed on some projects.

As you can see from the above examples, checklists can be valuable management, scheduling, and control tools.

Daily To-Do Lists and Planners

One of the most basic scheduling methods, and the only one that some managers use, is a prioritized list of activities that need to be accomplished on a daily basis: the daily to-do list. It is similar to the checklist, only it is prioritized. The to-do list typically consists of activities to be done rather than a reminder of what needs to be taken to the job site. The to-do list is developed either at the end of the day for the following day's work, or at the beginning of each day. Some managers prefer to do it each evening claiming they sleep better if the next day is already thought through or planned out. They don't lie in bed at night thinking of tomorrow's activities because they have already taken the time to schedule them. Other managers prefer to make this list first thing in the morning by arriving at the job site early to have some quiet organizing and thinking time. Many very successful people attribute their success in life to the development of a daily to-do list.

To create a to-do list, simply write down (or key on a computer) all the activities that need to be accomplished in a day and then prioritize those activities (see Figure 3.6). The goal is to always be working on the most important activity. Making the list of activities starts with a brainstorming session. This involves listing the activities as you think of them, not being concerned about the priority; that will be taken care of later. It is acceptable, and even recommended, to include activities of a personal nature—things that need to be done for your family, health, neighbor, community, and so on.

After the basic list of daily activities is completed, it is prioritized. This is done by putting an *A* by the items that *have* to be done today, meaning the day is not over until the "A" items are done. Next, put a *B* by the items that *should* be accomplished today, a *C* by the items that *could* be done today, and a *D* by the items that, should a miracle occur, *might* be accomplished today. Likely, the "C" and "D" activities will be on tomorrow's list along with a "B" or two. The next step is to number the letters to obtain the final priority. Look at all the "A" activities and select the most important. Mark that

FIGURE 3.6   A daily to-do list

To-Do List	Date
Priority	**Activity**
A7	Call Bill @ Beaner Concrete
A4	Test Asphalt
C2	Check Repair on Scraper
D1	Schedule Maintenance of Cat #306
A3	Send Flowers to Wife
A10	Check Compaction of Exit 38
C1	Check Soil Reports of SR 208
A6	Get Check to Frank
A11	Call Jayson about Football Tickets
C3	Call L&M Travel about DC Trip
A8	Buy Shotgun Shells
B4	Check Status of Portable Concrete Plant
D3	Order Hydraulic Ram
B1	Order the Dozer Cushion Blade
B3	Calculate Haul Units on Project #2005-56
A9	Check on Delivery of Piles
B2	Estimate Asphalt Production for Next Week
A5	Order Ribbed Tires for the Backhoe
A2	Get the Fuel Tank Refilled
A1	Check with Fred on the Condition of the Fuel Tank

activity with a "1," the next important with a "2," and so forth. Then, do the same with the "B" activities and so on. until the list is fully prioritized (see Figure 3.6).

Now, it is a simple matter as to where the attention is focused first—"A1," of course. Once "A1" is completed, there is the thrill of crossing it off the list and then focusing on "A2" without getting drawn to other less important activities. This helps the manager concentrate on the important activities rather than just the "fun" activities. This technique not only gives focus to the day's activities but also ensures that even if everything is not done, the most important things have been completed first and you have done the best you could. Some managers find this daily to-do list to be the only scheduling method they need. Others use it in conjunction with other methods of planning and scheduling.

The problem with daily to-do lists is that it is not uncommon, at the end of the day, for activity "A1" to still not be completed even though it was only a 20-minute activity. The day has been filled with an untold number of crisis activities that were not even on the list. Some say that is simply the way life is as a manager, especially a manager of construction projects. However, as discussed previously, many crisis activities are really the result of poor planning. Nevertheless, daily to-do lists are still the favorite time management method of many successful managers. To-do lists can be used as a stand-alone method or in conjunction with other scheduling techniques. Some

FIGURE 3.7   The Palm V, a type of electronic planner

managers use more sophisticated methods of scheduling and then download the information to a daily to-do list because they like their simplicity and practicality. The to-do list is a serious time management tool that every manager needs to consider.

ELECTRONIC PLANNERS

Many managers use the electronic version of the to-do list—the Palm Pilot or personal digital assistant (PDAs)—to do the same process, only electronically (see Figure 3.7). One of the advantages of the electronic planner is the ability to keep the list updated and copy and paste the remaining activities to tomorrow's list. You can use an electronic planner to schedule meetings or other calendar items far into the future. The contact information and addresses are always listed in alphabetical order, which saves time when finding a contact person. Many other programs run on these small computers such as appointment calendars, memos, to-do lists, loan interest programs, calculators, punch list programs, astronomy programs, games, and spreadsheets. You can also download books, contracts, articles, and other kinds of information to the electronic planner.

Carrying a binder full of papers to the job site can be cumbersome and inconvenient. These electronic devices fit in a shirt pocket or a small belt holder, so they are easy to carry at all times. Another advantage to electronic planners is that all the data in a handheld device is easily backed up to a desktop computer, providing two copies of your critical information. If the planner crashes or is lost or destroyed, there is a backup, whereas with a hard-copy planner, when it is lost, it is gone for good. In spite of these advantages, some managers still prefer to see the information in hard-copy format. The important thing is to find the method that works best for you, so you can stay better organized and in control.

MAGNETIC SCHEDULING BOARDS

Some projects and companies prefer to use a large metal-backed calendar or set of calendars installed on a wall similar to the one shown in Figure 3.8. The activity names are written on magnets and placed on the calendar on the projected dates by which the activities should be completed. These moveable magnets can be color-coded to represent specific crews or people responsible so that the manager can better analyze the schedule. As changes occur, the manager can reposition the magnets (activities) to represent the new, revised schedule. This simple scheduling technique has been used very successfully by some subcontractors to show which projects their crews are working on, on

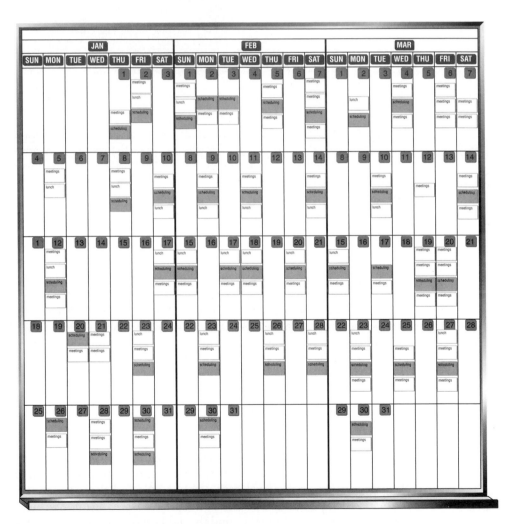

FIGURE 3.8 Magnetic scheduling board
Courtesy of Magna Visual

a day-by-day basis. This method does require the manager to think through the project in advance and becomes the method of communication to all other team members as to where everyone should be working and when. Of course, all team members need to have easy access to the board or must visit the location where the schedule is kept.

A disadvantage of magnetic scheduling boards is that any change in the schedule causes the manager to have to rethink each of the remaining activities. A significant amount of the manager's time can be spent rescheduling and adjusting the entire board to keep it up-to-date. Yet, it is ideal for some people and some projects. In an effort to look sophisticated, don't overlook these simple methods if they work.

CONCLUSION

Some of the simpler methods of planning and scheduling include checklists, daily to-do lists (whether on hard copy or on an electronic planner), and magnetic scheduling boards. These may be all that is needed for controlling some projects. Don't overlook the simple methods of scheduling a project if one of the techniques does the job. One of the complaints about graduates from four-year construction management programs is they try to use the computer to do everything. They seem to prefer to be computer operators, rather than project managers. They sometimes make a simple project complex by trying to be too sophisticated. A good rule used by many managers is to keep the scheduling system as simple as possible and yet keep in mind its main purposes: to force detailed thinking and planning and then communicate that thinking and planning to everyone involved in the project.

APPLICATION

1. Think of an activity or simple project you need to do in the near future and make a checklist of the tasks that must be accomplished. You might also make a checklist for a subcontractor or other person you manage to clarify what tools, materials, or equipment needs to be available to accomplish a task.

2. If you are not currently using daily to-do lists, try out the technique for an eight-week period. Each morning, take a few minutes to list the activities you need to do that day and prioritize them as discussed in this chapter. Work through the list during the day, transferring to the next day the activities you did not finish. See if your productivity improves or if you feel more in control.

3. If you have tried to use the three-ring planners and have disliked having to carry them with you, investigate the electronic versions and see if you want to give them a try.

4. Create an automated checklist schedule in Microsoft Excel using the WORKDAY function as explained in this chapter. See the example checklist included on the CD accompanying this text.

CHAPTER 4

BAR CHART SCHEDULES

■ I N T R O D U C T I O N ■

The bar chart method of scheduling is what most managers think of when they hear the word *schedule.* The bar chart is by far the most popular method for scheduling construction projects; in fact, it is considered the default scheduling method. Sometimes, bar charts are used in conjunction with other scheduling methods, such as critical path method (CPM), but many times they are used as a stand-alone method for planning and scheduling. The bar chart gives a visual or graphic representation of the project plan. It includes the activities, their durations, and the dates the activities are scheduled to happen. As a bar chart is created, the manager is forced to think through the construction process and organize the activities for successful completion of the project objectives. Bar chart schedules are easily read and understood; therefore, they are frequently the primary method used to communicate the project plan to everyone that is concerned with the schedule.

HISTORY OF BAR CHARTS

The development of the bar chart dates back to World War I when Henry L. Gantt used the bar chart method of scheduling to plan and control military operations. In honor of Gantt's early development of bar chart scheduling you will often hear the term *Gantt chart* when referring to a bar chart. For practical purposes, the terms *Gantt chart*, *Gantt schedule*, or *bar chart schedule* are one and the same.

CREATING BAR CHARTS

The creation of a hand-drawn bar chart schedule is a relatively simple process. Using a piece of graph paper, write the calendar date across the top of the page as shown in Figure 4.1. Some managers like to list the work day as well. Skip the nonwork days (holidays and weekends) as you enter the calendar dates.

Work day	1	2	3	4	5	6	7	8	9	10	11	12	13	14	15	16
Calendar Date	7/1	2	3	5	8	9	10	11	12	15	16	17	18	19	22	23

FIGURE 4.1   Hand-drawn bar chart heading with nonwork days excluded

The bar chart heading in Figure 4.1 shows a project starting on Monday, July 1. Notice that July 4 is not listed because it is a holiday. Also notice that the weekends are not listed, signifying a five-day work week. The work days are consecutive.

Some creators of bar charts prefer to show the calendar date as consecutive and block out the nonwork days as shown in Figure 4.2.

Notice that the holidays are indicated by an *H* and the weekends by a *W*. Many methods communicate well, so it is just a matter of personal preference which method the manager chooses to use. The time scale is typically based on units of days, but for a summary bar chart or long-range planning (when less detail is necessary) it is common to use units of weeks, months, quarters, or even years. It can also be made using minutes or hours if more detail is important.

After the time line is created, the next step is to list the first activity on the left side of the paper and show a bar on the dates when that activity is expected to take place (see Figure 4.3). As the activities are listed, try to put them in chronological order. If the activities are not in chronological order, it is much more difficult to follow the sequence of work.

This beginning bar chart shows *Survey* as the first activity, which is scheduled to take place on the first work day, July 1. Continue listing the activities in chronological order with their corresponding bars as shown in Figure 4.4.

Another way to show the nonwork days is to show the weekends and holidays shadowed as in Figure 4.4.

In the schedule illustrated in Figure 4.4, "FRIPS" stands for *Form, Reinforce, Inspect, Pour,* and *Strip.* Notice from the schedule that the *FRIPS Footings* crew is scheduled to work on the Fourth of July holiday and the *FRIPS Foundation* crew has agreed to work on Saturday, July 6. Also notice that the scheduled activities are listed in chronological order, or early start and early finish sequence. If two activities start on the same day, such as *W Proof & Plaster Fdn.* and *Cure Foundation,* the one with the earliest finish date is listed first.

Work day	1	2	3	H	4	W	W	5	6	7	8	9	W	W	10	11
Calendar Date	7/1	2	3	4	5	6	7	8	9	10	11	12	13	14	15	16

FIGURE 4.2   Hand drawn bar chart heading with nonwork days included

Work day	1	2	3	4	5	6	7	8	9	10	11	12	13	14	15	16
Calendar Date	7/1	2	3	5	8	9	10	11	12	15	16	17	18	19	22	23
Survey	■															

FIGURE 4.3   Hand-drawn bar chart schedule showing an activity and its expected completion date

Work day		1	2	3	H	4	W	W	5	6	7	8	9	W	W	10
Month		July														
Calendar Date		1	2	3	4	5	6	7	8	9	10	11	12	13	14	15
Survey		■														
Install Temp. Power		■														
Excavate			■													
FRIP Footing				■	■											
FRIPS Foundation							■	■		■						
W Proof & Plaster Fdn.											■					
Cure Foundation											■	■	■	■	■	■

FIGURE 4.4   Hand-drawn bar chart schedule listing various activities and expected completion dates

Watching these little details improves a bar chart and makes it look more professional. That is particularly important if you are going to use it to impress potential owners while making presentations for negotiated projects. These types of bar charts can be made by hand or, for a more professional look, on any spreadsheet program such as Microsoft Excel, Corel Quattro Pro, or IBM Lotus. The computer also makes it easier to update the schedule by copying and pasting the bars to their actual start and finish positions. Later chapters in this book discuss using dedicated scheduling programs such as Primavera Project Planner, SureTrak, Project Manager, and Microsoft Project to create bar charts.

Obviously, the length of the bar represents the duration of the activity. The duration should not be a guess or based on some arbitrary assumptions. The duration should be based on productivity records, available resources, and experience. Most managers obtain information about the amount of work to be performed from the quantity survey or estimate. Once the quantities are determined, you divide those quantities by the production rate to determine the activity duration. More information about determining activity durations is contained in Chapter 7 of this text.

To create as much teamwork as possible, as the scheduled activities and their bars are created, there should be consultation with other members of the management team. Some managers prefer to make a list of the activities and their durations while discussing the project with other team members prior to the actual development of the bar chart.

Figure 4.5 shows a bar chart schedule for the construction of a small home. Notice that the activities are listed in chronological order or early start and early finish sequence, as was discussed earlier.

The schedule shows the home is to start on July 1 and finish 35 work days later on August 19. This bar chart is easy to read with the vertical and horizontal sight lines. Without the sight lines, it is easy to get off a row or column and select the wrong activity dates.

Month	July																						August												
Calendar Date	1	2	3	5	8	9	10	11	12	15	16	17	18	19	22	23	24	25	26	29	30	31	1	2	5	6	7	8	9	12	13	14	15	16	19
Work Day	1	2	3	4	5	6	7	8	9	10	11	12	13	14	15	16	17	18	19	20	21	22	23	24	25	26	27	28	29	30	31	32	33	34	35
Survey																																			
Install Temp. Power																																			
Excavate																																			
FRIP Footings & Fdn.																																			
Strip, WP & Plstr. Fdn.																																			
Plumb Sub Slab																																			
Form & Pour Bsmt. Slab																																			
Back Fill & Rough Grade																																			
Frame & Install Windows																																			
Exterior Concrete																																			
Install Roofing																																			
Rough HVAC																																			
Rough Plumbing																																			
Masonry																																			
Rough Electrical																																			
Wall Insulation																																			
Exterior Trim																																			
Drywall Tape & Finish																																			
Paint Exterior																																			
Insulate Ceiling																																			
Interior Carpentry Finish																																			
Landscape																																			
Paint Interior																																			
Install Hardware																																			
Electrical Finish																																			
Install Cabinets																																			
Ceramic Tile Baths																																			
Cabinet Tops																																			
Floor Coverings																																			
Install Appliances																																			
Finish Plumbing																																			
Finish HVAC																																			
Clean-up																																			

FIGURE 4.5 Bar chart schedule for the construction of a small-home

Determining the Level of Detail

It is always difficult to know how detailed to make a bar chart. Should there be one activity for footings and foundations or should they be separate activities? Remember, the primary purposes of the schedule are to force detailed thinking that provides control of the project and then to communicate that thinking to all parties involved. Let that be a major guide. Don't make the schedule more complex than necessary, and yet give it enough detail to provide control of the job. Watch out for information overload, where you give more information than needed.

Updating Bar Charts

A typical problem with bar charts is in the updating process. As the schedule is updated with some activities being ahead of the original schedule and others behind, or there is an approved change, each remaining activity needs to be rethought and adjusted on the chart. One of the advantages of computer CPM schedules, where there is logic built into the schedule, is when an activity gets ahead or behind, the computer automatically updates all later activities dependent on that activity. It is not necessary to totally rethink the schedule and readjust it manually. This will be discussed in detail in later chapters.

Showing Progress on a Bar Chart

Many managers have found that a key to improving the performance of their crews or the people they manage, is to measure performance and then report it back. Create simple methods of comparing the scheduled date of the activities with the actual dates of the activities and report on the variance. By doing so, an opportunity is created to reward outstanding performers. This becomes a motivating factor for many people.

An outstanding superintendent or foreman will know the performance standards and productivity of the people he or she is supervising. If a finish electrical crew was approached and reminded that the average crew in the company was able to install 5 outlets per person an hour and that the company record is 6.2 outlets per hour, would that improve productivity? It's almost a guarantee that it would.

Performance in the installation of a concrete curb and gutter would likely be measured in lineal feet per person or crew hour. The placing of concrete flat work would likely be measured in square feet per person or crew hour. The placing of concrete for a large dam would likely be measured in cubic yards per person or crew hour. Each of the last three examples are all working with concrete, yet performance is measured differently for each activity. The unit of measurement must be practical.

Safety performance is frequently measured with a large sign on the job site that tracks the number of days since a lost time accident. Does that help remind the workers to work in a safe manner? It does! It is always great to beat the old record.

The world of sports relies on the principle of beating past records and to outscore the other teams or individuals. Without measuring performance, there would be little interest in the world of sports. Measuring performance and reporting it back certainly could increase the excitement and productivity of construction operations if this concept was used.

If we measure performance and report it back in a highly visible manner, it is a subtle motivator for everyone on the job. No one likes to be seen as the person who delayed the project. If a bar chart was created that shows the planned schedule along with the updated schedule and that chart was displayed where everyone would see it (similar to the safety sign), it would become a motivator to many workers. This can be done with a bar chart as shown in the following example.

Figure 4.6 shows an updated schedule where the planned schedule is indicated by the black solid bars on top and the as-built schedule is indicated by the crosshatched bars below the planned bars.

Notice that the project started a day late with the *Survey*. Also, it can be seen that the *Excavate* activity took two days rather than the one as originally planned. Therefore, the project is two days behind the original schedule. Updating the schedule could be done with a magic marker on the original schedule in the job site office or on a computer spreadsheet program.

Month	July																					
Calendar Date	1	2	3	4	5	6	7	8	9	10	11	12	13	14	15	16	17	18	19	20	21	22
Work Day	1	2	3	H	4	W	W	5	6	7	8	9	W	W	10	11	12	13	14	W	W	15
Survey																						
Install Temp. Power																						
Excavate																						
FRIP Footings																						
Termite Treatment																						
FRIPS Foundation																						
WP & Plaster Fdn.																						
Cure Foundation																						

FIGURE 4.6 Bar chart showing progress—comparing the planned schedule to the as-built schedule

USING THREE-WEEK LOOK-AHEAD BAR CHARTS

One of the most popular uses of bar charts on construction projects is the three-week look-ahead bar chart. It is concerned with only the activities that are scheduled during the next three weeks. Because it is limited to the next short period of time, it typically breaks the activities into a greater level of detail. The three-week bar chart is developed using the same techniques as the overall project schedule as discussed earlier. It is typically created by the superintendent to the level of detail needed to analyze tools, equipment, workers, and material needed during this short time interval. Some companies call this schedule a short interval production schedule (SIPS) or a construction activity plan (CAP). It should be in agreement with the master project schedule as far as milestone dates are concerned.

CREATING BAR CHARTS WITH MICROSOFT EXCEL

Microsoft Excel is an excellent spreadsheet program that will help in the creation of bar charts. See the Excel bar charts on the CD included with this textbook. Basically, enter the dates across the top of the spreadsheet. Next, enter the activity names down the left column of the spreadsheet. Then, format the cells and shade them to show the bars on the dates desired. The activities could be double-spaced, leaving room to mark the schedule with a highlighter showing the actual start and finish dates so that performance can be measured and reported.

EXAMPLES OF COMPUTER-GENERATED BAR CHARTS

Figure 4.7 shows a bar chart created with Excel that leaves room to update the project with the actual start and finish dates. The actual bars could be entered by hand with a highlighting marker. Also notice the weekends and holidays are shaded to show them as nonwork days. This bar chart shows only a portion of the complete schedule. Refer to the CD included with the text under the file name Bar Chart Example.xls to see the complete schedule. It could be used to create bar charts for commercial, industrial, residential, or highway projects.

The bar chart schedule illustrated in Figure 4.8 details construction of the first floor of a hotel. It was created with the use of SureTrak Project Manager, a dedicated project management software program.

In Figure 4.9 you can see a portion of a bar chart schedule for a highway overpass. Primavera Project Planner, another dedicated project management software program, was used to create the schedule.

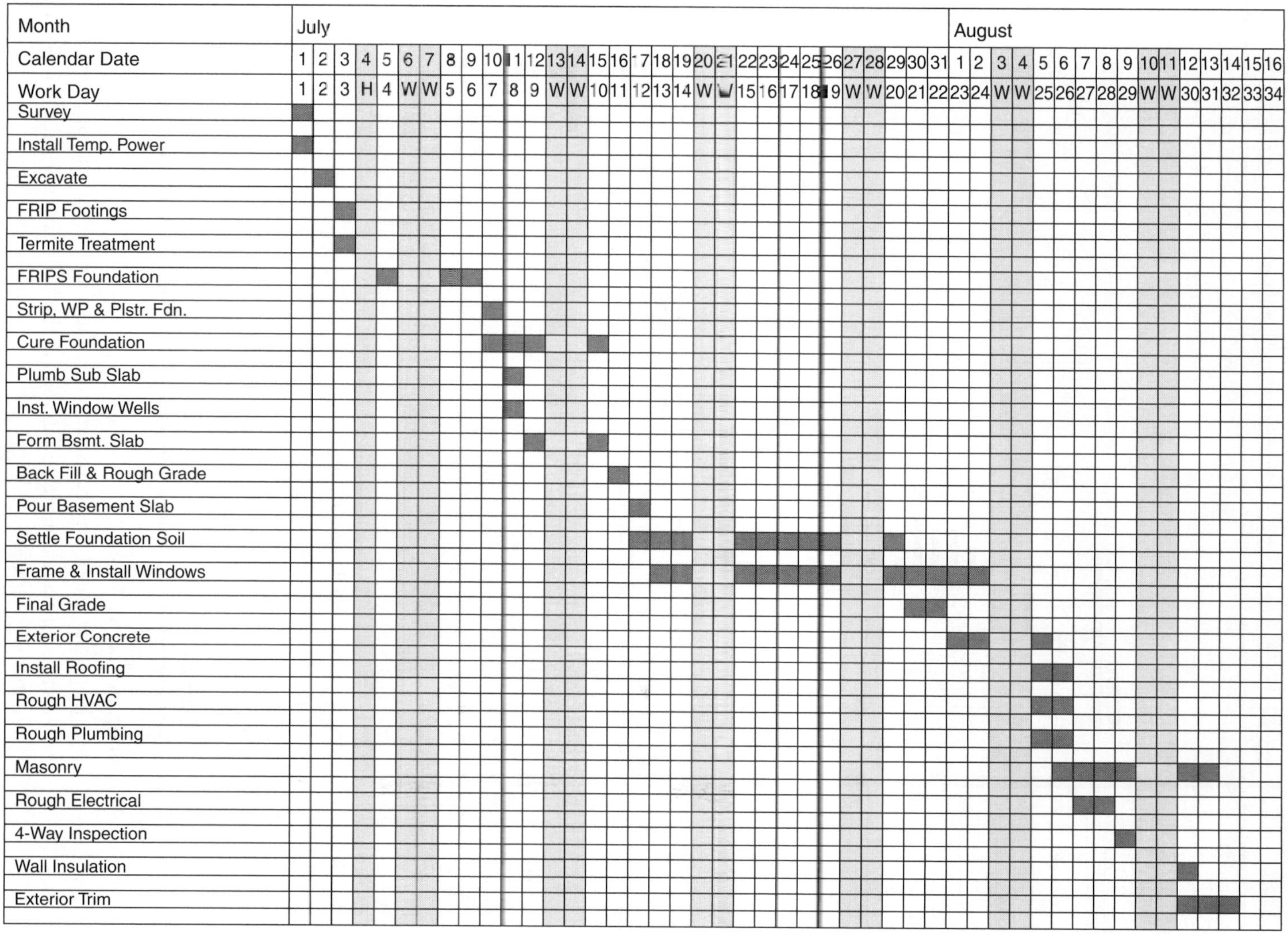

FIGURE 4.7 Bar chart with space for updating

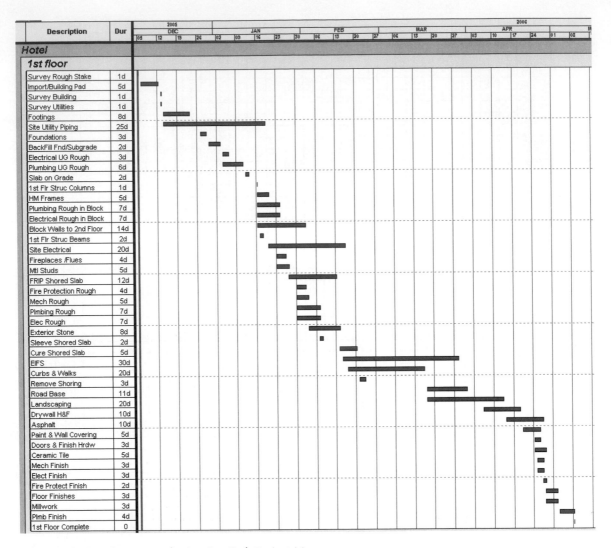

Description	Dur
Hotel	
1st floor	
Survey Rough Stake	1d
Import/Building Pad	5d
Survey Building	1d
Survey Utilities	1d
Footings	8d
Site Utility Piping	25d
Foundations	3d
BackFill Fnd/Subgrade	2d
Electrical UG Rough	3d
Plumbing UG Rough	6d
Slab on Grade	2d
1st Flr Struc Columns	1d
HM Frames	5d
Plumbing Rough in Block	7d
Electrical Rough in Block	7d
Block Walls to 2nd Floor	14d
1st Flr Struc Beams	2d
Site Electrical	20d
Fireplaces /Flues	4d
Mtl Studs	5d
FRIP Shored Slab	12d
Fire Protection Rough	4d
Mech Rough	5d
Plmbing Rough	7d
Elec Rough	7d
Exterior Stone	8d
Sleeve Shored Slab	2d
Cure Shored Slab	5d
EIFS	30d
Curbs & Walks	20d
Remove Shoring	3d
Road Base	11d
Landscaping	20d
Drywall H&F	10d
Asphalt	10d
Paint & Wall Covering	5d
Doors & Finish Hrdw	3d
Ceramic Tile	5d
Mech Finish	3d
Elect Finish	3d
Fire Protect Finish	2d
Floor Finishes	3d
Millwork	3d
Plmb Finish	4d
1st Floor Complete	0

FIGURE 4.8   Bar chart created using SureTrak Project Manager

CONCLUSION

Advantages of bar charts:

- The proper use of bar charts can make them a powerful management tool.
- The total management team can look at the bar chart and get the vision or big picture of the job.

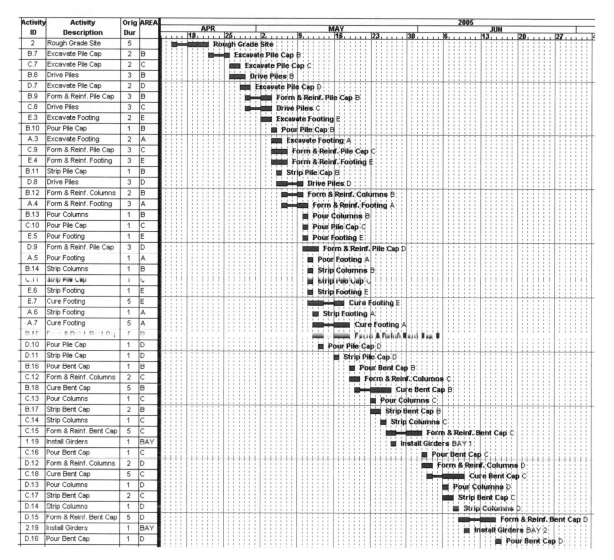

Activity ID	Activity Description	Orig Dur	AREA
2	Rough Grade Site	5	
B.7	Excavate Pile Cap	2	B
C.7	Excavate Pile Cap	2	C
B.8	Drive Piles	3	B
D.7	Excavate Pile Cap	2	D
B.9	Form & Reinf. Pile Cap	3	B
C.8	Drive Piles	3	C
E.3	Excavate Footing	2	E
B.10	Pour Pile Cap	1	B
A.3	Excavate Footing	2	A
C.9	Form & Reinf. Pile Cap	3	C
E.4	Form & Reinf. Footing	3	E
B.11	Strip Pile Cap	1	B
D.8	Drive Piles	3	D
B.12	Form & Reinf. Columns	2	B
A.4	Form & Reinf. Footing	3	A
B.13	Pour Columns	1	B
C.10	Pour Pile Cap	1	C
E.5	Pour Footing	1	E
D.9	Form & Reinf. Pile Cap	3	D
A.5	Pour Footing	1	A
B.14	Strip Columns	1	B
C.11	Strip Pile Cap	1	C
E.6	Strip Footing	1	E
E.7	Cure Footing	5	E
A.6	Strip Footing	1	A
A.7	Cure Footing	5	A
D.?	Form & Reinf. Columns	?	D
D.10	Pour Pile Cap	1	D
D.11	Strip Pile Cap	1	D
B.16	Pour Bent Cap	1	B
C.12	Form & Reinf. Columns	2	C
B.18	Cure Bent Cap	5	B
C.13	Pour Columns	1	C
B.17	Strip Bent Cap	2	B
C.14	Strip Columns	1	C
C.15	Form & Reinf. Bent Cap	5	C
1.19	Install Girders	1	BAY
C.16	Pour Bent Cap	1	C
D.12	Form & Reinf. Columns	2	D
C.18	Cure Bent Cap	5	C
D.13	Pour Columns	1	D
C.17	Strip Bent Cap	2	C
D.14	Strip Columns	1	D
D.15	Form & Reinf. Bent Cap	5	D
2.19	Install Girders	1	BAY
D.16	Pour Bent Cap	1	D

FIGURE 4.9   Bar chart created using Primavera Project Planner

- The bar chart forces the management team to think and plan the project in detail and it enables them to control the project and communicate that plan to all involved.
- A bar chart is the familiar and accepted schedule for most field personnel.
- A bar chart gives a visual or graphic presentation of the process of construction which helps the management team, as well as the field workers, see what is planned and when activities should happen.

- A bar chart provides a goal to work toward.
- A bar chart can be used to measure progress and performance.

Disadvantages of bar charts:
- The bar chart does not automatically show the effects of changes. The manager must rethink and redraw the schedule continually.
- The bar chart also does not help the manager identify the critical activities that determine the completion date of the project. However, intuition tells experienced managers which project activities are not urgent and which are critical and must be done on the days specified.
- It is very difficult, if not impossible, with a bar chart to see the effects of a change and whether or not a potential change will affect the project completion date. This becomes a point of contention between the owner and the contractor when changes are proposed.
- Most of the disadvantages are resolved with bar charts based on CPM schedules, as is discussed in the following chapters.

APPLICATION

1. If you are currently working on a project, using Excel or graph paper, create a bar chart schedule for the remainder of that project, or at least for the next three months. Make it a bar chart that can easily be updated to show the actual schedule compared to the as-planned schedule. If you are not currently working on a project, do activity 2.

2. You have been asked by your boss to create a first draft bar chart that will be used in a presentation for a negotiated contract for the construction of a warehouse. Using Excel or a piece of graph paper, create an impressive bar chart schedule that will be included in the proposal to the owner. The owner has furnished the following brief scope of work. Fill in other details as needed. The detailed plans will be developed later. The warehouse is 40 × 120 feet with a concrete footing and floor slab. It is a steel structure with the sections between the structural posts filled in with metal studs. It has exterior finish insulation system (EFIS) exterior wall coverings. The roofing material is a single-ply roof membrane. The roof is insulated with fiberglass insulation on the inside with a heavy plastic protection on the bottom side of the insulation. The exterior walls will be insulated with fiberglass batts. The only interior partitions are for a small office and restrooms. The inside wall coverings are drywall that will be finished and painted. The heating system consists of natural gas unit heaters suspended from the ceiling. There is no cooling system. There are two large overhead doors and two man doors for access to the building. There are also some landscaping and paved parking areas around the building.

INTRODUCTION TO CPM SCHEDULING

I N T R O D U C T I O N

This chapter introduces the critical path method (CPM) of planning and scheduling. It explains the advantages of CPM as compared to other scheduling methods, and discusses why so many sophisticated project managers prefer CPM and consistently use it to help manage construction projects.

DEVELOPMENT AND FEATURES OF CRITICAL PATH METHOD (CPM)

There were two projects taking place in the United States in the mid-1950s that have been credited for the major development of CPM scheduling. One was the Polaris missile project for the U.S. Navy and the other was a joint effort of DuPont and Remington Rand to manage plant overhaul, maintenance, and construction. By developing the schedule and analyzing the work to be accomplished with the aid of a flowchart or network diagram, the detailed relationships among the activities could be carefully evaluated. The network showed the predecessors and successors to each activity. This way, if an activity was changed, behind, or ahead of schedule, the following activities' dates were automatically adjusted based upon the relationships among all the activities.

The Navy titled its method PERT (Project Evaluation and Review Technique). Besides being a network flowchart, PERT used three time estimates: an optimistic time, a most likely time, and a pessimistic time. The final activity duration was determined by taking the optimistic time, plus four times the most likely time, plus the pessimistic time, and dividing the results by six $(O + 4L + P \div 6)$. This gave the most likely time a weighted average or placed four times more emphasis on that most likely time.

CPM was also a network flowchart method, but it simply used one time estimate for the duration of each activity. These methods of planning and scheduling were developed concurrently and independent of each other. Neither the Navy nor Dupont & Remington Rand knew of the other parties developments.

There are two types of networking methods: activity on arrow (sometimes called AOA) and activity on node (sometimes called AON or precedence diagram method). The Navy used the AOA method. This text will predominately discuss the AON diagram method. There is a more in-depth discussion of AOA techniques in Chapter 18. AOA had some major advantages with the early software programs because it was an easier method to computerize. With the power of modern computers, however, the AOA method has almost dropped out of existence. The AON method is significantly easier to develop and understand.

The CPM precedence logic diagram shown in Figure 5.1 provides a basic understanding of CPM and how it relates to the focus of this textbook—construction scheduling. It is recommended that you photocopy this diagram and refer to it while reading the Chapter.

The triangles with numbers in them represent subnetworks of this main or super network diagram. Subnetwork number 1 is a detailed schedule of how the management team plans on doing the excavation, foundation, and sitework. That subnetwork could

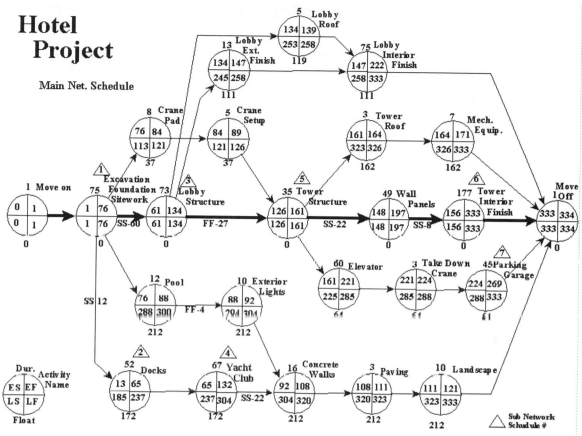

FIGURE 5.1   CPM logic diagram—main network for a hotel project

be an even larger diagram than the main network diagram. Subnet number 7 is a detailed logic diagram of how the parking garage will be built.

CPM Shows the Construction Logic

As a basic introduction, notice the network or flowchart nature of the diagram in Figure 5.1. The arrows represent relationships of logic. An arrow leaving one activity and entering the next identifies the prior activity as a predecessor and the later activity as a successor. The arrows labeled *SS* or *FF* indicate a lag, meaning the later activity starts or finishes the number of days indicated after the prior activity. For example, the arrow labeled *SS-60* between the *Excavation* and *Lobby Structure* means the excavation starts and then 60 days later the lobby structure starts. The *FF-27* between *Lobby Structure* and *Tower Structure* means the *Lobby Structure* is finished and then 27 days later, the *Tower Structure* is finished. If there is no *SS* or *FF*, it means the earlier or predecessor activity must finish prior to the start of the later or successor activity. This is called a finish-to-start relationship and it is the most common or default relationship.

The legend in the lower left corner of the hotel schedule shows the following: *ES*, the early start day; *EF*, the *early finish* day; *LF*, the late finish day; *LS*, the late start day; and *Dur.*, the duration. The *activity name* is outside the circle to the upper right, and the activity *float* is under the circle. As you look at the activity *Yacht Club* toward the bottom of the diagram, you see it can start as early as the end of day 65, in which case it should finish as early as the end of day 132. Or, it could start as late as the end of day 237, in which case it should finish as late as day 304. If it is not finished by day 304, it will delay the project completion date. The *Yacht Club* activity has 172 days of float or what some people call slack, which simply means extra days. Therefore, it is not critical.

CPM Identifies the Critical Activities

Continuing to examine Figure 5.1, notice the activities going down the center of this particular project where the relationship arrow is bolded. Those activities have "0" days of float and so they are identified as critical activities. Their early start and late start days are the same. Their early finish and late finish days are also the same. They have no extra days, no float; therefore, they are critical.

Note that the hotel project should be completed in 334 work days. If the *Excavation* activity's start is delayed by 5 days, the project will now be scheduled to finish 5 days late because excavation is a critical path activity. If the *Pool* takes 12 days longer to finish than originally planned, will that cause a delay in the project completion date? As long as the pool is finished by day 300, it will not cause a delay in the project completion date. If the contractor for the *Yacht Club* started on time but took an additional 60 days to finish, is that contractor responsible for liquidated damages? That contractor could have taken an additional 172 days without being responsible for project delays. That is why it is so important for subcontractors to be able to read these types of schedules. If the subcontractors take longer than they agreed to, that does not necessarily mean they have delayed the project because there may be float in their activities. But if their activities are critical, and they take extra time, they are obviously responsible.

If the *Lobby Structure*, which is a critical activity, takes 78 days to complete, instead of the 73 originally planned, which later activities need to be accelerated in order to meet the original project completion date? It wouldn't benefit the project to finish the *Pool*, the *Parking Garage*, *Paving*, *Lobby Interior Finish*, *Mechanical Equipment*, or many other activities any faster. The management team can see that they need to focus on the remaining critical activities following the *Lobby Structure*: the *Tower Structure*, *Wall Panels*, *Tower Interior Finish*, and *Move Off*, in order to make up the 5 extra days the *Lobby Structure* took.

This management method helps managers know specifically which activities to focus on in order to make up time. Managers will not needlessly accelerate activities that have no impact on getting the project finished on time. Think of the typical unscheduled project, where the management team has just figured they will probably not finish on time. The manager likely would send a notice to all project personnel that, from now on, everyone will work Saturdays or multiple shifts or overtime in order to get the project back on schedule. Everyone is accelerated because it is not known specifically whom to accelerate. This is no longer necessary with CPM scheduling. With CPM, a manager can see exactly which activities would benefit from acceleration and then focus on those activities that will have the least negative impact on time, cost, quality, or safety.

There is a management principle discussed in many management circles called the 80:20 rule. It is also called Pareto's law, named after Vilfredo Pareto, an Italian economist and avid gardener who, in the late 1800s observed that 20 percent of the Italian people owned 80 percent of their country's accumulated wealth. While gardening, Pareto also observed that 20 percent of the pea pods in his garden yielded 80 percent of the peas that were harvested. Over time and through application in a variety of environments, this analytic has come to be called Pareto's principle or law, the 80:20 rule, or the "vital few and trivial many rule." Roughly 80 percent of your management problems are caused by 20 percent of the people you manage. Roughly 80 percent of your daily results come from just 20 percent of the items on your to-do list. The problem is that most of us are so busy going from crisis to crisis that we never get around to the vital few activities that will lead to the greatest results. In a scheduling context, this rule of thumb states that roughly 20 percent of the activities account for 80 percent of the results. The key is to identify those 20 percent of the activities and manage them carefully, and the theory is that the (trivial many) others will just follow along. CPM helps us to identify those critical activities that account for the project meeting its major objectives.

CPM Helps Determine the Effects of Change Orders or Delays

Using CPM as a management tool helps identify if a change order will or will not affect the completion date. It is not necessary to go to court in order to determine the effects of delays or changes. The CPM logic and calculations determine the effects of a proposed change or an actual delay. Most important, the manager knows where to focus, in order to get back on schedule, or knows that the project will finish late based on the change or delay. If a critical activity has a change or delay associated with it that will prolong the finish of that critical activity, the project completion date will be delayed. That is, unless something is done with the remaining critical activities to get back on schedule. If an activity with float has a change or delay that is less than the available float, it will not result in a delay or extension of project time. But if that float activity goes beyond its late finish date, it subsequently causes a delay in the project completion date.

CPM Allows Management to Set Priorities

By using CPM, managers are able to prioritize their activities more accurately. When many activities need the same equipment or resource, it can be determined which activity gets the resource first, generally based upon the amount of float the activities have. The CPM schedule can also help accurately determine when the materials for the activities need to be delivered. The team can specifically watch for the materials for the critical activities and not consume too much of the float time for the noncritical activities. The procurement of the activities could be included in the schedule, which would further help the managers keep abreast of problems with getting materials to the project site on time. CPM helps determine and manage the cash flow on the project by allowing the noncritical activities to use some of the allocated float time.

CPM Adapts to Any Project—Simple or Complex

During the 1970s and 1980s it was common practice to not use CPM on smaller projects. It was generally thought that it would not be worth the cost or time to use CPM unless the project exceeded at least $2 or $3 million. That thinking has disappeared for even small projects in the past few years. Today's software is more user-friendly and more people are familiar with the basics of CPM. Many home builders use this management tool, and CPM is finding use in the manufacturing industry, the software and computer industry, in engineering projects, military projects, business projects, medical projects, and many other applications and industries. Anytime there is a project consisting of several activities, where one activity must be finished prior to the start of another activity, CPM can help define and manage those relationships and activities for a successful project completion. A few hours spent in planning and organizing the project in the early days can eliminate days, weeks, and even months of frustration during the life of the project.

CPM Is Easy to Follow Visually

Many managers state the aspect they like best about CPM is how it gives them a vision of the whole project. As the logic diagram is developed, it forces the management team to think at a much higher level than bar charts or any other scheduling system. The logic diagram forces detailed thinking about each activity and the relationships that exist among all activities. As stated, the CPM logic diagram gives a vision of the entire project from beginning to end. A management team is able to begin with the end in mind. As another person then looks at that logic diagram, that person is able to see the project the same way as the original developers visualized it. This visual advantage cannot be overlooked; it is a major advantage of network scheduling methods. If something changes, it is easy to visually see the effects of that change and respond accordingly. CPM potentially is the most effective scheduling and planning system that has been developed to date.

CPM Allows Analysis of Different Methods or Sequences of Construction

With CPM and the computer, the management team is able to analyze the options available on how to manage the project. They can play "what if" scenarios and perform cost-benefit analysis. What if we bring in another crane? What if we double this or that crew? What if we work weekends or multiple shifts on this or that activity? Then, with CPM and the computer they can choose which scenario gives the best results. With a computer, it also becomes manageable to update the schedule, to know precisely where the project is, time wise, as compared to where it should be.

CPM Is Useful for Court Cases—Proving Responsible Party for Delays

Some companies use CPM scheduling for this reason alone—to help keep them out of court. They are tired of trying to prove who is responsible for delays. Some of the biggest lawsuits relating to construction are related to delay claims. Sometimes a delay of a few days in the fall may delay the completion of the project for months due to bad weather in the winter.

When CPM scheduling is used, it is much more obvious who or what caused the delay. This is a two-edged sword; it cuts in both directions. Some owners are reluctant to force the contractor to use CPM because it vividly shows the effects of the delays caused by the owner as well.

CPM Creates Teamwork

Another major advantage of CPM is that it creates opportunities for teamwork better than any other scheduling method. Everyone who looks at the logic diagram sees the same vision of the project. Everyone also can see the importance of his or her part in the total process. The development of the logic diagram is an opportune time to get input from the prime subcontractors and stakeholders on how the project is organized and will be managed.

The typical construction project begins with a lot of enthusiasm and good feelings among the major players. The first construction progress meetings go something like this: "This is going to be a great project, it will be a win–win opportunity for everybody." "This is going to be a quality project; we are going to finish on time, within budget, and without any accidents." "Everyone work hard and it will be a joy to work with you."

A construction project can be compared to a football game where, in the first huddle, the quarterback says, "Let's get a touchdown on this first play." "Everyone run hard, hit someone; let's make a touchdown—break!" What would happen with that type of play called in the huddle? The quarterback would be smeared—no one knows if it's a run or pass, what, when, or where. Each player would be putting maximum effort into blocking someone, running somewhere, tackling anyone around, and total chaos would ensue. Some construction projects are similar to that—a plan for disaster. In order to make a play, everyone needs to have a specific assignment. The team needs to know if it is a pass or a run and specifically what the patterns and assignments are in detail. If one offensive lineman misses his assignment, another team player will do everything possible to take care of his teammate's responsibility as well. This desire, commitment, and teamwork attitude must also be present in construction teams if they want to win the contract and finish the project with success. There must be a plan of how the project is going to be built. Many construction project managers start projects without a schedule or a specific plan. Their only plan is to work hard and finish on time. It is surprising some times how successful the construction industry is without a more specific plan or formal schedule. However, many times the price paid is high: overtime, poor work, unsafe conditions, and years of litigation.

The CPM logic diagram looks somewhat like a football play. Every team member knows exactly what they are supposed to do and when to do it. Everyone can easily see the effects of one person not filling the assignment or dropping the ball. CPM creates a much better plan for success than just "working hard."

WHY CPM IS NOT BETTER KNOWN OR USED

As CPM was first publicized, many project managers became excited about the possibilities of using this new management tool. The construction industry was one of the first to apply this new method to their major projects. However, the industry shortly lost interest in CPM because it was too difficult to learn and it needed the use of computers to do the calculations and to keep it up-to-date. Not many companies had access to computers and, if they did, the turn-around time on updating and printing new reports was too excessive. Instead of getting management reports, they got historical reports because the job changed daily and the old computer reports were generated monthly. In order for CPM to truly be a management tool, the manager needs to interact with the computer on a real-time basis, which has been possible only in the past few years.

Formerly, field managers were reluctant to accept CPM because they did not understand it and it seemed to be just a lot of paperwork. One of the problems with an inexperienced manager using CPM and the computer is the tendency to produce more reports and schedules than necessary. With the computer, you can generate a pile of complex reports resulting in a stack of paper in a few minutes. The experienced manager has learned to keep the reports as simple as possible to control the project and communicate the plan to all involved. A good rule of thumb is one piece of paper for each crew leader, showing their activities for the next few weeks.

The advent of the personal computer has created a new world in project management. With a good basic understanding of CPM, the user-friendly software that project managers and superintendents are learning to use is having an impact on their projects, helping them to achieve greater levels of success. CPM is an idea of the 1950s whose time has finally come.

DISADVANTAGES OF CPM

CPM can become complex and requires training to become an effective user. Many find CPM difficult to teach, even if they are good at using it themselves. It typically requires formal training and then applied use. As the most sophisticated scheduling and planning system in use today, CPM requires tremendous commitment, especially in the early learning stages, in order to use it effectively. Without training, the field personnel are reluctant to accept it, especially if they have not had input into the development of the schedule. To overcome this, many companies have found success in providing in-house training to all their project managers and superintendents.

Conclusion

CPM has the potential of being a great asset to the management team as they learn how to develop accurate and complete schedules. CPM's features or benefits include showing the construction logic, identifying the critical activities, helping determine the effects of a change order or delay, allowing management to set priorities, adapting to any project, being easy to follow visually, allowing analysis of different methods or sequences, being useful for court cases, and creating teamwork.

CPM scheduling will enjoy only limited success until it is made a team effort. The whole management team must learn and understand the basics so they can take advantage of this management tool and avoid the pitfalls that are caused by misuse and a lack of understanding. The schedule should be developed with input from the superintendents, the prime subcontractors, and key project players. It then becomes "their" schedule and they will take responsibility for their activities.

This concludes the introduction to CPM. The next few chapters will discuss in detail how to develop the CPM network logic diagram, calculate the start and finish dates, calculate the float, and how to use CPM as an effective tool to help manage projects.

Application

1. Visit a significant commercial construction project and ask to interview the project manager or superintendent. Ask his or her opinion about critical path method and its use with construction projects. How does the manager or superintendent develop the schedule? What does he or she like or dislike about CPM?

2. Attend a local Associated General Contractors (AGC) or an Associated Builders and Contractors (ABC) meeting and informally talk to several of the general contractors as well as subcontractors to get their opinions of CPM. Ask the subcontractors if many general contractors they have worked with actually scheduled projects using CPM. Did the subs have the opportunity to give input into the development of the schedule? Did having a CPM schedule make a difference to the subs' own productivity and profitability?

3. If you can find a project where CPM is being used, ask to see the logic diagram. Does it make sense to you? You will become much more proficient and capable of analyzing a CPM logic diagram as you continue with this text.

CHAPTER 6

CREATING THE NETWORK LOGIC DIAGRAM

▄▄▄▄▄▄▄▄▄▄▄▄ I N T R O D U C T I O N ▄▄▄▄▄▄▄▄▄▄

The next few chapters will take the reader through the logic development and use of CPM one step at a time. This chapter focuses on specifically how to develop the network logic diagram. Because this is the first step in developing a CPM schedule, an entire chapter is devoted to the subject. After the logic diagram is developed the durations are assigned, which is the focus of Chapter 7. Once the durations are assigned the start and finish date calculations are done (Chapter 8).

There are several methods that experienced management teams like to use to develop the logic diagram. This chapter discusses the most common methods used and provides ideas on what must be done prior to the actual development of the logic diagram. Creation of the logic diagram is the most important step in CPM scheduling. If the logic diagram is inaccurate the scheduled dates will be incorrect and the schedule will not properly serve anyone. This chapter will help the reader understand how this is to be done.

THOROUGHLY FAMILIARIZE YOURSELF WITH THE PROJECT

Before a manager can begin to create a schedule, he or she first should become very familiar with the project by studying the plans and specifications thoroughly. The General Conditions, Submittals section of the specifications typically will contain details of the schedule, including the number of activities, software requirements, types and number of reports, and so on. As you examine the plans, think of the methods of construction that will be used to build the project. Analyze access to the site. Is there room for storage and delivery of materials? What equipment will be needed? Which area of the project will be best to start on first? Where will the work move to from there? There are many questions the management team needs to consider.

There is no one right way to build any project, but there may a better way or a way this specific team desires to build this particular project. The architectural plans must become very familiar to the management team. The team must think particularly about how they are going to move throughout the project and then determine the best sequence of operations. They should also look for unusual or unique aspects about this project that may differ from other similar projects they have managed. The team must try to anticipate problem areas in constructing the project. For example, what major parts of the project are the most important, that may need to be finished first? If they are done first, does this limit access to other areas? Is it important to schedule the delivery of materials to arrive just in time for installation? Be creative in the thinking at this point. Don't be afraid to think "outside the box."

INTERVIEW KEY MANAGEMENT PERSONNEL

The management team should talk with the estimators about problem areas relating to the project that estimators may have seen as they prepared the bid. Make sure all superintendents and project managers are consulted and have an opportunity to be involved in the planning and development of the schedule. Don't forget to involve the owner as an additional source of information. It is also important to have help, when needed, from the superintendents of the prime subcontractors that will be working on the project. If this is to be a team project, involve the team members. Too many times, project schedules are developed without any input from other members of the team or subcontractors. This may lead to a breakdown in communications and a lack of support for the schedule. If the schedule is really to be used to help manage the project, this is an important step in developing the network logic diagram. There is more information on how to involve subcontractors and others in the development of the schedule in Chapter 17.

BREAK DOWN THE PROJECT INTO ACTIVITIES

This step is more difficult than it may appear. It is always a challenge to determine how detailed to make the activities. Remember, the overall goal is to plan, organize, direct, and control—to force detailed thinking and then communicate the schedule with all team members. If the activities are too large or are more summary-type activities, the team won't plan in detail and there will be little control or direction. If the activities are broken down into unnecessary detail, however, confusion and additional work can result in order to control and update the schedule later. Watch out for information overload, where you provide more information than is needed. As an example, the framing of a simple house could be one activity: "frame." Or, it could be broken down into a few more activities such as "frame floor," "frame load-bearing walls," "frame roof," "frame interior partitions." It also could be broken down into needless detail: "place mud sill on foundation," "mark location of foundation bolts," "drill 5/8" hole," "apply sill sealer," "put mud sill on top of foundation and sill sealer," "slide on washer," "put on nut," "tighten nut." Of course that would be way too much detail, but somewhere between this needless detail and one activity, "build the project" is the correct level of detail. Every management team wrestles with this on every project. Don't make the schedule more complex than necessary and yet give it enough detail to allow control and communication.

A few guidelines for breaking down projects are as follows: Consider who the schedule is designed for. If the management team is very experienced, larger scaled activities may be appropriate. If the management team is less experienced, they may need a more detailed breakdown of activities. Typically, keep trades separate. Don't schedule one single activity for mechanical, electrical, and plumbing. Break down the activities to the level that can be managed and that provides control. A schedule may show one activity that goes from the beginning of the job to the end that is titled "electrical." This level of detail does little to give direction to the subcontractor or crews. All they know is that they are on the job somewhere during those days. At least break down the electrical to "sub slab electrical," "rough electrical," "electrical service," and "finish electrical." However, that level of detail still may not communicate to the electrician what is needed to control the job. The level of detail that results from a well-thought-out schedule (that communicates and provides control) is a schedule that shows the electrical crew, for example, when they will be doing finish electrical on the fourth floor of the east wing. Some project managers schedule summary-level activities and then expect the superintendents to schedule in greater detail for the next few weeks, to give them the ability to communicate and control the project on a day-to-day basis.

Then there is the question of whether or not the procurement activities should be included in the schedule? For instance, should the schedule include the approval of submittals, the manufacturing of the materials, and the shipping of the materials to the site? Should the schedule include the preparation and submission of shop drawings, catalog cuts, and samples? Testing of materials, equipment, and systems are other items that possibly should be included. Samples or mockup installations for testing or review may also need to be included in the schedule. If these are frequent problems that come up during the execution of projects that cause a loss of control, include them in the schedule. A good rule of thumb is to include in the schedule the items that usually cause problems—the activities that a manager has a tendency to forget or overlook.

USE A WORK BREAKDOWN STRUCTURE (WBS)

Some companies prefer to use a work breakdown structure (WBS) to help identify the activities prior to developing the schedule. This is a systematic means of defining the activities so that each activity can be readily identified by its WBS number. The WBS number builds intelligence into the activity ID number. The numbering system is typically unique for a company or project. Some prefer to divide the project by the responsible person, firm, or subcontractor. Others divide the project or break it down according to building or area of work. Sometimes it makes sense to break it down according to the divisions in the specifications. A common method is to break down the project according to phases. For example, with a building, start with the major phases of the project and number them accordingly:

Phase 1	Project Feasibility
Phase 2	Design and Engineering
Phase 3	Job Mobilization
Phase 4	Site Preparation
Phase 5	Foundation
Phase 6	Structure
Phase 7	Interior Rough-ins

After the main phases are determined, break down the main phases to the next level of detail. Then break down "Footings" to the next level as shown below:

5 Foundation
    5.1 Footings
        5.1.1 Lay out footings
        5.1.2 Excavate footings
        5.1.3 Form footings
        5.1.4 Reinforce footings
        5.1.5 Pour footings
        5.1.6 Strip footings
    5.2 Foundations

Thus, the WBS code 5.1.2 would be interpreted as follows. The "5" ties the activity to the "Foundation" phase. The "1" ties the activity to "Footings." The "2" is the second activity under "Footings" which is "Excavate footings." The WBS can continue to the level of detail desired.

Rather than using a WBS, some managers prefer to simply start creating the logic diagram and thinking directly on the activity level as the logic diagram is drawn. When identifying the project activities many managers feel it is good scheduling practice to use an action verb, object, and location to describe the activities. Rather than "Footings," use "Form" (the action verb), "footings" (the object), on the "north end" (location). When the schedule is input into the computer and a daily list of activities is produced, that level of detail will communicate "Form footings north end." If the report said only "Footings," the workers would not know if they were to form the footings, reinforce the footings, or pour the footings, nor would they know which footings. This technique provides for communication to the workers and control of the project. Everyone knows where they need to be, what they should be doing, and when it should be done.

With experience, managers learn what is the most effective level of detail to break down a project. Sometimes a summary-level schedule is enough to help with the estimating and to get a project started. Then, later the project is broken into greater levels of detail as needed for the three-week look-ahead schedules discussed in Chapter 4. Those three- or four-week look-ahead schedules should match the main milestone dates of the summary schedule.

CREATE THE NETWORK LOGIC DIAGRAM

A simple warehouse project will be used in our example of how to create a schedule. This warehouse has a slab on grade monolithic footing, wood framing, trussed roof, asphalt shingles, face brick on the side facing the street, wood siding on the other exterior surfaces, a few windows, and an overhead door. With that scope of work in mind, the CPM logic diagram will be created. A popular way to do this is with a rubber stamp as shown in Figure 6.1.

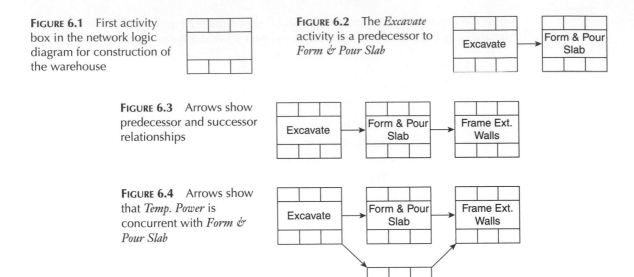

FIGURE 6.1 First activity box in the network logic diagram for construction of the warehouse

FIGURE 6.2 The *Excavate* activity is a predecessor to *Form & Pour Slab*

FIGURE 6.3 Arrows show predecessor and successor relationships

FIGURE 6.4 Arrows show that *Temp. Power* is concurrent with *Form & Pour Slab*

This rubber stamped diagram is called a "node" or an "activity box." One diagram is stamped for each activity. For now, only the large center section will be used to write the name of the activity. Typically, the activity name is abbreviated enough to fit into the center box. Some managers prefer to use sticky notes rather than a rubber stamp.

To create the CPM schedule, obtain a piece of paper large enough to plan out the project. Some schedulers like to use meat wrapping paper from the butcher shop. They can roll the paper out to the length desired as they create the schedule.

Next, stamp an activity box at the beginning of the piece of paper as shown in Figure 6.2 and write in the name of the first activity, *Excavate*.

Now stamp the second activity box, *Form & Pour Slab*. Because *Form & Pour Slab* can't start until *Excavate* is done, draw an arrow from *Excavate* to *Form & Pour Slab*. In scheduling terms, *Excavate* is a *predecessor* to (occurs before) *Form & Pour Slab*. *Form & Pour Slab* is a *successor* to (occurs after) *Excavate* as shown in Figure 6.2.

The management team decides that *Frame Ext. (Exterior) Walls* is the next activity and it can start after the slab is formed and poured. In scheduling terms, it is said that *Form & Pour Slab* is a predecessor to *Frame Ext. Walls*. Stamp it accordingly and draw the arrow as shown in Figure 6.3.

The next activity the management team plans is *Temp. (Temporary) Power*. They want to do *Excavate* first. They also agree that *Temp. Power* needs to be done in order for the carpenters to do the *Frame Ext. Walls* activity. So, the diagram now looks as illustrated in Figure 6.4.

Figure 6.4 shows that *Temp. Power* is *concurrent* with (occurs at the same time as) *Form & Pour Slab*. The logic diagram, with its relationships of predecessor, successor, and concurrent activities, is the heart and soul of the schedule. Therefore, these relationships must be thought through in detail. If they are wrong, all the dates and reports will be incorrect. A bogus schedule will result.

According to the logic of the schedule in Figure 6.4 the concrete forming crew will not have electrical power; they will need to use battery-operated tools for what little sawing they need to do, or a chainsaw, or a handsaw. If it is desired that the forming crew needs *temporary power*, change the logic of the diagram and show *Temp. Power* inserted between *Excavate* and *Form & Pour Slab*.

ELIMINATE REDUNDANT ARROWS

As the network logic diagram is created, there is no need for redundant arrows.

Figure 6.5 shows a redundant arrow from *Excavate* to *Frame Ext. Walls*. If *Excavate* is a predecessor to *Form & Pour Slab*, and *Form & Pour Slab* is a predecessor to *Frame Ext. Walls*, it is redundant to have the arrow from *Excavate* to *Frame Ext. Walls*. That arrow is not necessary. Redundant arrows just confuse the logic diagram, so avoid them. Also avoid backward arrows; they tend to be confusing as well, as do crossing arrows. Oftentimes crossing arrows cannot be avoided, but strive to keep the logic diagram as simple and easy to visually follow as possible.

It is important to also eliminate logic loops.

A logic loop, shown in Figure 6.6, is impossible logic and therefore not acceptable in the logic diagram. If Activity A precedes Activity B, and Activity B precedes Activity C, it is not logical that Activity C could precede Activity A.

FIGURE 6.5 Redundant arrows cause confusion in the logic diagram

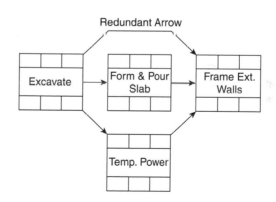

FIGURE 6.6 Logic Loop

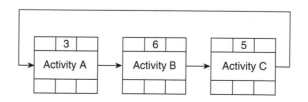

The scheduler or management team next adds *Frame the Roof*, after *Frame Ext. Walls*. Then comes *Shingle Roof*. They also want *Rough Electrical* to follow *Frame Roof*. Next, *Inst. Windows & Doors* is added to the diagram. The new logic diagram is shown in Figure 6.7.

The rest of the logic diagram is developed until the management team is satisfied that the network logic diagram is indeed the way they plan on building the project. Figure 6.8 shows the team's completed network logic diagram for the construction of the warehouse.

Normally, the last two activities would continue in a horizontal line, but here it was done with a vertical line in order to keep the diagram large enough to easily

FIGURE 6.7 Progression of logic diagram

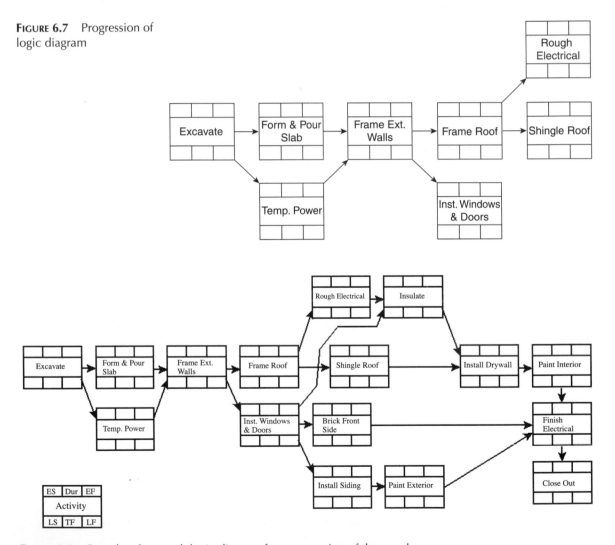

FIGURE 6.8 Completed network logic diagram for construction of the warehouse

read and yet fit on one page. Windows and doors are each a predecessor to insulate so that the insulation can be fitted around the rough window and door openings. The team wanted the roof shingled prior to the drywall so the drywall would not be damaged in case of bad weather. The brick, exterior paint, and interior paint are all predecessors to the finish electrical because this warehouse has electrical lights and outlets on all exterior walls and the electrician wanted to do all finish electrical in one trip.

It is important to remember that the creation of a schedule is a team process that should involve input from all key members of the team. Don't overlook the superintendents and prime subcontractors. They can furnish time and money-saving ideas if they are given the chance. As the network logic diagram is created, most managers find they are thinking on an entirely different level of detail than when they create a bar chart schedule. As discussed earlier, one of the greatest advantages of CPM scheduling is that it forces the management team to think through the project in detail and thus eliminate mistakes during the actual construction of the project. Some managers have stated that if the creation of the logic diagram is used for this purpose only, it is well worth the time required developing it.

That is all there is to creating the network logic diagram. Some project management software programs call this a "pure logic diagram," whereas others call it the "PERT view." (You may recall that PERT refers to Project Evaluation Review Techinque, used by the Navy in its early development of network scheduling.) "Network view" or "logic diagram" are more accurate descriptions of this flowchart diagram.

Figure 6.9 shows a network logic diagram created with the use of a rubber stamp. The diagram does not need to be extremely neat at this point. It just needs to be legible enough to accurately input this logic into the computer.

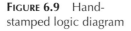

FIGURE 6.9 Hand-stamped logic diagram

CONSIDER OTHER METHODS FOR CREATING THE LOGIC DIAGRAM

Most experienced schedulers prefer to create the logic diagram by hand rather than on a computer. The project management software of today provides the possibility of creating the logic diagram right on the computer. The problem is that the computer screen is small and allows only a few activity boxes to display on the screen at one time. For a small project this will work fine, but for a project of many activities, it is difficult to locate the proper predecessors and successors in order to draw the arrows between them. This results in excessive scrolling up and down and to the left and right, making it easy to create errors. Another advantage of the hand-drawn schedule is that it gives the management team the vision of the entire project.

If the logic diagram is created by hand, there will be many revisions as the project comes together. A large eraser is frequently needed because the team's thinking processes evolve as the project schedule develops. Also, as more people are given the opportunity for input into the schedule, new ideas come forth and cause a revision in the logic diagram. This should be encouraged. If the schedule is as well thought out as possible, the project will run much more smoothly. It is easier to erase a pencil mark than it is to remove reinforced concrete. Normally the logic diagram is drawn a couple of times in order to simplify it and make it communicate accurately. The first draft generally results in backward arrows, inserted activities, potential loops, and basically looks like a bowl of spaghetti. Once it is drawn more neatly and the durations are included, along with any special notations, it is ready to be input into the computer.

Inputting the hand-drawn logic diagram into the computer is a fairly simple process; an assistant or staff person can be trained quickly. If the network logic is developed on the computer, the scheduler needs to input the information. This eliminates input from other team members and requires a lot of the manager's time. If it is developed on paper, the critical and detailed thinking is done by management and then the staff person inputs the schedule information into the computer.

Most project managers prefer to create the project from the beginning to the end—and some prefer to create the project from the end to the beginning. Creating a schedule "in reverse" means beginning with the last activity—close-out. Before that can be done, the final clean must be completed, and so on. That "backward" way of planning is acceptable; simply stamp out the logic diagram from the end to the beginning. As always, it is important to get the team's thoughts down on paper.

Planning is everything—the logic diagram is primarily a planning process, not a scheduling process—and the logic diagram is the result. The final schedule will be the primary tool used to communicate that planning process to all involved in the construction of the project. After a manager is experienced at developing a few of these logic diagrams, it becomes much easier. Once the logic diagram is completed and the durations are entered along with the start and finish dates, it then shifts from a planning process to a scheduling process.

Another technique that pays off later is to create the project logic diagram with only one beginning activity and finish the logic diagram with only one ending activity. If the project starts with two or more activities, create a single start activity and label it

FIGURE 6.10 A page of mail labels used to help create the logic diagram

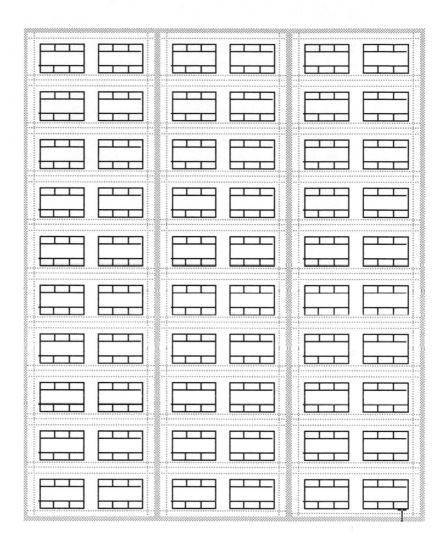

"start" or "begin" and give it a duration of zero days. Do likewise if there are two or more ending activities. This is a good scheduling practice that helps check the computer input. It is easy to overlook a predecessor or successor while inputting the schedule into the computer. A helpful method for finding obvious computer input errors is to see if there is only one activity with no predecessors (the first activity) and only one activity with no successors (the last activity).

The use of the rubber stamp to create the logic diagram has already been discussed. The stamp decreases the amount of time it takes to create the network. Another idea is to use mail labels (Figure 6.10) to represent the activities. A sheet of mail labels with a similar activity box as used with the rubber stamp could be created on your computer and then printed. A typical mail label is large enough to handle two activity boxes. The mail label is then pasted onto the paper as the network is being created. Avery 5160 is a common mail label to use. The original is created by using a word processing program with the page formatted for mail labels.

Another aid some managers like to use to help create the logic diagram is sticky notes. Write the activity name on the sticky note and apply it to the network diagram. The different colors of notes can represent different trades, equipment, or other resources or problems that are being solved. The notes can be easily repositioned as needed. One caution, however, is that after the network is completed, take a few minutes to tape or glue the notes in their final position. When the paper is rolled or folded up, unattached sticky notes reposition themselves at will.

It doesn't matter which method is used to create the logic diagram. The important thing is that it represents the thinking of the management team as to how they plan on constructing the project.

MAKE SURE THE LOGICAL RELATIONSHIPS ARE ACCURATE

Because of the reluctance of some managers to develop the logic diagram, it must be stated one more time that this is the *most important part of CPM scheduling!* The schedule dates, as you will see in the next chapters, are calculated from this logic diagram. If the logic diagram does not reflect the way the management team really intends on building the project, the dates, bar charts, and other reports created from it will all be incorrect. Updating the schedule will be a time-consuming and confusing ordeal. The schedule reports will also be confusing, and everyone will hate the computer, the scheduler, and CPM scheduling in general.

To make sure the logic diagram represents the way the team desires to construct the project, double-check the diagram and ask yourself these two questions of each activity: (1) Does this activity *really* have to be done before each of the following activities can start? (2) What *other activities* need to be done before this activity can start? The above two questions seem to be key to make the mind think of other relationships or activities that may have been forgotten in the development of the first logic diagram. It is important to take the time to double check the network.

CONCLUSION

The careful development of the logic diagram is the most important step in the creation of a CPM schedule. The thought and time required to develop an accurate logic diagram will pay off later as the schedule is input into the computer and updated. A primary reason schedules are not used or are later abandoned is due to not taking sufficient time to think through the logic and failing to obtain team input into the development of the logic diagram. Too many schedulers today overlook this important step. The first step in creating a diagram is to familiarize yourself with the project. Next, management team members and others involved with the project should be consulted and given an opportunity to give their input. With the overall goals in mind, the project must be broken down into activities. The work breakdown structure (WBS) is frequently used to help identify the activities before developing the schedule. Once the management team is ready to create the handdrawn network logic diagram, several methods can be used: the rubber stamp, mail labels, or sticky notes. The most critical aspect of the network logic diagram is that it accurately reflects the way management intends to build the project. The industry needs schedulers who understand the construction process—or at least obtain input from team members that do understand construction processes—rather than just computer operators who know the software and can make impressive-looking bar charts that have no technical merit. The thinking and development of the logic diagram is essential to success with the critical path method. This important step cannot be overlooked, nor can it be delegated to a person with good computer skills but poor construction and management skills.

APPLICATION

1. Create a logic diagram of the same project you created a bar chart for in Chapter 4. Do not look at the previous bar chart as you create this logic diagram. How does your thinking process compare with the thinking process that went into the development of the bar chart? Write a short paragraph on the differences in the thinking process required to create a bar chart versus that required to create a logic diagram.

2. Which scheduling technique (the network or the bar chart) resulted in the most accurate and well-thought-out schedule?

3. If you are currently working on a project, create a logic diagram of that project covering the construction operations planned for the next few months. Then show that plan to other members of the management team and seek their input to revise and improve the plan.

4. From the logic diagram developed above, ask the 2 key questions of every activity and note the improved changes they make to the logic diagram.

DETERMINING DURATIONS

I N T R O D U C T I O N

Now that the network logic diagram has been developed and the management team has thought through the project and developed a plan of exactly how they intend to construct the project as far as activities and relationships are concerned, it is time to add the duration to each activity. Most of the software has the ability to schedule by the hour or even by the minute. However, with construction applications, it is difficult to get a tradesperson to show up anytime during a single day to do a 20-minute job. Therefore, the durations typically are rounded up to the next full day. If it is realistic to have one activity completed in the morning and another activity completed in the afternoon, it is still suggested that the schedule be done by the day. Simply show the activities as concurrent in the network logic with a duration of one day each. Then in the activity description, include *A.M.* or *P.M.* to communicate the time of the day that activity should be done as shown in Figure 7.1.

For some specific projects, such as in manufacturing or maintenance, it may be realistic to schedule by the hour, minute, or shift. The challenge is to make the durations realistic in practical real-world applications.

THE RELATIONSHIP OF ACTIVITY DURATION TO ACTIVITY COST

The duration of the activity is typically the duration that meets or exceeds quality standards, provides for a safe work environment, is within budget, and gets the project done on time. This is particularly true of the activities on the critical path. It is important to select a duration that represents a realistic cost. If the activity duration is much shorter than a typical duration (by working overtime or increasing the number of workers or pieces of equipment) the costs go up because of a crowded work space or

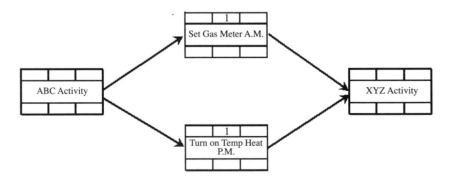

FIGURE 7.1   Scheduling half-day activities concurrently

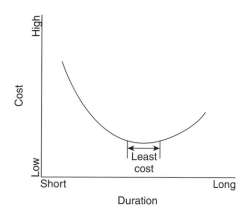

FIGURE 7.2   Activity time–cost curve

fatigue which decreases productivity. If the activity duration is much longer than a typical duration (by having a less than desirable crew size, inexperienced workers, or people working short days or weeks) the overhead costs of supervision and other overhead increases, again causing the costs to increase. This time–cost relationship is shown in Figure 7.2.

An examination of Figure 7.2 shows how the activity duration typically affects cost. Extremely short durations increase costs and extremely long durations also increase costs. So the key is to use the duration that will give the lowest cost, without sacrificing quality or safety.

THE TEXTBOOK APPROACH

The typical textbook approach to determining durations is as follows: First, obtain the quantity of work to be done from the estimate or quantity survey. Then (preferably from company records) obtain the productivity rate of the crew. Let's use the activity "Form & Pour Footings" as an example. If there are 500 lineal feet of 12 × 36-inch reinforced footings to form and pour and the productivity records indicate that it takes one hour of work to form and pour 2 feet, then one worker can do 16 feet in eight hours. A crew size of four should be able to do 64 feet per day. So, 500 total feet ÷ 64 = 7.81 days. This would be rounded up to 8 days for the duration of this activity.

If the work is new or unusual for a company, they could use an estimating manual such as the *Means Estimating Handbook* or *Walker's Manual for Construction Cost Estimating* to obtain productivity information. *Means* generally lists the productivity of a typical crew. This may be more accurate than the example above, because a crew of four may not be the ideal crew size. Sometimes a crew of two can do more than twice the work of one. An extra-large crew may have one or more workers standing around much of the time. Assuming *Means* shows a crew of four to have an average daily output or a productivity rate of 65 feet per day, the duration is equal to the quantity divided by the productivity rate: $500 \div 65 = 7.69$, or 8 days.

$$\text{Activity Duration} = \frac{\text{Quantity}}{\text{Productivity Rate}}$$

As you can see, if the crew size is increased, the productivity rate should increase and therefore decrease the duration.

Typically, it is better to use a company's own productivity rates because productivity may change in different parts of the country and under differing weather conditions. No one is more familiar with durations than an experienced project manager or superintendent who knows the company's own productivity rates.

The textbook approach is an excellent method to obtain accurate durations when the productivity rate and the quantities are known. This is probably the most accurate method to use, especially with self-performed labor on very large construction projects. With smaller major projects an experienced superintendent may be more accurate in estimating durations than all the productivity figures and texts combined. Certainly, in the light commercial and residential construction industries the estimate from the superintendent or project manager is sufficient.

DURATIONS FROM SUBCONTRACTORS OR VENDORS

Perhaps the easiest way to get durations is from the people who will be doing the work. It is common to simply ask the subcontractor how long it will take to do the assigned work. However, this duration may not fit the general contractor's schedule, which may cause a conflict. Generally, subs are selected by the lowest bid, without considering the duration. Assume a subcontractor was thinking he or she could do this work in five weeks and for x amount of money. The general contractor awards the contract to the subcontractor and then a few weeks later, as the schedule is developed, the subcontractor is notified that the activity must be done in one week. Assume the subcontractor has the workforce available to do that activity in one week. Can it be done in one week at the same cost as it was bid when the subcontractor was thinking of five weeks? Can it be done in one week with the same quality and safety standards? Most likely not, so a dispute is created. Another problem with simply asking the subcontractor for a duration, after the sub has been awarded the contract, is the sub may state an excessive amount of time to ensure it will be done within that time period. This gives the subcontractor a little time cushion for doing the job. If this practice is repeated by most of the subcontractors on each of their activities, the total project duration will be greatly inflated and the schedule will be excessively long.

Remember, the overall objectives are to build a quality project, on time, within budget, and in a safe work environment. If contracts are always awarded to the lowest bidder, what is really being managed? Cost, cost, cost, and cost. A better approach would be to prequalify the subcontractor by inspecting a prior job to validate that the sub's work meets the quality standards. Then validate the subcontractor's safety record to make sure the tradespeople have safe work habits. Once the safety and quality are approved, then ask the sub for a cost *and* a duration, knowing the contract will be awarded on a combination of cost and time. This keeps the cost and the duration competitive and holds the subcontractor accountable for the duration of the activities as well as the costs.

An additional method to use after prequalifying the sub, is to furnish a duration that meets the needs of the project and then ask for a price with that duration. Somehow, not only the cost but also the duration must be agreed upon because unrealistic time frames increase costs. If cost and time can be agreed on early in the job, potential problems can be eliminated. Communication and agreement in these vital areas will help a project move more smoothly.

Weather conditions and the time of year are other factors to consider in determining durations. Climates where the weather and temperature vary will also have productivity figures that vary. It takes much longer to do some jobs during bad or freezing weather than it does in good weather. Some activities, such as paving and landscaping, cannot happen during the winter months in many northern climates. Likewise, too hot of conditions also affect productivity.

DURATIONS FROM EXPERIENCED SUPERINTENDENTS OR CREW LEADERS

When the person preparing the schedule receives input concerning the project logic from each team member, that is a good time to also get the activity durations. If an experienced superintendent says it will take so many days to do an activity, it is amazing how accurate he or she is. That may be all that is necessary to determine an accurate duration. It is not based on productivity reports, national estimating manuals, or quantity surveys, yet it may be the most accurate duration in this case because a person with a high experience level considers all kinds of difficult-to-quantify information to make that duration decision.

SCHEDULING FOR INCLEMENT WEATHER

There are several methods used to schedule and adjust durations for bad weather. One method would be to simply increase the duration if the activity must be done during adverse weather conditions. An excavation in the summer may take only 12 days, whereas the same excavation in frozen earth in the winter may take twice that long. Highway work is greatly impacted by weather. Another method of scheduling for inclement weather is to add a weather contingency activity at the end of the schedule with a duration of the number of forecasted nonwork days. This would show the project completing at the end of the weather contingency. Another method used by some schedulers is to insert several weather contingency activities into the critical path during the phases of the project that are more susceptible to weather delays. An additional method is to input the number of projected weather delays each month into the calendar as nonwork days, similar as is done with holidays. By creating a weather calendar these weather days can be tracked.

Whatever method is used, it is important to schedule for bad weather days. The number of days to consider can be determined from the local weather data. It must be agreed upon how much snow or rain defines a nonwork day. Then, from the local weather data, the average number of weather days in a month can be determined and scheduled. If the management team has scheduled for normal weather delays and then the weather is unusually severe and additional days are needed, the contractor generally has the right to receive a time extension or additional compensation to accelerate the project in order to finish on the original completion date. However, if weather days were not considered in the makeup of the durations in the schedule, and then normal bad weather delays the job, the contractor should not be compensated for the weather delays.

A few inches or fractions of an inch of snow may delay a project being constructed in the southern portion of the United States. In Salt Lake City, Utah, it may take a foot of snow to delay the project. Or, maybe in Salt Lake City, with a foot of new snow, the roads are still open but the contractors would not show up for work because they would all be skiing. It sounds silly, but situations like this might be considered in creating the schedule. In Arizona, a small amount of rain may delay a project in the summer, whereas in Seattle, rain is a common occurrence and tradespeople know how to work in raincoats and boots.

Another effect on durations in some states is the opening of the annual deer or elk hunt. If a large percentage of the working population is involved in these types of activities, this should be considered in the schedule.

ADDING THE DURATION TO THE NETWORK LOGIC DIAGRAM

The duration is entered into the predetermined area of the activity box in the network logic diagram. Using the activity box defined earlier, the duration of the activity goes in the top center cell as shown in Figure 7.3.

The network logic diagram of the warehouse, with the durations included is shown in Figure 7.4.

Now that the durations are included in the activity boxes, it is time to calculate the start and finish dates as explained in the next chapter.

FIGURE 7.3   Placement of duration in an activity box

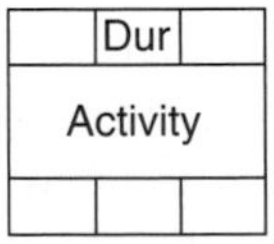

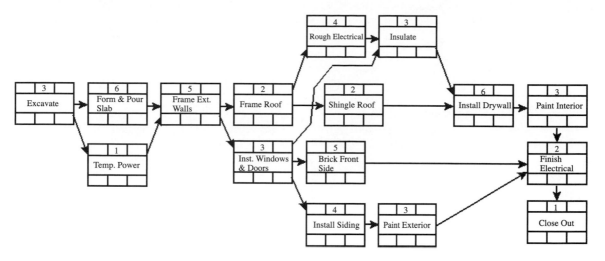

Figure 7.1   Durations added to the logic diagram for the warehouse project

Conclusion

Durations should not be just a guess. They should be based on crew size productivity and the quantities from the estimate. If durations are given by an experienced superintendent the plans and the estimate should be consulted and a thoughtful assumption made. Weather conditions and special considerations should be taken into account when determining durations. Involve the whole management team, including the subcontractors, to determine the most likely duration for each activity. Manage the duration of each activity just as you manage the cost of each activity.

Application

1. Using the logic diagram developed in Chapter 6, add the durations to the activity boxes.
2. Examine any estimating book and look for productivity rates of given crews and see how activity durations could be determined once the quantity survey is completed.

CHAPTER 8

CALCULATING START AND FINISH DATES

■ I N T R O D U C T I O N ■

Once the network logic diagram has been created and the durations have been added to the activities, the calculations can be done to determine the start and finish dates. This step is generally done by the computer. However, any person involved with CPM scheduling needs to understand where the dates come from and exactly how they are determined. Without understanding this, CPM scheduling is somewhat of a mystery. In fact, some project managers prefer to calculate the early start and finish dates by hand before the schedule is input into the computer to verify that the project completion date is acceptable.

CALCULATING EARLY START AND EARLY FINISH DATES— THE FORWARD PASS

With the network logic diagram completed and the activity durations included for the warehouse project, the next step is to calculate the early start and early finish dates. This process is typically referred to as the **forward pass.** The calculations start at the beginning of the project and move to the end of the project, or from left to right.

In the activity box shown in Figure 8.1, the early start day typically is noted in the upper left corner and the early finish day is noted in the upper right corner. The box could be divided differently, or even be a different shape, but the box layout shown is a popular design.

To begin the calculations, put a zero (which represents the morning of the first day) in the early start (ES) area of the activity box as shown in Figure 8.2. Add the duration to the ES and that results in the early finish (EF) day for the first activity.

The forward pass moves from left to right or from the beginning to the end of the job as shown in Figure 8.3.

The second activity can start as soon as the first activity has finished; therefore, the next step is to transfer, or copy, the EF of the predecessor activity to the ES of the successor activity.

FIGURE 8.1   Activity box layout for forward pass

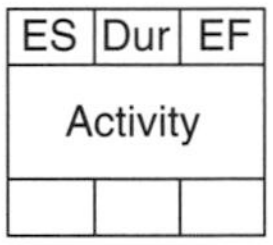

FIGURE 8.2   Early start and early finish days for *Excavate*

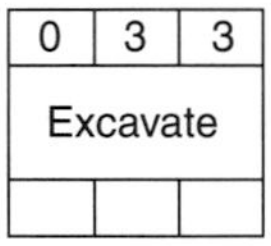

FIGURE 8.3   The forward pass moves in this direction

As shown in Figure 8.4 *Excavate* has an EF of the end of day 3, so *Form Pour Slab* and *Temp. Power* can both start (ES) the end of day 3. Adding the durations of each activity to the ES day gives an EF day for *Form Pour Slab* at the end of day 9, and *Temp. Power* the end of day 4, as show in Figure 8.4.

Look at the early dates in Figure 8.4 for *Temp. Power.* The ES day is the end of day 3 and the EF day is the end of day 4. Although stating that an activity will start at the end of a day is a little confusing, that is the way the system works. Therefore, the real work day for *Temp. Power* is day 4, and it has a one-day duration. That could be corrected by starting the first activity with an ES of 1, but then all the days would begin in the morning. The start day would then make sense, but it would be confusing to say the activity ends the morning of the next day. Some schedulers keep adding and subtraction a "1" from the numbers, but that is even more confusing. Most schedulers prefer to use the "0" start and then simply remember that all days really begin at the end of the day. This way, if someone misreads the schedule, they show up a day early rather than finishing a day late. It may take a few minutes analyzing the above example to understand this concept. The bottom line is, remember to start the first activity with a zero and keep in mind that all dates represent the *end* of the day. Therefore, the start dates are really the morning of the next day, but finish dates are the end of the day stated. Project management software helps simplify this and shows the schedule in calendar days rather than work days.

If there are two activities (arrows) as predecessors to a single activity, choose the one with the largest EF day to insert into the successor activity. This is done because both activities need to be finished before the successor activity can start.

Notice in Figure 8.5 the ES for *Frame Ext. Walls* is the largest EF of the predecessor activities, the 9, not the 4. Then, add the duration to get the EF day: $9 + 5 = 14$.

Figure 8.4 Second and third activities begin as soon as first activity has finished—day 3

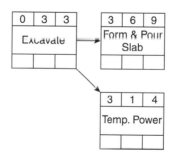

Figure 8.5 Select the largest EF of the predecessor activities

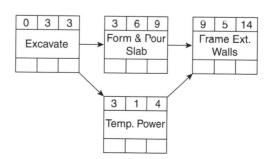

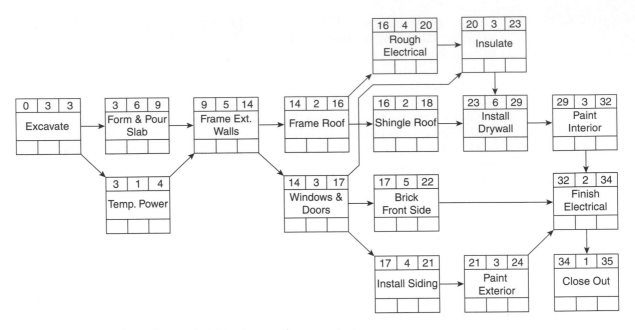

FIGURE 8.6   Forward pass is completed for the warehouse project

Hence, the EF for *Frame Ext. Walls* is the end of day 14. Continue in a like manner, always choosing the larger of the predecessors for the ES day, adding the duration to get the EF day and continuing this through the rest of the network as shown in Figure 8.6.

As can be seen from the network in Figure 8.6, the project is scheduled to finish on the end of day 35. Also note that the ES day for *Insulate* is the larger of its two predecessors, *Rough Electrical* (20) or *Windows & Doors* (17), so the 20 was chosen. Further notice that *Finish Electrical* has three predecessors with the largest being 32; therefore, 32 was chosen as the ES day for that activity.

You learn to schedule by scheduling, not just by reading about it. You must practice the concepts learned. In order to get some experience with the forward pass calculations before going on in this chapter, calculate the early start and early finish dates for Practice Problem #1 shown in Figure 8.7. You may want to photocopy these practice problems and do the work on the hardcopy rather than in the text. Do the forward pass on this project and compare your results with the answers provided at the end of the chapter.

CALCULATING LATE START AND LATE FINISH DATES— THE BACKWARD PASS

With the forward pass completed, the early start and finish days have been established. To establish the late start and finish days, the same concept is followed, except everything is done backward. Consequently, it is called the **backward pass.** The calculations

FIGURE 8.7 Practice
Problem #1

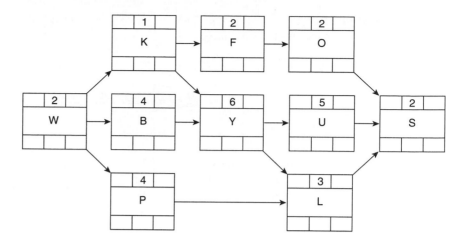

FIGURE 8.8 Activity box
layout for backward pass

FIGURE 8.9 Backward
pass calculations

FIGURE 8.10 The
beginning of the backward
pass

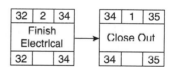

begin at the end of the project and move to the beginning of the project, or from right to left. If two arrows back into an activity, the lowest number is chosen.

The activity box in Figure 8.8 displays the late start (LS) day in the lower left corner and the late finish (LF) day in the lower right corner.

To begin the backward pass calculations, go to the last activity and copy the EF day (top right cell) into the LF (bottom right) cell of the activity box as shown in Figure 8.9. This is the standard or default method of starting the backward pass because it is typical to want the late finish day to be the same day as the early finish day. Then, subtract the duration from the LF day and that gives the LS day for that last activity as shown in Figure 8.9.

Next, move to the predecessor of the last activity and copy the LS day of the successor to the LF of the predecessor as shown in Figure 8.10.

Close Out has an LS day of 34, so this becomes the LF day for *Finish Electrical*. Then, subtract the *Finish Electrical* duration of two days (34 − 2 = 32) and this calculates the LS for *Finish Electrical* to be day 32. The LS and LF are going backward on the bottom of the activity boxes. Ignore the numbers on the top of the boxes, with the exception of the duration. They are the early days used on the forward pass and have nothing to do with the backward pass.

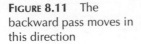

FIGURE 8.11 The backward pass moves in this direction

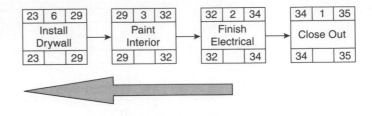

FIGURE 8.12 Always choose the earliest late finish day (14, from *Frame Roof*) for the backward pass

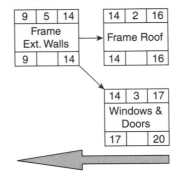

Continue in this manner, copying the EF of the successor to become the LF of the current activity, subtracting the duration to get the EF of the current activity as shown in Figure 8.11. Again, focus on the numbers (late dates) along the bottom of the activity box as shown.

During the backward pass, when there are two successor activities (noted by arrows) backing into a single activity, choose the one with the *earliest* LS day to become the LF day to insert into the predecessor activity as shown in Figure 8.12.

For example, both *Frame Roof* (LS of 14) and *Windows & Doors* (LS of 17) are backing into *Frame Ext. Walls*. So, the number to enter into the LF of *Frame Ext. Walls* (lower right) is 14, the earliest or smallest. Remember to focus on the bottom numbers in the activity box. Then subtract the duration of 5 days to get the LS day for *Frame Ext. Walls*. (14 − 5 = 9). Continue in this manner, always choosing the smaller number backing into the activity, then subtracting the duration, to get the LS day.

Continue backing through the rest of the network as shown in Figure 8.13.

When the backward pass is complete, the ES and the LS of the first activity should both be zero as shown in Figure 8.13. To review what has been calculated to this point, examine the *Shingle Roof* activity in Figure 8.13. *Shingle Roof* can start as early as the end of day 16 and finish as early as the end of day 18. Or, it could start as late as the end of day 21, and finish as late as the end of day 23 without delaying the project completion date.

For experience, now do the backward pass on Practice Problem #1 and compare your results to the solution provided at the end of the chapter.

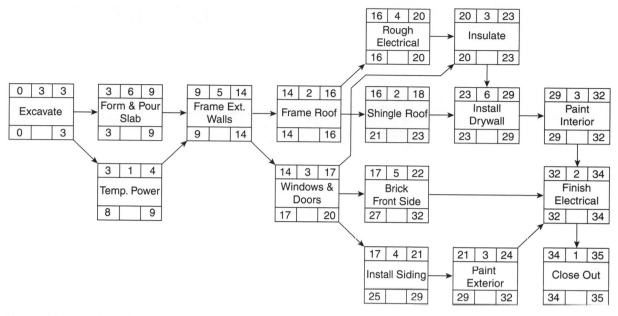

FIGURE 8.13 Backward pass is completed for the warehouse project

FIGURE 8.14 Activity box with total float (TF) added

CALCULATING TOTAL FLOAT

Total float is the difference between the early start and the early finish date or the difference between the late start and late finish date. To learn how to calculate total float, focus on the activity *Shingle Roof*. It has an ES of the end of day 16 and an LS of the end of day 21. That is a difference of 5 days in the start days. Therefore *Shingle Roof* has 5 extra days, which is called total float or, according to some schedulers, total slack. Slack and float mean the same thing. A closer look at the finish dates of *Shingle Roof* shows an EF of the end of day 18 and an LF of the end of day 23. That is also a difference of 5 days. *Shingle Roof* has 5 extra days for a total duration of 10 days that it could take without delaying the project's finish date. The mathematical formula for total float is LS − ES = Total Float, or LF − EF = Total Float. With normal relationships, as are being used here, the same number of days of float or slack are arrived at whether the ES is subtracted from the LS or if the EF is subtracted from the LF.

Total float is entered into the activity box in the bottom center cell as shown in Figure 8.14.

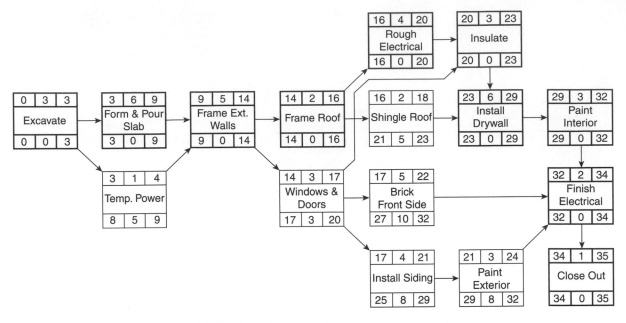

FIGURE 8.15 Warehouse project with all calculations completed

This activity box is commonly used when the calculations are done by hand. Yet, it could be used in any way that would help the project team analyze and plan the project. If the hand-drawn logic diagram will input into the computers these cells are typically used for other purposes. For example, you could record the activity ID number, the subcontractor or person responsible, the equipment needed for that activity, the crew size, the activity cost or value, or anything else that is of interest.

To complete the calculations on the warehouse schedule, look at the difference in the start days or the finish days and record that number as the activity's total float. Figure 8.15 shows the warehouse project with all the calculations completed.

For experience, do the float calculations on Practice Problem #1 and compare it to the solution at the end of the chapter.

DETERMINING THE CRITICAL PATH ACTIVITIES

Critical activities are the activities that have no total float. The activities that have zero total float obviously have no extra days, therefore they are critical. They have to start and finish on those days. In the diagram shown in Figure 8.15 the critical path activities have bolded activity boxes. Their ES and LS days are the same day. Their EF and LF are also the same day; therefore, they are critical activities. This path of zero float activities that goes from the beginning of the project to the end is called the **critical path** of the project. These are the activities that must be managed carefully. Many times a project will have more than one critical path. However, the critical path, typically will not just pop up somewhere amid noncritical activities. The only time the critical path would start out in the middle of non-critical activities is if there is a date constraint or a different calendar assigned to some activities. These characteristics of CPM scheduling will be discussed in greater detail later. For now, focus on the standard or typical CPM conventions discussed above.

Another definition of critical path is the longest path through the network of activities. The shorter paths have float. It is possible to do the backward pass with a greater number (later date) than the forward pass calculated. In the above schedule for the warehouse, if the backward pass was started on the end of day 40, there would be float of five days or more on every activity in the schedule. In this case the critical path would be the path with the least amount of float.

DETERMINING THE EFFECTS OF A CHANGE OR DELAY

All projects incur change, and these changes require adjustments to work sequences as well as work performed. Changes naturally impact the original schedule which now must be altered to reflect the naturally occurring changes in individual task durations and sequencing. In fact, the old adage "the only thing that is constant is change" is very true in many construction projects.

On the warehouse schedule shown in Figure 8.15, let's say the carpenters who are to frame the exterior walls start on time, but take 7 days to complete rather than the 5 original days duration and, therefore, finish on day 16. Is this a problem? Notice that framing the walls is a critical activity. By finishing on day 16, they are 2 days beyond their late finish date and so they have caused a delay in the entire project. In order to make up for that delay, which later activities would be considered for acceleration in order to get on schedule? If the brick, windows, siding, or exterior paint were to be accelerated, would that make up for the delay? The only way to make up for the delay would be to focus on the critical path activities. The challenge is to determine which activity or activities to be accelerated would have the least effect on project quality, cost, or safety. There are three things that can be done to accelerate the activities on the critical path: (1) decrease the duration by using more equipment or people; (2) schedule to work on weekends, overtime, or multiple shifts; and (3) change the logic to have two or more critical activities work concurrently.

Let's look at another scenario: The *Install Siding* activity (Figure 8.15) starts on time but ends up taking 7 days to complete rather than the 4 originally agreed to, finishing the end of day 24. Is that a delay to the project? According to the CPM logic diagram, *Install Siding* does not have to finish until the end of day 29, so that does not constitute a delay. However, that would affect the early start day of *Paint Exterior*, and a new calculation would show *Paint Exterior* to now have only 5 days of total float.

Let's say that the owner is proposing to change the roof shingles from asphalt to tile, which would take 5 days to install, rather than the 2 days originally planned (Figure 8.15). Would that affect the completion date of the project? As long as the roofing material can be available in time, that change would not affect the project completion date. *Shingle Roof* does not need to be finished until the end of day 23, thus *Shingle Roof* could take 7 days without creating a delay in the project completion date.

Consider another potential change. The owner is proposing to change the slab to a 12-inch-thick slab, which will increase the time to form and pour the slab to 8 days instead of 6. Does this justify an extension of contract time (Figure 8.15)? Absolutely; *Form & Pour Slab* is a critical activity and if it is delayed, the project completion date is extended. Are there any other choices? Yes, the remaining critical activities could be accelerated and accordingly the project could still finish on time. Would there be an extra cost to accelerate the later activities that goes above and beyond the extra cost to form and pour the thicker slab? Certainly! More equipment possibly would be needed or people would be required to work overtime in order to make up for the delay caused by the change order. Is it necessary to hire a team of attorneys and go to court to determine that? It depends on whether or not the owner is an attorney looking for business to keep his staff busy. Other than that, definitely not.

GAINING ADDITIONAL EXPERIENCE WITH CPM

For additional experience, perform all calculations, including total float, to Practice Problem #2 (Figure 8.16) and mark the critical path. Before you begin, are there any redundant arrows?

There is a redundant arrow between activity *P* and activity *T*. If *P* precedes *U*, and *U* precedes *T*, there is no need for the arrow from *P* to *T*. Remember to keep the logic diagram as simple as possible. After completing Practice Problem #2, compare your calculations with the solutions at the end of the chapter.

For additional experience and a little challenge, do Practice Problem #3 (Figure 8.17). The contract for this project states it must finish in 40 days from today or the liquidated damages are $2 million per day late. The total project cost is esti-

FIGURE 8.16   Practice Problem #2

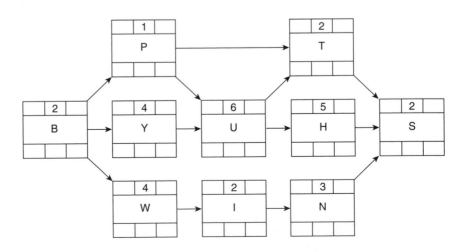

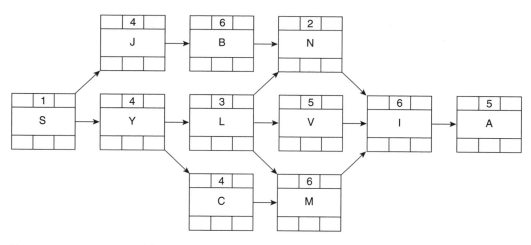

FIGURE 8.17   Practice Problem #3

mated at $45 million. It is a small, but expensive project with high risks. The owner is not willing to pay any progress payments. Payment will only be made 40 days from today or at the completion of the job, whichever is greater. Also, the owner is not willing to pay too early. If the project can be finished next week, the contractor will still not get paid until approximately day 40. The big question then is, when should the contractor begin the project? If it is started too early, the contractor will lose money in interest invested in the project. If it is started too late, the contractor will lose money in liquidated damages.

After careful consideration, the contractor wants to know the latest day possible from today to start the project. Once that is determined, the contractor decides to start the first activity 5 days earlier than absolutely necessary in order to put a little cushion or float in the project and to lessen the risks.

To determine the project start date, do the backward pass first. In Figure 8.17 enter the contractual finish day (40) in the LF cell (lower right cell) of the last activity box (activity *A*) and work backward. When you have calculated the LF date of the first activity, start 5 days earlier for the ES day for the forward pass. To check for correct calculations, see the solutions at the end of the chapter. It makes sense that if the project starts 5 days early, it should finish 5 days early. So the early finish day of the last activity should be the end of day 35. See the answer to Practice Problem #3 at the end of the chapter.

From this example, you can see that once you understand the theory and details of CPM, it is a tool that can be used in many different ways.

It is even possible to determine the project start and finish dates based on the constrained date of an internal activity. From that constrained activity, a backward pass could be done to the beginning of the project, then the forward pass could be done to the end of the project and the total project would be calculated based on the constrained date of the internal activity.

CONVERTING WORK DAYS TO CALENDAR DATES

Knowing the work day on which an activity must start or finish on is of little value to the workers responsible for completing that activity; they need to know the calendar date. When the hand-drawn schedule is input into the computer, the reports automatically convert from work days to calendar days. The computer also takes care of the end of day problem discussed earlier. When the computer-generated report shows an activity starting on Tuesday, it is meant to start the morning of that day. When the report shows a finish date, it is meant to be finished before the end of that day. The forward and backward pass calculations on a hand-drawn schedule could be done with calendar dates, skipping the weekends and holidays, but would be error prone. If a manager wants to schedule a project by hand, there needs to be an easier method of converting from work to calendar days.

Consider adding a conversion chart to the schedule shown in Figure 8.18.

The work days are consecutive. The calendar days are based on a five-day work week and the holidays are omitted. The project is scheduled to start on Monday, July 1. July 4th is a holiday, so it is skipped, along with all Saturdays and Sun-

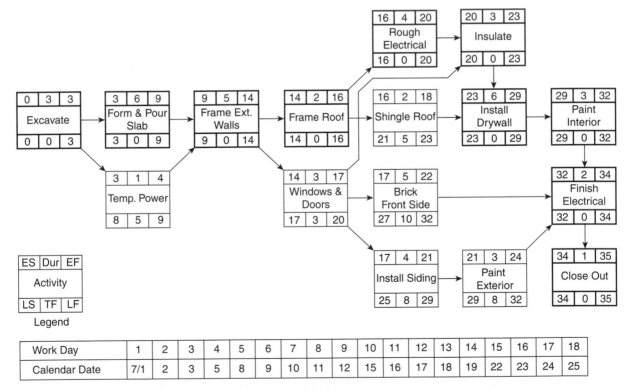

Work Day	1	2	3	4	5	6	7	8	9	10	11	12	13	14	15	16	17	18
Calendar Date	7/1	2	3	5	8	9	10	11	12	15	16	17	18	19	22	23	24	25

FIGURE 8.18   A conversion chart converts work days to calendar dates

FIGURE 8.19 Solution to Practice Problem #1

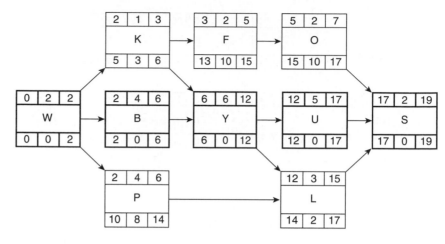

FIGURE 8.20 Solution to Practice Problem #2

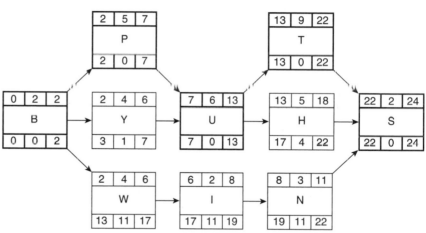

days. The calendar date for *Excavate* will be July 1 through July 3. *Form & Pour Slab* starts the end of work day 3 (which is July 5) and ends work day 9 (which is July 8). Remember that the start dates are the end of the day, so the conversion is the morning of the next day. The finish days are also the end of the day, so they can be read right off the chart.

Using a conversion chart is much easier than trying to do the calculations using calendar dates, if a manager is scheduling by hand, without the use of computer software.

SOLUTIONS TO PRACTICE PROBLEMS

It can be seen from Practice Problem #3 (Figure 8.21) that there really is no critical path in this project of zero days of float. The least number of days of float is 5. Therefore, the *most critical* path is the path of 5 days of float.

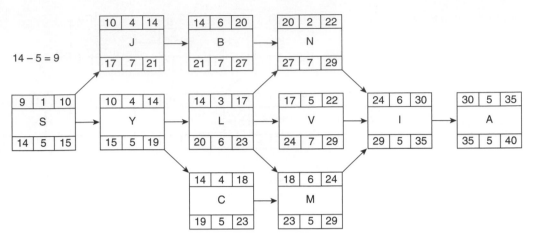

FIGURE 8.21 Solution to Practice Problem #3

CONCLUSION

Using the forward pass, which establishes the early start and early finish dates, you add, move from the beginning of the project to the end, and use the largest number of all predecessors. With the backward pass, which establishes the late start and late finish dates, you subtract, move from the end of the project to the beginning, and use the smallest number of all successors. Total float or slack is the number of extra days an activity has and is determined by the difference between the early start and early finish dates or the difference between the late start and late finish dates. The critical activities are the activities with the least amount of float, typically, zero total float.

With CPM the effects of a change order can be accurately determined. No longer is it a guess as to whether or not a change will delay the project completion date. The logic diagram, and specifically each arrow, determines the scheduled dates of a project. That is why the original planning that goes into the logic diagram is so vitally important. If the logic diagram is not accurate the rest of the scheduled dates are all bogus because they depend on that logic. This, again, is the problem with most CPM schedules. The logic diagram is quickly created without the proper planning and thinking. The creation of the logic diagram must be well thought out and representative of how the management team really plans on constructing the project. If it is quickly developed, without input from other members of the management team, the results will be confusion and eventual abandonment of the schedule. It is one thing to use the computer and sophisticated software to create an impressive bar chart that impresses an owner and quite another to develop a CPM schedule that will help to truly manage the project. By the way, the properly prepared logic diagram will also result in an impressive looking bar chart that is founded on proper logic. A few hours of planning and scheduling will save many hours and days of project time. If the logic diagram is developed as suggested in Chapter 6, and the durations are determined as suggested in

Chapter 7, then the calculations of the start and finish dates arrived at as shown in this chapter will be accurate. If the prior steps are not done with some accuracy the scheduled start and finish dates will not be realistic. A conversion chart helps convert word days to calendar days.

On large projects you will not do the calculations by hand; it is difficult to do them without errors. This is where the computer comes in. Although the computer does the calculations perfectly, the computer knows nothing about the logic of constructing a project. That is where a good management team comes in. The team knows how they plan on constructing the project. Then with the computer it is possible to keep up with the calculations as the project is updated. That is why many experienced managers develop the network logic diagram on a piece of paper where they can plan and analyze and then simply have that logic input into the computer for the calculations, printing of reports, and updating of the schedule.

Now you can also see that as one activity is accelerated or delayed, that change is automatically adjusted throughout the remainder of the project. The managers do not need to rethink the project out as in the case of a bar chart. Some activities will be affected by the change and others will not. The logic diagram automatically calculates the effects of the potential change.

APPLICATION

If you have done the practice problems associated with this chapter, you have already had some experience working with these concepts. For more application of these principles, consider the following:

1. Take the warehouse project you developed in Chapter 6, and added durations to in Chapter 7, and do the following calculations: early start, early finish, late start, late finish, and total float. Also mark the critical path with a highlighter or red pen.

2. As you examine and think about the schedule you have just calculated, do you feel more confident in your ability to build and manage that project? Even on a simple project like this, do you think your planning and scheduling efforts would save actual construction time? Can you now see the potential of this method of management? Explain.

CHAPTER 9

CALCULATING TOTAL, SHARED, FREE, INDEPENDENT, AND NEGATIVE FLOAT

INTRODUCTION

Once a manager understands the basics, CPM can become even a more powerful management tool with additional information and experience. It has been the author's experience, after consulting with and training several hundreds of project managers and superintendents in all aspects of CPM, that many managers are not aware of the implications of the different types of float. Many express frustration with allowing activities to use only the float shown on the computer, and yet by using that float a delay resulted without the manager understanding why. With the increased use of computer project management programs to help manage projects of all types and sizes, it is becoming apparent that the different types of float are not well understood, resulting in mismanagement of the project. With a thorough understanding of float, the management team can be more proficient at controlling the project and relieving some of the pressure caused by tight project objectives.

The different types of float are not easy to understand when you are first introduced to them. These concepts are not covered in most scheduling texts or project management software manuals. You may need to review some of the points in this chapter several times until they are understood.

As most managers get into CPM, they feel the main benefit is the ability to identify the critical activities. This is admittedly important, yet as one becomes more experienced, the realization comes that with the critical activities, there is really no flexibility in when those activities are to happen. It is the job of management and the responsibility of the entire project team to make sure the critical activities are done as scheduled. The critical activities are important to the timely completion of the job and are the point of focus to reduce or change the project completion date. However, the critical activities provide no opportunity for adjustment in order to manage cash flow or level resources. It is the float activities that allow for more precise management. The manager can make decisions to start, interrupt, or complete the float activities as desired to fine-tune the project. Correct use of float takes the pressure off many aspects of the project and provides the opportunity of leveling and controlling resources and costs. A detailed discussion of cost and resource leveling will be covered in a later chapter; suffice it to say that float is the key to this process and the correct identification of the different types of float is very beneficial.

After using CPM for a short time, the manager may notice some interesting things about float. As the project is updated and adjusted, the float changes and many times an entire string of activities have the same number of days of float and they all adjust together. This chapter explains the different types of float and helps a manager better understand what these differences are and how to use them to the project's advantage. As the managers understand these concepts, they become more effective with the use of CPM.

TOTAL FLOAT

First of all, take a closer look at total float, the only float discussed to this point. Total float is the difference in the early start and the late start days or the difference in the early finish and late finish days as explained in Chapter 8. A manager who is inexperienced with CPM may give the schedule to a typical subcontractor or vendor who thinks their activity has float that belongs to that activity alone. However, when that float is used, it is realized that it takes float from several other activities as well. For example, note the solution to Practice Problem #2 shown in Figure 9.1.

SHARED FLOAT

If the schedule in Figure 9.1 was given to the subcontractors and they thought it was OK to use their float, notice what happens.

Subcontractors $W, I, \& N$ see the 11 days of total float and each plans on using the extra days. So activity B uses 2 days, W uses 15 days (the 4 days of duration, plus the 11 days float), I uses 13 days, N uses 14 days, and S uses 2 days. The total project duration becomes $2 + 15 + 13 + 14 + 2 = 46$ days. The project now takes 46 days when originally it was supposed to take only 24 days, and no subs used more than their days of float. Obviously, there is a problem. This is why only a basic understanding of CPM is inadequate for the manager to really control and manage the project.

FIGURE 9.1 Solution to Practice Problem #2

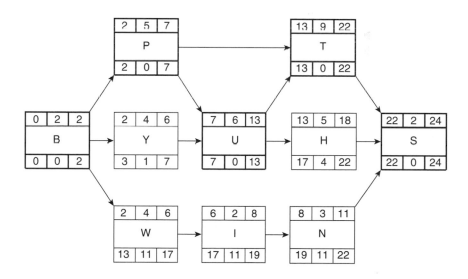

Shared float is a difficult concept to understand. Keep looking at the logic diagram for Practice Problem #2 (Figure 9.1) as you read the following information. On closer examination, if activity *W* used those 11 days and finished on day 17, activity *I* could no longer start on day 6 because *W* didn't finish until day 17, which is activity *I*'s *late* start date, Now *I*'s *early* start day is 17, the same as its *late* start day, so activity *I* is now critical, with no days of float. Therefore *N* is also critical because *N* can't start until day 19 when *I* finishes due to *W* using the 11 days. Therefore, it is realized that float can be shared. Those 11 days are shared among *W*, *I*, and *N*. If *W* uses even one day, that robs a day of float from *I* and eventually *N*. If *W* finishes on day 7, *I* cannot start until day 7, one day of *I*'s float is gone. Review Figure 9.1 carefully until you grasp the concept of shared float. Although it is sometimes a difficult concept to understand, it is critical if the manager doesn't want the activities with shared float to cause a delay to the project.

A careful manager would not want to give all 11 days of total float to *W*, causing *I* and *N* to become critical. Float is like money in the bank: you would like to save it for a later date when it may be of greater need. Notice if *Y* and *H* used their float days it would not affect later activities, nor could earlier activities rob them of their float. Therefore, they do not share float. Activities *Y* and *H* have float that affects only them. This will be discussed in more detail later. For now, just realize *Y* and *H* do not share float.

Because shared float belongs to the path or string of activities, it is frequently called **path** or **string float**. Occasionally it is referred to as *interference float* because, if used, it interferes with the float of later activities. In this text it will be called shared float.

An examination of the solution to Practice Problem #3 (Figure 9.2), with the calculations completed in the traditional manner, shows the shared float.

If activity *J* uses those 2 days of available float, finishing on day 7, the 2 days are also robbed from *B*'s float. Activity *B* becomes critical and finishes on day 13, making *N* critical also. Therefore, *J*, *B*, and *N* all share those 2 days of total float. Notice that

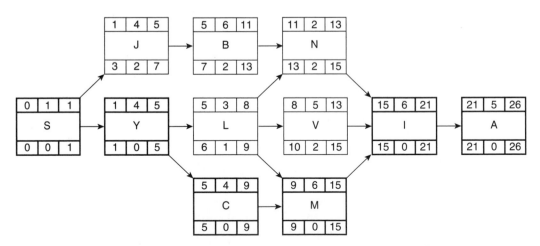

FIGURE 9.2   Solution to Practice Problem #3

activity *L*, if it uses that one day of float, robs one day from *V*. If *L* finishes on day 9, *V* can't start on day 8. Therefore, *L* and *V* share one day of float. Activity *V* does not have to start until day 10, so it would still have one day that is not shared with *L*. This 1 day would be considered independent float which will be discussed later. Looking back at the hotel project in Chapter 5, you will realize that almost all of the hotel activities share float with other activities.

FREE FLOAT

Free float, by definition, is the amount of time an activity can be delayed without delaying the early start of activities following it. Or, stated another way, free float is the amount of time an activity can be delayed without taking away float from later activities. Free float of an activity is determined by subtracting its earliest finish time from the earliest of the early start times of the activities that directly follow. Let's look again at the solution to Practice Problem #2 in Figure 9.3.

If activity *Y* uses that 1 day of float, it does not affect *U* because *U* cannot start until day 7 anyway; therefore *Y* has 1 day of free float, float that can be used without affecting later activities. Free float does not look at earlier activities, just later activities.

Let's look at activity *H*. If *H* uses 4 days of float it will not affect *S*. Activity *S* cannot start until day 22 anyway. Therefore, *H* has 4 days of free float. Notice that if *W* uses any of those 11 days it does indeed affect *I*, delaying *I*; therefore *W* has no free float.

Look at activity *I*. If *I* uses any of the 11 days of float, it does affect *N*, delaying *N*. Therefore, *I* has no free float.

Looking at activity *N*, if *N* uses any of those 11 days, it does not affect *S*; therefore, *N* has 11 days of free float. In the case of *W*, *I*, and *N*, remember that they all share those 11 days of float, but at *N* it becomes free float because it does not affect later activities, even though it is shared with earlier activities. Activity *N* is the last activity in

FIGURE 9.3 Solution to Practice Problem #2

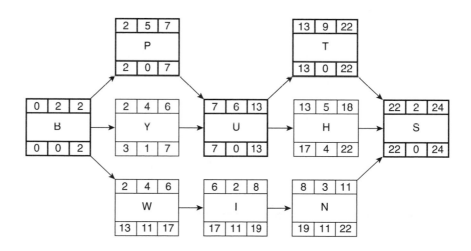

the string that shares float; that is why the float is free at *N*. That is always the case: In a string of activities that share float, the last activity in the chain will have free float. If *W* or *I* used the float, later activities would be affected. Just because there is free float does not mean it could be given away, because *N*'s free float may be used by earlier activities, such as in the case of *W* or *I*, and then *N* would have no float.

Examine the solution to Practice Problem #3 (Figure 9.4) for free float.

Notice that if *J* uses any float it will be robbing float from *B*, because *J*'s early finish is day 5 and *B*'s early start is also day 5; therefore, *J* has no free float.

Let's look at activity *B*. If it uses any float, it will delay or rob float from *N*; therefore, *B* has no free float.

Notice activity *N*. If it uses any float, that will not affect the later activity *I*; therefore, *N* has 2 days of free float. Realize *J* or *B* could have used it prior because *J*, *B*, and *N* all share those 2 days of float. Hence, *N*'s chance of having float is small, even though it has free float.

Activities *L* and *V* also share 1 day of float. If *L* uses it, *V* is delayed; therefore, *L* has no free float. Activity *V*, however, could use both of those days of float, as long as *L* does not steal 1 of them. Activity *V* can use both days without affecting *I*; therefore, *V* has 2 days of free float.

From a management point of view it is difficult to see any real advantage to free float. Free float tells the manager only if that activity uses it; no later activities will be affected. However, free float could be shared with prior activities and if the prior activities use it, it will not be available for the last activity. Therefore, it is crucial to not give away free float or commit free float too early in the job. Those extra days may be needed later. If the float is used early, that creates more critical activities and a higher risk of the job finishing late if problems do (and they will) occur later. There is only one type of float that may be given away—independent float—which is discussed next.

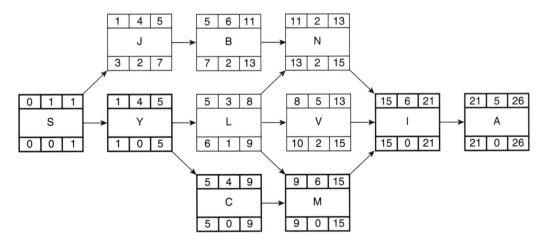

FIGURE 9.4 Solution to Practice Problem #3

INDEPENDENT FLOAT

Independent float is float that belongs to one activity and that activity alone. It is not shared with any other activities, earlier or later. Independent float is float a management team could give away because it has no effect on other activities.

Let's look at the solution to Practice Problem #2 again (Figure 9.5), only this time the focus is on independent float.

Notice activity *Y*. If it uses the float, it does not affect any later activities—the float is free. Also note that it does not share float with earlier activities; therefore, it is independent. No earlier activity could steal that float, nor if used, would it affect a later activity. The same is true for activity *H*—all 4 days are independent. A careful observation will show that each of those two activities have a predecessor that is critical and a successor that is also critical. Both activities sort of hang from the critical path with no other activities interfering. It is easy to identify independent float if the activity comes from the critical path and goes to the critical path. But that is not always the case.

Activities *W*, *I*, and *N* have no independent float because they all share the 11 days they have together. The only chance for that path or string of activities to have independent float is at the point where *I* is 100 percent complete. If any of those 11 days of shared float are still unused, they then become independent float at activity *N*. Accordingly, free float does have the chance to become independent if all the predecessors are finished and there is float still available. Another way to look at it is, free float looks behind the activity (to the right) to see if the float is shared. Independent float looks behind *and* ahead of the activity (to the right and also to the left) to see if the float is shared in either direction. If it is not shared in either direction, it is independent.

FIGURE 9.5   Solution to Practice Problem #2

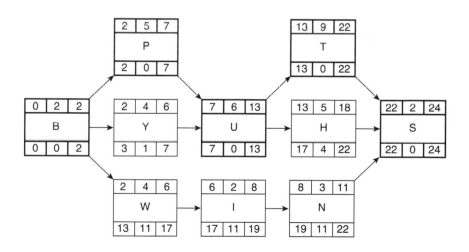

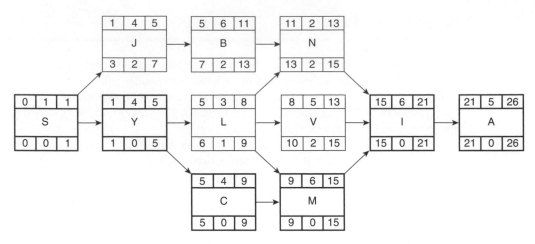

FIGURE 9.6   Solution to Practice Problem #3

FIGURE 9.7   Activity box showing the different types of float

ES	Dur	EF
Activity		
LS	TF	LF
SF	FF	IF

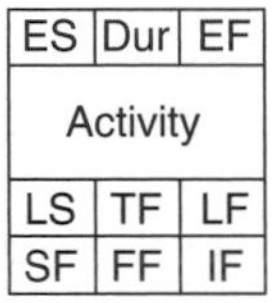

Now let's look at the solution to Practice Problem #3 (Figure 9.6) for independent float. Earlier in the chapter, it was determined that *J*, *B*, and *N* share those 2 days of float. So at *N* the 2 days of float are free in that *N* could use the float without affecting any later activity. At the early completion of *B*, the float remaining with *N* would be independent.

Note activity *L*. Activity *L* shares that 1 day of float with *V*. The other day of float belonging to *V* is independent. It affects no later activity and only 1 day can be robbed by *L*. Hence, again, *V* has one day of independent float.

Most texts and project management software discuss and calculate total float and free float, but not shared and independent. The ability to analyze these types of float prevents the manager from making the mistake of giving away float that may end up damaging the project. *It is essential to realize that most of the time float is shared, and it is not independent.*

A method preferred by the author to show the different types of float in the activity box of the network logic diagram is shown in Figure 9.7.

Shared float (SF) is in the lower left corner cell.

Free float (FF) is in the lower center cell.

Independent float (IF) is in the lower right corner cell.

Total float (TF) is where it has always been shown in this text, in the center between the late start (LS) date and the late finish (LF) date.

It would be nice if the computer software would identify and calculate the shared and independent float. As managers continue to pressure the software developers, this

FIGURE 9.8 Solution to Practice Problem #2, with floats shown in the activity box

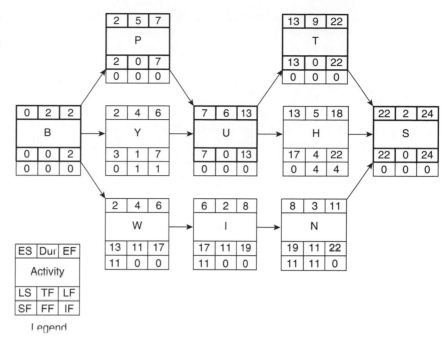

2	5	7
	P	
2	0	7
0	0	0

13	9	22
	T	
13	0	22
0	0	0

0	2	2
	B	
0	0	2
0	0	0

2	4	6
	Y	
3	1	7
0	1	1

7	6	13
	U	
7	0	13
0	0	0

13	5	18
	H	
17	4	22
0	4	4

22	2	24
	S	
22	0	24
0	0	0

2	4	6
	W	
13	11	17
11	0	0

6	2	8
	I	
17	11	19
11	0	0

8	3	11
	N	
19	11	22
11	11	0

Legend:

ES	Dur	EF
	Activity	
LS	TF	LF
SF	FF	IF

may become a reality in the future. Software developers are reluctant to do so because it makes CPM scheduling appear to be even more complex, for which they are already criticized. In addition, it is surprising that more managers have not realized these different types of float exist and, therefore, have not encouraged the software developers to differentiate among them. Free float is often hidden by most of the software programs even though the software is developed with the ability to show it.

An activity box showing the different floats is added to the diagram in Practice Problem #2, as illustrated in Figure 9.8. Notice that the critical path has no float in any category.

A legend, as shown in the lower left corner of the schedule in Figure 9.8, should be included to ensure that those using the schedule understand the format.

NEGATIVE FLOAT

The last type of float to discuss is negative float. **Negative float** is obtained by having a fixed project start date and a fixed project finish date, where the finish date is set at a time earlier than would be calculated by the forward pass. Looking at Practice Problem #2 in Figure 9.8, if the backward pass was done with a number smaller than 24, the results would be negative float. Negative float means the project is already that many days behind schedule. A manager typically does not want to see negative float on the project. There are, however, times when it is beneficial. If there is a forced completion date and negative float appears, it shows the management team the path or paths of activities where acceleration is needed and exactly how many days need to be eliminated from each path of activities in order to get the project back to just critical. The negative float is typically shared; the team does not need to reduce each activity by the number of negative days. Just eliminate that many days from each path or string of activities.

Many experienced managers do not like the practice of inputting a firm start date and also a firm finish date into the computer. If the forced finish date is earlier than the finish date calculated by the forward pass, negative float results. If the forced finish date is later than the finish date calculated by the forward pass, there will be positive shared float on every activity. The critical path will now be the path of least total float because there will be no zero float. Many experienced managers input into the computer only the start date and then keep an eye on the finish date to make sure it meets project requirements. Many management teams prefer the original planned schedule to have a calculated finish date earlier than project requirements because they know things will not work out exactly as planned and delays will probably be incurred. Projects with more risk should be planned originally to finish much earlier than contract completion date. A good project team learns how to evaluate and manage the risk.

USING FLOAT TO HELP MANAGE THE PROJECT

Once a manager has the knowledge and understanding of the different types of float, that manager can use the information to help manage the project. To help understand this, examine the warehouse schedule shown in Figure 9.9.

WHEN TO GIVE AWAY FLOAT AND WHEN TO KEEP OR HIDE IT

A closer examination of the schedule in Figure 9.9 shows *Temp. Power* with 5 days of independent float. A manager would be safe in simply telling the electrician to install the temporary power sometime this week. It really does not have to start on day 4 (end of day 3). If the electrician is the type of person whose word is his bond, tell him he could start on day 4 and end on day 9. If the electrician is a little slow or undependable, tell him to start on day 4 and to be finished on day 6, saving the 3 extra days in case the electrician doesn't finish as requested.

Use the same concepts on *Shingle Roof*, where its 5 days of float are also independent. *Shingle Roof* just needs to be done sometime within that week. There is no real need to push people beyond what is reasonable. The scheduler could change the durations of these two activities to give away some or all of this float. If the roofers said they would do it in 2 days and they are given a few more days, that just ensures they will be able to finish on time. The scheduler could keep some of that shared float hidden, depending on how many days the duration is increased. Of course, notes would be kept for future purposes showing the increase in the durations to share the float. These notes could be made within the software and then shown or hidden, as desired, on the reports.

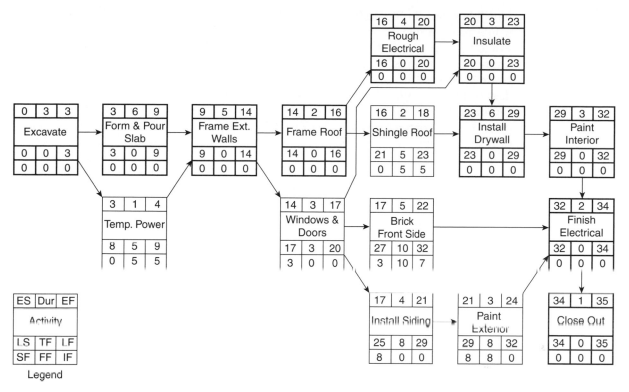

FIGURE 9.9 Completed warehouse schedule with float

A closer look at *Windows & Doors* and *Brick Front Side* in Figure 9.9 shows they share 3 days of float, and that *Brick Front Side* has an additional 7 days that are independent. The management team could decide to give *Windows & Doors* 2 or 3 of those days and *Brick Front Side* would still have plenty of float left. However, if 3 days of float are given to *Windows & Doors* by changing the duration to 6 days, that would take 3 days of shared float that *Windows & Doors* also shares with *Install Siding* and *Paint Exterior*, leaving them with only 5 days of shared float between them. Therefore, the team could give 2 additional days to *Install Siding*, increasing its duration to 6 days and still have 3 days of float left for *Paint Exterior*. In other words, if float is shared, a sophisticated manager could choose to share that float in order to ensure success and make the project easier to manage.

TO WHOM DOES FLOAT BELONG?

Many general contractors have the attitude that all the float belongs to them. They would simply give the early start and finish dates to the subcontractors and would not increase the durations as explained above. If this was the case, with the warehouse schedule shown in Figure 9.9, and the windows sub took a couple of extra days, that would have an impact on brick, siding, and paint exterior. All their early start days would be delayed and the manager would have to make three phone calls in order to notify them of the delay. Then it could be possible that one or even all of those sub-contractors have already scheduled their crews to be somewhere else on those later days so they won't be able to get back to this warehouse job for days or even weeks, causing a delay to the project. The sharing of shared float could have eliminated this delay. If a subcontractor is a professional who really understands CPM and the types of float, give the computer disk to that subcontractor if it helps manage the project. Don't try to hide information from team members. The fear is that someone who does not understand these concepts, uses shared float, causing later activities to be critical and potential delays to the project completion date.

If the whole management team is professional enough to recognize these different types of float and realizes when they are shared or independent, it certainly will make the job run more smoothly. But if they do not, and instead think that total float belongs solely to them when in fact it is shared (and they count on those extra days), the schedule will be in a state of confusion and the project will be delayed. That is why it is not a bad management idea to increase the durations a few days on the shared float activities and then give only the early start and early finish dates to the subs and suppliers. That way, the manager can hide some of the float in case it is needed later to better control the project and ensure the project will finish on time.

Sometimes the project owner feels all the float should belong to the owner. The contract could even state that all activities must start as early as possible and finish as early as possible, taking away all the float. From a management point of view, this makes every activity critical. That would not be a very wise move, even from the owner's point of view. In Chapter 5, the hotel project had an excess of 200 days of shared float on many activities. That type of owner requirement would force those activities to be completed around 200 days early and the owner would then have to pay interest on that money without being able to get a return until the project is finished. If the owner did not want to be a team player and, instead, wanted to use all the float to his or her advantage, the contract would state that all activities would start and finish as late as possible without delaying the project completion date. This would then make each activity start on the late start date and finish on the late finish date and keep the owner from paying more interest than necessary. It would also make each activity critical. A popular notion with experienced management teams is that the float belongs to the project and should be used by the activities that can benefit most by it.

Conclusion

It is important to be able to identify the types of float and then to develop a management style on how to use those floats to manage the project to help ensure the project's success. As float is shared, it can take the pressure off as many of the activities as possible. It is float that gives the management team an opportunity to relax a little; every activity is not critical. With a traditional bar chart schedule, which is not based on a network, there is no float. Therefore, the team's understanding is that each activity must be done on the days shown. The correct identification and use of float can be a great asset to all working on the project.

If the attitude can be developed that the project really is a team project, all the float should belong to the project and as a team member needs it, it should be available as long as it does not have an adverse effect on other team members. Float could be negotiated for the advantage of the team and the project based on prioritized needs. A later chapter shows additional applications of using float in order to balance resources, such as the number of workers or equipment and cash flow.

APPLICATION

Additional Examples of the Different Types of Float

Those who are having difficulty understanding the different types of float or who want to strengthen their ability to recognize the types of float may find the following example problems helpful. Most people find it easier to learn to distinguish the different types of float by understanding the logic rather than trying to memorize a formula. A formula would be complex because it is necessary to look at all predecessors and all successors to each activity. The explanations in Figure 9.10 focuses on the logical relationships.

Using the schedule in Figure 9.10, first we will look for independent float. Anytime an activity is between critical activities, without other relationships, this is a case where the float will always be independent. There are other cases where there may be independent float even if the activity is not between critical activities without other relationships. Notice activity D. It comes from a critical activity and goes to a critical activity. If D uses the float and finishes on the end of day 8, it does not rob float from later activities. Therefore, D has 2 days of independent float. Activity D does not share float with anyone.

FIGURE 9.10 An example of a schedule showing independent and shared float

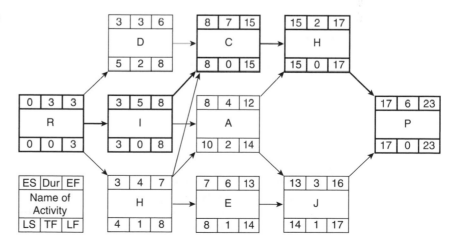

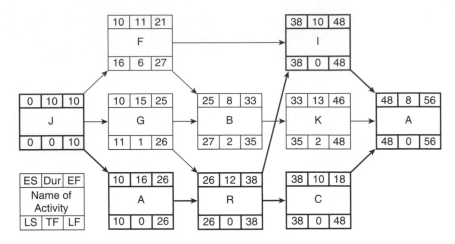

FIGURE 9.11 Another example of a schedule showing independent and shared float

Next look for shared float in Figure 9.10. Whenever you see a string or path of activities with the same number of days of total float, it is a good guess the float may be shared with those activities in that string or path. Notice activities *H*, *E*, and *J*; they all have one day of total float. If *H* uses that day and finishes on the end of day 8, then *E* can't start until day 8 and it now has zero float, it is critical. Activity *J* is in the same situation—*H* or *E* can rob *J* of its float. Therefore, *H*, *E*, and *J* all share that 1 day of float.

A closer examination of activity *A* in Figure 9.10 shows that if *A* uses both days of float, it will rob 1 day from *J*, forcing *J* to be critical. Therefore, *A* and *J* share a day of float. Also notice that *A* can finish on day 12 and *J* can't start until day 13, so *A* has 1 day of independent float that can be used without affecting *J*. Because that day is not shared with earlier activities, it is independent. Therefore, *A* has 1 day that is independent and 1 day that is shared with *J*.

As another example of the different types of float, see Figure 9.11.

As Figure 9.11 is closely examined, notice that *B* and *K* both have 2 days of float and they are in a string together. It is probably shared. A closer examination reveals that if *B* uses those 2 days of float and finishes on day 35, that will rob *K* of all float forcing *K* to become critical. Therefore, *B* and *K* share those 2 days of float. Now examine *G*. If *G* uses the 1 day of float and finishes on day 26, then *B* can't start on day 25. Therefore, *G* can rob *B* and eventually *K* of 1 day of float each. Now we can see how *G* shares 1 day of float with *B* and *K*.

Next look closely at activity *F* in Figure 9.11. Activity *F* looks somewhat independent with a critical predecessor and a critical successor. However, *F* also has *B* as a successor. Without the relationship with *B*, *F* would definitely have those 6 days as independent float. Notice if *F* uses the 6 days and finishes on day 27, that will rob *B* and eventually *K* of two days of shared float. Hence, *F* shares 2 days with *B* and 2 days with *K*. Now notice that *B* can't start until the end of day 25. Activity *F* could finish on the end of day 21, so *F* could go from day 21 to day 25 without robbing *B* of float. Those 4 days are independent to *F*.

FIGURE 9.12 An additional example of a schedule to help analyze the different types of float

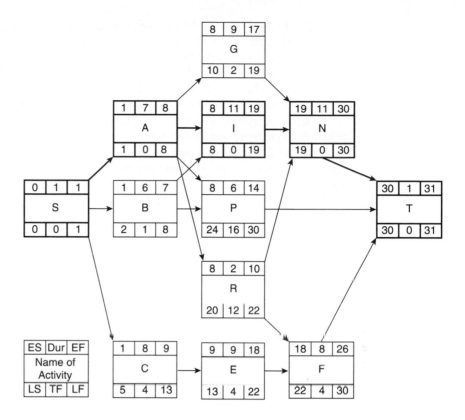

If you are still having a little difficulty recognizing the different types of float, study the schedule in Figure 9.12. If you are still having difficulty with these concepts, review some of the prior schedules in this chapter.

To evaluate the different floats within the schedule in Figure 9.12 we will first look for shared float. As you look for shared float, look for strings of activities with the same number of days of float. Notice C, E, and F, they are in a string and each has 4 days of total float. Upon close examination, it can be seen that if C uses the 4 days and finishes on day 13, E's float is taken, forcing E and F to become critical. Therefore, C, E, and F share those 4 days of float. Does F also share with R? If R finished on the late finish day of 22, that would also rob F of all float. Therefore, F shares float with C, E, and R.

Taking a closer look at R in Figure 9.12, it is realized that R does not share float with the predecessor activity A. Activity R could finish on the end of day 10 and F can't start until the end of day 18. Therefore, the 8 days are independent to R. Activity R continues to share the remaining 4 days with F.

Now examine activity B. If B used the 1 day of float and finished on the end of day 8, that would not affect any other activity because P and J cannot start until the end of day 8 anyway. Therefore, B's 1 day of float is independent.

If activity *P* uses the 16 days of float and does not finish until the end of day 30, that does not affect later activities, nor does *P* share float with earlier activities. Therefore, those 16 days of total float are independent to *P*.

Continue looking at Figure 9.12 and examine activity *G*, which has a critical predecessor and a critical successor. If *G* uses the 2 days of float it does not affect any other activity; therefore, those 2 days are independent to *G*.

A final application of the principles in this chapter is to examine the warehouse schedule you developed in the prior chapters and identify the independent, shared, free, and total floats in that project. Remember, the current computer software will not figure the different types of float for you. To benefit from this information you need to see the relationships for yourself and that will improve your ability to manage using CPM. Review the prior information and examples and eventually it will click between your vision and your mind and these concepts will make sense. Don't give up being able to recognize the different types of float. It will make you a better manager and leader. You will understand what many others do not.

next activity. Or, time may be needed for the soil to settle or the drywall compound to dry prior to the next step, and so forth. Another common place to use finish-to-start lags is when you place an order and then have a finish-to-start lag of the number of days it takes to receive the material.

Figure 10.3 shows how the same scheduled activities could be drawn without lags; however, this requires three activities, rather than two as shown in Figure 10.2. Therefore, it can be seen that lags reduce the number of activities to deal with while using or updating the schedule. However, the example in Figure 10.3 communicates better. With the FS lag, an inexperienced person reading the schedule in Figure 10.2 may not understand why the 5 is on the arrow and the significance of that.

The logic diagram in Figure 10.4 indicates that activity B starts two days before activity A finishes. This causes an overlap in the activities rather than a delay between them. The total duration for the two activities would be 5 days.

START-TO-START RELATIONSHIPS

Figure 10.5 illustrates a start-to-start relationship with a 2-day lag. The logic here indicates that activity A starts and then 2 days later activity B can start. This again allows the activities to overlap. A start-to-start lag is a common relationship in medium- to large-sized construction projects. Soon after the interior studs are started, the electrical and mechanical rough-ins can begin. They do not need to wait until all the studs are completed. A day or two after the form work on a large concrete slab is begun, the concrete can start to be poured. There are many activities in construction projects that would be appropriate for a start-to-start relationship with

FIGURE 10.3 Using an activity rather than a finish-to-start lag

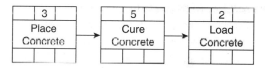

FIGURE 10.4 A finish-to-start relationship with negative lag

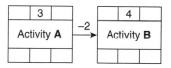

FIGURE 10.5 A start-to-start relationship with a 2-day lag

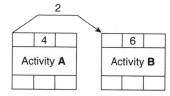

a lag. Typically, a start-to-start lag is not a negative number. A negative start-to-start lag would mean the successor would start that many days prior to the predecessor, which is illogical.

FINISH-TO-FINISH RELATIONSHIPS

Figure 10.6 depicts an example of a finish-to-finish relationship with a 2-day lag shown. The logic here indicates that activity *A* finishes and then 2 days later activity *B* finishes. Finish-to-finish is also a common relationship in large construction projects. A successor activity frequently can finish a few days after a predecessor activity finishes. The taping and texturing of the drywall can't be finished until a few days after hanging of the drywall is finished. Painting the stripes on the highway can't be finished until a few days after the pavement is finished.

The confusing aspect for most managers is to determine which relationship is best, a start-to-start or a finish-to-finish. With the start-to-start relationship shown in figure 10.5, if activity *A* goes for 3 days and then has a delay due to lack of materials or such, can activity *B* really finish without activity *A* being finished first? Generally, with construction activities, the prior activity must finish prior to the later activity being able to finish. The placement of concrete cannot be finished until the forming is finished. The drywall cannot be taped and finished until the last piece is hung. Therefore, maybe a finish-to-finish lag should be the most common lag. The problem with that is the later activity typically cannot start until the earlier activity has started. A general rule some managers use is if the later activity has a longer duration than the earlier activity, use a start-to-start lag. If the later activity has a shorter duration than the earlier activity, use a finish-to-finish lag. Using this rule will avoid problems in many situations.

A better recommendation is when it seems logical to use either a start-to-start or a finish-to-finish lag, consider using both. Using both lags on the same activities will eliminate a delay in the predecessor allowing the successor to go ahead and finish first, which typically is not logical. Generally, when a start-to-start is first considered, upon thinking about the logic of the activities, a finish-to-finish should also be used and vice versa. All the popular scheduling software allows the use of multiple relationships, so this is not a problem as far as the software is concerned. Many managers consider it a good scheduling practice to use both a start-to-start lag and a finish-to-finish lag together.

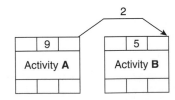

FIGURE 10.6 A finish-to-finish relationship with a 2-day lag

If a scheduler is after a quick and easy, but not as accurate schedule, it may be simpler to input into the computer a finish-to-start negative lag to show an overlap in activities in the bar chart generated from the network logic diagram.

START-TO-FINISH RELATIONSHIPS

Figure 10.7 is an example of a start-to-finish relationship with a 2-day lag. The logic here indicates that activity A starts and then 2 days later activity B finishes. This is a very uncommon relationship in any type of construction project. It is difficult to think of a situation where a start-to-finish relationship would be better than a combination of start-to-start and finish-to-finish, as discussed above. This is such an unusual relationship that most of the scheduling software programs did not even accommodate this relationship in their early releases.

Therefore, it is the manager's choice when and where to use lags. In some ways, lags simplify the schedule by reducing the number of activities. In other ways, lags make the schedule more difficult to understand and therefore interfere with effective communication.

Example Project Using Lags

Lets look at a simple case study that illustrates the use of lags to schedule a trowel finish on a 40×80-foot concrete floor slab. It will be formed and placed with a two-person crew. The management team thinks that a crew of two people should be able to place 1/4 of the slab each day. So, the plan is to form and reinforce 1/4 of the slab on the first day. On the second day, the first quarter that was formed and reinforced yesterday would be placed while the same two workers would form and reinforce the second quarter of the slab, which would be placed the next day. This sequence would continue until the slab is completed. The project could be scheduled with lags as shown in Figure 10.8.

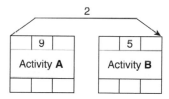

FIGURE 10.7 A start-to-finish relationship with a 2-day lag

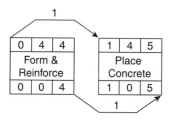

FIGURE 10.8 Illustration of both a start-to-start and a finish-to-finish lag

The logic diagram in Figure 10.8 shows that *Form & Reinforce* would start the end of day 0, which is really the morning of day 1, and finish the end of day 4. *Place Concrete* would start one day after forming starts, which would be the end of day 1 (really the morning of day 2) and finish the end of day 5. The schedule is a simple illustration of SS and FF lags. The FF lag is used to make sure that if *Form & Reinforce* is delayed after the first day, the placement of the concrete will finish 1 day after forming and reinforcing is finished, which is logical.

This is a simple schedule for the construction of this slab. It would be the field personnel's responsibility to determine which quarter of the floor to begin with and how to move throughout the project. This is one of the advantages of lags in that it gives greater flexibility at the job site. It also allows the field managers to adjust the work in progress without having to adjust the schedule. They could work on whichever quarter of the floor they desired. Which quarter to work on might be determined by such simple things as where they parked the truck, or where it is shady as they start work.

That advantage of flexibility is in some ways a disadvantage. Many times there is a reason to start the slab in a particular area and complete the work in a specific sequence. For example, as soon as one end of the slab is complete, the structure could be started on that end. There may be a reason to start the structure on one end because of more detailed interior partitions or finishes in that end. Or perhaps, equipment may need to be installed on that end, and so on. The schedule shown in Figure 10.8 would not communicate that additional information. It would be left up to the concrete crew to determine the starting place and the work sequence, and they may not have the vision of the entire project like the project manager has. Therefore, it would be important to communicate these details to the workers in order for the project to be completed in the correct order.

To communicate this schedule more precisely, a more detailed schedule would be required. If the management team wanted to move through the project in the following sequence NE to NW to SE to SW, the logic diagram may look as shown in Figure 10.9 without the use of lags.

This is a more complex-looking logic diagram, but it communicates the schedule to the concrete crew exactly the way the management team desires the project to be completed. With this level of detail, the schedule communicates the work flow to the concrete crew without the project manager or superintendent needing to verbally communicate the information.

Tabular Report of a Project with Lags

To communicate the schedule, the report format probably would not be the network logic diagram shown in Figure 10.9. That would be too confusing for many tradespeople. Rather it would be a bar chart or a simple tabular report generated by the computer from the logic diagram. Figure 10.10 shows a tabular report schedule developed from the data in the logic diagram for a specific subcontractor.

Of course, the week days shown in Figure 10.10 would be calendar dates. A simple project as discussed here would not need the logic diagram in order to develop this

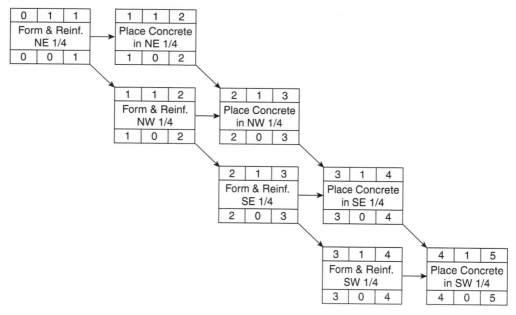

FIGURE 10.9 Detailed schedule for the concrete slab project

Activity	Start Date	Finish Date	Notes
Form & Reinforce NE 1/4	Monday	Monday	
Place Concrete in NE 1/4	Tuesday	Tuesday	
Form & Reinforce NW 1/4	Tuesday	Tuesday	
Place Concrete in NW 1/4	Wednesday	Wednesday	
Form & Reinforce SE 1/4	Wednesday	Wednesday	
Place Concrete in SE 1/4	Thursday	Thursday	
Form & Reinforce SW 1/4	Thursday	Thursday	
Place Concrete in SW 1/4	Friday	Friday	

FIGURE 10.10 Concrete subcontractor's tabular schedule

tabular report. However, with more complex projects the logic diagram would be input into the computer and the computer would generate tabular reports as shown in Figure 10.10.

This simple schedule (Figure 10.10) tells *who* (the concrete crew) is doing *what, where,* and *when.* A properly developed schedule should communicate that precise information in simple form. If this level of detail is not needed because the management team does not care which quarter is done first, the schedule with lags would be

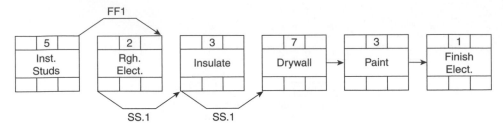

FIGURE 10.11   Simple interior finishes schedule with single lag relationships

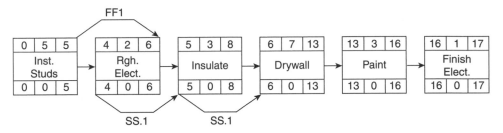

FIGURE 10.12   Start and finish date calculations with single lags

sufficient. The experience and knowledge of the concrete crew may also determine the desired level of detail.

Many times the management team chooses to create the main schedule with the use of lags and then breaks down the project into this additional level of detail for the three-week look-ahead schedule. As the project details become clearer the superintendent may use the three-week look-ahead schedule to better plan for the necessary equipment, people, and other resources needed for the near-term activities.

Start and Finish Date Calculations with Lags

The example above (Figure 10.11) shows a simple Interior finishes schedule with single lag relationships.

The logic diagram in Figure 10.11 shows that the *Rgh. (Rough) Electrical* can't finish until 1 after *Inst. Studs* is done. Then *Insulate* can start 1 day after *Rgh. Electrical* has started. According to the logic diagram, *Drywall* can start 1 day after *Insulate* has started. This will allow *Inst. Studs, Rgh. Electrical, Insulate,* and *Drywall* to overlap. The calculations would be done as shown in Figure 10.12.

When performing the calculations, let your eyes and the arrows guide you. Start with *Inst. Studs* with 0 as normal. Add the duration of 5 and put 5 in the EF space for *Inst. Studs.* Remember, the days still begin at the *end of the day,* just as before. *Rgh. Electrical* finishes 1 day after *Inst. Studs* finishes, so add 1 day to the EF of *Inst. Studs*

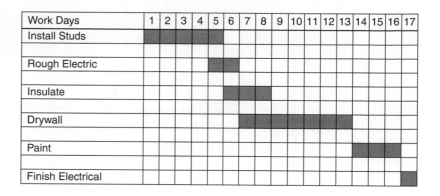

FIGURE 10.13 Bar chart showing overlaps caused by activity lags

$(5 + 1 = 6)$ and write 6 in the EF space of *Rgh. Electrical*. Then subtract the duration of *Rgh. Electrical* (2 days) from the EF of *Rgh. Electrical* $(6 - 2 = 4)$ to get the ES of the end of day 4. Now *Insulate* starts 1 day after *Rgh. Electrical* starts, so add 1 day to the ES day of *Rgh. Electrical* $(4 + 1 = 5)$ and write 5 in the ES day for *Insulate*. Now *Insulate* starts 1 day after *Drywall* starts, so add the 1 day lag to the ES of *Insulate* $(5 + 1 = 6)$ to get the ES day for *Drywall* at the end of day 6. Then add the 7-day duration to the ES for *Drywall* $(6 + 7 = 13)$ to get the EF of the end of day 13. The rest of the calculations with a finish-to-start relationships for *Paint* and *Finish Elect.* are the same as normal.

The backward pass is calculated in the reverse order just as before. With the lags, subtract the amount of lag and follow the process in reverse. *Drywall*'s LS day is the end of day 6, so subtract the SS lag of 1 day to get the LS for *Insulate* at the end of day 5. Then add the duration of 3 days to get the LF of day 8 for *Insulate*. Continue in a like manner, following the arrows backward to the beginning of the project.

Bar Chart of a Project with Lags

A bar chart based on the above network would appear as illustrated in Figure 10.13. The chart shows the overlaps caused by the activity lags.

The calculations of the dates for activities with lags are somewhat confusing. They are even more confusing if there are more than one relationship. The above example showed just one relationship. Visualize how much more difficult it would be with multiple relationship arrows, choosing the largest and the smallest numbers. When using lags it is common to let the computer do the calculations without doing even the forward pass by hand.

Figure 10.14 shows a portion of a bar chart created with SureTrak from a network where several lags were used. The critical activities are the darker color and careful observation shows that many of the critical activities are overlapped.

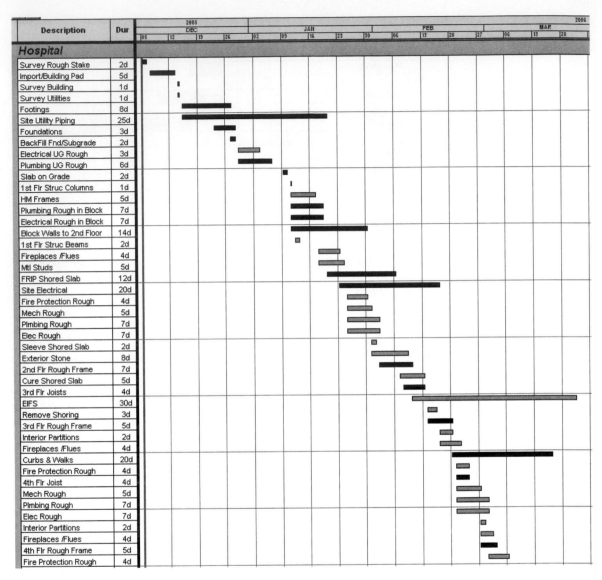

Description	Dur	2005 DEC				JAN				FEB				MAR		2006

Hospital

Description	Dur
Survey Rough Stake	2d
Import/Building Pad	5d
Survey Building	1d
Survey Utilities	1d
Footings	8d
Site Utility Piping	25d
Foundations	3d
BackFill Fnd/Subgrade	2d
Electrical UG Rough	3d
Plumbing UG Rough	6d
Slab on Grade	2d
1st Flr Struc Columns	1d
HM Frames	5d
Plumbing Rough in Block	7d
Electrical Rough in Block	7d
Block Walls to 2nd Floor	14d
1st Flr Struc Beams	2d
Fireplaces /Flues	4d
Mtl Studs	5d
FRIP Shored Slab	12d
Site Electrical	20d
Fire Protection Rough	4d
Mech Rough	5d
Plmbing Rough	7d
Elec Rough	7d
Sleeve Shored Slab	2d
Exterior Stone	8d
2nd Flr Rough Frame	7d
Cure Shored Slab	5d
3rd Flr Joists	4d
EIFS	30d
Remove Shoring	3d
3rd Flr Rough Frame	5d
Interior Partitions	2d
Fireplaces /Flues	4d
Curbs & Walks	20d
Fire Protection Rough	4d
4th Flr Joist	4d
Mech Rough	5d
Plmbing Rough	7d
Elec Rough	7d
Interior Partitions	2d
Fireplaces /Flues	4d
4th Flr Rough Frame	5d
Fire Protection Rough	4d

FIGURE 10.14 Bar chart created with SureTrak showing several lags used

CONCLUSION

Lags can significantly reduce the number of activities needed in a schedule. Allowing critical activities to overlap also reduces the number of days required to complete the project. Lags also reduce the time required to develop, maintain, and update the schedule, and allow for more flexibility in the field. However, lags may not show the level of detail needed to eliminate communication problems. If the schedule is to communicate, it needs to show the detail of who is doing what, when, and where. Lags also complicate the schedule calculations if the manager is scheduling by hand, without the use of computer software. This is not a big issue, however, because there are very few, if any, managers using CPM without the help of a computer.

APPLICATION

1. Look at the warehouse schedule you created and have been using throughout this textbook. Are there places in the logic diagram that would be more realistic by using lags? Can you see how overlapping the activities, especially the critical activities, will reduce the overall number of days to complete the project?

   Some project managers do not bother to use lags on noncritical activities; they like the simpler methods of construction without congestion. However, they prefer to overlap the critical activities because it shortens the project life span and is a more realistic way to schedule and manage a project.

2. If possible, talk to other experienced project managers or schedulers and get their opinion on the use of lags. When do they prefer to use lags? For what type of activities do they use lags? Which type of lags do they use? How comfortable are they with using lags?

CHAPTER 11

REVIEWING AND ANALYZING THE SCHEDULE

I N T R O D U C T I O N

After the initial development of the schedule and prior to creating reports it is important to review and analyze the schedule to make sure it is complete, reasonable, meets primary goals, and satisfies contract requirements. If inaccurate or faulty reports get into the field it is difficult to get rid of them. Schedule addendums can be sent out to replace the faulty schedule, but for some reason the faulty schedule keeps popping up and the revised version gets lost. It is much better if only the proper schedule is disseminated. A careful review not only eliminates these problems but also strengthens the schedule. This chapter points out what to look for in that review process.

ARE THE RELATIONSHIPS VALID?

Physical Relationships

First, managers review the schedule to make sure the physical relationships are valid. Is it physically possible to construct the project in the manner shown by the relationship arrows? To check this out, ask the same two questions suggested in Chapter 6: (1) Does this activity *really* need to be done before each of the following activities can start? (2) What *other activities* should take place before this activity can start? If the time is taken to ask these two questions of each and every activity, the resulting schedule will be even more accurate and there will be few, if any, logic or activity relationship errors.

Figure 11.1 illustrates a portion of a logic diagram for the construction of an office building with a full basement for storage area. A first glance at the logic diagram

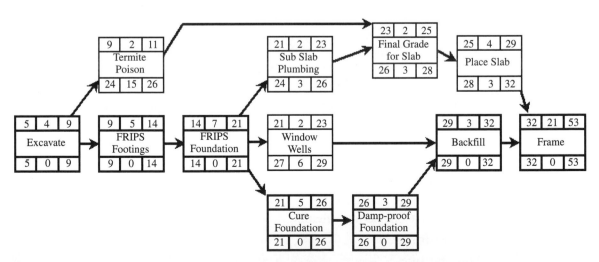

FIGURE 11.1   Some of the relationships in this office building project are invalid

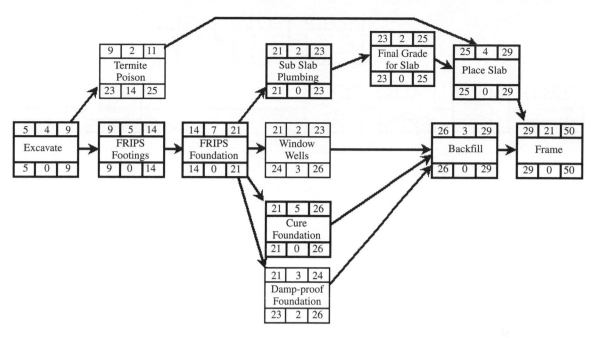

FIGURE 11.2   Adjusted logic diagram for the office building project—with valid relationships

shows a well-thought-out plan. Asking the two questions above may help improve it. Does *Excavate* really need to happen before *Termite Poison* and *FRIPS* (Form, Reinforce, Inspect, Pour, and Strip) *Footings?* Yes, so they are OK. Are there any other activities that should happen before *Termite Poison?* No, so that is OK. Does *Termite Poison* need to be done before *Final Grade for Slab?* Probably not, so the logic should be adjusted. Also ask, does *Cure Foundation* really need to be done before *Damp-proof Foundation?* No, *Damp-proof* can start right after *FRIPS Foundation* and be concurrent with *Cure Foundation.* The adjusted logic diagram would appear as shown in Figure 11.2.

An examination of Figure 11.2 shows *Frame* to finish on day 50, whereas in Figure 11.1 *Frame* was to finish on day 53. So, making *Damp-proof Foundation* concurrent with *Cure Foundation* saves 3 project days. Answering those two questions helps the manager think through the process and makes it easier to spot problems. Also, notice that the critical path has changed (activities with zero float) in Figure 11.2.

Safety Relationships

Managers must review the activities and logic relationships, focusing on safety and a safe work environment. Look at activities that may have a higher safety risk and examine concurrent activities to make sure no one is working under the high-risk activity. If unsafe conditions are noticed, change the logic diagram (arrows) to eliminate the unsafe working condition. For example, on a simple residential schedule you would not want to be installing roof trusses while another crew is working under the trusses installing subfloor plywood. When changing the logic, select the activity that

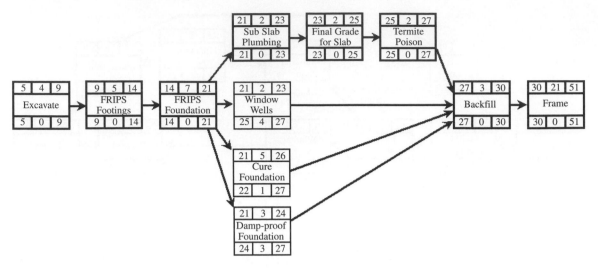

FIGURE 11.3 Office building logic diagram adjusted due to safety concerns

is less critical to become the successor. Try to eliminate conflicts without lengthening the critical path or the duration of the project.

With safety in mind, look carefully at Figure 11.2 again. As currently planned, the *Backfill* activity is done prior to *Frame*. From a safety standpoint that is a good idea; the carpenters will not have the big hole around the project to contend with. But what about *Termite Poison* being concurrent with *Sub Slab Plumbing* and *Final Grade for Slab?* If *Termite Poison* is done near its early dates, the plumbers and grading crew will be working in poisoned soil! That would be a safety concern. Therefore, the logic should be changed to have *Termite Poison* done after *Sub Slab Plumbing* and *Final Grade for Slab.* The new adjusted logic diagram is shown in Figure 11.3. Notice in Figure 11.3 that the *Frame* activity now is going to finish on day 51, 1 day later than in Figure 11.2, but the project is being built in a safe work environment. The project is still 2 days ahead of where it was prior to this evaluation process. Note that the critical path has changed again.

Quality Relationships

Examine the relationships focusing on quality. Make sure the logic diagram shows the activities in the proper sequence of construction in order to maintain high-quality standards. Think of past projects where activities that were done out of order caused poor quality results. Double-check those activity sequences. For example, make sure the nailing of siding or brick ties has been done on the outside of the exterior walls prior to drywall finishing on the inside to eliminate the number of nail pops in the drywall finish. With residential construction, make sure the insulation is scheduled after the exterior windows are installed so that the space around the rough window frame and the window jamb is able to be filled with foam insulation. Continue to think about and check those types of relationships so that quality is maintained.

Cost Relationships

Look closely at the scheduled activities focusing on costs. Are the schedule's logic and durations creating excessive costs anywhere? Are there too many people working in one area at the same time, creating a crowded condition? Are there areas where two activities that are currently scheduled in a straight line could be concurrent in order to shorten the project duration? Take a close look for this especially on the critical path. Do all the durations seem reasonable based on past experience with the same subcontractors?

DOES THE PROJECT COMPLETION DATE MEET CONTRACT REQUIREMENTS?

Check the contract documents to make sure the scheduled completion date meets all contract requirements. Also make sure the completion date meets the management team's requirements. With most projects you have the right to complete earlier than the contract requires. This would decrease project overhead costs. Does the management team want to consider this? Even more important, does the project's total duration feel right? Don't get so scientific with scheduling that common sense is overlooked. A good "gut check" is simply, does the total duration make sense and seem right based on past construction experience? If it does not, double-check the logic and durations of the critical path until it looks right.

Compressing the Schedule

If the original schedule is too long or as it is updated it goes beyond the contract completion date, it becomes necessary to compress the schedule. Compressing the schedule is also called "crashing" or "shortening" the schedule. Generally, compressing the schedule results in one or more of the following: higher costs, lower quality, or a less safe work environment. That must be kept in mind as the schedule is compressed. What is the best method to use that will have the least negative impact on the project and the people doing the work? Some managers have tried to come up with more scientific methods with spreadsheets and graphs to make these decisions, but generally, a good conversation with the management team will do the job most efficiently. The three following items need to be considered when compressing the schedule:

1. *Changing the durations of critical and near critical path activities.* It is obvious that if the durations of the critical activities are shortened, the project completion date will also be shortened. Less obvious is that the path or string of activities with low float may also need to be revised. If the schedule is to be shortened by 15 work days, it is necessary to shorten not only the critical path by 15 days but also every other path where there is 15 days or fewer of shared float. Of course, this typically increases resource demands of more workers and possibly equipment which may affect productivity and increase costs. Another option that may be considered is to go to multiple shifts for a short period of time on critical activities.

Don't forget to also assess the impact that shortening durations may have on quality and safety.

2. *Changing the calendar to have selected critical path activities work on the weekends or holidays.* This choice obviously requires the additional costs of overtime, but typically has less effect on creating additional safety problems or decreasing quality. Another method, if there are a sufficient number of workers available, is to work people 11.5 hours per day for 3.5 days which gives them their 40 hours. Then work another crew 11.5 hours per day for the other 3.5 days. A crew works for 3.5 days and then has 3.5 days off. This provides for 80 hours of work on the job. Of course, this would be done only on the critical path activities. That way no one works overtime, but productivity will suffer due to the long work days. Think creatively about other work hour adjustments that might be acceptable to solve special problems.

3. *Revising the schedule logic to have more or longer lags and/or more concurrent critical activities.* If the logic can be changed to take a critical activity off the critical path and make it concurrent or even to create an additional critical path, that will take days off the total project duration. This probably was not desirous in the original planned schedule, but in order to decrease the project duration it may be the best choice. This choice may create crowded conditions with the additional concurrent work taking place, but still may be the best choice. Also where there is a lag between critical activities, if the overlap is increased the project will finish earlier. Again, consider the effects of this choice on costs, quality, and safety.

Expanding the Schedule

Expanding the schedule is doing the opposite of compressing the schedule. If it is desirous that the project finish later than the first draft, you would consider the same choices as above but to increase rather than decrease the total project duration. Another reason to expand the schedule would be to decrease congestion or decrease total project costs through improved productivity by giving people more room in which to work. If the draft schedule is quite tight, expanding the schedule may decrease costs.

As the schedule is expanded the noncritical activities will have more float. This allows for more opportunity to level and manage resources. The more float in a schedule the more flexibility. Also, having additional activities with more float decreases the risk in the project. The more critical activities or higher percentage of critical activities the more likely there is to be delays.

IS THE CRITICAL PATH WHERE EXPERIENCE SAYS IT SHOULD BE?

The critical path should not be a surprise. Don't overlook your common sense and construction experience. The critical path or paths should be where you would expect them. Also check the near critical path, the paths or strings of activities with a small amount of shared float. Are the near critical activities about as you would expect them? Again, don't get so tied into the computer and the calculations that you overlook your common sense based on experience.

Milestones

Are the project milestones (major achievements) about where you would expect them? Think of the project in big chunks. For example, on a commercial building project think of the following: Is the project duration about right to get from the excavation to the completed foundation? Is the duration from the foundation to the finished structure about right? Is the duration on course for all the interior rough-ins? Is the duration accurate for the amount of time scheduled for all the exterior finishes? the interior finishes?

Procurement

Has the schedule included the key items of procurement? Double-check, especially the items that have a long lead time. Should they be included as part of the schedule? Think of past projects where procurement items have created problems and make sure those items are taken care of. Make sure the critical path activities receive their materials just prior to the installation of those materials. Materials delivered to the job site too early incur damage and possible theft. Check to make sure the procurement activities do not consume all the float shared with other construction activities, making those other activities critical.

Time of Year

Double-check the activities that must be done during a particular time of year. Will it be too cold or too hot for the seasonal activities? If temporary heat must be provided, it might be a good idea to make it part of the schedule so that it is not overlooked. Is there special weather protection needed during part of the construction process? Will it be necessary for some activities to be accelerated to make sure weather-sensitive activities are completed prior to bad weather?

Float Paths

Check the paths or strings of activities that have large amounts of float and see if that is really the case. Do those activities actually need to be completed prior to the start of other activities? Do you want to show that much float, or could you finish that part of the project and lock it off, or get the punch list items done in that area and then make that area off-limits? When a path or string of activities share float, it is not a bad idea to increase their activity duration in order to share that shared float. Take the pressure off those activities. However, save some of the shared float in case future problems arise.

Organize to Simplify

Is there any way you can reorganize the schedule to simplify it or make it communicate better? Ways to simplify include listing all the activities for one area together on the logic diagram; scheduling the activities in order from top to bottom—for example, the roofing activities would be on the top of the diagram and the footings and foundations on the bottom; showing floor levels from the bottom to the top as the building is being completed, or in reverse sequence as long as they are grouped together; with highway or lineal construction, showing the mile markers or other things to consider to make the schedule appear more organized and easy to follow.

Color-Code Some Activities

Would color-coding of key activities help the schedule? Having each trade represented by a specific color? Or showing a specific color for each activity that requires a particular piece of equipment, person, or other key resource? Would the schedule communicate better if a specific color was used to identify each inspection?

Figure 11.4 shows a portion of a highway overpass schedule where the activities that use the crane are highlighted by the darker colored activity box. Having the crane activities stand out helps in evaluating the schedule to make sure it is realistic in its use of the crane.

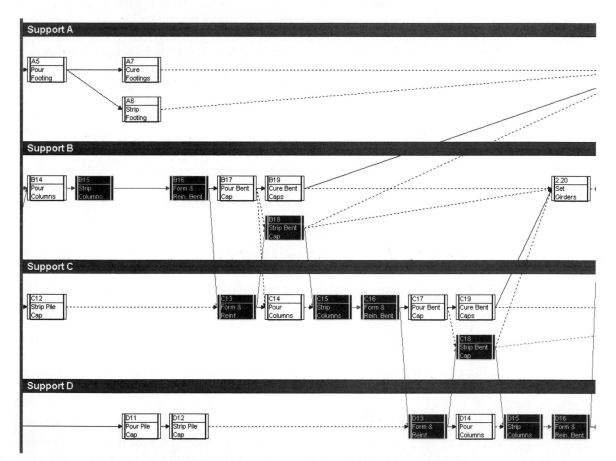

Figure 11.4 A highway overpass project schedule with crane activities color-coded

CONCLUSION

The management team must review and analyze the schedule before communicating it to the subcontractors and workers and anyone else involved in the project. The team should ask themselves these questions as they review the schedule: (1) Does this activity really need to be done before each of the following activities can start? (2) What other activities should take place before this activity can start? Managers must also review the activities and logic relationships to ensure that the working conditions are safe and that all activities will be done in the proper sequence to maintain high-quality standards and keep costs at a minimum. If a schedule is too long or goes beyond contract completion date, or there is a need to decrease congestion at the job site, managers have the option to either compress or expand the schedule using various methods. Throughout the project, managers need to constantly assess such factors as durations, procurement, the weather, float paths, and schedule organization in order to maximize their success.

Many major problems on construction projects are traceable to poor planning. Reviewing and analyzing the schedule will eliminate many potential problems. It does take a few minutes to double check but it is worth it. Remember it is easier to erase on paper than to remove concrete and welds. Let's eliminate the old saying: "There is never time to do it right but there is always time to do it over." Schedule and plan to do it right the first time.

APPLICATION

1. Go back to the warehouse project you scheduled in earlier chapters, double check the items discussed in this chapter, and record changes made. Was the review worth it? Is the reviewed schedule better than the original schedule?

2. Make a checklist of activities where an improper sequence caused quality problems. Keep this list and keep adding to these activities as you manage projects. Then you can consult this list on future schedules to make sure you will not experience those problems again. If you are a student and have not had sufficient experience to do this, interview an experienced project manager for this information.

3. Follow the same instructions as for activity 2, but focus on issues relating to safety.

4. Look at your warehouse schedule and consider cutting two weeks off the schedule. How would you do it to cause the least negative effect on quality, costs, and safety?

CHAPTER 12

CREATING BAR CHARTS AND TABULAR REPORTS FROM NETWORK LOGIC DIAGRAMS

INTRODUCTION

The network logic diagram forces the management team to think through the project in detail and then the diagram communicates that thinking and planning to all involved in the project—provided they have been taught to read and understand the logic diagram. That is a major problem with CPM networks. The typical field workers have had no training in reading logic diagrams. They see the logic diagram as a confusing bunch of arrows, boxes, and way too many numbers. When field workers, and many times managers, hear the word "schedule," they automatically think of a bar chart, not a network logic diagram. Bar charts are the default schedule that most people think of, but they lack the detailed information and clarity of network logic diagrams. Plus, as a bar chart is updated and the schedule falls behind in an area or two, the manager must rethink the future schedule based on what has been done. Whereas, with CPM scheduling the updated future activities are automatically adjusted based on the logic diagram.

How do we overcome this problem? The answer is to plan the project using CPM and then print bar charts or even tabular reports on the computer to communicate the schedule to those who would prefer simpler scheduling methods. This chapter will take the power of the CPM network logic diagram and create a bar chart using that detailed information. The advantage of using a bar chart created from a network is not only that the bar chart is simpler to understand but also that it can be designed specifically for the person receiving it. For example, you can show or not show the float or the critical activities. Most important, the bar chart is based on the detailed thinking required for the development of the network logic diagram.

This chapter will show the development of three bar charts for three different team members. The first bar chart will be for in-house use by the project manager or the project team that understands CPM logic and float. The second bar chart will be for the subcontractors, which will not show float. This keeps the subs from misusing shared days of float. The third bar chart will be for the owner, showing the late start and late finish dates so the owner will not become alarmed if the activities do not start on the early dates.

To clarify, the use of different dates is not intended to mislead anyone. The intent is to keep those who are not completely knowledgeable of CPM and its features—the early dates, late dates, and the different types of float—from misinterpreting the schedule information and creating problems for the project.

Figure 12.1, Practice Problem #1, which was used in Chapter 8, will be used in this chapter as an example project. There is a work-date to calendar-date conversion chart at the bottom of the logic diagram. You may want to copy this page as a reference to look at while reading the rest of the chapter.

BAR CHARTS FOR THE PROJECT MANAGER

This bar chart will show the bars positioned in their early dates (rather than the late dates) and it will also show the total float on the bars. The person reading this schedule must realize that the float shown may be shared with other activities, and that it is not independent float that belongs to that activity alone, as discussed in Chapter 9.

Notice that in the schedule in Figure 12.2 the activities are listed in chronological order, or, in scheduling terms it is called early start (ES), early finish (EF) sort or order. The first sort criteria is ES. If two activities have the same ES day, then the next criteria would be EF, so the one with the earliest finish would be listed first. Activity *W* is obviously the first activity. As you examine the network logic diagram in Figure 12.1, the second activity could be *K*, *B*, or *P*. They all three start at the same time, but because *K* finishes first, it is listed first. Activities *B* and *P* could be interchanged because they both start and finish on the same days. Continuing to look at the logic diagram in Figure 12.1, activity *F* is next because it has the next ES day. Then comes *O* and *Y* in order of their ES dates. Activities *L* and *U* have the same ES date, but *L* has the earliest EF date, so it is listed first. Finally, activity *S* is listed last.

Another common sort is ES, total float (TF). With this sort, the first sort criteria is ES, but if two activities have the same ES day, then the next criteria would be TF. Therefore, the most critical activity (the one with the least float) would be listed first. The ES, TF sort would look very similar to the schedule in Figure 12.2, except *B* would be listed before *K* or *P* because they all have the same ES date, but *B* has the least amount of total float. Activity *K* would be next and finally *P* would be the last of the

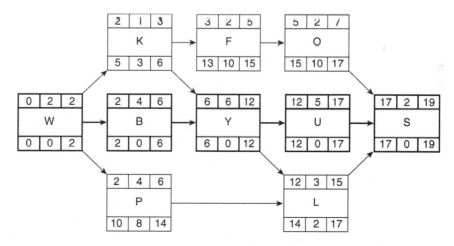

Calendar Date	7/1	2	3	5	8	9	10	11	12	15	16	17	18	19	22	23	24	25	26
Work Day	1	2	3	4	5	6	7	8	9	10	11	12	13	14	15	16	17	18	19

FIGURE 12.1   Practice Problem #1

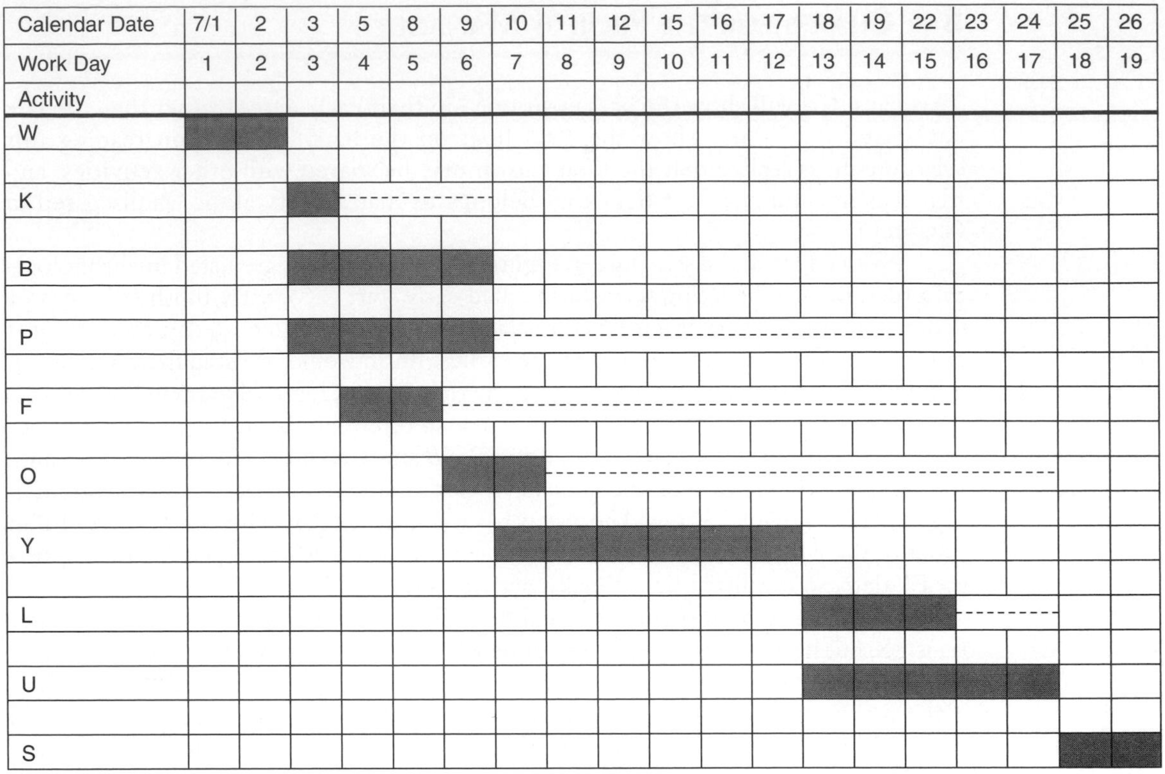

Calendar Date	7/1	2	3	5	8	9	10	11	12	15	16	17	18	19	22	23	24	25	26
Work Day	1	2	3	4	5	6	7	8	9	10	11	12	13	14	15	16	17	18	19
Activity																			
W	■	■																	
K			■	┄	┄	┄													
B			■	■	■	■													
P			■	■	■	■	┄	┄	┄	┄	┄	┄	┄	┄					
F				■	■	┄	┄	┄	┄	┄	┄	┄	┄	┄					
O						■	■	┄	┄	┄	┄	┄	┄	┄					
Y							■	■	■	■	■	■							
L													■	■	┄	┄			
U													■	■	■	■	■		
S																		■	■

FIGURE 12.2 This bar chart for the project manager shows float

three because *P* has the most total float. Also, *U* would be listed above *L* because *U* has zero float and *L* has two days of total float.

In Figure 12.2, note that the time scale shows both calendar and work days. The project starts on July 1, which appears to be a Monday. July 4th is skipped because it is a holiday. Saturdays and Sundays are also skipped signifying a 5-day work week. So as the bars are entered, the scheduler looks at the work days that correspond with the logic diagram in order to create the bars in the proper locations. Also, remember that on the hand-drawn schedule, the work days begin at the end of the day. Thus, activity *W* starts on the end of day 0 (really the morning of day 1) and ends on the end of day 2. Likewise, activity *B* starts on the end of day 2 (really the morning of day 3) and finishes the end of day 6. As discussed previously, the computer software is programmed to eliminate this problem and to show just the calendar days. When the computer says an activity starts on July 14, that means the morning of July 14. When the computer says an activity finishes on July 20, that means the end of the day on 20.

If a hand-drawn bar chart is being developed without the aid of the network, the creator of the chart will not be thinking at the same detailed level required for the development of the network logic diagram. On the other hand, the bar chart that is developed based on the network will reflect this detailed thinking. In fact, the bar chart developed from the network is simply displaying the network information in a different form—a bar chart. Bar charts based on networks are much more accurate than non-network based bar charts.

BAR CHARTS FOR THE SUBCONTRACTORS

The prior bar chart for the project manager would not be ideal to give to the typical subcontractor because it shows the total float. The subcontractor may think all float shown belongs to that activity (is independent float) and not realize that most of the time total float is shared with other activities, thus creating major problems for the project. The bar chart in Figure 12.2 could be drawn by hand showing only independent float, if that is the desire of the project management team. The current computer software programs do not identify independent float, so that is not an option with the software. The only option with most software is whether or not to show total float. It is possible to show free float with some software, but from a management point of view, that would be of little help because free float could still be shared with prior activities in the same path or string.

Therefore, the typical bar chart for the subcontractors would be one that does not show any float, with the activities displayed in their early dates and sorted or ordered by ES, EF, as shown in Figure 12.3.

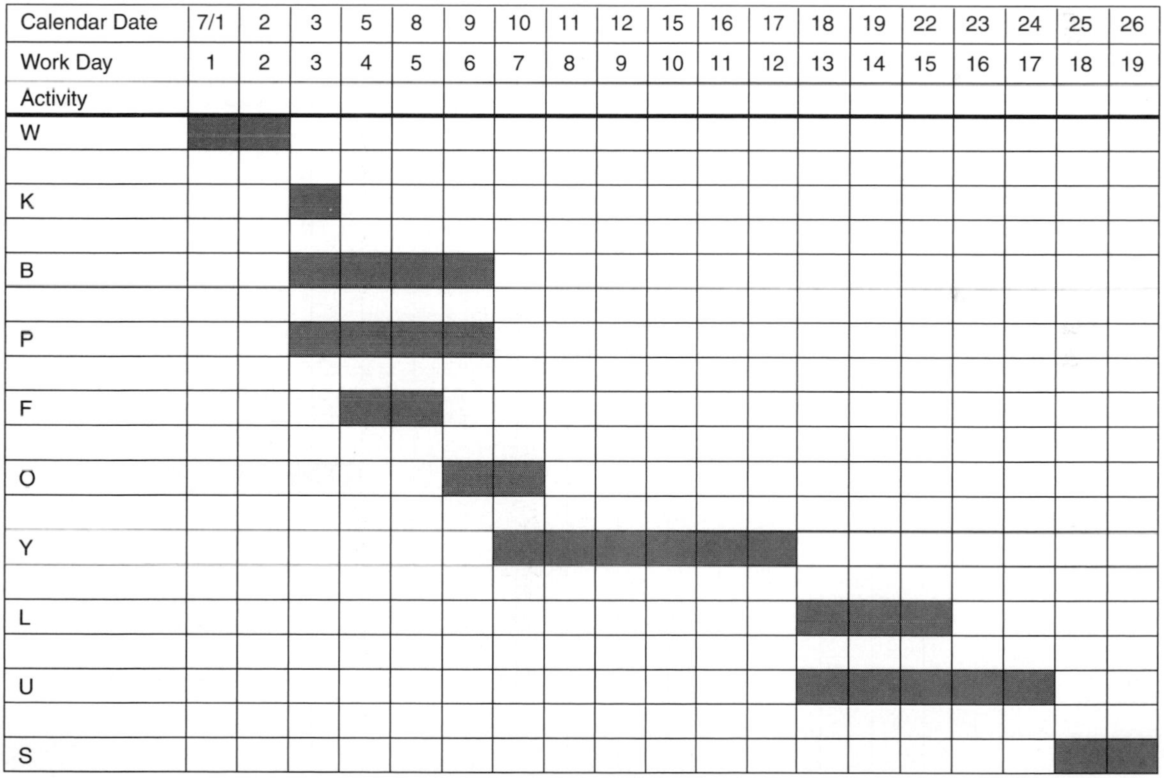

Calendar Date	7/1	2	3	5	8	9	10	11	12	15	16	17	18	19	22	23	24	25	26
Work Day	1	2	3	4	5	6	7	8	9	10	11	12	13	14	15	16	17	18	19
Activity																			
W	▓	▓																	
K			▓																
B			▓	▓	▓	▓													
P			▓	▓	▓	▓													
F				▓	▓														
O						▓													
Y							▓	▓	▓										
L													▓	▓	▓				
U													▓	▓	▓	▓			
S																		▓	▓

FIGURE 12.3 This bar chart for the subcontractors does not show float

As a subcontractor examines the schedule in Figure 12.3, there is no chance he or she will see float and, therefore, misuse it. Notice that because it shows only the early dates it forces the subcontractor to focus on those dates, ensuring the subcontractor will not delay the project as long as he or she finishes the activities as scheduled.

BAR CHARTS FOR THE OWNER

If the same (prior) bar chart developed for the subcontractors was given to the owner it could create some possible problems for the project. If the owner focused on the early activity times and then an activity starts later, within the float dates, the owner may think the project is behind schedule when it isn't. This could cause communication problems between the owner and the contractor. For example, let's say activity K used the 3 days of float and actually started on its LS day (the end of day 5) and finished on its LF day (the end of day 6). It's probable the owner will compare the actual schedule with the as-planned schedule in Figure 12.3 and become alarmed, thinking the project is behind when in fact it is not; it is within the days of float. Therefore, an experienced scheduler likely would provide the owner with a bar chart showing the bars displayed on their late dates—without showing float—and the activities sorted by LS, LF, as shown in Figure 12.4.

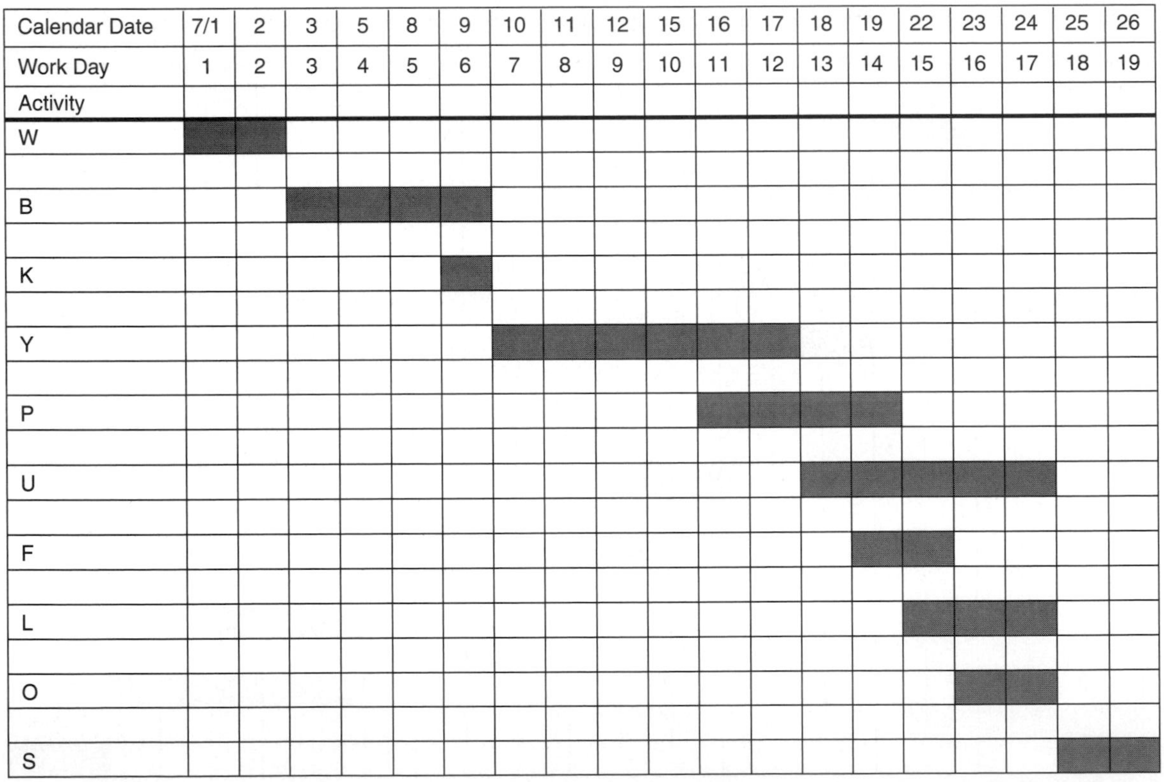

Calendar Date	7/1	2	3	5	8	9	10	11	12	15	16	17	18	19	22	23	24	25	26
Work Day	1	2	3	4	5	6	7	8	9	10	11	12	13	14	15	16	17	18	19
Activity																			
W	■	■																	
B			■	■	■	■													
K						■													
Y							■	■	■	■	■	■							
P											■	■	■	■					
U														■	■	■	■		
F														■	■				
L															■	■	■		
O																■			
S																		■	■

FIGURE 12.4   This bar chart for the owner shows late dates without float

Notice in Figure 12.4 that activity *K* is now scheduled for work day 6 (its late date), where on the subcontractors' schedule it was scheduled to happen on day 3 (its early date). All the bars are shown to happen on their late dates, rather than their early dates.

As the owner now focuses on the bar chart shown in Figure 12.4, he or she has no reason for concern if some of the activities use the float. In fact, as some of the activities are finished prior to their LS and LF dates, it actually makes many of the activities and the project look ahead of schedule, as shown in the updated bar chart that will be discussed next.

UPDATED BAR CHARTS

A careful examination of the bar chart schedule in Figure 12.5 shows the as-planned schedule represented by the solid dark bars. The vertical lined bars underneath represent the actual dates that each activity started and finished on. This project is updated through the end of work day 12 where the bold vertical line appears. That line represents the project data date, which is the date the project was updated.

Calendar Date	7/1	2	3	5	8	9	10	11	12	15	16	17	18	19	22	23	24	25	26
Work Day	1	2	3	4	5	6	7	8	9	10	11	12	13	14	15	16	17	18	19
Activity																			
W	█	█																	
		▓																	
B			█	█	█	█													
			▓	▓	▓	▓													
K						█													
				▓	▓														
Y							█	█	█	█									
							▓	▓	▓	▓	▓								
P											█	█	█						
										▓	▓								
U													█	█	█	█	█		
F														█	█				
											▓								
L														█	█				
O															█				
S																		█	█

FIGURE 12.5 In this updated bar chart the as-planned schedule is indicated by the solid dark bars and the actual start and finish dates by the shaded bars

When comparing the bar chart schedule in Figure 12.5 with the dates in the logic network diagram shown earlier (Figure 12.1), you can see that some of the activities actually happened on their ES and EF dates such as activities W and B. Others, like activity K, started on day 4, after the ES date but prior to the LS date. Activity K also took 2 days to complete, rather than the 1 day originally assigned, but K finished prior to the LF date, making the project look good. Then, to see activities P and F appear to be ahead of schedule makes the project team look great!

Providing the target schedule to the owner with the late dates and then doing several of the activities on earlier dates, makes the project appear to be ahead of schedule when it is really on schedule with the critical activities. Notice the critical activity Y in Figure 12.5. As compared with the logic diagram shown earlier, the critical activities are right on schedule; therefore, the project as a whole is not ahead of schedule. But it sure makes everyone look good. That is why many owners, who are familiar with CPM scheduling, require specific reports in the contract documents—so they know what is happening with the schedule. However, if the owner is not experienced with CPM scheduling, the bar chart in Figure 12.5 is more effective than the bar chart developed for the subcontractors because it makes the project appear to be behind when, in fact, it may be within its float. As stated earlier, it should not be the intent to furnish false or misleading information, but neither should it be the intent to cause the owner to become overconcerned when there is no reason for concern.

When the total management team (general contractor, subs, suppliers, vendors, architect, engineers, owner, etc.) members are all professional and experienced with CPM and understand the different types of float, there is no reason to try and fool anyone or make schedules look deceiving. The problem is with team players who do not understand the implications of CPM and the different types of float, who may overreact when they perceive an activity is behind, when it is really within its float time. Or even worse, when shared float is used because a project team member thinks it is independent float. Many experienced owners require a target, or as-planned, schedule that displays the bars in their early date positions and shows total float.

TABULAR REPORTS

Another way to display the information from the network logic diagram is with tabular reports. Tabular reports are basically just rows and columns of information without any graphic representations, such as bars. They are simple and communicate the desired information from the CPM network.

Tabular Reports for the Project Manager

Using the same philosophy as was used for the bar charts, the tabular report headings, designed for in-house use for the project manager or superintendent who understands CPM and the types of float, would look similar to the column headings in Figure 12.6. The data included in each column would be the same as the column title.

Activity	Duration	Total Float	Early Start	Early Finish	Late Start	Late Finish
(Data)	Duration	TF	ES	EF	LS	LF

FIGURE 12.6   Example of tabular report headings and data to be included for the project manager

Activity	Duration	Total Float	Early Start	Early Finish	Late Start	Late Finish
W	2	0	7/1	7/2	7/1	7/2
K	1	3	7/3	7/3	7/9	7/9
B	4	0	7/3	7/9	7/3	7/9
P	4	8	7/3	7/9	7/16	7/19
F	2	10	7/5	7/8	7/19	7/22
O	2	10	7/9	7/10	7/23	7/24
Y	6	0	7/10	7/17	7/10	7/17
L	3	2	7/18	7/22	7/22	7/24
U	5	0	7/18	7/24	7/18	7/24
S	2	0	7/25	7/26	7/25	7/26

FIGURE 12.7   Project manager's or superintendent's tabular report

Activity	Start Date	Finish Date	Other Information as Desired			
(Data)	ES	EF				

FIGURE 12.8   Example of tabular report headings and data to be included for the subcontractors

The full tabular report for the project manager would look similar to Figure 12.7, with the data supplied from the network logic diagram and the work days converted to calendar dates.

This report has a simple format that gives the project manager who understands CPM the basic data needed to help manage the project. However, this format is of no help in understanding the types of float, so care must be taken to not overuse shared float.

Tabular Reports for the Subcontractors

The tabular report headings for the subcontractors would put the focus on the early dates but not show any indication of late starts, late finishes, or float as shown in Figure 12.8.

The column heading would state "Start Date," but the data from the network would be ES dates. Likewise, the "Finish Date" data would be EF dates. This protects the project from subcontractors who do not understand that float may be shared and, therefore, use it to the detriment of the total project.

Activity	Start Date	Finish Date	Notes
W	7/1	7/2	Remember to bring dynamite
K	7/3	7/3	
B	7/3	7/9	
P	7/3	7/9	
F	7/5	7/8	Interior paint is Whisper White
O	7/9	7/10	
Y	7/10	7/17	Check with the electrician prior to installation
L	7/18	7/22	
U	7/18	7/24	
S	7/25	7/26	

FIGURE 12.9   Subcontractors' tabular report

The full tabular report for subcontractors would look similar to Figure 12.9, except it likely would contain only the information for that specific sub, with the data supplied from the network logic diagram and the work days converted to calendar dates.

Notice in Figure 12.9 that the "Notes" column is used to convey any additional information desired to the subs. Also notice that the "Start Date" column heading is the early start data and the "Finish Date" is the early finish data, and that the activities are listed in chronological order.

Tabular Reports for the Owner

The tabular report for the owner would put the focus on the late dates and then, as some of the activities actually finish earlier, it eliminates unnecessary concern for the owner. This keeps the owner from becoming alarmed if some of the activities used float. The report column headings for the owner may appear as shown in Figure 12.10.

The column heading would state "Start Date," but the data from the network would be LS dates. Likewise, the "Finish Date" data would be LF dates. This protects the project from owners who do not understand that float may be available and therefore noncritical activities can start late without delaying the project.

The full tabular report for the owner would look similar to Figure 12.11, with the data supplied from the network logic diagram and the work days converted to calendar dates.

Note in Figure 12.11 that all the dates are the late start and late finish dates even though the column headings state "Start Date" and "Finish Date." Also notice that the activities have been arranged in chronological order for the owner based on their late start and late finish dates.

The tabular format is the favorite report for many managers because it communicates the project information to the different parties as desired in a simple and easy-to-understand format. Because of the tabular report's simplicity, it eliminates the problem of misinterpreting information or receiving more information than is needed. The tabular report can be included with spreadsheets containing other project infor-

Activity	Start Date	Finish Date	Other Information as Desired			
(Data)	LS	LF				

FIGURE 12.10   Example of tabular report headings for the owner

Activity	Start Date	Finish Date	Comments
W	7/1	7/2	The extended family is welcome to the groundbreaking
B	7/3	7/9	This is the last date changes to plans can be made
K	7/9	7/9	
Y	7/10	7/17	
P	7/16	7/19	
U	7/18	7/24	Decision on landscaping needs to be made by the 10th
F	7/19	7/22	
L	7/22	7/24	
O	7/23	7/24	
S	7/25	7/26	

FIGURE 12.11   Owner's tabular report

mation as desired. This tabular report information could even be downloaded to a Palm Pilot or other handheld computing device. Tabular reports are also easy to attach to e-mail messages. For all of these reasons it has become the favorite report for many experienced managers. However, tabular reports would not be effective in a proposal for a negotiated contract where impressive and flashy graphics would be the best choice.

LINEAR BAR CHARTS

A linear bar chart is another type of bar chart that has been developed. It is particularly well suited for repetitive elements in projects, such as the interior finishes in a multistory office building. A linear bar chart is also useful for repetitive projects such as homes or multiunit housing projects. As is the standard bar chart, the linear bar chart is also based on the network logic diagram. There is no current software on the market that creates this type of bar chart. For project management teams who are not computer oriented, it may be an ideal method of planning and scheduling the project.

The linear bar chart is created from a logic diagram. Therefore, the first step is to create the logic diagram.

Figure 12.12 is a logic diagram of the interior finishes for one floor of a small office building. The critical path activities are bolded. Notice that *Rgh. Mech.* has 1 day of independent float and *Floor Coverings* and *Finish Mech.* have 2 days of shared float.

The next step is to create the linear bar chart showing the schedule information, as shown in Figure 12.13.

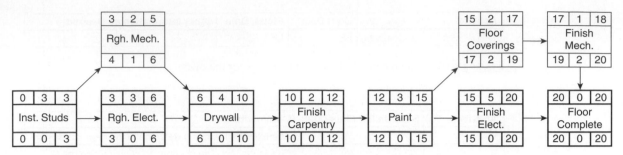

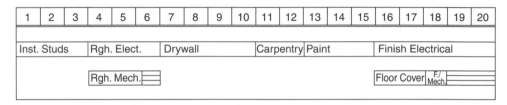

FIGURE 12.12   A linear bar chart can be created from this logic diagram

FIGURE 12.13   A linear bar chart based on the logic diagram in Figure 12.12

The critical path is the first line of activities with the bolded bars end-to-end. If there are multiple critical paths, those additional critical activities are drawn attached to the bottom of the first critical bar activities. The duration can be determined by comparing the individual activity bar with the time scale on the top. Float is shown by the multiple horizontal lines. Shared float is shown by placing the activity bars that share float end-to-end and then showing the shared float after the last activity as in *Floor Cover* and *F. Mech*. Independent float is shown by locating that activity all alone as in *Rgh. Mech*. The resulting bar chart is called a linear bar chart because the activities' bars are aligned in a linear rather than vertical fashion as in the case of a standard bar chart.

Many managers would feel comfortable giving the linear bar chart to subcontractors because it shows both the activities with shared float and the activities with independent float. Consequently, it is less likely that a subcontractor would think that the shared float belongs to his or her activity alone and, therefore, would misuse the float.

The linear bar chart takes on additional power when it is used in a master schedule for the construction of repetitive activities. A master schedule of the interior finishes in a four-story office building could be scheduled as shown in Figure 12.14.

Each floor level appears as a single bar in this linear bar chart schedule. The floor levels are offset by 5 days because the longest critical duration is 5 days. This provides for a schedule where the crews could go from floor level to floor level without having any crew scheduled to be in two places at one time.

The schedule could be updated by hand using a highlighter to show progress on each bar where progress has been made. If this schedule is mounted on a wall or bulletin board, a string with a weight on the bottom (like a plumb bob) could be tacked on the time scale representing the current day, and then progress could be noted by comparing

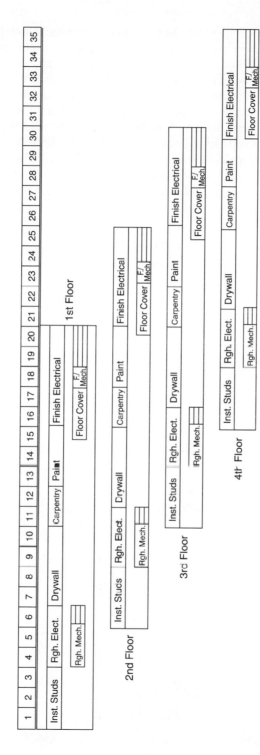

FIGURE 12.14 There is a separate linear bar chart for each floor level in this four-story office building schedule

141

the highlighted activities with the position of the string. If each floor level bar was printed on a separate piece of paper, that long, narrow piece of paper could be moved to the right or left to update the schedule in comparison with the string representing the current day.

The linear bar chart can be updated and scheduled by hand quite easily. There are no software programs that make this linear master schedule from the CPM information input into the computer. The linear bar chart is most easily made by using a spreadsheet program such as Microsoft Excel. The master linear bar chart schedule works well with repetitive projects such as units, floor levels, houses, buildings, or apartments. The updated master schedule would show the current status of the project and precisely which activities are ahead of or behind schedule. If this master linear bar chart schedule is located in a highly visible place, it puts subtle pressure on everyone to adhere to the schedule.

COMPUTER-GENERATED BAR CHARTS DEVELOPED FROM NETWORKS

The following examples were developed with the CPM scheduling program SureTrak Project Manager, created by Primavera Systems, Inc.

The network logic diagram that the bar charts are developed from is displayed in Figure 12.15.

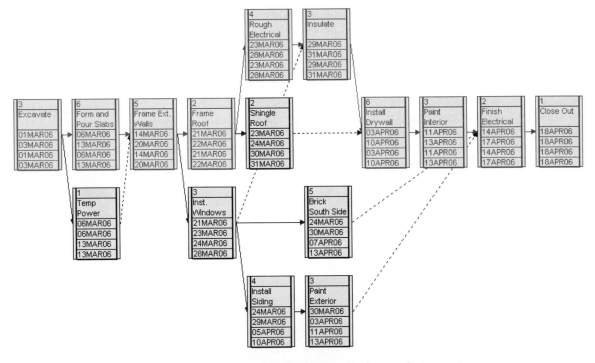

FIGURE 12.15 SureTrak Project Manager network logic diagram for the warehouse project

This schedule is for the construction of the simple warehouse project that has been referred to throughout this textbook. The first row in the activity box is the duration. The second row is the activity description. The first row of dates is ES, the second is EF, the third is LS, and the last row is LF.

Figure 12.16 illustrates a standard bar chart for the project manager. Notice that the schedule shows total float as a column and also on the bars. The management team decides what information to include on the reports.

Figure 12.17 shows a standard bar chart for the subcontractors. Notice that the schedule shows no sign of total float or late start or finish dates.

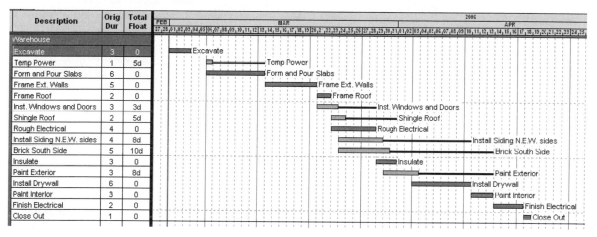

FIGURE 12.16   SureTrak standard bar chart for the project manager

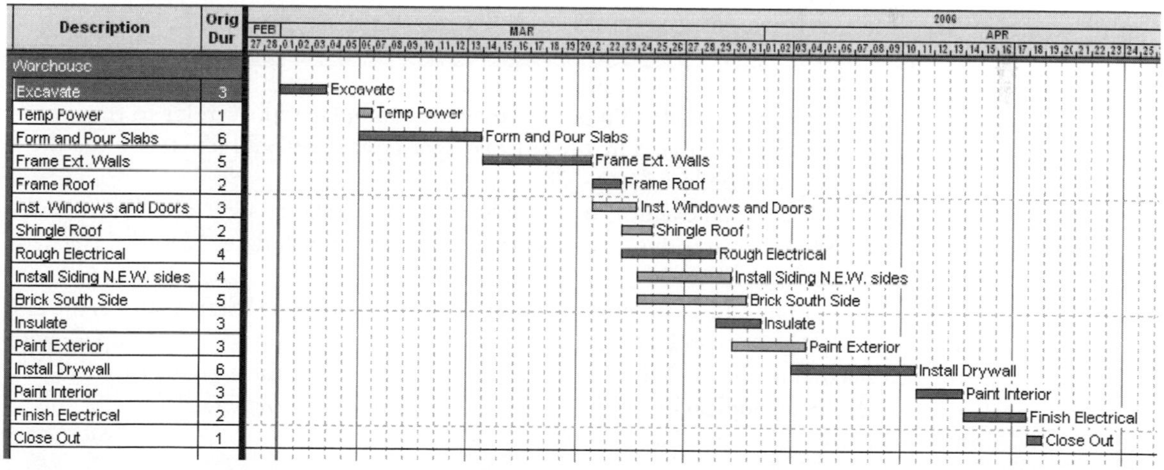

FIGURE 12.17   SureTrak standard bar chart for the subcontractors

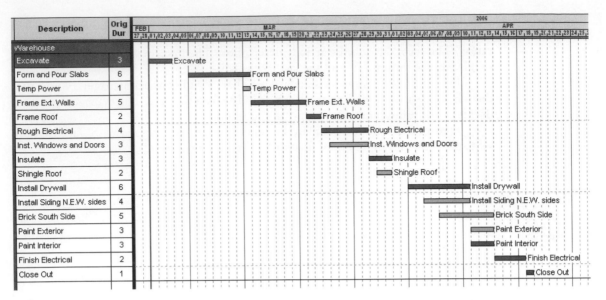

Description	Orig Dur						
Warehouse							
Excavate	3	Excavate					
Form and Pour Slabs	6	Form and Pour Slabs					
Temp Power	1	Temp Power					
Frame Ext. Walls	5	Frame Ext. Walls					
Frame Roof	2	Frame Roof					
Rough Electrical	4	Rough Electrical					
Inst. Windows and Doors	3	Inst. Windows and Doors					
Insulate	3	Insulate					
Shingle Roof	2	Shingle Roof					
Install Drywall	6	Install Drywall					
Install Siding N.E.W. sides	4	Install Siding N.E.W. sides					
Brick South Side	5	Brick South Side					
Paint Exterior	3	Paint Exterior					
Paint Interior	3	Paint Interior					
Finish Electrical	2	Finish Electrical					
Close Out	1	Close Out					

FIGURE 12.18   SureTrak standard bar chart for the owner

Figure 12.18 depicts a standard bar chart for the owner. Notice that the bars are in the late start and late finish positions.

COMPUTER-GENERATED TABULAR REPORTS DEVELOPED FROM NETWORKS

In Figure 12.19, an example of a project manager's tabular report, refer to the scheduled dates for *Paint Exterior*. The project manager typically would like to see the float, the early dates, and the late dates.

Figure 12.20 is an example of a subcontractors' tabular report. The "Start Date" is the early start date and the "Finish Date" is the early finish date. Notice the scheduled dates for *Paint Exterior*.

Finally, Figure 12.21 shows an owner's tabular report. The "Start Date" is the late start date and the "Finish Date" is the late finish date. Again, notice and compare with the prior schedule the dates for *Paint Exterior*. Also note that the activities are listed in the proper chronological order (late start, late finish) for the owner.

Act ID	Description	Orig Dur	Total Float	Early Start	Early Finish	Late Start	Late Finish	Notes
Warehouse								
1	Excavate	3	0	01MAR06	03MAR06	01MAR06	03MAR06	
3	Temp Power	1	5d	06MAR06	06MAR06	13MAR06	13MAR06	
2	Form and Pour Slabs	6	0	06MAR06	13MAR06	06MAR06	13MAR06	6,000 psi concrete
4	Frame Ext. Walls	5	0	14MAR06	20MAR06	14MAR06	20MAR06	2 X 6 ext. walls
5	Frame Roof	2	0	21MAR06	22MAR06	21MAR06	22MAR06	
6	Inst. Windows and Doors	3	3d	21MAR06	23MAR06	24MAR06	28MAR06	Vinyl #3685 Windows
9	Shingle Roof	2	5d	23MAR06	24MAR06	30MAR06	31MAR06	Dark Brown Shingles
7	Rough Electrical	4	0	23MAR06	28MAR06	23MAR06	28MAR06	
11	Install Siding N.E.W. sides	4	8d	24MAR06	29MAR06	05APR06	10APR06	Doe Skin Brown,
10	Brick South Side	5	10d	24MAR06	30MAR06	07APR06	13APR06	Navaho Brown Brick
8	Insulate	3	0	29MAR06	31MAR06	29MAR06	31MAR06	R-19 Walls R -40
12	Paint Exterior	3	8d	30MAR06	03APR06	11APR06	13APR06	Tan # 48
13	Install Drywall	6	0	03APR06	10APR06	03APR06	10APR06	5/8" type X
14	Paint Interior	3	0	11APR06	13APR06	11APR06	13APR06	Winter Cloud White
15	Finish Electrical	2	0	14APR06	17APR06	14APR06	17APR06	
16	Close Out	1	0	18APR06	18APR06	18APR06	18APR06	

FIGURE 12.19   SureTrak tabular report for the project manager

Act ID	Description	Orig Dur	Start Date	Finish Date	Notes
Warehouse					
1	Excavate	3	01MAR06	03MAR06	
3	Temp Power	1	06MAR06	06MAR06	
2	Form and Pour Slabs	6	06MAR06	13MAR06	6,000 psi concrete
4	Frame Ext. Walls	5	14MAR06	20MAR06	2 X 6 ext. walls
5	Frame Roof	2	21MAR06	22MAR06	
6	Inst. Windows and Doors	3	21MAR06	23MAR06	Vinyl #3685 Windows
9	Shingle Roof	2	23MAR06	24MAR06	Dark Brown Shingles
7	Rough Electrical	4	23MAR06	28MAR06	
11	Install Siding N.E.W. sides	4	24MAR06	29MAR06	Doe Skin Brown,
10	Brick South Side	5	24MAR06	30MAR06	Navaho Brown Brick
8	Insulate	3	29MAR06	31MAR06	R-19 Walls R -40
12	Paint Exterior	3	30MAR06	03APR06	Tan # 48
13	Install Drywall	6	03APR06	10APR06	5/8" type X
14	Paint Interior	3	11APR06	13APR06	Winter Cloud White
15	Finish Electrical	2	14APR06	17APR06	
16	Close Out	1	18APR06	18APR06	

FIGURE 12.20   SureTrak tabular report for the subcontractors

Act ID	Description	Orig Dur	Start Date	Finish Date
Warehouse				
1	Excavate	3	01MAR06	03MAR06
2	Form and Pour Slabs	6	06MAR06	13MAR06
3	Temp Power	1	13MAR06	13MAR06
4	Frame Ext. Walls	5	14MAR06	20MAR06
5	Frame Roof	2	21MAR06	22MAR06
7	Rough Electrical	4	23MAR06	28MAR06
6	Inst. Windows and Doors	3	24MAR06	28MAR06
8	Insulate	3	29MAR06	31MAR06
9	Shingle Roof	2	30MAR06	31MAR06
13	Install Drywall	6	03APR06	10APR06
11	Install Siding N.E.W. sides	4	05APR06	10APR06
10	Brick South Side	5	07APR06	13APR06
12	Paint Exterior	3	11APR06	13APR06
14	Paint Interior	3	11APR06	13APR06
15	Finish Electrical	2	14APR06	17APR06
16	Close Out	1	18APR06	18APR06

FIGURE 12.21   SureTrak tabular report for the owner

CONCLUSION

Efficient managers realize the potential for standard and linear bar charts and tabular reports developed from the detailed thinking required of the network logic diagram. Each of these different types of reports has its benefits, and is designed specifically for the person receiving it. This makes the simple bar chart or tabular report a powerful communication tool to help manage the project. Once the logic diagram is developed and input into the computer it becomes easy for a manager experienced with the software to print these different types of charts and reports.

APPLICATION

1. Create a standard bar chart with the bars in the early position and showing the total float, based on the network logic diagram of the warehouse you created in Chapter 6. Add the durations from Chapter 7, the calculations from Chapter 8, and the types of float from Chapter 9. This bar chart will resemble the chart discussed in this chapter for the project manager. It can be created using graph paper or on the computer if you know Microsoft Excel or another spreadsheet program.

2. Compare the bar chart you created in activity 1, based on the logic diagram, with the bar chart of the same project you created as a stand-alone bar chart in Chapter 4. Are the two bar chart schedules different? How do you account for this difference—they were both done by the same person on the same project? Which one is more accurate? Which one gives you greater confidence in building the project?

3. Using the techniques discussed in this chapter, create a bar chart for the subcontractors that will be working on your warehouse.

4. Create a bar chart for the owner of the warehouse project. Use the techniques learned in this chapter.

5. Create a tabular report for the manager of the warehouse project. Use the techniques discussed in this chapter.

6. Create a tabular report for the subcontractors of the warehouse project.

7. Using the techniques discussed in this chapter, create a tabular report for the potential owner of the warehouse project

CHAPTER 13

LINEAR OR LINE-OF-BALANCE SCHEDULES

I N T R O D U C T I O N

Linear schedules, sometimes called line-of-balance schedules, have their roots in the manufacturing industry. They are particularly well suited for projects where the activities are of a repetitive nature. The construction projects that lend themselves to linear scheduling are typically horizontal rather than vertical projects. Projects such as highways, pipelines, and railroads are common examples. However, high-rise buildings and even residential construction could be scheduled with linear scheduling methods due to the repetitive nature of those projects. This type of scheduling helps project managers visualize time and space conflicts between activities.

HOW TO CREATE LINEAR SCHEDULES

The steps to develop a linear schedule are as follows:

1. Identify the activities
2. Estimate activity production rates
3. Develop activity sequence
4. Create a velocity diagram for the first activity
5. Add the velocity diagram for each additional activity
6. Look for conflicts and buffers

Following is an example project for laying 5,000 feet of pipeline that we will create a linear schedule for. The project consists of five activities: *Survey & Layout, Clear & Grub, Trench, Lay Pipe, and Backfill.* Figure 13.1 shows their **production rate** and the calculated duration based on that production rate. For example, Survey & Layout has a production rate of 500 ft per day. The project consists of a total of 5,000 ft. Therefore, the duration is calculated to be 10 days (5,000 ft ÷ 500 ft per day = 10 days). Partial days are rounded up to the next full day.

The activities are to be done in same **sequence** as they are listed.

FIGURE 13.1 Production rate and duration for the pipeline project

Activity	Production Rate (Feet per Day)	Duration for 5,000 Feet
Survey & Layout	500	10
Clear & Grub	400	13
Trench	200	25
Lay Pipe	300	17
Backfill	250	20

VELOCITY DIAGRAMS

The velocity diagram is simply a chart plotting productivity on the *y* axis and time on the *x* axis. The velocity diagram for *Survey & Layout* would be as shown in Figure 13.2.

Figure 13.2 shows a production rate of 500 ft per day, therefore, taking 10 days to complete. *Survey & Layout* would start on the morning of day 1 and continue until the end of day 10. If the activity had a lower production rate, the slope of the line would be less steep. If the production rate were higher, the slope of the line would be steeper.

Figure 13.2 depicts an activity with a constant productivity rate. However, it is possible that the productivity rate would not be constant, as shown in the velocity diagram in Figure 13.3.

In Figure 13.3 *Survey & Layout* has a productivity rate of 500 ft per day for the first 2,000 ft and then rugged terrain is encountered which slows down the productivity to 200 ft per day for the next 1,000 ft, at which time productivity should continue at 500 ft per day for the remaining 2,000 ft.

For the pipeline example we will use the constant productivity velocity diagram (Figure 13.2) for *Survey & Layout*. The next step is to add *Clear & Grub* to the linear schedule. *Clear & Grub* has a lower productivity, therefore, we know the velocity diagram will be less steep than *Survey & Layout*. The management team wants to start *Clear & Grub* two days after *Survey & Layout* to make sure these two activities will not conflict. *Clear & Grub* has a duration of 13 days. The linear schedule now looks as shown in Figure 13.4.

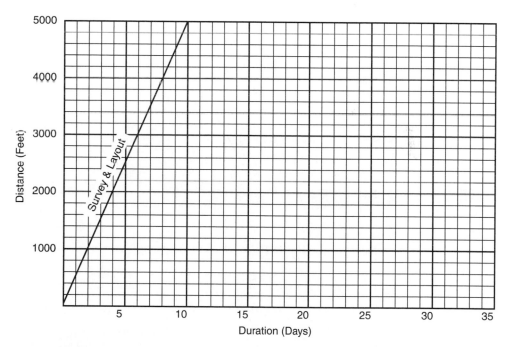

FIGURE 13.2　Velocity diagram showing a constant production rate activity *Survey & Layout*

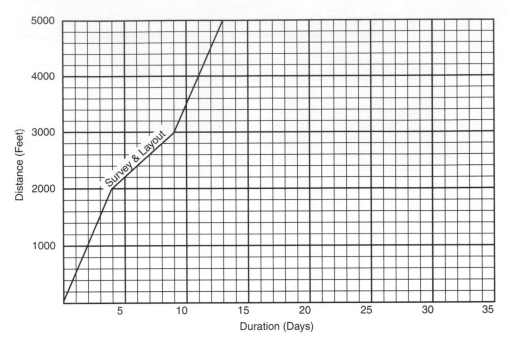

FIGURE 13.3 Velocity diagram showing an unconstant production rate

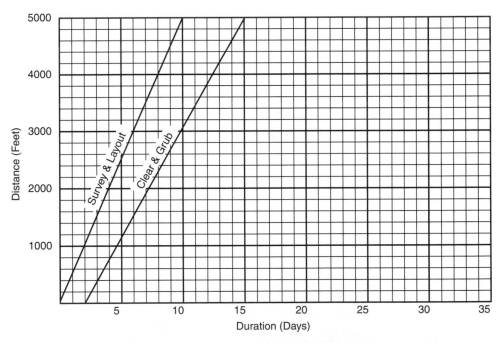

FIGURE 13.4 *Clear & Grub* has a lower productivity rate than *Survey & Layout* and starts two days after *Survey & Layout* starts

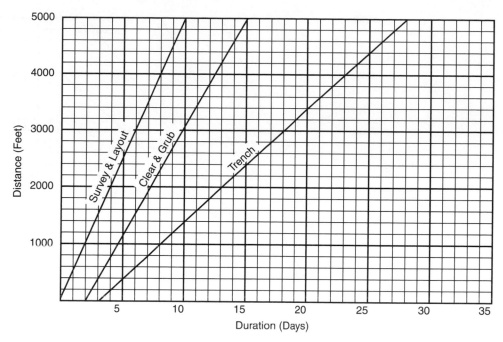

Figure 13.5 *Trench* has an even lower productivity rate than the first two activities and starts one day after *Clear & Grub* starts

The next activity is *Trench* which has a productivity rate of 200 ft per day and therefore a duration of 25 days. The productivity rate for trenching is even lower than it was for *Clear & Grub*, so the velocity diagram will be even less steep. Therefore, the management team desires to start trenching 1 day after *Clear & Grub* starts. The linear schedule with the *Trench* activity added now looks as shown in Figure 13.5.

Forecasting Conflicts

The next activity to add is *Lay Pipe* with a duration of 17 days. *Lay Pipe's* productivity is higher than the trenching productivity so the velocity diagram may intersect if it is started too soon. For example, if it is desired to start laying the pipe a day later than the trenching started, the lines will intersect sometime during the evening of day 6 or morning of day 7, creating a conflict as shown in Figure 13.6.

As can be seen from Figure 13.6, *Lay Pipe* will overrun the *Trench* activity in just a few days where the two lines cross. This is a conflict. The pipe obviously cannot be laid until the trench is dug. One of the benefits of the linear scheduling method is to be able to forecast such conflicts and change the schedule to avoid the conflict. This conflict likely would have been easy to determine without the linear schedule. However, with the linear schedule it can be accurately forecast when the conflict would happen. If the conflict were later in the schedule it may have been more difficult to forecast. The linear schedule gives the management team confidence that there won't be a schedule conflict or the ability to forecast and adjust the schedule to avoid the conflict.

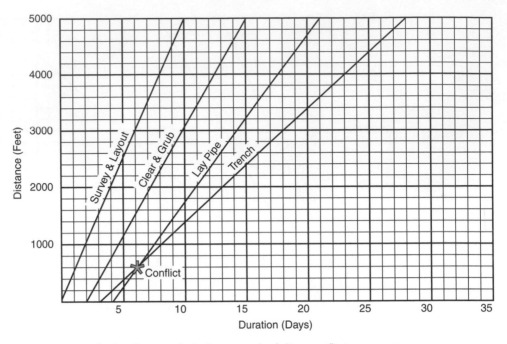

FIGURE 13.6   Velocity diagrams help forecast scheduling conflicts

The diagram in Figure 13.7 shows how to solve this potential conflict. Because *Lay Pipe* has a steeper slope velocity, look at the *finish* of the *Trench* activity and decide how many days after trenching is finished the *Lay Pipe* activity should also finish. In this case, the management team desires to finish laying the pipe 2 days after the trenching is finished. They want a 2-day time buffer. Therefore, the velocity diagram is drawn *backwards* from the finish date to determine the start date for laying the pipe as shown in Figure 13.7.

Notice in Figure 13.7 that *Lay Pipe* is scheduled to finish 2 days after *Trench* is finished. Drawing from this point backward determines that *Lay Pipe* should start on day 14. Or, *Lay Pipe* could start a little earlier and then be suspended for a time period to be continued later as long is it does not conflict with the *Trench* activity. Or, *Trench* could be speeded up by using more equipment or other resources to eliminate the conflict and finish the project earlier. Another option, if it reduces cost, would be to slow down the productivity of the *Lay Pipe* activity by employing fewer people or using less equipment to avoid the conflict with the *Trench* activity. It is up to the management team. The linear schedule helps them visually identify problems and then find solutions to those problems.

The last activity to include is *Backfill* with a duration of 20 days. *Backfill* has a lower productivity rate than its predecessor, so the slope of the line will be less steep. The management team desires to start *Backfill* 2 days after *Lay Pipe* has started. The completed linear schedule is shown in Figure 13.8.

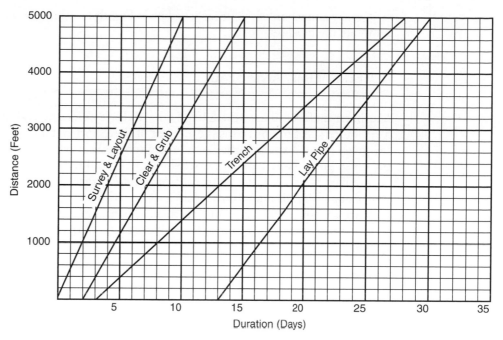

FIGURE 13.7 This velocity diagram is drawn backward to determine the *Lay Pipe* start date

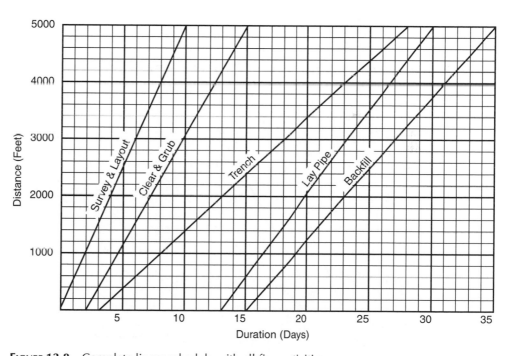

FIGURE 13.8 Complete linear schedule with all five activities

155

An examination of the linear schedule in Figure 13.8 shows it will take 35 days to complete the pipeline project.

BUFFERS, TIME, AND SPACE

Another benefit of linear scheduling is the ability to examine and plan for time and space buffers. A **time buffer** is the amount of time, horizontally, between activities at any given point. A **space buffer** is the amount of space, vertically, between activities at any given point. Notice the linear schedule in Figure 13.9.

There is a time buffer between *Trench* and *Lay Pipe* on the morning of day 24 of approximately 3.5 days and a space buffer of approximately 1,000 ft. The closer the two lines are together, the greater the risks. The management team can change the production rates or the start or finish times of each activity to obtain the amount of buffer desired.

Bars similar to regular bar charts could be added to the linear schedule to note special activities happening during the project as shown in Figure 13.10.

A full bar chart could, in fact, be shown in the background if there were such a need.

Figure 13.11 shows how a curtain could be used to show a "curtain of time" when something is happening.

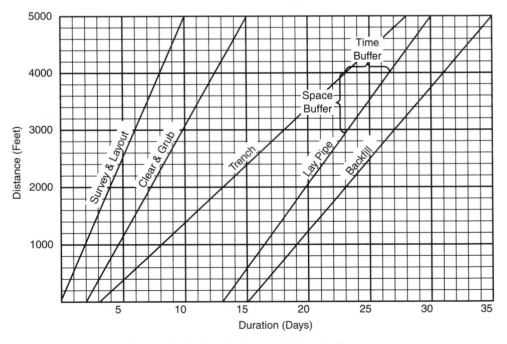

FIGURE 13.9 Linear schedules help identify time and space buffers

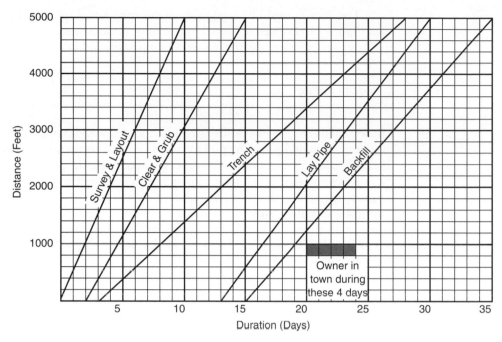

FIGURE 13.10 Special activities can be added to the linear schedule via a bar chart

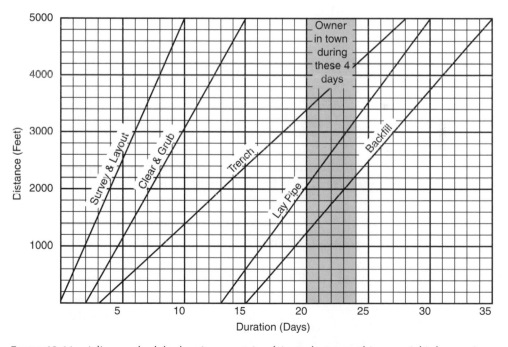

FIGURE 13.11 A linear schedule showing a curtain of time when something special is happening

The curtain could be used to show the dates when special visitors are expected, as in Figure 13.11, dates of special inspections, periods when strikes are planned, special dates available for specific pieces of equipment, and so on.

CONCLUSION

Linear scheduling, or line-of-balance, methods show the project schedule in a unique format that would be very helpful for some types of construction projects. Creating a linear schedule requires a six-step process: identifying the activities, estimating activity production rates, developing activity sequence, creating a velocity diagram for the first activity, adding the velocity diagram for each additional activity, and looking for conflicts and buffers. Any management tool that helps improve the vision of the management team and can be of assistance in helping to see bottlenecks or other problems is worthwhile considering. The manager who has a full toolbox of these management and scheduling tools is so much better off than the manager who has only a small toolbox with just a scheduling tool or two. You will find that some projects lend themselves better to one method or another. The linear schedule could be the ideal scheduling tool on some projects.

If you feel you need additional detail in order to understand this chapter, be sure to work the second application problem.

APPLICATION

1. Visit a highway construction site or highway construction firm's home office and ask a superintendent or project manager: How familiar are you with linear scheduling techniques? What do you think about them? Ask to see some examples, if possible. Write a report on your findings.
2. Create a linear schedule for the construction of a 15-mile-long highway with the following activities and production rates. Have a time buffer of not less than 2 days and a space buffer of not closer than half a mile. Use the graph paper in Figure 13.12 to create the linear schedule. The correct solution is found in Figure 13.13.

Survey & Layout	3 miles per day
Clear & Grub	0.75 mile per day
Earthwork	0.5 mile per day
Subbase	1 mile per day
Base	1 mile per day
Paving	3 miles per day
Signage & Striping	5 miles per day

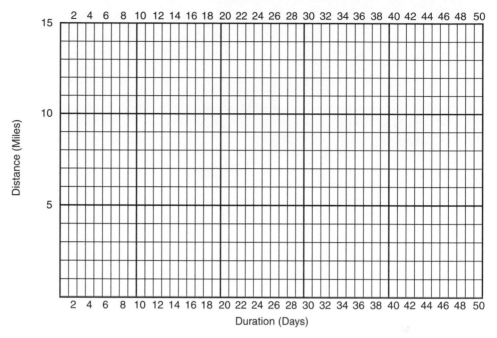

Figure 13.12   Graph paper for creating a linear schedule

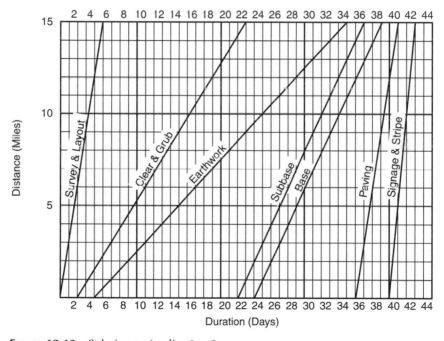

Figure 13.13   Solution to Application 2

CHAPTER 14

UPDATING THE SCHEDULE

INTRODUCTION

After the CPM schedule has been developed and reviewed, bar charts or tabular reports have been generated and sent to the appropriate participants, and the project is under way, it is important to keep the schedule accurate by updating it. Updating the schedule could be as simple as just declaring the actual start (when meaningful work begins) and actual finish dates (when the activity is substantially finished). Or, if an activity has started but not finished, the actual start date is declared and either the percent complete or number of days remaining is also declared. The update could also include declaring the actual number of resources used, such as workers, money spent, equipment hours utilized, and so on. This is when the computer becomes a necessity. With CPM scheduling every update requires a new forward and backward pass to determine the new project completion date. This is much too laborious and prone to errors to do by hand. This chapter deals with the details of updating the project and determining percent complete.

CREATING A TARGET OR BASELINE SCHEDULE

Before updating the schedule, make sure you have created a target or baseline of the as-planned schedule. This way you will be able to compare the current schedule with the target schedule in the bar chart format as discussed in Chapter 4. You will also be able to use the management technique of "When performance is measured, performance improves. When performance is measured and reported back, the rate of improvement accelerates" as was also discussed in Chapter 4. The target schedule is created differently in each software package and it is easy to forget to create it prior to the first update. It is an important step to remember. If the schedule is updated prior to creating the target, the original thinking and planning is lost. You will no longer have an as-planned schedule to compare performance to.

Figure 14.1 depicts the as-planned target schedule of a project (top bars) compared to the updated schedule (bottom bars). As the schedule is updated the management staff can measure and compare performance. This schedule is now ready to be updated.

KEEPING HISTORICAL INFORMATION

Before every major update make sure to rename the schedule, saving the old schedule for historical information in case of future legal action. Historical information is also valuable when planning future projects similar to this one. Many schedulers name the

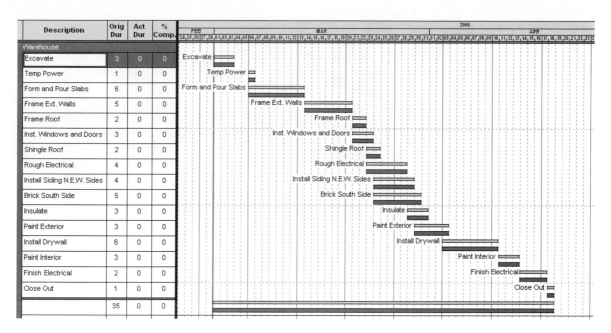

Description	Orig Dur	Act Dur	% Comp.
Warehouse			
Excavate	3	0	0
Temp Power	1	0	0
Form and Pour Slabs	6	0	0
Frame Ext. Walls	5	0	0
Frame Roof	2	0	0
Inst. Windows and Doors	3	0	0
Shingle Roof	2	0	0
Rough Electrical	4	0	0
Install Siding N.E.W. Sides	4	0	0
Brick South Side	5	0	0
Insulate	3	0	0
Paint Exterior	3	0	0
Install Drywall	6	0	0
Paint Interior	3	0	0
Finish Electrical	2	0	0
Close Out	1	0	0
	35	0	0

FIGURE 14.1 Target schedule (Top bars) compared to updated schedule (bottom bars) for warehouse project

as-planned schedule using two numerical digits for the last two characters—for example, *Chicago Office Bldg00*. Before the project is started, a new schedule is copied from *Bldg00*, leaving the original schedule showing the project team's thinking prior to the start of the project. The new schedule is named *Bldg01* which will be used for the first month's daily updating. At the end of the first month's update, the project is saved to a new name of *Bldg02* for the second month's daily updating. This process is continued until the project is completed. There may be occasions when the schedule would be renamed in the middle of the month due to changes or project problems where it is desired to show what the schedule was like just prior to the problem.

Figure 14.2 shows the file structure of the *Bldg* project. It is easy to follow the audit trail and know which schedule represents which updates.

Make sure you back up these old schedules to a disk or other storage device in case you need to refer to them in the future. It is a good idea to back up to disk all data on your personal computer at least once a month. It is not a matter of *if* the hard disk in your computer will crash, but *when* it will crash. Many companies automatically back up all data daily. If you are not on a network system, but rather working on a stand-alone computer, make sure you back up your own data at least monthly. You may even want to keep the backup in a location other than your office in case of a fire or major disaster. This will ensure you have multiple copies of critical historical data. If this process is used and a company finds it is in litigation several years later, it is easy to find the old backups and reconstruct the happenings on the job site. Having this capability may save the company many tens of thousands or even millions of dollars. Historical data also can be valuable to plan and schedule similar future projects.

FIGURE 14.2   SureTrak
Open Project dialog box
showing updated names of
the *Bldg* project file

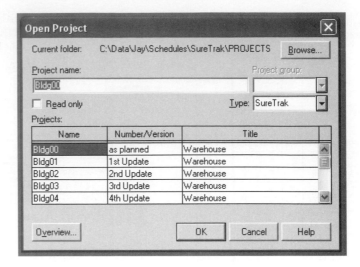

UPDATING THE PROJECT SCHEDULE

Monthly Updates

Most project specifications require an update every month. Some contracts require an update weekly. The typical monthly update is done by reading the daily logs to determine when each activity actually started and finished. The daily logs should be accurate because they are done daily. In reality, however, many superintendents do the daily logs weekly just prior to when they need to be delivered to the main office. If they are done weekly rather than daily, their accuracy suffers. Either way, updating the schedule requires reading the daily log.

Daily logs developed by hand are sometimes difficult, at best, to read. Updating a schedule by this technique will take several hours. Most likely the project manager or scheduler will resent the amount of time required to update at the end of each month, along with all the other monthly reports, and so the schedule is put off and then likely abandoned. The schedule remains abandoned until the management team realizes things are out of control and then a new effort is made to reschedule the job starting from the activities currently happening through the end of the project. This is an all-too-familiar scene on many projects.

If the contract requires monthly updates, the schedule is somewhat accurate, but the time necessary to update is still resented. Updating is done more for contract purposes rather than to help manage the project. If a few critical activities are late at the beginning of the month, it may not come to anyone's attention until the end of the month. This loses a month of action time that could have been used to get back on schedule.

One thing that can be done to simplify this process for those who update monthly, is to create a schedule turnaround report at the beginning of the month. This report will have the activity description and the planned start and finish dates of the activities to be under construction that month, with blank columns for the actual start and finish dates or percent complete to be written in by the superintendent. This is much better than relying on the daily log for actual start and finish information.

Weekly Updates

Updates that are done weekly, although similar to the monthly updates, takes much less time and therefore might actually get done and help with managing the project. Following this process, the management team will never be less than a week away from being apprised of schedule problems. Weekly updates still take considerable time to do, however, and are sometimes resented or abandoned but are typically more accurate than monthly updates.

Daily Updates

Daily updates—a third option—consist of the following:

1. Opening the project on the computer.
2. Thinking "what old activities finished today" and inputting the actual finish dates.
3. Thinking "what new activities started today" and inputting the actual start dates.
4. Having the computer calculate the remainder of the schedule and check the project completion date to make sure the project is still on track.

The daily process may take only a few minutes. On major projects it is common that no new activities have started or old activities finished so the update is a quick thinking process and requires no input. Daily updates are also more accurate than weekly or monthly updates because you are not relying on handwritten reports. The biggest advantage to daily updates is that they keep the management team up-to-date with any potential problems. It is not necessary to include in the daily update the percent complete or days remaining of activities under progress. This will only be necessary on the last day of the month to show activities under progress for progress payments and the monthly reports and analysis.

Other criteria for how often the schedule should be updated include how complex it is and how often new schedule information needs to be communicated to other team members. Daily updates solve these problems as well. If the schedule is updated daily and then posted to the Internet on the project's home page, each team member and especially the subcontractors could look on the Internet each evening or morning and know exactly where they need to have their crews work that day.

Using a PDA to Update the Schedule

Some companies are updating the schedule with Palm Pilots or other PDAs (personal digital assistants). The field manager inputs the actual start and finish dates on his or her PDA and then synchronizes the portable handheld computer to the desktop computer in the office or sends the data over the Internet and the schedule is updated from the PDA. All of the popular project management software allows this interface.

After the schedule has been updated on the base computer, new current schedules can be e-mailed or, with an Internet connection, sent back to the field manager. That way the field manager always has an updated schedule. This has the potential of eliminating a lot of paperwork and double entry on the computer.

Using Remote Cameras to Gather Project Information

One of the problems with updating the schedule is to gather the information from the job site. Consider installing cameras in key areas of the project. The cameras broadcast the pictures to your computer where you can rotate the camera and see the project site, similar to the way the traffic is reported on TV in major cities. Cameras in critical locations on the job would provide views showing which activities in that location are complete and therefore ready for the next activity.

Determining Whether to Use Percent Complete or Days Remaining

For activities that are under way (already started but not complete, at the end of the monthly update), is it best to use percent complete or the number of days remaining to determine progress? Basically, it is a matter of company preference. The important thing is that the method is consistent so there is an understanding of how progress is to be measured. If half of the total units are installed in a 20-day duration activity, that does not necessarily mean there are only 10 more days to go. The final half of the units may take longer to install due to height, difficult access, or more details. Days remaining is sometimes the method preferred because it is easier to quantify, but percent complete is the most commonly used. Most software programs link percent complete and days remaining together: if you input one, the other is automatically calculated. Most software will allow the unlinking of these, enabling you to input both percent complete and days remaining if you desire. Check with the default options of the software.

Determining Percent Complete

It isn't as easy as it may sound to determine the percent complete of an activity under progress. Should it be based on percent of quantities in place, percent of budget expended, percent of time expended, or percent of labor hours (or other key resources) used? If 50 percent of the brick is installed, is the activity 50 percent complete? What if the remaining brick is to be installed on the top story of a multistory building? Does it take more money, effort, and time to install brick on the top story versus the ground level? Or maybe there is a special pattern and many cuts in the laying of the final bricks that consumes a great deal of time. It is also possible that the final bricks are in a very tight area which slows productivity enormously. Due to these varied conditions, measuring percent complete is more difficult than first assumed.

PERCENT OF QUANTITIES IN PLACE.   The most common method of measuring percent complete is based on the percent of quantities physically in place. If the activity "install drywall on the 3rd floor" requires 16,000 square feet (sq ft) of drywall and 4,000 sq ft have been installed and there is no anticipated change in expected productivity, the activity is 25 percent complete. To get a percent value,

$$\text{Percent complete} = \text{Quantity Installed} \div \text{Quantity Planned} \times 100$$

Or, in this case

$$\frac{4,000}{16,000} = .25 \times 100 = 25\%$$

In this example, this would be a good method to measure percent complete. If there is an expected change in productivity of the remaining units to be installed, this would not be an accurate method to use to measure percent complete. Or, at least this method would need to be modified or adjusted to be more accurate.

PERCENT OF ACTIVITY BUDGET EXPENDED.   This would be a comparison of the actual costs at the time of the update to the planned total activity costs. This method is accurate if the actual costs have not varied too much from the planned costs. For example: if the planned cost of an activity was $4,000 and the actual cost at the time of update was $2,000 the activity would be 50 percent complete. To get a percent value,

$$\text{Percent Complete} = \frac{\text{Actual Cost}}{\text{Planned Cost}} \times 100$$

Or, in this case

$$\frac{\$2,000}{\$4,000} = .50 \times 100 = 50\% \text{ complete}$$

PERCENT OF ACTIVITY TIME EXPENDED.   This would be a comparison of the actual duration to the point of the update to the planned duration for the total activity. This method is accurate if the productivity upon which the original duration was based is being met. For example: if the planned duration of an activity was 10 days and the actual duration at the time of update was 3 days, the activity would be 30 percent complete. To get a percent value,

$$\text{Percent Complete} = \frac{\text{Actual Duration}}{\text{Planned Duration}} \times 100$$

Or, in this case

$$\frac{3 \text{ days}}{10 \text{ days}} = 3 \times 100 = 30\% \text{ complete}$$

PERCENT OF LABOR HOURS OR OTHER KEY RESOURCES USED. This would be a comparison of the actual labor hours consumed at the time of the update to the total planned labor hours for the activity. This method is accurate if the labor hours are estimated to be used evenly throughout the activity; in other words, no planned major adjustment of crew size from the start of the activity to the finish of the activity. Also, as in the other cases, the number of labor hours has not varied significantly from the way it was anticipated. For example, if the planned labor hours of an activity were 150 and the actual labor hours at the time of update were 112, the activity would be 74.67 percent complete. To get a percent value,

$$\text{Percent Complete} = \frac{\text{Actual labor Hours}}{\text{Planned labor Hours}} \times 100$$

Or, in this case

$$\frac{112}{150} = .7466 \times 100 = 74.67\% \text{ complete}$$

As stated earlier, even though one of the above methods may be the best for a particular activity, most companies prefer that a consistent method be used throughout the company. That way reports are consistent and everyone knows how progress is being measured. The method most common in use today is percent complete based on actual quantities physically in place.

Determining the Number of Quantities in Place

Once you have determined how you are going to measure percent complete, how will you arrive at that figure? How are the data collected? The data could be determined by reporting processes. Some companies get the information from the daily log, which has some concerns as stated previously in this chapter. A turnaround report could be created where the field managers fill in the percent complete column on each activity under progress as they walk the job. That person typically needs training on how percent complete is to be measured. It is important that the data are measured accurately because this measurement typically becomes the basis of the progress payment from the owner to the general construction company and then from the general to the subcontractors. It needs to be based on a direct observation of the project. That is another reason the project manager or superintendent is in an excellent position to be the scheduler.

EVALUATING THE PROJECT STATUS BASED ON THE UPDATE

Now that the project schedule has been updated, it is important to look at the status of the project on a weekly or monthly basis. Is the project on schedule from a time point of view? Are costs in line with the budget? Is quality where it should be? Is safety being managed properly? Are there any adjustments needed in the logic of the remaining activities? Has anything been learned on the project at this point that makes the original plan not as efficient as it should be? Are there any new activities that need to be planned that were originally not thought of or originally were thought unnecessary? Are any additional concerns appearing?

If the project schedule is cost or dollar loaded, the cost analysis can be done with the scheduling software. The time analysis is obviously done with the scheduling software by simply comparing the planned project completion date with the new updated or forecast project completion date. If there are problems noticed, take action immediately to correct the problems. They only get worse if ignored. Keep the schedule in front of the team members during all periodic progress meetings. Print adjusted schedule reports to disseminate to all the team members. Review and analyze the schedule as suggested in Chapter 11 with the original schedule. How are the future critical path activities doing? How is the shared float holding up? How are the procurement activities doing? If the project is behind schedule, what does the project team want to do to get back on schedule? Generally, small deviations from the original completion date are not worthy of significant changes to the schedule. The updated completion date will be a little ahead on some updates and behind on others without being of concern. But when the variance becomes significant to the project team, act on it.

EXAMPLE OF AN UPDATED SCHEDULE

Figure 14.3 shows an as-planned schedule bar positioned above the current (as-built) schedule bar. The vertical line in the middle of the bar chart represents the date of the update. As seen from this update, the schedule is now 2 days behind where it was originally scheduled to complete (notice the dates of the last activity). By comparing the as-planned

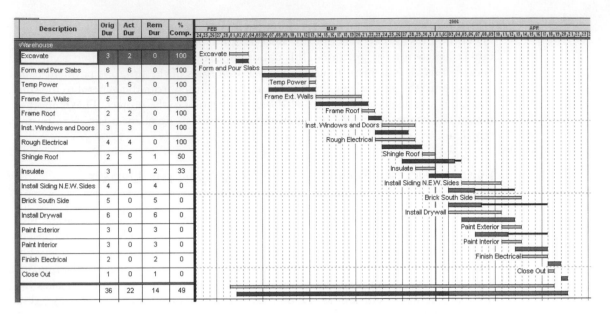

Description	Orig Dur	Act Dur	Rem Dur	% Comp.
Warehouse				
Excavate	3	2	0	100
Form and Pour Slabs	6	6	0	100
Temp Power	1	5	0	100
Frame Ext. Walls	5	6	0	100
Frame Roof	2	2	0	100
Inst. Windows and Doors	3	3	0	100
Rough Electrical	4	4	0	100
Shingle Roof	2	5	1	50
Insulate	3	1	2	33
Install Siding N.E.W. Sides	4	0	4	0
Brick South Side	5	0	5	0
Install Drywall	6	0	6	0
Paint Exterior	3	0	3	0
Paint Interior	3	0	3	0
Finish Electrical	2	0	2	0
Close Out	1	0	1	0
	36	22	14	49

Figure 14.3 Updated warehouse construction schedule with as-planned dates shown in the top bar and current dates shown in the bottom bar

schedule with the as-built schedule you can see where delays occurred. If it were desirable to adjust the future schedule, the management team would focus on the remaining critical activities and decide which activities to accelerate by decreasing durations, working on weekends, or changing the logic to allow critical activities to be concurrent.

Conclusion

Updating the schedule is a key to evaluating the project progress. The updated schedule will determine if there are any adjustments to the completion date. A management team will know where they are as compared with the original schedule and where they are going with the remainder of the project. Is the construction plan progressing satisfactorily or do adjustments need to be made? The updated schedule gives the management team the opportunity to make midcourse corrections to ensure that the project will still hit its target. It is important to ensure the project is still meeting the goals of being a quality project, finished on time, within the budget, and in a safe work environment. It is a common occurrence for everyone working on a project that is not updated to assume things are going fine until it nears completion—they realize they are not going to achieve their goals. Problems went unnoticed months ago because they failed to update the project schedule. Valuable time is now lost and the cost to accelerate the project now could be extremely significant.

APPLICATION

Interview current project managers to determine the following:

1. How often do they prefer to update their schedules?
2. How do they measure percent complete for activities under progress at the time of updating?
3. Why do they prefer that method of measuring percent complete?
4. Typically, how often do they need to significantly adjust the remainder of the project based on an updated schedule?
5. Who does the actual updating of the schedule and how long does it take to update?

CHAPTER 15

USING THE SCHEDULE TO FORECAST AND BALANCE RESOURCES

▌I N T R O D U C T I O N▐

Another major advantage of critical path method (CPM) scheduling over other scheduling methods is that CPM provides the opportunity to balance resources. By examining the activities with float, the project team can alter the start and finish dates of the activity to coincide with when a specific resource is available. Or, by delaying the start of some activities with float, the project team can balance or level out specific resources, such as the number of workers on the project at one time or the cash flow. By using activity float, the management team can fine-tune the project to control the resource usage.

The examples in this chapter consist of simple practice problems so the reader can understand the principles without getting lost in the details. While reading this chapter, keep in mind these basic principles and carefully examine the example problems. When applying resource management to major projects the principles are the same, just on a larger scale.

CREATING RESOURCE RELATIONSHIPS

A common method used to balance and to solve resource problems is to create a resource relationship. Typically as the logic diagram is developed, the management team first thinks of the *physical relationships*. Then the team determines the durations, based on available resources, that will provide for a timely completion without excessive costs or safety risks. Next, the *quality relationships* need to be considered. It may not be physically necessary to have one activity as a predecessor to another activity, but to ensure quality, the management team may create those relationships. For example, in the construction of a home, it is not physically necessary to have the siding on the outside installed prior to the finishing of the drywall on the inside; however, to eliminate excessive nail pops in the drywall finish, the schedule would show the siding as a predecessor to finishing the drywall. That way, as the siding is being nailed on the outside, there is no drywall finishing to cause nail pops on the inside. Next, consider the *safety relationships*. Make sure the schedule has eliminated people working over the top of other workers, creating an unsafe work environment. Finally, the *resource relationships* are considered. If two activities need the same piece of equipment, the management team determines which activity goes first by making that activity a predecessor over the other activity that needs that same piece of equipment. The precise order of those relationship considerations is not absolute, but all four must be considered. Too many times the schedule represents only the physical relationships and then the management team wonders why the schedule is unrealistic.

This chapter helps the management team learn how to determine the resource needs, level the resource demands, and better control the project from a resource point

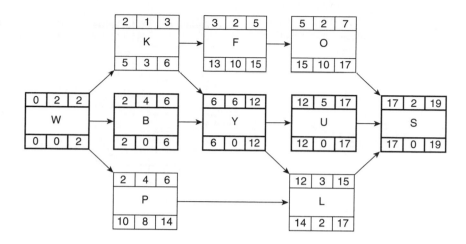

FIGURE 15.1 Logic diagram for learning resource management

of view. Activity float is a key consideration in determining and managing the resource demands. To understand how to use float to forecast and control cash flow, equipment, and human resources, we will use the project illustrated in Figure 15.1.

Figure 15.1 shows the schedule for a large excavation project that you are in charge of. You work for the excavation company and have met with your management team and developed the schedule. The letters represent areas of the project to be excavated. Area *W* will be excavated first and then areas *K, P,* and *B* can begin. The durations are in months. It will take 2 months to excavate area *W.* You can't work in area *Y* until areas *K* and *B* are completed, and so forth. You are confident in your durations and the logic. What you are not comfortable with is whether you can do this project with the 10 D8 Caterpillars you have available. Also, the owner is very concerned with the cash flow on this project. The owner can finance up to $110,000 maximum per month. The owner wants to know, in advance, what the monthly progress payments are forecast to be.

In order to do this you need to tie the resources to the project activities. This will enable the schedule to provide the management team with the ability to forecast and control equipment and costs. Virtually any resource can be forecast and controlled using these techniques. Typical resources of concern are equipment, costs, materials, and workers.

FORECASTING AND BALANCING CASH FLOW

When costs are included in the schedule it is generally called a "cost loaded" or "value loaded" schedule. To cost load a schedule in order to forecast cash flow the activity value needs to be calculated for each activity. The *activity value* is the amount the owner owes at the completion of the activity. The activity value consists of all direct and indirect costs including labor, equipment, tools, materials, project site overhead, home office overhead, and profit. The total amount of the contractor's bid becomes the project

FIGURE 15.2   Activity values for excavation project

Activity	Total Value $1,174,200	Duration in months	Monthly Value
W	$ 45,000	2	$ 22,500
K	12,000	1	12,000
B	192,000	4	48,000
P	144,400	4	36,100
F	96,000	2	48,000
O	115,000	2	57,500
Y	289,200	6	48,200
L	72,000	3	24,000
U	185,000	5	37,000
S	23,600	2	11,800

budget once the contract is awarded. All of the individual activity values should equal the project budget. The estimating department has supplied the following activity values for this project as shown in Figure 15.2.

In order to forecast the monthly cash flow, the monthly value needs to be determined. This is done with the following formula:

$$\frac{\text{Estimated Total Activity Value}}{\text{Duration}} = \text{Monthly Value}$$

The next step in forecasting and managing the cash flow is to create a bar chart, showing float, that is based on the logic diagram. Then load the bar chart with the monthly value of each activity based on the early start and early finish as shown in Figure 15.3

The resource profile in the lower half of the cost-loaded bar chart in Figure 15.3 is sometimes called a histogram, showing the costs in chart form to help visualize and analyze the data.

The owner can guarantee to finance the project up to $110,000 per month. So, we can see by examining Figure 15.3 that we are in trouble during months 4, 5, and 6.

In attempting to solve the problem, first focus on the activities with float that are scheduled to happen in the problem months. It would not help solve the problem to use some of some of the float belonging to area K. That would only make the problem worse. A close examination of the logic diagram shows area P has 6 days of independent float and 2 days that are shared with L. If we choose to start area P 5 months late, on month 8, so it would be after area O (by making O a predecessor), area P would finish on month 11 and still have 3 months of float. However, that would take away almost all the float from areas K, F, and O. (If this were on the computer it would be much easier to analyze. You could make the changes on the computer and immediately see the results without needing to redo the forward and backward passes and recalculate the new cash flow.)

Activity	Months 1	2	3	4	5	6	7	8	9	10	11	12	13	14	15	16	17	18	19
W	22.5	22.5																	
K			12																
B			48	48	48	48													
P			36.1	36.1	36.1	36.1													
F				48	48														
O						57.5	57.5												
Y							48.2	48.2	48.2	48.2	48.2	48.2							
L													24	24	24				
U													37	37	37	37	37		
S																		11.8	11.8
Total in Thousands	22.5	22.5	96.1	132.1	132.1	141.6	105.7	48.2	48.2	48.2	48.2	48.2	61	61	76	37	37	11.8	11.8

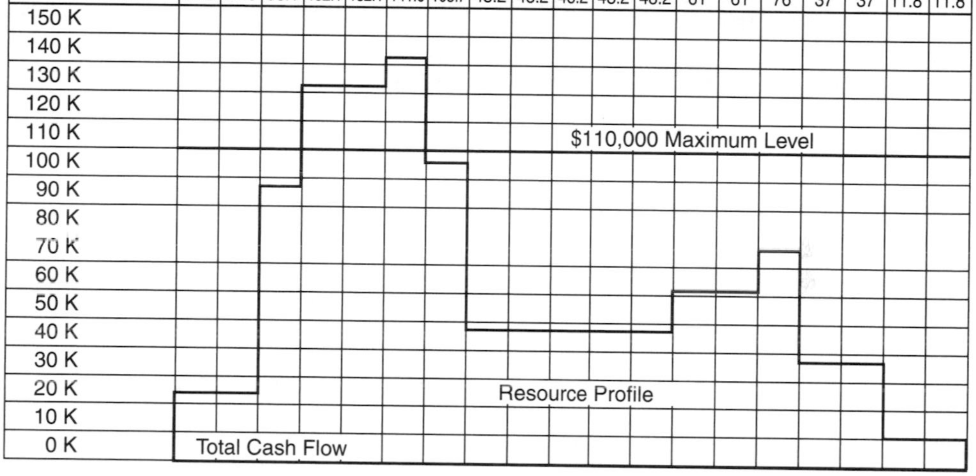

Resource profile (y-axis in thousands): 150 K, 140 K, 130 K, 120 K, 110 K, 100 K, 90 K, 80 K, 70 K, 60 K, 50 K, 40 K, 30 K, 20 K, 10 K, 0 K

$110,000 Maximum Level

Resource Profile

Total Cash Flow

FIGURE 15.3 Cost-loaded bar chart showing float (top half) and a resource profile (lower half)

Another choice would be to delay the start of area *F* until area *P* is finished (make *P* a predecessor to *F*). From the logic diagram it can be seen that areas *F* and *O* share those 10 days of float. Therefore if *F* is delayed, that will in turn delay area *O*. That adjustment would have no effect on areas *P* or *L*. It appears this latter choice may have the least effect on the project as a whole and so for whatever other reasons, this is the choice the management team makes. With those changes the new cash flow would appear as shown in Figure 15.4.

With that adjustment, the monthly cash flow never exceeds $105,700. We were able to avoid a potential crisis with the owner, which we would have had, if we had not been able to forecast the cash flow and then later, submitted a pay request to the owner for months 4, 5, and 6 in excess of the $110,000 max the owner could guarantee.

From this example, it can be seen that it is really float, and being able to recognize the different types of float, that gives the management team the ability to manage the resources of the project. In some ways, float is more important than the critical activities.

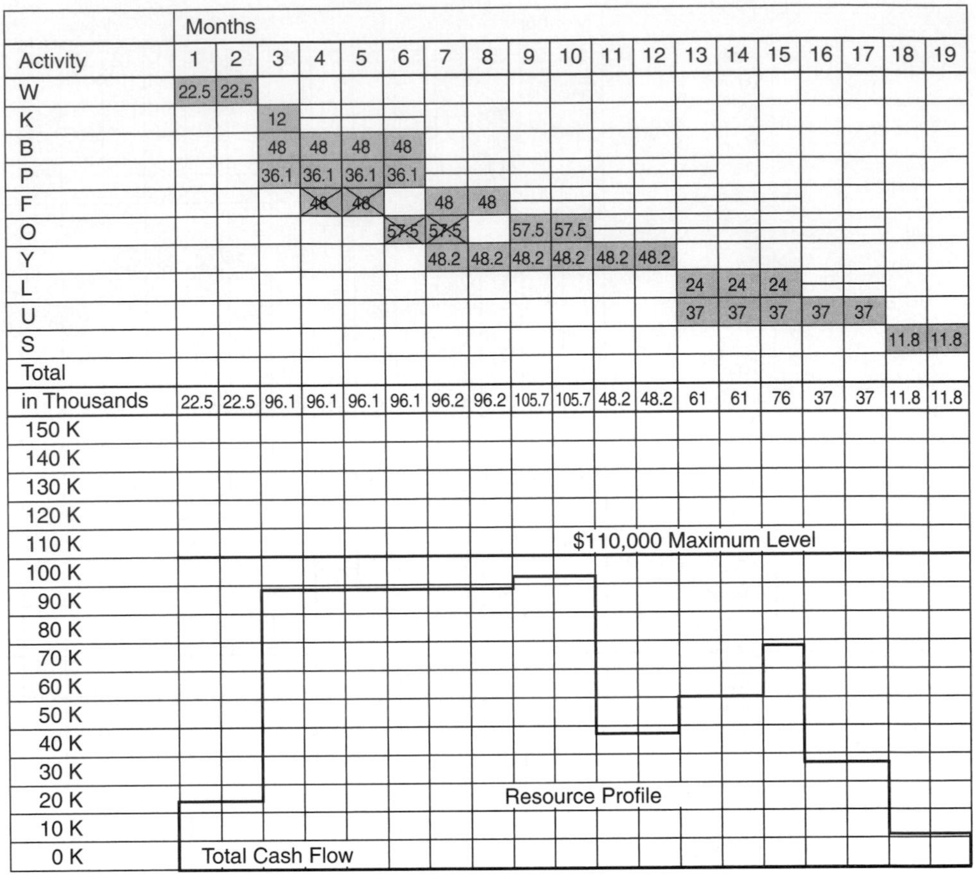

Activity	Months																		
	1	2	3	4	5	6	7	8	9	10	11	12	13	14	15	16	17	18	19
W	22.5	22.5																	
K			12																
B			48	48	48	48													
P			36.1	36.1	36.1	36.1													
F				48	48		48	48											
O						57.5	57.5		57.5	57.5									
Y							48.2	48.2	48.2	48.2	48.2	48.2							
L													24	24	24				
U													37	37	37	37	37		
S																		11.8	11.8
Total																			
in Thousands	22.5	22.5	96.1	96.1	96.1	96.1	96.2	96.2	105.7	105.7	48.2	48.2	61	61	76	37	37	11.8	11.8

$110,000 Maximum Level

Resource Profile

Total Cash Flow

(Resource level scale: 0 K, 10 K, 20 K, 30 K, 40 K, 50 K, 60 K, 70 K, 80 K, 90 K, 100 K, 110 K, 120 K, 130 K, 140 K, 150 K)

FIGURE 15.4 Bar chart adjusted to level cash flow

With the critical activities the management team has no choice as to when the activities are to happen. They must happen on the dates calculated. But with float, it is the management team's choice as to when the activities happen within their float time. This gives the sophisticated manager a chance to fine-tune the project and really manage cash flow and other resources without delaying the project completion date.

USING PROGRESS S-CURVES AND BANANA CURVES

Progress S-Curves

Another type of cost analysis is illustrated with a progress S-curve. The progress S-curve plots the cumulative costs, rather than the daily, weekly, or monthly costs. Using the same excavation project, the following early start progress S-curve is generated.

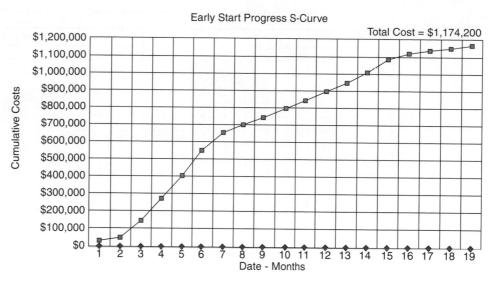

FIGURE 15.5   Early start progress S-Curve for the excavation project

To understand Figure 15.5, look back at the monthly cash flow in Figure 15.4 and you see—if all the activities are started and finished as early as possible—that the first month's billing is $22,500. During the second month another $22,500 is billed for a total of $45,000. An additional $96,100 is billed in the third month, for a total of $141,100. As you examine the progress S-curve in Figure 15.5 you see these cumulative costs plotted. The curve is generally in the shape of an *S* because as the project starts out, there is slow progress (as measured by money spent). During the midportion of the project a lot of progress is being made. There are a number of workers on the job and a high volume of materials is being installed. Then, as the job finishes, there are fewer workers and progress typically slows down. If this curve starts out unusually steep, it may be a sign of "front-end loading"—where the contractor is overbilling the owner to work off the owner's cash or to make up for the owner withholding retainage. Obviously, the owner does not approve of this practice. The practice of front-end loading has been known to create a lack of trust between the owner and the contractor.

If all the bars are shifted to their late start and late finish positions a late start progress curve could be generated. The cash flow would be determined from a late start and late finish bar chart showing each bar positioned in its late position, with the float showing in front of the bar as illustrated in Figure 15.6.

You will notice from the cost-loaded bar chart in Figure 15.6 that there are 4 months where the cash flow is in excess of the owner's guaranteed maximum of $110,000 (months 14–17).

Based on sliding all the bars to their late dates, the late start progress S-curve would then look something like as shown in Figure 15.7.

Activity	Months																		
	1	2	3	4	5	6	7	8	9	10	11	12	13	14	15	16	17	18	19
W	22.5	22.5																	
K						12													
B			48	48	48	48													
P											36.1	36.1	36.1	36.1					
F														48	48				
O																57.5	57.5		
Y							48.2	48.2	48.2	48.2	48.2	48.2							
L															24	24	24		
U													37	37	37	37	37		
S																		11.8	11.8
Total																			
in Thousands	22.5	22.5	48	48	48	60	48.2	48.2	48.2	48.2	84.3	84.3	73.1	121.1	109	118.5	118.5	11.8	11.8

FIGURE 15.6 Shifting all the bars to their late dates shows the cash flow based on LS, LF

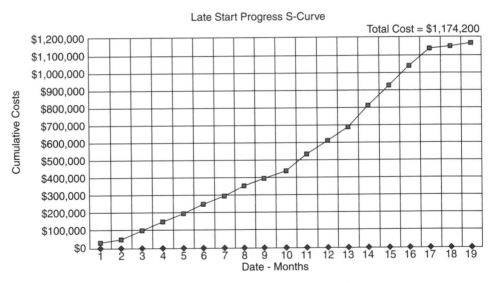

FIGURE 15.7 Late start progress S-Curve for the excavation project

Looking back at the late start and late finish monthly cash flow in Figure 15.6, if all the activities are started and finished as late as possible, we see a first month's billing at $22,500. The second month another $22,500 is billed for a total of $45,000. The third month an additional $48,000 is billed for a total of $93,000 as shown in Figure 15.7, whereas with the early data the end of the third month was $141,100. Again, as you examine the progress S-curve you see these cumulative costs plotted. The total cost for the project is still $1,174,200.

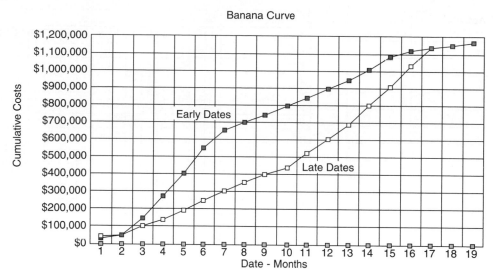

FIGURE 15.8   A banana curve shows early and late dates plotted together

Banana Curves

If both the early S-curve and the late S-curve are plotted together, a banana curve results, as shown in Figure 15.8.

This chart is called a banana chart or banana curve because it resembles the shape of a banana. As the schedule is updated, the actual progress line should be between the early dates and the late dates or within the banana. If the actual progress line is above the banana, the project is either overbudget or ahead of schedule. If the actual progress line is below the banana, the project is either underbudget or behind schedule.

This is a good example of management by exception. The rule is, the actual progress line will be within the banana. If the line is outside the banana—manage it! It is an exception to the rule. A quick glance at this report gives the manager a good idea of the status of the project as compared to where it should be. It is a good early warning system to alert a sophisticated project manager if there are cash problems showing up on the job. This report is a favorite by some upper managers. For your information, SureTrak and Microsoft Project can produce only the early curve or the late curve, not both. P3 will print both the early curve and the late curve, resulting in the banana curve.

FORECASTING AND BALANCING EQUIPMENT

When equipment is added to the schedule it is often called an "equipment-loaded" schedule. Forecasting and balancing equipment is very similar to forecasting and balancing cash/flow. First, analyze the number of pieces of equipment of interest needed for each activity. Then create a bar chart showing float and load the bars with the

Activity	Number of D8 Cats
W	2
K	1
B	4
P	3
F	4
O	5
Y	4
L	2
U	3
S	1

FIGURE 15.9 Number of Caterpillars needed per activity

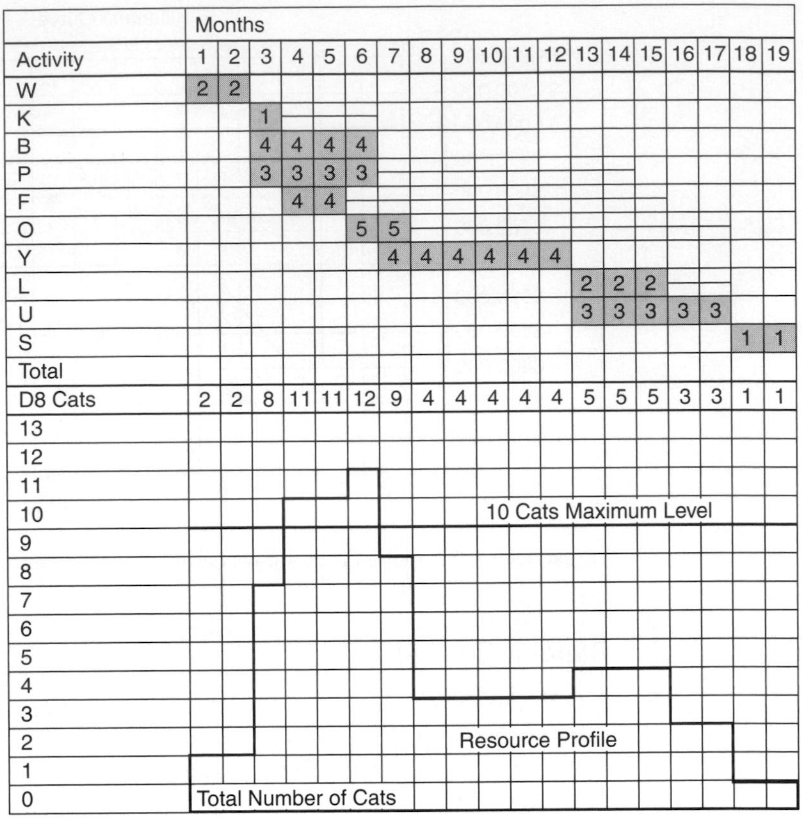

Activity	1	2	3	4	5	6	7	8	9	10	11	12	13	14	15	16	17	18	19
W	2	2																	
K			1																
B			4	4	4	4													
P			3	3	3	3													
F				4	4														
O						5	5												
Y							4	4	4	4	4	4							
L													2	2	2				
U													3	3	3	3	3		
S																		1	1
Total																			
D8 Cats	2	2	8	11	11	12	9	4	4	4	4	4	5	5	5	3	3	1	1

(Months header spans columns 1–19. Resource profile chart below, y‑axis 0–13: "10 Cats Maximum Level", "Resource Profile", "Total Number of Cats.")

FIGURE 15.10 Equipment (Cats) loaded bar chart

equipment to be analyzed. Next, examine the loadings, and adjust the bars within the float as desired. To help understand this we are going to examine our need for D8 Caterpillars (Cats) on the excavation project. The company owns 10 D8 Cats and we want to know how many need to be on this project on a monthly basis.

Figure 15.9 lists the activities and the optimum number of D8 Cats for each activity. Area *W* is a tight area where it is estimated that only two pieces of equipment will be able to work efficiently, whereas in area *B* there is sufficient space for four pieces of equipment.

The next step is to create a bar chart, showing float, based on the network logic diagram of the project. Then load the bars with the equipment of interest, in this case the D8 Cats. Then create the resource profile, as shown in Figure 15.10.

In the resource profile, notice that the number of Cats needed exceeds the number available during the fourth, fifth, and sixth months of the project. Using the same logic as was used for the cost-loaded schedule, it is determined to make area *P* a predecessor to area *F*. Because area *F* and area *O* share float, area *O* must also be adjusted. This results in the equipment-loaded bar and resource profile illustrated in Figure 15.11.

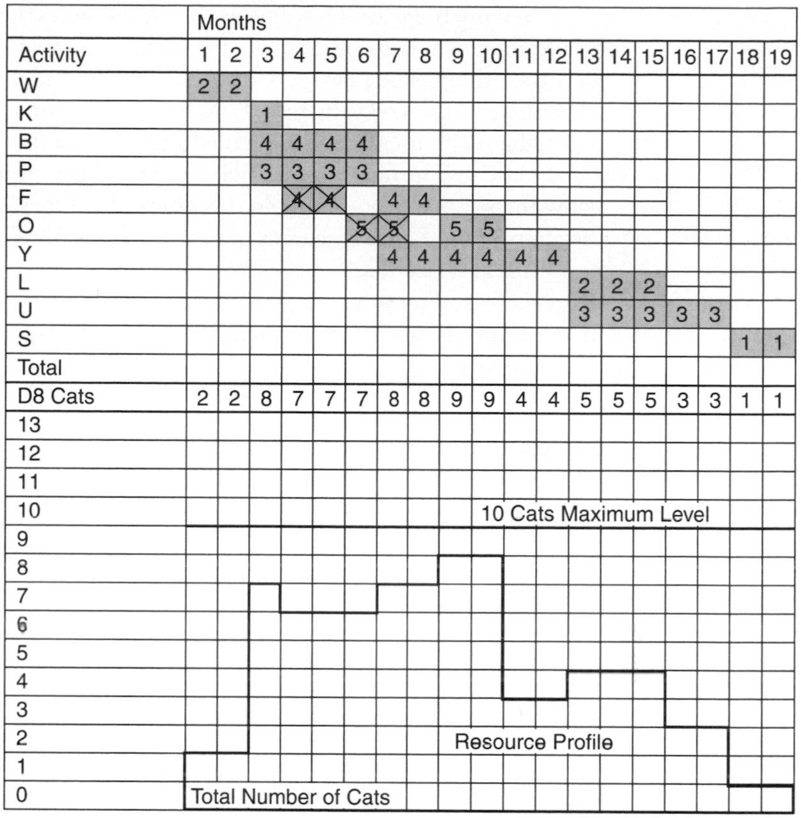

FIGURE 15.11 Adjusted
equipment loaded
schedule to level
equipment resources

Activity	Months

Activity	1	2	3	4	5	6	7	8	9	10	11	12	13	14	15	16	17	18	19
W	2	2																	
K			1																
B			4	4	4	4													
P			3	3	3	3													
F				X	X		4	4											
O						X	X		5	5									
Y							4	4	4	4	4	4							
L													2	2	2				
U													3	3	3	3	3		
S																		1	1
Total																			
D8 Cats	2	2	8	7	7	7	8	8	9	9	4	4	5	5	5	3	3	1	1

10 Cats Maximum Level

Resource Profile

Total Number of Cats

The profile now shows the project can be completed with only nine Cats assigned to the project. In fact, if areas *K*, *F*, and *O* could use only seven pieces of equipment and, therefore, take a little more time, using some of the available float, the project could be further adjusted to use just seven Cats during the third through the eighth month, and still finish on time. Again, the management team can determine and balance resources by deciding when they want to start and finish activities with float. This provides an opportunity to fine-tune a project to possibly save costs, without sacrificing time, quality, or safety. Understanding the different types of float and how to use float is a key to this process.

FORECASTING AND BALANCING HUMAN RESOURCES

When the crew size is added to the schedule it is many times called a "labor loaded" schedule. The number of workers on the job at any one time can be forecast and balanced in the same way as equipment and costs. Determine the number of workers or crew size for each activity and then load the activities with the number of workers on that activity.

Making these forecasts and analyzing resources by hand, without a computer, would be a time-consuming and frankly difficult job. As one resource is adjusted, it of course affects the others. The managers would need to spend a great deal of time evaluating and adjusting and then reevaluating. However, with a computer, this analysis and adjustment is possible. The use of CPM, coupled with the computer, can be a great aid in resource management. The manager just needs to have a through understanding of CPM and also know the software enough to do this efficiently. Once the data are in the computer, it is easy to play the "what if" games to see the effects of resource adjustments on the project.

It is also possible to have the computer automatically level resources, without the managers needing to make all the decisions. But, most managers are hesitant, at best, to trust a computer to make such decisions not knowing where the computer will put the emphasis.

COMPUTER DEFAULT METHODS TO AUTOMATICALLY BALANCE RESOURCES

Most computer project management software programs use one of two methods to automatically determine which concurrent activity gets first priority to the common resource: (1) the minimum float rule or (2) the minimum duration rule. Using one of these two rules, the computer assigns the activity that has either the least amount of float or shortest duration, as the activity that gets the competing resource first, the next one second, and so forth. Of these two rules the minimum float rule is the most common.

The problem with the minimum float rule is it may not be the most efficient on the project site. If the competing resource is a piece of equipment, it would make more sense to use the equipment in one location and then move it to the next nearest location and continue moving from activity to activity based on physical location. The computer has no way of knowing that sequence, although it can easily figure float or durations, which may have that piece of equipment going all over the place in an inefficient manner. Do to all the soft, but important, reasons to give priority to one activity over another, many experienced managers prefer to make those resource calls themselves, rather than have the computer make those decisions. They use a relationship line, assigning predecessors or successors, to manage the resource. The computer can aid in this process by filtering for all the activities that have a common resource assigned. Those activities can then be listed in chronological order based on start and finish dates, with the float and durations shown, and then the manager can assign the predecessors necessary to make the project feasible based on the resources required and available.

DURATION-DRIVEN VERSUS RESOURCE-DRIVEN SCHEDULES

Another way to handle resources is to have the schedule driven by the resources. To this point this text has dealt only with duration-driven schedules. The management team has determined the duration of each activity and then made sure there are sufficient resources to complete the activities within that predetermined amount of time. This is the normal method of managing projects because there is a definite date the project must be completed by. That date is generally stated in the contract documents.

Another method of scheduling projects is to have the project resource driven. For example, the number of labor hours and the number of workers are determined for each activity. Then the computer calculates the activity's duration. If an activity is estimated to take 400 labor hours and there are four workers available it will take 100 total labor hours to do the activity:

$$\frac{100 \text{ labor Hours}}{8 \text{ labor Hours per Day}} = 12^{1}/_{2} \text{ days}$$

This would then be rounded up to 13 days duration based on the resources available. To change an activity's duration the resources would be changed and the new duration would be calculated. So resources, typically labor hours, are entered into the computer, rather than durations. This would, therefore, be a resource-driven schedule rather than a duration-driven schedule.

It is uncommon for this type of scheduling to be used for most construction projects. Construction managers typically think in durations and then make sure there are sufficient resources to complete the activities within those given durations.

CONCLUSION

For any project to be realistically scheduled the management team must consider the resources required and the availability of those resources. It is not practical to assume infinite resources. Labor, equipment, money, and material must be made available in the required quantities when needed to make a feasible or realistic schedule. CPM scheduling and the computer can be a great asset in identifying resource conflicts and an aid to solving those problems before they become a crises on the project site. Understanding the different types of float and how to use float is key in the balancing of project resources. The ability to forecast and manage resource conflicts, along with the ability to level resources, is a required skill that ensures a greater level of success for practically any project.

APPLICATION

Using Practice Problem #2 (Figure 15.12) and the accompanying data (Figure 15.13), create the following. You must calculate the daily value in Figure 15.13.

1. A daily cash-loaded bar chart and daily cash flow histogram based on the project's early dates.
2. An early start progress S-curve of the cumulative daily cash flows.

FIGURE 15.12   Practice
Problem #2

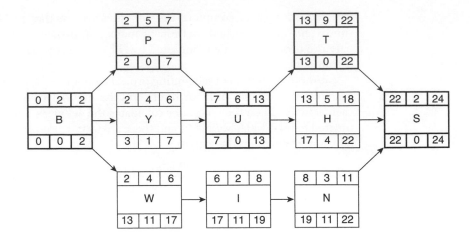

FIGURE 15.13

Activity	Duration (Days)	Activity Value	Daily Value	Crew Size
B	2	$10,600		4
Y	4	24,400		6
P	5	30,500		2
W	4	20,000		3
I	2	28,000		7
U	6	15,960		8
N	3	9,000		5
H	5	25,000		2
T	9	18,000		2
S	2	5,330		3

3. A banana curve of the cumulative daily cash flows showing both the early and the late S-curves.

4. A human resource-loaded bar chart and histogram based on the project's early dates showing the total number of workers on the job each day.

5. Analyze the above reports and write a paragraph on what could be done to balance the resources.

CHAPTER 16

COST SCHEDULE CONTROL SYSTEM CRITERIA (C/SCSC)

INTRODUCTION

Generally, companies get serious about using CPM scheduling to control time. Later, after they are somewhat comfortable with scheduling to control time, quality, safety, and costs to some degree, they realize they want to get better at controlling time and costs *together*. Time and costs on construction projects typically are tracked separately. The problem with this type of monitoring is that a project may be ahead of schedule from a time perspective and so everything looks good on paper. However, in order to be ahead of schedule there may have been extreme cost overruns, excessive use of equipment, tradespeople working overtime, too many workers on the job site resulting in crowded conditions and therefore a loss of productivity, and so on. This obviously would put the project ahead of schedule but create a serious budget problem. This chapter discusses a method that measures progress considering both time and costs. This method was developed by the U.S. Department of Defense and is called Cost/Schedule Control System Criteria (C/SCSC). Some managers call it the earned value system. The objective of the C/SCSC is to have an integrated time-cost progress monitoring and control system. It is frequently required by owners of large projects and common on NASA and Department of Defense contracts.

PERFORMANCE MEASURES

The system utilizes three key performance measures: (1) budgeted cost of work scheduled; (2) budgeted cost of work performed; and (3) actual cost of work performed.

BUDGETED COST OF WORK SCHEDULED. **Budgeted cost of work scheduled (BCWS)** is the original budgeted, estimated, or planned cost of the work scheduled to be accomplished through the analysis date. For activities that are complete, it is simply the budget for those activities that should have been complete by the date of analysis. For activities that should have been in progress, it is the budget for those activities multiplied by the percent scheduled. If the contract is silent as to which dates (early start and finish or late start and finish dates) the planned schedule is based on, the contractor typically will use the late dates. An average of the early and late dates could also be used in this analysis.

BUDGETED COST OF WORK PERFORMED. **Budgeted cost of work performed (BCWP)** is the original budgeted, estimated, or planned cost of the actual work that has been accomplished. For activities that are complete, it is simply the budget for those activities that have been completed by the date of analysis. For activities in progress, it is the budget for those activities multiplied by the percent complete. Budgeted cost of work performed is sometimes called "earned value" of work accomplished. On a hard bid project, this is the total amount of money the owner owes the contractor at this time—or, the amount of money the contractor has earned.

ACTUAL COST OF WORK PERFORMED.   **Actual cost of work performed (ACWP)** is the cost of the actual work that has been accomplished.

VARIANCES

To analyze the costs and the schedule there are three variances that are used. A **variance** is a deviation from the planned costs or schedule to the actual costs or schedule. Variances are either favorable or unfavorable. The three variances are as follows: (1) cost variance (CV); (2) schedule variance (SV); and (3) total variance (TV).

Cost Variance

Cost variance (CV) is a comparison between the budgeted cost of work performed and the actual cost of work performed, or CV = BCWP − ACWP. A positive cost variance would be a favorable condition or costs coming in underbudget. A negative cost variance would be an unfavorable condition or costs coming in overbudget.

Sometimes a management team desires to know the percent cost variance (PCV) rather than a monetary cost variance. This can be calculated as follows:

$$PCV = \frac{CV}{BCWP} \quad \text{or} \quad PCV = \frac{BCWP - ACWP}{BCWP}$$

Schedule Variance

Schedule variance (SV) is a comparison between the budgeted cost of work performed and the budgeted cost of work scheduled, or SV= BCWP − BCWS. If activity progress is measured based on the budget (if 50 percent of the budget is expended the activity is 50 percent complete), then comparing the BCWP with the BCWS gives an indication of project schedule status because they both are measured based on budgeted cost. A positive schedule variance is a favorable condition in that the project is ahead of schedule.

This variance does not indicate the number of days the project is behind or ahead the planned schedule. That can be determined only by examining the planned project completion date with the updated or actual project status and then projecting the current status through to the end of the project as discussed in Chapter 14.

If the management team wants to know the percent schedule variance (PSV), similar to the PCV discussed above, the formula would be as follows:

$$PSV = \frac{SV}{BCWS} \quad \text{or} \quad PSV = \frac{BCWP - BCWS}{BCWS}$$

Total Variance

Total variance (TV) is a comparison between the budgeted cost of work scheduled and the actual cost of work performed, or TV = BCWS − ACWP. A positive total variance would again be a favorable condition indicating that, as a whole, the project is underbudget at the time of analysis. There has been less spent by the analysis date than had been planned. However, that could be because the project is behind schedule.

If the management team wishes to know the percent total variance (PTV), the formula would be as follows:

$$\text{PTV} = \frac{\text{TV}}{\text{BCWS}} \quad \text{or} \quad \text{PTV} = \frac{\text{BCWS} - \text{ACWP}}{\text{BCWS}}$$

PERFORMANCE INDEXES

Some managers prefer to use cost and schedule performance indexes. The **cost performance index (CPI)** is calculated as follows:

$$\text{CPI} = \frac{\text{BCWP}}{\text{ACWP}}$$

A CPI value of greater than 1 indicates costs below the budget.

The **schedule performance index (SPI)** is calculated as follows:

$$\text{SPI} = \frac{\text{BCWP}}{\text{BCWS}}$$

An SPI value of greater than 1 indicates the project is ahead of schedule.

GRAPHICAL REPRESENTATION OF THE C/SCSC DATA AND VARIANCES

A Graphical Representation of the C/SCSC (Cost/Schedule Control System Criteria) data and variances is shown in Figure 16.1 The warehouse project is overbudget and behind schedule, consequently the CV and the SV are negative. The TV is positive because less money has been spent than planned as a result of the project being behind schedule.

Figure 16.2 is an example computer printout from SureTrak showing some of the cost control information.

The bold vertical line in the bar chart area represents when the schedule was updated or data date. The columns at the left are typical cost information. Note the "BCWS," "BCWP," "ACWP," "CV," and "SV" columns. Examine the data carefully while looking at the bars to the right of the report and see if the information makes sense to you. If it doesn't, do the application problem at the end of the chapter and then reexamine Figure 16.2.

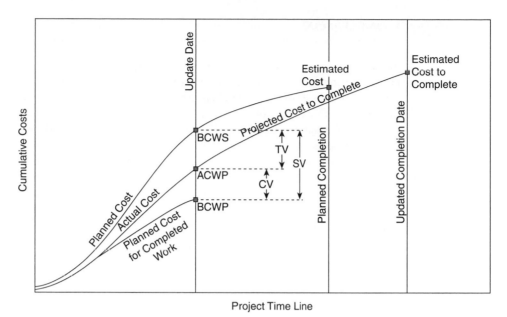

FIGURE 16.1 Graphical representation of the C/SCSC data and variances

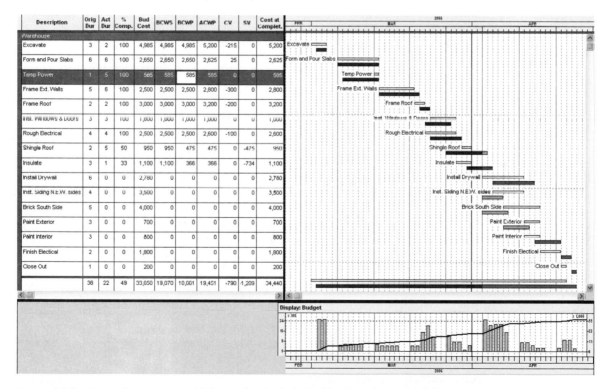

Description	Orig Dur	Act Dur	% Comp.	Bud Cost	BCWS	BCWP	ACWP	CV	SV	Cost at Complet.
Warehouse										
Excavate	3	2	100	4,985	4,985	4,985	5,200	-215	0	5,200
Form and Pour Slabs	6	6	100	2,650	2,650	2,650	2,625	25	0	2,625
Temp Power	1	5	100	585	585	585	585	0	0	585
Frame Ext. Walls	5	6	100	2,500	2,500	2,500	2,800	-300	0	2,800
Frame Roof	2	2	100	3,000	3,000	3,000	3,200	-200	0	3,200
Inst. Windows & Doors	3	3	100	1,800	1,800	1,800	1,800	0	0	1,800
Rough Electrical	4	4	100	2,500	2,500	2,500	2,600	-100	0	2,600
Shingle Roof	2	5	50	950	950	475	475	0	-475	950
Insulate	3	1	33	1,100	1,100	366	366	0	-734	1,100
Install Drywall	6	0	0	2,780	0	0	0	0	0	2,780
Inst. Siding N.E.W. sides	4	0	0	3,500	0	0	0	0	0	3,500
Brick South Side	5	0	0	4,000	0	0	0	0	0	4,000
Paint Exterior	3	0	0	700	0	0	0	0	0	700
Paint Interior	3	0	0	800	0	0	0	0	0	800
Finish Electical	2	0	0	1,800	0	0	0	0	0	1,800
Close Out	1	0	0	200	0	0	0	0	0	200
	36	22	49	33,050	19,070	10,001	19,451	-790	-1,209	34,440

Display: Budget

FIGURE 16.2 Example cost control information included with a bar chart schedule

CONCLUSION

The Cost/Schedule Control System Criteria helps a management team integrate time and costs into one data stream. The typical control system keeps time and costs separate, comparing the variances of actual costs to budgeted costs and the actual durations to the planned durations. This involves two separate streams of information: time information and cost information. The C/SCSC makes it possible to deal with only one data stream. Knowing the budgeted cost of work scheduled, the budgeted cost of work performed, and the actual cost of work performed, the cost variance, schedule variance, and total variance of the project can be monitored. As the management team sees variances beyond acceptable allowances, action can be taken to bring the project back into control.

This more sophisticated system is typically used on larger projects, but some managers prefer to use it with smaller projects as well. Once a management team gets familiar with these concepts they can be helpful in completing projects on time and within budget.

APPLICATION

You are currently working on the warehouse project shown in Figure 16.3.

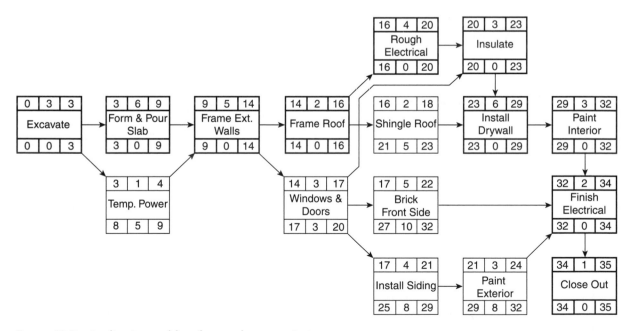

FIGURE 16.3 Application problem for warehouse project

The project has been updated through the end of March. Figure 16.4 shows the compiled data.

1. Calculate the following:

   CV _____   SV _____   TV _____

   PCV_____   PSV_____   PTV_____

   CPI _____   SPI _____

2. Explain the status of the project based on the data collected and calculated. Check your answers with those on page 194.

Description	% Complete	Budgeted Costs	BCWS	BCWP	ACWP
Excavate	100	$ 4,958	$ 4,958	$ 4,958	$ 5,200
F & P Slab	100	2,650	2,650	2,650	2,625
Temp. Power	100	585	585	585	585
Frame X Walls	100	2,500	2,500	2,500	2,800
Frame Roof	100	3,000	3,000	3,000	3,200
Windows/Doors	100	1,600	1,600	1,600	1,600
Rgh. Electrical	100	2,500	2,500	2,500	2,600
Shingle Roof	50	950	950	475	475
Insulate	33	1,100	1,100	366	366
Drywall	0	2,780	0	0	0
Siding	0	3,500	0	0	0
Brick S. Side	0	4,000	0	0	0
Paint Exterior	0	700	0	0	0
Paint Interior	0	800	0	0	0
Finish Electrical	0	1,800	0	0	0
Close Out	0	200	0	0	0
Total		33,650	19,870	18,661	19,451

FIGURE 16.4   Data for the warehouse project

Answers:

1. CV _____−790_____   SV _____−1,209_____   TV _____419_____

   PCV _____−4_____   PSV _____−6_____   PTV _____2%_____

   CPI _____.96_____ .   SPI _____.94_____

2. An explanation of the above:

   A CV of a negative $790 indicates the project is overbudget at this point by that amount.

   An SV of a negative $1,290 indicates the project is behind schedule.

   A TV of a positive $419 indicates the project has cost $419 less to this date than planned because it is behind schedule.

   A PCV of a negative 4% indicates the project is overbudget by 4%.

   A PSV of a negative 6% indicates the project is behind schedule by 6%.

   A PTV of a positive 2% indicates that there has been 2% less money actually spent to date than planned.

   A CPI of .96 indicates the project is overbudget (a value less than 1 indicates overbudget).

   An SPI of .94 indicates the project is behind schedule (a value less than 1 indicates behind schedule).

   Look back at Figure 16.2 which is a printout of this same problem done with the project management software SureTrak.

CHAPTER 17

CREATING TEAMWORK AND GETTING SUBCONTRACTORS TO CONFORM TO THE SCHEDULE

Introduction
Provide Formal Training
Hold a Preliminary Scheduling Meeting
Create the Logic Diagram and Then Share It
Use the Gilbane Method
Manage Durations
Plan for Undependable Subcontractors
Reward Subcontractors for Schedule Compliance
Other Methods for Getting Subcontractors to Conform to the Schedule
When to Use a Scheduling Consultant
Conclusion
Application

■ I N T R O D U C T I O N ■

This textbook has emphasized time and again the importance of teamwork in creating a schedule. Too often the schedule is created by the general contractor's scheduler or project manager with little input from other members of the management team. This chapter will explore ideas of how to make the schedule a team process and how to get the subcontractors and other team members to conform to the schedule.

One of the major problems relating to scheduling today is the development of the schedule by a single person with great computer skills, who creates impressive-looking bar charts printed in multiple colors with assorted fonts of varying sizes that are absolutely fictitious. There is little thought that goes into the logic diagram. In fact, the schedule is probably an old one from a past project that has simply been renamed, redated, and spruced up by adding company logos and clip art or photos to look even more impressive. One of the values of CPM scheduling is the ability to make impressive bar charts for presentations and negotiations, but they need to be based on thought, experience, and planning. The schedule needs to be factual and realistic. To make it that way, it needs to be a team effort.

As stated repeatedly throughout this textbook, it is essential in the development and updating of the schedule, to get input from all team members, especially the superintendents and subcontractors. It has to be viewed as "our schedule," not the "general contractor's schedule." To accomplish this, the key team members, including the subcontractors, need to be involved in the creation of the schedule logic and the durations. The schedule should be maintained as a focus point not only during the planning of the project but also throughout the entire construction process.

PROVIDE FORMAL TRAINING

In order for each member of the management team, including the superintendent of each of the major subcontractors, to have input into the schedule, he or she needs to be familiar with the basics of CPM scheduling. This generally means providing professional training for most of these people. Many superintendents do not really understand the basics of CPM even though they may claim they do. They often do not have a good grasp on the importance of the logic diagram, the durations, and the different types of float. General contractors could greatly benefit if they provided this training not only to their own managers but to the subs as well. This generally means hiring a consultant or trainer.

The training must be well received and presented in a manner that will motivate and excite all involved. There are many people who are very good at CPM scheduling, but not very effective at training others. You need a trainer who is experienced in teaching these concepts. A potential source of experienced trainers is professors in major universities that have accredited construction management programs. It is common for this training to take a full 6 to 8 hours, including some hands-on exercises. The training typically focuses on the basics of project management: breaking down the project into activities; developing the logic diagram, lags, and durations; calculating the early and late start and finish dates and total, free, shared, and independent float; identifying the critical path; and evaluating and updating the schedule. The training must be practical and include the development of a project schedule.

HOLD A PRELIMINARY SCHEDULING MEETING

A method used by many project managers is to hold a preliminary scheduling meeting or preconstruction conference with all the major team players to discuss the project and specifically to brainstorm the schedule. The purpose of this meeting is to come to some agreement on where to start the project and how to move through it in an organized manner. This meeting should be a brainstorming environment where everyone feels free to voice ideas and think creatively. Encourage cooperation and improvement. You may want to try to get people to think "outside the box" and explore methods never used before to build this project. Don't limit your thinking to traditional methods. Explore, be a little crazy, and you may be surprised at what the team will come up with if given the chance.

CREATE THE LOGIC DIAGRAM AND THEN SHARE IT

Once everyone has an understanding of the basics of CPM, they are at a point where they can assist in the development of the schedule. A method used by some companies is to have the project manager and the project superintendent develop the original logic diagram. This is developed on a large piece of paper or a roll of butcher paper as suggested in Chapter 6. After the initial logic diagram has been developed they meet with superintendents of all the prime subcontractors. Generally, for this logic diagram to communicate, it requires a redraw of the first logic diagram to make it a little neater, avoiding backward arrows, inserted activities, and excessive crossing of logic lines prior to showing it to the subcontractors. Everyone is given a chance to provide input into the schedule. All subs are responsible especially to check the logic of the activities that need to be finished before their activity can start. They should be looking for the opportunity to overlap activities with lags as well as to make sure the logic is acceptable. The subcontractors need to make sure they have sufficient workers and equipment available to meet the planned schedule. Durations and lag amounts are checked and agreed upon. This may take some negotiation and team play. It may also be wise to discuss this logic diagram with the prime suppliers or others to make sure the procurement activities are planned for sufficiently. The schedule does not need to be computerized at this point. If it is hand-drawn, it appears more flexible and open to change. Once it is computerized and printed out, subcontractors and others will not feel as welcome to make changes. Remember, it is still a "draft" copy.

It is not always necessary to draw out the total project schedule at this time. It may be more efficient to make a schedule that focuses on the general plan and then another schedule (or schedules) that focuses on the repetitive components of the project (such as the interior finishes of one area of one floor level) due to the fact that in the final schedule, this portion will be repeated many times. Make this repeated section accurate and then, during the computer input, it can be copied and pasted to create a detailed final and complete schedule.

This does take time and effort, but the time will be more than made up by having a project plan and schedule that represents the thinking of the management team, not just the scheduler. When everyone has a chance for input into the schedule they take ownership of it and everyone benefits. Everyone works harder to make it come to pass and everyone feels like they are an important team member. If given the opportunity, subcontractors will come up with many money- and time-saving ideas about how to construct a project. It is this type of prior planning and communicating that makes projects challenging, productive, and enjoyable to work on.

After the key players have had a chance to provide input into the schedule, it is computerized and then rechecked prior to sending out reports. If the purpose of the schedule is to simply look organized and professional for a project presentation or negotiated contract proposal, this detailed work is not necessary. Go with an impressive, not-so-detailed schedule, but mark it as a "preliminary" schedule. Then don't try to manage the project with this preliminary schedule. There are few things better than to begin a project being organized and prepared. The well-thought-out schedule with input from the key players will help provide this. The idea that you will eventually get organized typically does not work.

USE THE GILBANE METHOD

Another method used to get input from the prime subcontractors and involve the whole management team in the development of the schedule is to use a technique attributed to the Gilbane Building Company. This technique is addressed as a case study in *Construction Planning & Scheduling*, written and published by the Associated General Contractors (1994, pp. 23–25).

The general process of the Gilbane method is as follows: First, a preconstruction meeting is held with all the key team players present. Everyone should be intimately familiar with the project plans prior to this meeting. The project is discussed and a basic method or plan for the construction process is agreed upon. The team reaches a conclusion of where operations will begin and how they plan on moving through the project. This is a fairly short meeting, lasting no longer than an hour or so in length. A followup meeting is scheduled within the next week to develop the schedule.

Each team member is supplied with colored 3 × 5-inch cards or sticky notes. Each person has his or her own unique color of note card. On their own, the team members list their activities on individual note cards. The activities are broken down the way team members feel is necessary to achieve control of the project following the process agreed to in the prior meeting. Each card or note contains the name of the activity and the duration of the activity at a minimum. The predecessors and successors could also be recorded as well as the crew size and major equipment needed, particularly if the schedule is to be crew loaded or equipment loaded.

At the schedule development meeting, the facilitator (typically the project manager) tapes butcher paper or poster paper on the conference room wall. Some facilitators prefer the butcher paper that has a plastic film on one side because it is very durable. It is not unusual for the paper to completely wrap around the conference room. The project manager then posts the first note card with the appropriate activity on it. Next, each team member comes to the wall in turn and tapes or posts the activities on the poster paper in the appropriate place. As this takes place, the project is scheduled and discussed by the entire management team. Each person coming forward and then steps back as others post their notes to the schedule. The appropriate predecessor and successor lines are drawn with a pencil showing the correct relationships as the project is developed and discussed. Everyone brings extra blank cards because new activities and a further refining of activities will happen as the meeting progresses. Each team member can easily recognize his or her individual activities in the schedule due to the unique color of the note cards.

After the schedule logic diagram is completed, it is a good idea to review the schedule to ensure the logic is correct and no major errors or omissions have been made. A quick forward pass could be done to determine if the project completion date is within the contract requirements. If the completion date does not meet contract requirements or team goals, the team addresses the problem now and adjusts the schedule to make sure it meets team goals and contract requirements. The attitude is what are *we* going to do in order to improve *our* project plan and schedule. It should be emphasized that it is the participants' schedule and they will have to live with it, so let's get it right.

This meeting typically will take a few hours. However, generally it is a lively meeting and the time goes by fast. There will always be those subcontractors or team members who are too busy to attend, so the rest of the team members do their best to take into account the missing members' responsibilities. It is not unusual for the missing members to be in contention with the schedule and to be the complainers at the job site. They will be reminded by the rest of the management team that they were too busy to attend the schedule development meeting or to send a capable replacement. Hopefully, they will not choose to miss that meeting again. This meeting is the best opportunity for everyone to have input into the project plan and schedule, and has the potential of making the project a real team project.

After the schedule development meeting, the schedule is computerized and the logic diagram is printed. It is then desirable to hold a followup meeting with all the major team players to review and reanalyze the schedule prior to printing the reports that will be sent to all participants. It also works well to project the schedule onto a large screen so that all participants can easily see and review it. If problems are identified they should be noted. For example, the person inputting the schedule into the computer must not make any adjustments or changes to the schedule.

This development process could be repeated as the job progresses. On very large projects this process is done for a specified period of the job, rather than doing it for the entire project at once.

MANAGE DURATIONS

It is common for team members to inflate their individual durations when they are given the opportunity to supply their own durations. They do this to minimize their individual risk. If that is allowed, the project completion time will be unrealistically long. To help eliminate inflated durations when using a team process to develop the schedule, discuss the amount of risk everyone feels is reasonable for that particular project. If it is a complex project, there may be a need for many more days added to the project duration to control that risk. If it is a straightforward or more familiar project, there would not be a need for additional days. As the team agrees with the amount of risk, those extra days are added to the project duration. The owner is given the completion date based on the extra days of risk added.

There are two common methods of adding the extra days. One is to add a contingency activity with a duration of those agreed-upon risk days as the last activity in the network logic diagram. Another method is to do a backward pass with a date that many days beyond the calculated early finish date. With the second method there is that many days of float on the critical path and the float of every activity is increased by that same amount of days. Those float days are shared with every activity in the schedule. Either way, it is understood that those extra days belong to the project team and all are free to use them *as needed*. They should be held sacred because if someone uses them, the remaining team players are more at risk. This technique helps eliminate the need for each person to add extra days to each of his or her activities to control the risk.

PLAN FOR UNDEPENDABLE SUBCONTRACTORS

It is important to realize and plan for the subcontractors who have a history of not finishing on time. That can be planned and scheduled for by hiding extra days in the schedule. This is a major concern, especially for residential builders. With large commercial projects, the subs are there for an extended period and they simply need to be told what to do, where, and when. Residential builders, especially those building on scattered lots, have an entirely different challenge. It can become a major problem to even get the sub to the job site. Whether residential, commercial, industrial, or heavy highway, undependable subcontractors have caused some contractors to abandon scheduling altogether. They simply fly by the seat of their pants and don't schedule the next sub until the prior sub is finished. This is not scheduling in the least—it is simply going from crisis to crisis.

There are too many undependable subcontractors who, by not showing up or finishing on time create chaos with the rest of the schedule. This can be partially planned for by inserting some finish-to-start lags between activities in the schedule. Let's say it is known from past history that the drywall sub frequently arrives on the job a day late and typically takes a day longer to finish. You don't want to increase the duration for drywall in order to plan for those extra days; the sub would see that and use the extra days. You just want to schedule the extra days without the sub seeing them. A finish-to-start lag of 1 day prior to drywall and a finish-to-start lag of 1 day after drywall will adjust the schedule for that scenario. This does add 2 days to the schedule, but they are planned days that the subcontractor is not aware of and, therefore, will not consume. It certainly would be better to work only with dependable people, but that is not realistic. Therefore, a method is needed to work with undependable people and still have an accurate schedule. It doesn't take long to realize dependable people are worth a little extra cost. A more expensive sub that is dependable may save a lot of time and therefore money in the long run.

REWARD SUBCONTRACTORS FOR SCHEDULE COMPLIANCE

Reward team players for superior performance. Provide "Sub of the Month" (or year) awards to outstanding subcontractors. The awards could range from a paper award (which has unbelievable results), to gift certificates, vacations, tools, recreational vehicles, and so on.

A common observation of successful companies is they reward their employees and associates with appreciation. As one visits job trailers, it is exciting to feel the pride of superintendents or subcontractors who proudly display the certificates of appreciation or accomplishments on their office walls.

One company takes all the employees and subcontractors who meet their individual goals on a vacation each year. This is a residential builder who develops and builds recreational properties. The individual goals consist of time, cost, quality, and safety measurements, and the schedule is heavily weighted in this assessment. The employees and subcontractors and their spouses are invited to a competing recreational property where a few meetings are held to discuss how this property compares to the property being developed by the company. What is liked or disliked? What seems to be working and what does not? What can be learned and taken back home?

Another company is a major user of Giftcertificates.com, an Internet company where you can give a gift certificate that can be exchanged for practically any merchandise from hundreds of retail companies.

Yet another company with an interest in Browning Arms has a reputation of giving exclusive gifts, including knives, rifles, and hunting accessories, to associates who meet or exceed expectations. Again, the schedule is a major part of those expectations.

Remember, many people work for reasons other than money. Many satisfied employees stay with a company because of the way they are treated and the relationships they have formed with fellow employees. This frequently ranks higher than salary.

A method used by some companies to get the subcontractors to stop by the office to receive an updated schedule is to attach the schedule for the next several weeks to the paychecks. When the subcontractors pick up the check, they also get the schedule.

OTHER METHODS FOR GETTING SUBCONTRACTORS TO CONFORM TO THE SCHEDULE

The key in getting subcontractors to conform to the schedule is to make it *their* schedule, as discussed. Some additional ideas to consider are as follows:

❏ treat subcontractors like you would want to be treated. Your relationships with them will be a key to your success or failure.
❏ don't schedule the same crew to be in two places at the same time.
❏ don't schedule two conflicting subcontractors in the same place at the same time.
❏ use the Internet to communicate an updated schedule to the project team. (This is discussed in greater detail in the chapters relating to each piece of software.)
❏ fax reminders to notify subcontractors of their schedule.
❏ give sufficient notice to the subcontractors as to when their activities are scheduled to start and finish. A day or two notice is not sufficient.
❏ make the schedule part of every progress review meeting.

WHEN TO USE A SCHEDULING CONSULTANT

If a company is just getting started with CPM scheduling it may need some consultant help to get going. Consultants can be a great asset and save a company considerable money to provide help at the right time. The consultant can be brought in without creating a long-term commitment of paying for insurance and benefits. A consultant can bring valuable experiences from working with many other companies. The right consultant can be a tremendous asset in providing training. It is a known fact that if the upper management of a company provides training it is not nearly as well received as if the company hired a consultant to come in and say essentially the same things.

In the author's opinion, it is not to a company's advantage to use a consultant to routinely develop and maintain construction schedules. If that is the case it is typically the consultant's thoughts that go into planning the sequence and durations of activities. The schedule then reflects the way the *consultant* would build the project, not the way the management team would build the project. The consultant likely is not familiar with local conditions, construction traditions, or processes. It is necessary for the consultant to then update the schedule and make adjustments on future activities to adjust the schedule due to delays or changes. This may meet contract requirements, but it does not represent the manner in which the project team envisions completing the project. Furthermore, when a change occurs, the management team needs to wait for the arrival of the consultant to determine the effect of the change.

It has been the author's experience, even when using the management team's input to develop the schedule, that it is largely abandoned if it is not created, evaluated, and updated by the management team on the job site. They need to be in control and feel the responsibility of the project schedule. In order to do this, they need to know the basics of CPM scheduling and have the ability to use the computer software to allow them to be in control. Use a consultant to help in that training so that you can become independent of the consultant. An experienced construction consultant can be a great aid in software training as well as training on the basics of critical path method.

CONCLUSION

Everything that can be done to make a construction team function like a team, including communicating, displaying teamwork, facing accomplishments and trials together, and sacrificing for each other will pay off in big dividends. Give everyone in key management positions the opportunity to have input into the development of the schedule. Construction is such a great industry to work in when, at the end of the project, positive relationships have developed rather than bitter fighting, feuding, and problems caused by a lack of communication, lack of trust, and poor management. A schedule created by a team can go a long way in providing an enjoyable, successful project, where a team has worked together to overcome unbelievable challenges and obstacles.

APPLICATION

1. Think of great teams you have been associated with, whether it is on the job, at school, in sports, at church, or in your community, and analyze what made that team successful. Write a short paragraph or two relating to that experience.

2. The next time you have the opportunity to schedule any kind of a project involving multiple people, use the concepts discussed in this chapter and see if they really work.

3. Apply the concepts discussed in this chapter to planning any project, work, school, family, church, community, recreation, etc.

OTHER SCHEDULING TECHNIQUES

■ I N T R O D U C T I O N ■

This chapter provides a description of other scheduling techniques that might be considered for particular applications. Some of these techniques are CPM principles that have not been covered in prior chapters and others are stand-alone scheduling techniques. One of these ideas may help with a particular challenge you have with a CPM schedule or aid in presenting a schedule in a unique or different format.

THREE-WEEK LOOK-AHEAD OR SHORT INTERVAL SCHEDULES

It is common practice on large projects to use a general schedule for the whole project and then to create a more detailed schedule covering the next several weeks or months as needed. As discussed in Chapter 4, a popular time increment is to look at the next three weeks. Consequently, these schedules are frequently referred to as "3-week look-ahead schedules." Other common names are short interval production schedules (SIPS) or a construction activity plan (CAP). It is possible to create the general schedule in a greater level of detail and then use a short interval schedule that simply includes a selection of the activities that are scheduled to take place within the designated period. Because creating the master schedule to this level of detail would be a very time-consuming job on a major project, it is common to rely on the look-ahead schedule to deal with details.

Schedule Format

Short interval schedules typically are created by the superintendent and are, therefore, in a bar chart format (see Chapter 4). Some superintendents who are familiar with CPM create these schedules on the computer using network scheduling techniques. Because this schedule is limited to the next short period of time, it breaks down the activities into a greater level of detail to analyze tools, equipment, workers, and material needed. The schedule may deal only with the activities of a single crew or relate to specific areas of the project at this level. Of course, it must agree with the master project schedule as far as milestone dates are concerned. Developed every week, the short interval schedule includes the detail for the next 3 to 8 weeks, with three weeks as the most common time period. However, it is important to understand the schedule is developed every week covering the next short interval of time. It is not just created every three weeks. Managers also frequently resource load these schedules, as discussed in the next chapter.

Details That May Be Included

Although not required, the short interval schedule could include the following additional detail:

❑ number of workers on the job
❑ materials to be ordered and delivered
❑ equipment to be installed
❑ equipment necessary for construction
❑ maintenance of equipment
❑ owner interfaces
❑ inspections
❑ safety concerns
❑ meetings
❑ production rates
❑ special material tests

Some managers will take the information from the short interval schedule and let that be a guide to creating the daily to-do lists discussed in Chapter 3 of this text.

Example Format for a Short Interval Schedule

Figure 18.1 illustrates a typical format for a short interval schedule. Note that the weekends and holidays are shaded to make those dates stand out. Using this form, the superintendent could create a detailed bar chart by hand for the next three weeks.

Even though this is a typical format for a short interval schedule, it could be made simply by using a calendar, a matrix, or a spreadsheet. Whatever helps to schedule the project detail for the next few weeks is great. Don't limit your thinking to the traditional methods.

HAMMOCK ACTIVITIES

A **hammock activity**—an activity that spans other activities—is a scheduling technique used in CPM. It can be best understood by looking at Figure 18.2.

The *Dewatering* activity shown in Figure 18.2 is the hammock activity—the duration is the result of the activities it spans. If there is a change in the duration of those five activities, the duration of the hammock activity automatically changes to equal the total duration of the activities spanned. The hammock activity in this case shows when the dewatering is operative. In the schedule in Figure 18.2, *Dewatering* must start after the building is excavated and continue until the permanent drainage system will be in effect as the slab is placed. Hammock activities are also used when haul roads are maintained or during the procurement process. Hammock activities are unique in that their duration automatically changes with the activities they span. Their duration is not input into the computer. However, they do need to be identified in the software as a hammock activity in order for this to happen. Each software program is unique in how this is done.

Short Interval Schedule	Project							Prepared by							Date Prepared							
Week Day	M	T	W	T	F	S	S	M	T	W	T	F	S	S	M	T	W	T	F	S	S	
Work Day	1	2	3	H	4	W	W	5	6	7	8	9	W	W	10	11	12	13	14	W	W	
Activity Description / Calendar Date	7/1	2	3	4	5	6	7	8	9	10	11	12	13	14	15	16	17	18	19	20	21	Comments or Notes

Scheduled \   Completed X

FIGURE 18.1   Example format for a short interval schedule

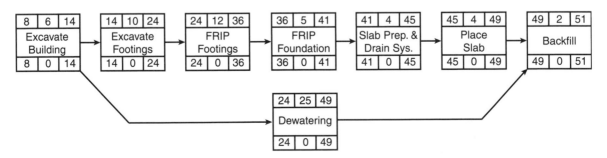

FIGURE 18.2   *Dewatering* is an example of a hammock activity

CONSTRAINTS

A **constraint** is a restriction or boundary on the start or finish data of an activity. Constraining an activity's start or finish dates is another technique used in CPM scheduling. Constraints are used to ensure that an activity meets a deadline or when an activity must happen before or after a certain date. The most commonly used constraints are deadlines (no-later-than constraints) and potential delays (no-earlier-than constraints). They can be attached to either the start or finish of an activity. For example, a deadline can be put on the start or finish of an activity (the activity must start or finish no later than the date specified) or a potential delay (the activity can start or finish no earlier than the date specified).

Typically, an experienced scheduler would enter the project into the computer without constraints first and examine the project purely on the CPM logic. Constraints are then added, one at a time—watching to see how each one affects the entire schedule. Remember, constraints override the CPM logic. If a mandatory start constraint is included on an activity, that activity will start on that date regardless of the CPM logic and whether or not the predecessors are finished. Or, if the project is ahead of schedule, the constrained activity will not automatically adjust to the possible new early date. Again, constraints overrides the logic, therefore, they must be used with care.

Date constraints are most often used for deadlines and delivery dates. They affect not only the constrained activity but also its predecessors and successors (and by extension the entire project). Therefore, they should be used sparingly. Too many constraints diminishes the value of using critical path method because activities that are constrained cannot be as freely rescheduled when other parts of the project are rescheduled. The next several sections describe the various types of constraints.

Start Constraints

Start constraints specify that an activity can start no earlier than, or no later than, a specified date. For example, if an activity cannot begin until the delivery of a piece of equipment on a particular date, make that date an early start constraint. The activity can start on or after that date, as calculated according to the logic of the schedule, but not before. If an activity must start by a certain date, attach a late start constraint.

Finish Constraints

Finish constraints are used to specify that an activity must finish no earlier than, or no later than, a specified date. For example, if an activity must finish by a certain date, attach a late finish constraint. If an activity can start at any time but cannot finish until a particular date, perhaps after a scheduled customer inspection, attach an early finish constraint.

Mandatory Constraints

Mandatory constraints force an activity to establish a definite date for its start or finish. No matter what happens, that activity will take place on the mandatory constrained date. Use these constraints with caution; they control activity dates whether or not they are consistent with schedule logic. Therefore, an activity with a mandatory constraint could be scheduled before its predecessor.

Start-on Constraints

Start-on constraints are equivalent to applying both a "start-no-earlier-than" and "start-no-later-than" constraint to an activity. It sets the early and late start dates equal to the specified date, but protects schedule logic (unlike the mandatory start constraint), so the activity can have positive or negative float.

Expected Finish Constraints

Expected finish constraints force the duration of an activity to depend on its scheduled finish date. Attach an expected finish constraint and the computer will calculate the duration for the activity from its early start date to the expected finish date you specify. If the activity is under way, the computer will calculate its remaining duration as the difference between the data date and the expected finish date. Because it is calculated, the software typically will display the duration with an asterisk.

Float Constraints

Float constraints affect the scheduling of an activity, but, unlike date constraints do not override schedule logic. There are two types of float constraints: zero total float constraint and as late as possible float constraint.

ZERO TOTAL FLOAT CONSTRAINTS.   A **zero total float constraint** causes an activity to be scheduled as soon as possible. It then has zero total float. The activity will be scheduled to occur on the first dates it can occur and it will appear critical. The float will disappear.

AS LATE AS POSSIBLE FLOAT CONSTRAINTS.   An **as late as possible float constraint** is used to set the dates of an activity so that the activity is scheduled as late as possible without delaying the early start date of its earliest successor. This eliminates any free float on the constrained activity. This constraint is commonly used for payments and deliveries.

FENCED BAR CHARTS

It is not uncommon for the contract documents to specify that a "fenced" bar chart be presented to the owner at certain intervals. A **fenced bar chart** is a bar chart developed from a CPM network that shows the logic relationships similar to the network. Rather than using boxes or nodes for the activities, the activities are represented by a bar and then arrows are added showing the predecessors and successors. Figure 18.3 is an example of a fenced bar chart.

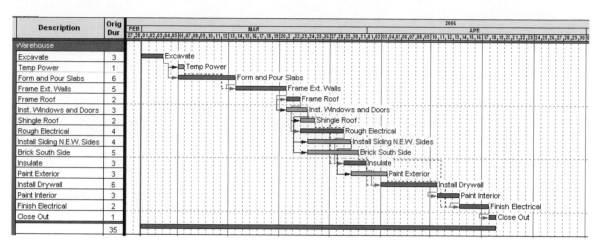

Description	Orig Dur	
Warehouse		
Excavate	3	
Temp Power	1	
Form and Pour Slabs	6	
Frame Ext. Walls	5	
Frame Roof	2	
Inst. Windows and Doors	3	
Shingle Roof	2	
Rough Electrical	4	
Install Siding N.E.W. Sides	4	
Brick South Side	5	
Insulate	3	
Paint Exterior	3	
Install Drywall	6	
Paint Interior	3	
Finish Electrical	2	
Close Out	1	
	35	

FIGURE 18.3 Example of a fenced bar chart

Notice the relationship arrows in the example fenced bar chart in Figure 18.3. *Excavate* is a predecessor to *Temp. Power* and *Form & Pour Slabs* because there is an arrow from the end of *Excavate* to the beginning of each of those successors. The fenced bar chart is popular with some managers because it strikes a balance between a bar chart and a logic diagram. However, the logical relationships in the fenced bar chart still are not as easy to follow as in the logic diagram. Many of the relationship lines tend to be grouped together and almost on top of each other, making it difficult to understand all the relationships. The larger and more complex the schedule, the bigger this problem becomes.

GRAPHIC SCHEDULES

A **graphic schedule** could be as simple as a marked-up set of drawings. Visualize the floor plan of a building where crosshatching or highlighting a portion of the floor plan shows when the drywall is to be installed in each area. One colored section shows the drywall dates written in and then another section of a different color shows the dates of the drywall written in for that section, and so on. Arrows could be drawn on the floor plan to show the planned sequence of moving through the area. This can be an effective, and yet simple schedule that has the power to force detailed thinking and communicate to everyone working on the project. This type of schedule is useful for concrete placement on the exterior of the project as well.

Figure 18.4 is an example of a graphic schedule for interior painting.

Figure 18.4 shows the schedule for painting one floor level. The shading shows the areas to be painted and the handwritten dates show the days the work is to be done. The arrows show the direction of how the painters are scheduled to work or move throughout the floor level.

Paint Schedule

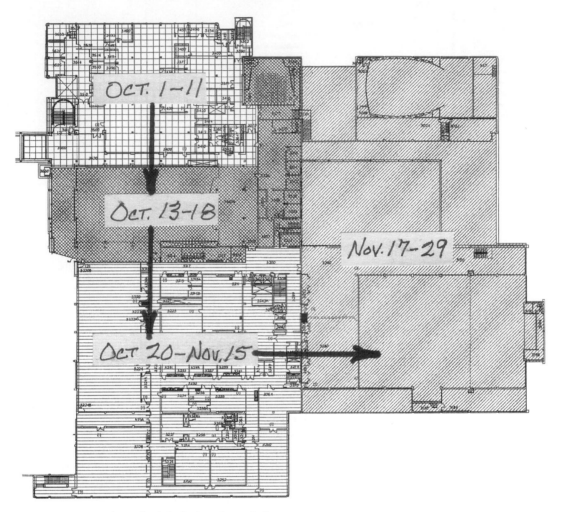

FIGURE 18.4 Graphic schedule for interior painting

MATRIX SCHEDULES

A **matrix schedule** shows desired summary information about when certain activities will happen. An example is illustrated in Figure 18.5.

The matrix schedule is a very user-friendly scheduling technique. If you want to know when drywall will be installed on the 9th floor, simply locate the 9th floor and move right to the drywall column.

Hotel - Interior Finishes - Matrix							
	Metal Studs	Rough-ins	Insulation	Drywall	Painting	Finishes	Carpet
Penthouse							
12th Floor							
11th Floor							
10th Floor							
9th Floor							
8th Floor							
7th Floor							
6th Floor							
5th Floor							
4th Floor							
3rd Floor							
2nd Floor							
1st Floor							
Basement							

Each Cell Contains the Following Information or Other Information as Desired.

Sch Start	Sch Finish
Act Start	Act Finish
Plan Dur	Act Dur

FIGURE 18.5 Example of a matrix schedule

Also, notice the schedule looks similar to a structural elevation of the building. This makes it very easy to find the information desired. The information contained in each cell is information of choice depending on what you desire to be tracked or measured.

The matrix schedule is not typical of CPM scheduling. None of the current project management software will create these schedules. Generally, the dates are taken from the CPM schedule and the matrix schedule is created with Microsoft Excel or similar software. Because this schedule is not tied to the CPM software it is not automatically updated as the schedule is updated on the computer. Thus, with each update a new matrix would need to be created. Matrix scheduling techniques are sometimes valuable in summarizing the project schedule to an owner during a proposal for construction services or at a meeting to report current progress and future plans.

ACTIVITY ON ARROW (AOA) OR ARROW DIAGRAM METHOD

This is a very brief description of activity on arrow (AOA) scheduling techniques that were previously mentioned in Chapter 5. Activity on arrow was a popular CPM scheduling method in the early years of CPM because it was easier to write AOA computer programs than for the activity on node (AON) method which has been used in this text. Even though AOA was more popular in the earlier years, with the added power of today's computers AOA has almost become a forgotten technique. None of the current popular software programs support AOA notation. It is discussed here so that if you see a schedule in that format, you won't feel intimidated.

Basically, the primary difference between AOA and AON is in the logic diagram. The activity description is located on the *arrow* with AOA, whereas with AON, the activity description is located on or in the *node* or activity box. That change creates a few other differences that will be further explained. Carefully observe the following AOA logic diagram in Figure 18.6.

Notice that the activity description is located on the arrows. The nodes (circles) represent the beginning or ending of the activity. The logic states that all activities coming into a node (circle) must be complete prior to the start of any activities coming out of the node. Therefore, according to the logic diagram in Figure 18.6, both

Warehouse

CPM, AO A Schedule

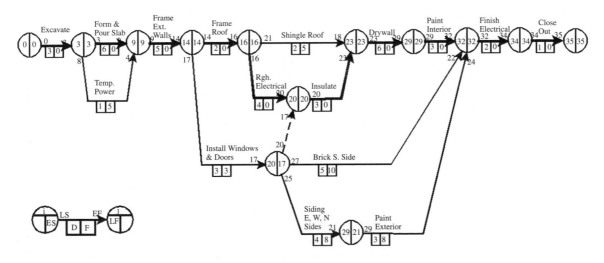

FIGURE 18.6   An activity on arrow CPM schedule of the warehouse

Form & Pour Slab and *Temp. Power* must be complete (are predecessors) before *Frame Ext. Walls* can start.

Another unique attribute of AOA logic diagrams is the use of dummies. A *dummy* shows relationships between activities, but is not an activity in and of itself. For that reason, it is typically drawn with a dotted or dashed line. Notice the dashed line (the dummy) in the schedule shown in Figure 18.6 going from *Install Windows & Doors* to *Insulate*. This means that *Install Windows & Doors* is a predecessor to *Insulate*. *Install Windows & Doors* is also a predecessor to *Brick S. Side* and to *Siding E, W, N Sides*. The dummy relationship is just as firm and important as any other relationship in the logic diagram. It is easy to read AOA logic diagrams if you simply remember those two items: *the activity description is on the arrow and dummies show predecessors*.

The remainder of the key concepts of AOA are the same as AON. The legend in the lower left of the schedule in Figure 18.6 indicates where early start, early finish, late start, late finish, duration, and total float are shown on the logic diagram. These dates will be exactly the same whether the logic diagram is drawn with AOA notation or AON notation. Bar charts developed from either logic diagram will look exactly the same. It is difficult to know how and where to use dummies with the AOA logic diagraming and it is not worth the effort to learn it today, unless you have a project where the specifications require an AOA logic diagram. You would have to find and use an old DOS version of Primavera in order to schedule using AOA techniques on the computer.

PERT (PROJECT EVALUATION AND REVIEW TECHNIQUE)

Project Evaluation and Review Technique (PERT) was the method developed by the Navy in the mid-1950s, as discussed in Chapter 5. PERT is a critical path technique that uses a logic diagram similar to other CPM techniques. Based on the logic diagram and the durations, a critical path is determined. However, the determination of the durations is where PERT differs considerably from other techniques. PERT uses three time estimates for each activity: an optimistic time, a most likely time, and a pessimistic time. The final activity duration is determined by taking the optimistic time, plus 4 times the most likely time, plus the pessimistic time, and dividing the results by 6: $O + 4L + P \div 6$. This gives the most likely time a weighted average or has 4 times the weight of the optimistic or the pessimistic durations. This accounts for some uncertainty in the durations of many projects. The more uncertain the durations are, the more valuable it would be to use the PERT method. The project's final duration would be determined using statistical procedures comparing the amount of variance in each of the three durations of all the critical path activities. The more variability in the three durations of each activity, the more likely it would be that the project would not finish on time. The PERT program would calculate the probability of the project finishing on the calculated finish date.

PERT techniques are used very little in the construction industry. It takes some knowledge of statistics to understand the process, along with a computer program designed for PERT techniques. Monte Carlo Simulation is the most common PERT method available that takes into account this difference in probable durations.

CONCLUSION

Even though all of these scheduling techniques are not required or used on every project, some of them will prove valuable to the project manager wishing to find creative ways to schedule unique projects and to report progress.

A short interval or three-week look-head schedule is an excellent technique used to plan the details for the next short period of the construction process. This schedule helps the superintendent think of the deliveries, tools, equipment, materials, crew sizes, and so forth to use in order to accomplish the milestones in the master schedule.

Knowing how to schedule hammock activities and apply the correct date and float constraints helps a manager create a reliable schedule that reflects the details of how the project is to be constructed. Fenced bar charts, matrix, and graphic schedules can be used to present the schedule information in different formats for specific uses, such as summary reports, or making the schedule easier for some people to understand.

APPLICATION

1. Visit a construction site and ask the superintendent or project manager to look at some of the short interval schedules he or she has created for the project. If there is a master schedule, compare the two.
2. Make a list of justified constraints on a construction project of choice.

CHAPTER 19

Introduction to Computerized CPM Scheduling

Introduction and Brief History
Tips for Learning Project Management Software
Comparison of Popular Project Management Software
General Suggestions for Computer Reports
Conclusion
Application

INTRODUCTION
AND BRIEF HISTORY

The basic principles of CPM were developed in the mid–1950s. Many major construction companies tried this new management technique for the next several years with some mixed success. The initial schedule was developed and input into the computers of the day. Then, the basic reports were printed and delivered to the project participants. One of the major problems with those early attempts was the updating process. If a company was very organized, the field personnel would update the activity's actual start and actual finish times and then submit the report to the home office where the data were transferred to keypunch cards and then delivered to the computer center for processing. The data were processed by the computer and new reports printed. The new reports were then delivered back to the home office to be taken to the field office. If this process was completed efficiently, the field managers received back the information in about a week after they submitted it. It was not uncommon for the process to take as long as 2 or 3 weeks. Consequently, the reports provided great historical information, but poor management information. The field managers were dealing with a completely new set of problems by then.

In order for CPM to be fully utilized at the project site, the field managers need to have real-time information to see the effects of potential changes and current delays. The management staff needs to have instantaneous feedback in order for CPM to be fully utilized. This was impossible in those early years without computers on the job site. Due to that, CPM scheduling became practically unknown for the vast majority of construction firms. Finally, with the advent of the personal computer in the early to mid–1980s it became possible to take advantage of this management tool. CPM gained much more attention and software was developed that worked on these new personal computers. CPM was an idea whose time had finally come. By the 1990s, many construction companies were finding success with CPM scheduling. However, a major problem that still persisted was the manager needed to have computer skills, as well as construction experience in order to make CPM scheduling reach its management potential. At that time there were people on both sides of the fence—some with computer skills and others with construction experience; but few had expertise with both. Some construction companies still wrestle with this problem today, but the computer skills of most project managers have greatly improved in the past several years.

The early computer programs utilized the activity on arrow notation system because it was easier to write the software for. Finally, by the 1990s computers had developed to the point that activity on node and precedence diagraming became not only feasible, but had to a large extent made the activity on arrow system obsolete. Some of the early software programs that gained respect and considerable market share were Project Management Systems II (PMS II), Time Line, Super Project Expert, MicroTrak, and Primavera Project Planner (P3). As the computer developed, so did the software. The most popular programs of today are Primavera Project Planner (P3), SureTrak Project Manager, and Microsoft Project. The software continues to be more user-friendly and more construction companies are finding success with this tool.

One major problem has not changed, however: Learning the basics of CPM to where a manager is effective is still a challenging issue. To go one step further, learning the software to the extent where the manager can efficiently analyze the updated project and produce the desired reports is critical. Project managers are busy people and it is difficult, at best, to devote the time necessary to become proficient with CPM and the computer. For managers to succeed in learning these newer management tools it takes persistence.

The difficulty of finding management people with computer skills is changing with the new breed of project management personnel that are graduating from major 4-year accredited construction management programs throughout the country. These graduates are entering the workforce with strong computer skills and quickly gain the construction work experience which enables them to become proficient at both the computer and managing the project.

TIPS FOR LEARNING PROJECT MANAGEMENT SOFTWARE

Once a manager has mastered one project management software program, it is easier to learn another. It is essential to know the basics of CPM first. A manager must understand what is going on inside the computer with the logic, calculations of dates, floats, and so on before having great success with the computer.

Some people are good at learning computer software programs on their own. However, most of us are not. We learn best by introductory training on the software. All the software companies provide training either at their facility, at announced locations throughout the nation, or at your facility. Typical complaints from managers about software company training is that it is too general and lacks specific information on how to apply the concepts to a construction project. Yet, the software companies take the challenge of training their customers and normally do an excellent job.

Another source of training is to contact the major four-year accredited construction management programs throughout the country. Some of them offer training at their university on the software and how to use it to manage construction projects. For a list of accredited four-year construction management programs, consult the home page of the American Council for Construction Education (ACCE) on the Internet at http://www.acce-hq.org. There are also professional consultants who offer software training.

Whatever choices you make for software training, expect it to take from two to three full days. Then, plan on some steep learning curve time back at the office soon after the training sessions to become proficient at the software. The time back at the office must follow. If a long time passes between training and application, a majority of the concepts learned will be forgotten. It must be applied immediately. Some managers take a project they are currently working on and schedule it from that point forward, at least for several months. Then, they enter that schedule into the computer and generate some basic reports while the training is still fresh in their minds.

Start with the basics. It is not necessary to know everything about each feature of the software to be a successful user. Simply input a schedule (Figure 19.1), print a few basic reports to communicate the schedule, update it, and get going. Then, learn more features as you need them.

Once you become familiar with the software and have developed your favorite reports and techniques, you will find it will save you time instead of taking it.

It is beneficial to have several employees from one company attend the software training together. That way, after they return, as one of them has a question, they may be able to help each other. Also, the Help menus on the software programs are beneficial and technical support is extremely valuable. The programs of today

FIGURE 19.1 A project manager enters schedule information into the computer

all contain a helpful tutorial that guides the learner through the main components. It is important to not get discouraged and give up. It will be worthwhile as you become more proficient and experienced.

COMPARISON OF POPULAR PROJECT MANAGEMENT SOFTWARE

This is a practical general comparison of the software from the author's point of view. Use it only as a general guide. Everyone should do their own detailed comparison for their specific purposes. The critical issue isn't which software package is used, but that you learn critical path method and are able to effectively use any one of the software packages available. The three programs to be discussed are the three that have the largest user base. They are Microsoft Project, of course from Microsoft, SureTrak Project Manager from Primavera, and Primavera Project Planner (P3), also from Primavera.

If you are managing large projects that are joint ventures with other companies, or projects where more than one project manager must be in the same schedule files at the same time (with different computers), the software choice is simple. Use P3. It is the only one that allows more than one person into the same schedule files at the same time. P3 is a powerful program that has been used on extremely large and complicated projects. Due to its power and capabilities, it is also more intimidating. Yet, it can be easy to learn if you stick to the basics and use it for fundamental scheduling. P3 is well written and has been the primary software choice for the commercial and industrial construction industries for many years. The current price for each copy of P3 is $5,000. However, if a company can save 1 week on a $4 million investment at 9 percent annual interest rate, the software has more than paid for itself (according to Chapter 2). From this point on, the company is saving money with the software. All future schedules are free—at least until the next upgrade. P3 will handle just about any kind of project and produce about any report imaginable.

The next two software programs, Microsoft Project and SureTrak Project Manager, are comparable in price. Microsoft Project retails at $599 and SureTrak retails at $499. They are both excellent choices. SureTrak is a junior version of P3. It is very similar to P3 in appearance and feel, however, it does not have the power of P3 but will do practically everything the single user needs in the way of project management. Being less powerful than P3, it is also easier to learn. SureTrak is also more Windows based than P3, with an Undo key, File and Save As commands, and other similar features.

With P3 you can create multiple target schedules, providing the opportunity to compare today's schedule with last month's schedule—or, to compare today's schedule with the as-planned schedule or any other update. Target schedules can be switched back and forth, whereas with SureTrak and Microsoft Project there may be only one baseline or target schedule at a time. When the target is updated to a new target, the old target is lost and comparisons to the older schedule can no longer be made.

If it is desirable to generate banana curves showing both the early S-curve and the late S-curve as discussed in Chapter 15, neither SureTrak nor Microsoft Project will perform that function. They only show either the early or the late S-curve. P3 will show both. Some managers state that SureTrak is more powerful and is more effective for heavy industrial and commercial scheduling needs than Microsoft Project. Due to the ease of importing SureTrak into P3, it is used by a large number of highway, industrial, and commercial firms. Many construction companies use SureTrak in the field and then import the schedule into P3 to meet owner contract requirements. That way they save considerable money by having several copies of SureTrak and only one copy of P3.

Outside the construction industry there is heavier use of Microsoft Project. Some experienced construction managers also prefer Microsoft Project because it uses all the familiar Microsoft conventions and thus is easier to learn and use. It also interfaces exceptionally well with other Microsoft programs such as Word and Excel. Residential construction companies that use CPM scheduling seem to be about split between Sure-Trak and Microsoft Project.

The above comments are strictly the opinion of the author based on extensive consulting and speaking experiences, and from contact with hundreds of commercial project managers and superintendents who attend the National Center for Construction Education and Research (NCCER) Academies taught at Clemson University four or five times a year, and from attendees at the International Builders Conference held by the National Association of Home Builders (NAHB) each year. Again, you must make your own comparisons and determine your own needs.

Ethically, it is important that software used by project managers is purchased, not copied. If the software is running on several machines by several project managers, a copy needs to be purchased for each computer. Keep in mind that if the software is used, it will pay for itself in a short period of time by reduced project time and better managed projects. Each of these programs is available for networked computers. If a company has 10 network licenses, then 10 managers can log on to use the software at one time. The 11th user will be denied access until someone else logs out. If company management expects suppliers, owners, and subcontractors to treat them fair and ethically, it goes both ways.

GENERAL SUGGESTIONS FOR COMPUTER REPORTS

Regardless of the software chosen, following are a few suggestions that might prevent some problems. As reports are developed, keep in mind that the purpose of the report is to communicate the schedule to the interested parties. Keep the reports as simple as possible to avoid overloading the receiver with nonpertinent information. Don't get caught up in fancy graphics and dazzling colors and fonts. One of the favorite reports used by experienced schedulers is a simple tabular report with columns of necessary information.

There are times when it is appropriate to create a graphical (such as a bar chart or a network) schedule that uses fancy graphics, dazzling colors, and varied fonts. When a schedule is needed in a presentation for a negotiated contract, that schedule needs to look organized, impressive, and professional. Sometimes, the monthly summary schedule delivered to the owner is also a graphical schedule with some enhancements. However, for day-to-day scheduling, keep the reports simple and don't overload people with too much information.

CONCLUSION

The advances of the computer have made it possible to effectively use CPM scheduling on construction projects today. In fact, the development of the personal computer caused a rebirth in the use of CPM. Practically all construction companies can benefit by learning to use this technology on their projects. It is important to not get discouraged by the amount of time it takes in becoming proficient with the basics of CPM or in learning how to use the software; it will pay off. There are excellent software programs available that can be learned, given some time and effort. Remember that as managers learn critical path method and the software, those managers have the potential to become more successful on every future project they will be involved in.

APPLICATION

1. Check the software company of choice to determine the availability of training in your geographical area.
2. Discuss with other project managers the learning process they went through to become proficient with the software.
3. Find out if there are any evening programs or classes in CPM and the software of choice, taught at major universities in your area.
4. If practical, arrange for several project managers and superintendents to be trained in your company facilities in the near future.
5. Dedicate some time each week to learn the CPM software program of choice.

CHAPTER 20

MANAGING PROJECTS USING PRIMAVERA PROJECT PLANNER (P3)

INTRODUCTION— PRIMAVERA PROJECT PLANNER VERSION 3.1

Primavera Project Planner, frequently referred to as "P3," is an extremely popular project management software program used by major construction firms. It is a product of Primavera Systems, Inc., headquartered in Bala Cynwyd, Pennsylvania. Contact information is listed at the end of this Chapter. Because P3 and SureTrak are both Primavera products, project scheduling information can be exchanged between the two. A major advantage to P3 as compared to SureTrak and Microsoft Project is that P3 has the capability of several managers creating and updating the same schedule at the same time.

The following instructions are presented chronologically and are based on *how managers use the software,* rather than explaining every detail and feature of the software. These instructions contain examples and assignments that teach how to use the software to communicate and manage the project. There is not unnecessary detail explaining how to do everything, rather, these chapters focus on helping you through the tough spots. However, these instructions are not foolproof and do not guarantee success. They are simply a guide to help you learn this dynamic program. If you find an error in the instructions, find a way around it. Keep in mind that with project management software it is not necessary to know everything in order to be an effective user. These instructions cover only the basics of P3. Learn these basics so you can start scheduling now, and then as you become proficient with scheduling you can learn additional details as you find a need for them. You will find this software to be extremely valuable in helping you control your projects rather than your projects controlling you.

The chapter starts by presenting many detail-instructions. As you work through the instructions, make sure you are thinking. Don't allow yourself to get into the mode of just carrying out the instructions without engaging your mind to make sure what you are doing is logical and makes sense. If you *think* as you do this, you will learn how to use P3. Don't get frustrated if everything doesn't work as you expect. Generally, with computer software, you learn the most when things go wrong. Keep thinking and trying and you will figure it out. Once you have followed the instructions in detail and accomplished a task, it is assumed you learned that task and from then on the instructions pertaining to that task will be less detailed. So, if later in the chapter you forget the details on how to do a task, go back to the beginning of the chapter to review the details pertaining to that task.

USING THE HELP BUTTONS

The Help buttons are very useful for when you feel lost or confused. There is also a Help feature and a tutorial under **Help** on the Menu bar. Each P3 window also displays a Help button that will provide help directly for that window. The schedules generated in this tutorial included on the CD accompanying this text are an additional source of help. They are contained in the P3 folder. These schedules are provided only as reference materials and contain the example exercises.

The schedule shown in Figure 20.1 for the construction of a warehouse will be used to help learn P3.

It shows the network logic diagram developed during a meeting with the management team.

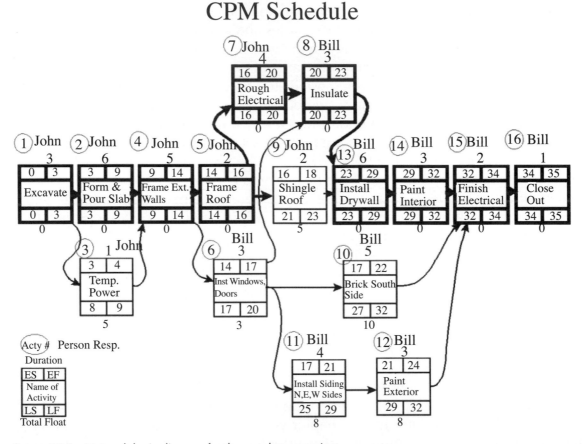

FIGURE 20.1   Network logic diagram for the warehouse project

The warehouse is to be supervised by two superintendents: Bill and John. John is particularly good at overseeing the earthwork and the structure activities. Bill will be brought in to manage the finishing activities, basically from the insulation to completion. The number in the circle represents the activity ID number. The 35 work days calculated to complete the project is in accordance with the contract provisions.

You are now ready to computerize the schedule.

MAKING A NEW PROJECT FILE

Load P3 from the Windows Program Manager. A user name and password is required in order for the program to boot. Obtain the user name and password from your computer specialist. Or, as the software was loaded that information was input. After the program comes up, create a new project file by going to the Menu bar and clicking on **File, New.**

Note: Use the following information to answer the setup questions at the beginning of the project. *Do not use the Enter key as you go from field to field; instead use the Tab key, arrow keys, or the mouse.* If you make a mistake and use the Enter key before entering all the information, P3 assumes you are done with that screen and it closes. To get it back to the Project Overview screen click on **File** from the Menu bar and then choose **Project Overview** to reopen this window.

The project name must be exactly four characters. Some managers prefer to use the first two characters to identify the project. For example, WH for this warehouse project. The last two characters are to identify the update number—for example, 00. The first or as-planned schedule would, therefore, be WH00. Then, as the project is updated, this first schedule will be copied and named WH01 for the updates through the first month. WH02 will be used for the updates through the second month, and so on.

Number/Version	"As Planned"
Project title	"Warehouse"
Company name	Enter your company name
Planning unit	Choose "Day" by clicking on the down arrow button and then selecting "Day."
Workdays/week	5
Week starts on	Monday
Project start	Enter next Tuesday's (date, or whatever is realsitic.)
Project must finish by	Leave blank—enter nothing. If you enter a date the backward pass will be computed based on this date, likely giving either negative or positive float.
Decimal places	Choose 2

Don't add the project to a project group (leave the check box blank). The Add a New Project dialog box should look similar to Figure 20.2.

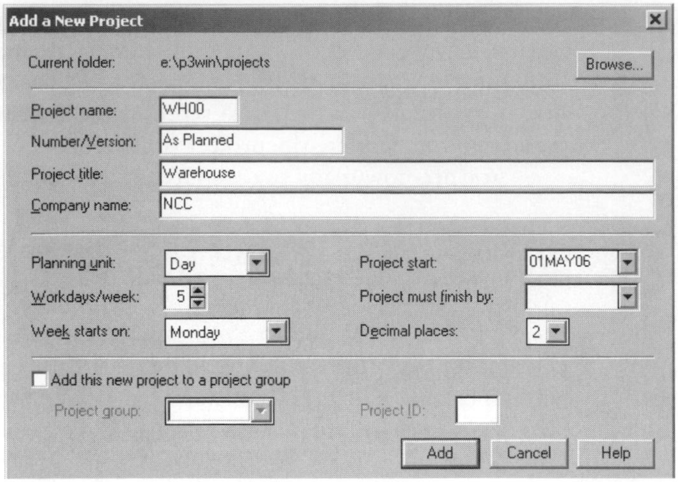

FIGURE 20.2 Create a new file in the Add a New Project dialog box

Notice the Browse button at the top right of the dialog box. You can use this to change the directory to where you want the file written, generally defaulted to the p3win/projects folder on the C drive of your computer or, if you are on a network, to whatever folder you want to save your schedules to.

Click on the **Add** button to accept this information and the computer will now begin creating this project. For your information, this program just created about 23 files for this project. It is not simply one file to copy or write to. This software is not like word processing or spreadsheets, where you are working in only one file at a time. Keep this in mind as you copy projects and files.

SETTING UP THE CALENDARS

Before you input activities and activity data you should set up the general parameters of the schedule. First we will set up the calendars for P3 to use. Do this by selecting **Data** and then **Calendars** on the Menu bar. (If Data is gray and not functional, press the Escape key to activate the Menu bar.)

Set the **Global Calendar** by clicking on **Global calendar.** Then make the following days as annual repeating holidays: Jan 1 (click on the Holidays button and then the plus (+) button). With the *right* mouse, click under **Start** and choose 01 Jan. Press the **OK** button. Have it **End** on 01 Jan. Then put a check mark in the repeating box by clicking in it twice. Add July 4, Dec 25, and any other holidays you want to set up as an annual repeating holiday.

To set up Thanksgiving, or other nonwork days that are not repeating, just click on the day and then click on **Nonwork.** The *G* means it is on the global calendar and the *R* is for repeating.

Next, check calendar #1 (click on 1-) and then **Standard.** Title it as your **5 day** calendar and put check marks on Monday through Friday and **OK** it. Click on the **Add**

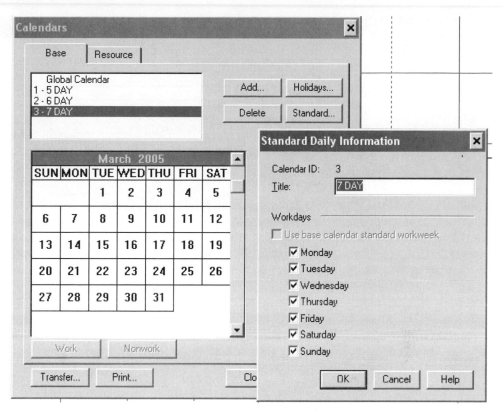

FIGURE 20.3   Calendars and Standard Daily Information dialog boxes

button to add calendar #2 and give it a name of **6 day** and make sure Monday through Saturday is checked (click on the Standard button). Then add calendar #3 as a seven-day calendar with all days of the week checked. The calendars should look similar to Figure 20.3.

You are now done with the calendars, so click on the **Close** button. You now have a five-, six-, or seven-day calendar that can be used for the various trades according to their work schedule and a global calendar that oversees all the individual calendars. You can create many more calendars as needed with additional holidays, and so on.

DEFINING ACTIVITY CODES

Next, set up the **Activity Codes (Data, Activity Codes).** First, delete the default codes **(minus (−) button or Delete key).** Create the first code by clicking on the **plus (+) button.** Give it a name of **"Supr,"** with **6 characters** in Length and description of **"Superintendent."** The second code will be **"Subs"** for the subcontractors and it will be **6** characters in length also, with a description of **"Subcontractors."**

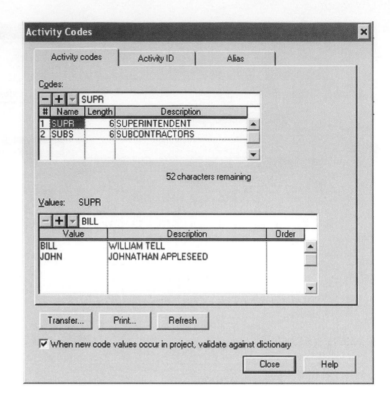

Now set the code **values.** To set the codes for the superintendents, highlight **Supr** at the top of the window (if it asks to save the structure edits, click yes) and enter the code values for **Bill** and then **John.** In the "Description" column you can give a full name, such as William Tell or whatever it is. Figure 20.4 shows how the Activity Codes dialog box should appear.

To set the code values for the subcontractors, highlight or select **Subs** in the Codes section and then type in a code value and description for each sub needed to complete the project being scheduled. When naming subs it is recommended you use the trade name, rather than real names, so that when you change subs you won't need to edit this field. For example, you might use a code title of Elect with a description of Electrician, rather than Mountain Electric.

Click on the down arrow to continue entering the subs and their descriptions. When finished with the activity codes, close the Activity Codes dialog box by clicking on the **Close** button.

Now that you have the basic parameters of the schedule, the calendar, and the activity codes defined it is time to enter the activity data. But before doing so, in order to have the activity ID number added automatically you will need to set the activity ID to be inserted by increments of 1. Do this by selecting from the Menu bar **Tools, Options, Activity Inserting,** and automatically number the activities to increment by 1. The Activity Inserting Options dialog box should look like Figure 20.5.

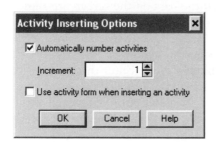

FIGURE 20.5 Use the Activity Inserting Options dialog box to automatically number activities in the increment desired

Primavera Project Planner - [W000]

File Edit View Insert Format Tools Data

Activity ID	Activity Description	Orig Dur
1	EXCAVATE	3
2	FORM & POUR SLAB	6
3	INST. TEMP POWER	1
4	FRAME EXT. WALLS	5
5	FRAME ROOF	2
6	RGH ELECTRICAL	4
7	INSULATE	3
8	SHINGLE ROOF	2
9	INST. WINDOWS & DOORS	3
10	INST. DRYWALL	6
11	BRICK SOUTH SIDE	5
12	SIDING, N.E. & W. SIDE	4
13	PAINT EXTERIOR	3
14	PAINT INTERIOR	3
15	FINISH ELECTRICAL	2
16	CLOSE OUT	1

FIGURE 20.6 Activity table with data entered

INPUTTING ACTIVITY DATA

There are three methods of inputting activity information: 1) Use the cells in the rows and columns area, (the activity table). (2) using the Activity Form, or (3) using the PERT view.

Input Using the Activity Table

You are now ready to input the individual activities from the schedule. Click in the first cell under "Activity ID" and enter the **Activity ID** number then click on the **check mark** button (on the edit bar) or press the Enter key to accept your input (see Figure 20.6). You will find this consistent throughout the program. To accept the data, select the check mark button or press the Enter key. Simply clicking on a new cell does not always save the last data input. Each activity must have a number assigned to it. You could use the numbers on the hand-drawn schedule or you could use the default numbers supplied by P3. It is typically easier to assign predecessors if you put activity ID numbers on the hand-drawn logic diagram and then input those same numbers.

Enter the activity **Description** or task name, then click on the check mark button. Next, enter the **Original Duration.** To get the *"Orig Dur"* column to show, position the mouse over the bold vertical line until the cursor turns into two vertical lines and then click and drag the line to the right to expose the column.

Repeat this for all the activities by clicking on the **plus (+) button** to add a new activity. If you cannot edit the "Activity ID" column proceed as follows: Close the project you are in by clicking on File, Close. After it closes, open it back up by clicking on File, Open. Highlight the name of your project by clicking on it and then find the little exclusive box and put a check mark in the box to give you exclusive rights to that project, and then OK it. (If a manager has exclusive rights, no other manager can access the same project.) At this point your screen should have the activities input as shown in Figure 20.6.

ASSIGN PREDECESSORS.   Once all the activities are entered you will assign the predecessors. You'll notice that all the bars on the screen are showing the same start date. This is because you have not told the computer which activities precede each other; the logic has not been input yet. Assign predecessors by selecting **View, Activity Detail,** and then **Predecessors.** Slide the window to a favorable position on the screen by clicking and dragging on the blue heading. Enter the predecessors to each activity by entering the predecessor activity ID. You do not need to enter the activity description. The computer knows the description associated with the ID. Double-check the hand-drawn logic diagram in and make sure the predecessors are correct. If there are lags, they are also entered at this time. The Predecessors window should look like Figure 20.7 for the *Form & Pour Slab* activity.

Carefully assign all predecessors to each activity. When finished, close the Predecessors window.

You do not need to exit P3 now, but when you are ready, do it properly.

1. Click on the *X* in the upper right corner to properly exit P3.
2. Then close Windows by clicking on the Start button at the bottom left corner of the screen and choose Shut Down. After Windows shuts down you can turn off the computer. If you do not exit Windows properly, files remain open which may fragment some of the files and cause you problems in the future.

Note: There is no File, Save or File, Save As option. P3 automatically saves all changes to the disk. Keep this in mind if you want to experiment with a schedule. Copy it first to a new name **(Tools, Project Utilities, Copy** and give it a new name under **Project Group)** so that you don't ruin the original schedule.

CALCULATE THE SCHEDULE.   You'll notice there still seems to be no predecessors assigned; the bars are still not staggered. That's because you haven't made the computer do the **forward and backward passes.** Do this by clicking on the tool

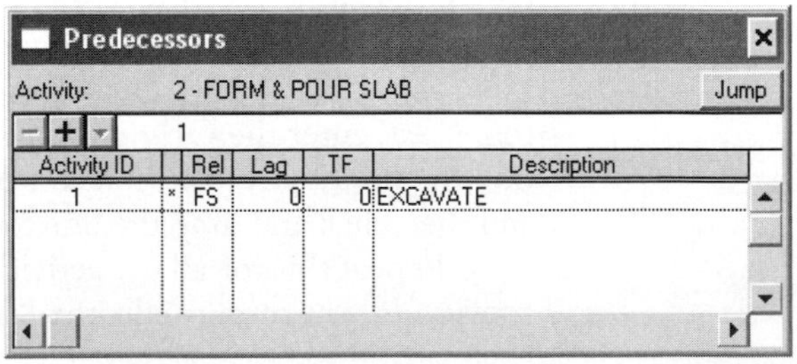

FIGURE 20.7
Predecessors window for
Form & Pour Slab

button that looks like a clock button 🕐. The **Data Date** is the start date of the schedule or the date of the update. The schedule button 🕐 gives you a calculations report. Look at the report to see if it makes sense. Close this report window by clicking on the *X* in the upper right of the window; you don't need to save the changes. Now you see a normal-looking bar chart with float similar to Figure 20.8.

Notice how the bars are shown in their proper location depending on their predecessors. Your schedule may look a little different due to the start date and the way the bars are formatted. However, the bars should be in their proper positions.

You can also have the computer calculate the forward and backward passes by pressing the F-9 key, which does the calculations, but does not provide the report.

ENTER ACTIVITY CODES.   Next enter the **activity codes** you set up a few minutes ago for the superintendents and subcontractors. Select **View, Activity Detail,** and then **Codes.** Highlight the activity first and then enter the activity codes (superintendent and subcontractor) for that activity. To assign the codes either right-click or click on the down arrow. If you forgot to create some activity codes you can enter them here and they will automatically be entered in the activity codes section. The activity codes for *Excavate* should look as in Figure 20.9.

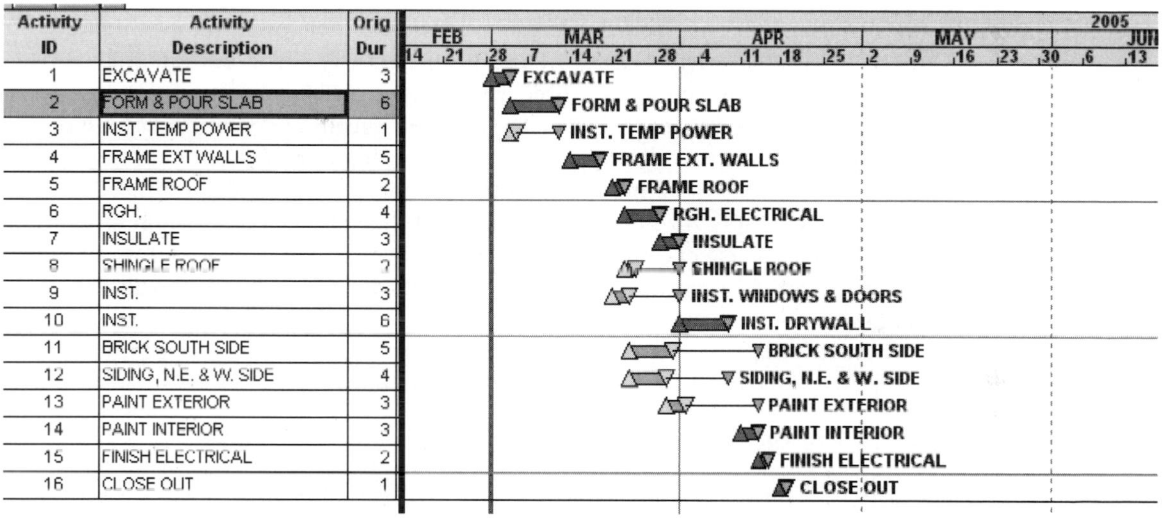

FIGURE 20.8   Bar chart showing total float

FIGURE 20.9   Activity Codes window for *Excavate*

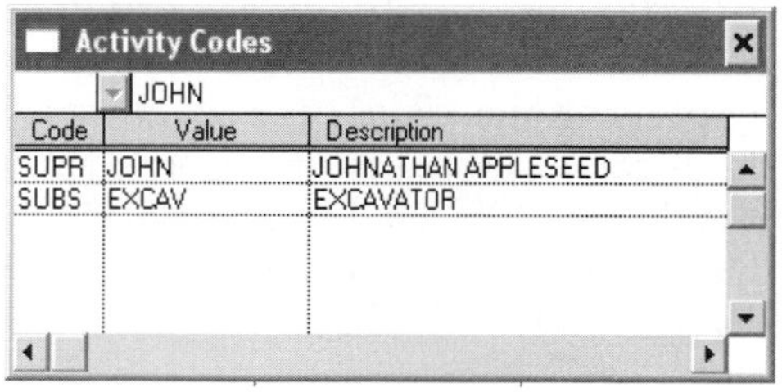

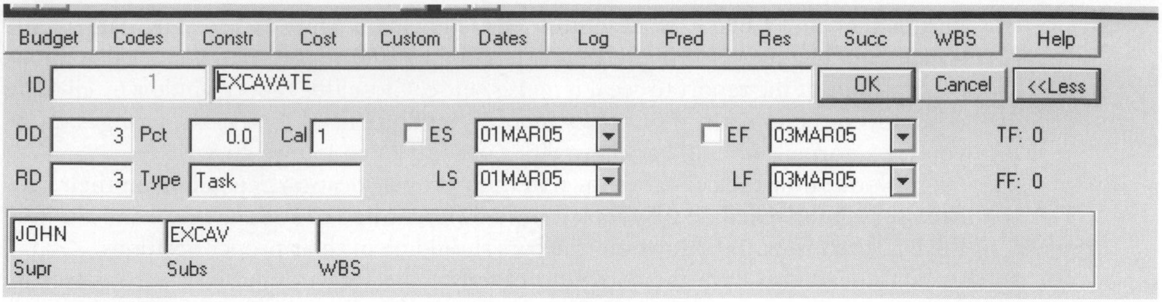

FIGURE 20.10   Activity form for *Excavate* with data entered

After entering all the activity codes (supr and subs) for each activity, close the Activity Codes dialog box. Some schedulers prefer to input all the information for one activity at a time, leaving the Predecessors window open and inputting all information for each activity, rather than the way we did it.

Input Using the Activity Form

Now input that same basic schedule again using the activity form. To open the activity form select **View, Activity Form** or click on the Activity Form button 🔲 . Predecessors are assigned by opening the predecessors window by selecting the **Pred** button at the top of the activity form. Click on the plus (+) button to create a new activity and then enter all the activity information in the activity form at the bottom of the screen. Don't input dates or remaining duration (RD); they are calculated. You need to deal with only the **ID, Activity Name, OD, Cal,** and the **activity codes** (Supr and Subs). All this information is entered using the activity form. Assign the predecessors as before using the Predecessors window. The activity form for *Excavate* will look like Figure 20.10.

After entering one activity, OK it and use the plus (+) button to start the next activity input. Continue until all the activities are input.

Input Using the PERT View

Now input the same basic schedule for the third time using the PERT view; click **View, PERT.** Play with this one; you will like it. Double-click where you want to create a new activity box and the activity box appears and the activity form shows at the bottom of the screen. Fill in the activity form just as before. To assign predecessors, click and drag from the end of the predecessor's activity box to the beginning of the successor's activity box. After predecessors are assigned calculate the schedule by pressing the F9 key. Notice all the critical activities are shown in red. Activity boxes can be moved to other locations by clicking on the activity box and dragging it to the new location. It is easier to input if the PERT view looks similar to the hand-drawn logic diagram. The PERT view with the activities input should look similar to Figure 20.11.

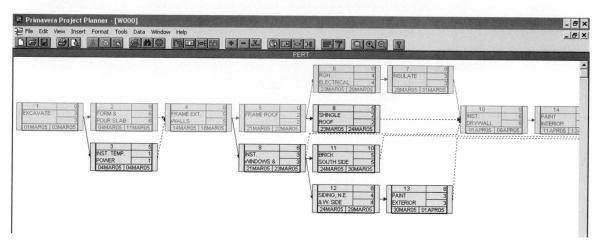

FIGURE 20.11   The PERT view with the activities input

To change the configuration of the activity box or node, click on **Format, Activity Box Configuration.** Then select **Modify Template** to have the activity box contain your information of choice. **Format** the **Relationships** to be **Direct** so they are easier to see. Experiment with other formatting options such as **View, Trace Logic,** and the **Cosmic View.** To return to the Bar chart view select **View, Bar Chart.**

Now that you know how to input the schedule using the three common methods, it is time to learn some of the abilities of the software to help you understand the schedule and manage the project.

ORGANIZING THE SCHEDULE

You will now notice that the bars show the proper start and finish dates on the screen, but the activities may not be listed in the desired order. To make them appear in chronological order or early start, early finish order, *organize* the schedule. Click on **Format,** then **Organize** (or click on the Organize icon on the tool bar) 🖿 and then change **Sort by** (bottom right of the dialog box) to **Early Start** and then **Early Finish** in ascending order. To do this, click in the cell and right-mouse click, then choose the order desired. It should show Early start in the first row and Early finish in the second row, in ascending order as shown in Figure 20.12.

Click on **Organize Now** and notice how good looking the bar chart is! It is in true chronological order of early start and early finish sequence. If two activities start on the same date the one with the earliest finish is listed first. Also notice the float and the critical (red) activities.

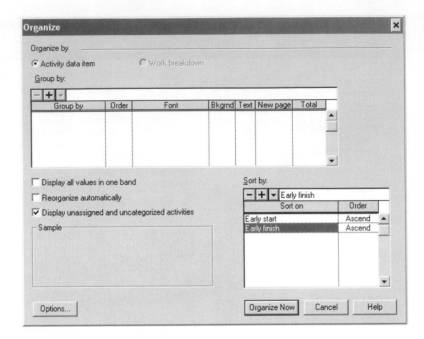

FIGURE 20.12 Organize activities to be sorted in chronological order, or early start, early finish order

Group Like Activities Together

Grouping similar activities is part of organizing the schedule. On the Menu bar, click on **Format, Organize,** and then **Group** by Superintendent. Now you see all of John's activities grouped together and the same with Bill's activities. You can summarize these bars to one bar by double-clicking on their name. The + next to their name signifies there is more detail under these bars. To expand them back, double-click again.

Check the Number of Days to Complete

To change the organization again, click **Format,** then **Organize** (or click on the Organize icon ![icon]). Under "Group by" right-click and choose "Project." Under "Total" select "Bottom." The Organize dialog box should look like Figure 20.13. Then click on **Organize Now.** Go to the bottom of the project (last activity), and slide the vertical bold line to the right to expose the duration column and note the total number of days after the last activity. For the warehouse project it should be 35 days. This is the total duration in work days for the project. If you have completed a forward pass by hand, this total duration should match your calculations.

Another way to check the total duration is to highlight the last activity, right-click in the column area, select **Activity Detail,** then **Dates,** and you see the dates and days in work days. Check some of the other dates with your hand-drawn schedule and note that P3 takes care of the end-of-day problem with the ES and LS dates.

FIGURE 20.13 Group the activities by project and total at the bottom to see the total duration

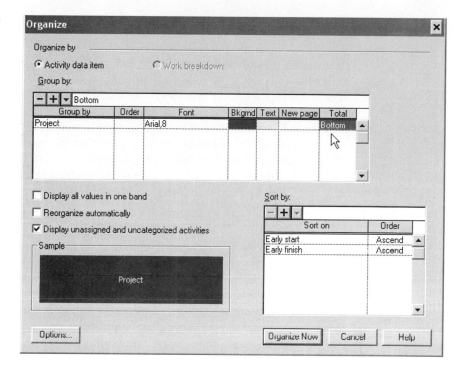

FILTERING FOR SPECIFIC ACTIVITIES

Filters help you focus on specific areas of a project by listing only those activities that match criteria you specify. Choose an existing filter or add a new one at the Filter dialog box. For example, to add a new filter for critical activities only, click Format, Filter (or select the Format Filters icon on the toolbar ▼) and then click the plus (+) button. Accept the number P3 assigns and enter a logical description such as **Critical Activities Only.** Then click Edit to specify (or, in some cases, to review) the filter criteria. Under "Select if" right-click and choose Total Float; under "Is" select Less than; and under "Low value" select 1. Press OK and then Run. Now you see only the critical activities.

Filter for all the activities John is responsible for. Create a new filter where Superintendent is equal to John and run it.

To get all the activities back, filter again and choose "All Activities." (All Activities is always at the top). Run it and all the activities appear again.

FORMATTING BAR CHARTS

The following sections explain how to format standard bar charts using P3.

Change the Date/Timescale

The timescale is the calendar heading that appears above the bar chart. To change a date, slide the bold vertical line to the left of the screen, exposing only the activity ID and the activity description. Now, move the cursor to the colored (yellow default) dates area at the top of the bar chart and double-click, or select Format, Timescale. Change the start date to SD −1d (*d* stands for days, *w* for weeks, or *m* for months) and the finish date to FD+ 10d. This shows the amount of timescale prior to the first activity and after the last activity. Change the Minimum time increment to **Days.** Next, slide the Density button (on top) all the way to the right, then **OK** it. Notice how long the bars are. If you want to change to a smaller scale, double-click again in the yellow heading area and slide the Density bar to the left, to the density or timescale you desire.

Format the Columns

To format the activity Columns, of information to the left of the bar chart slide the bold vertical line further to the right of the screen, exposing more of the columnar information and less of the bar chart. (If you slide it to the extreme right you lose it. To get it back, click and drag on the thin black line just to the right of the right arrow key on the bottom of the window.) To reformat the columns, click on Format, Columns, or select the Format Columns icon ▦ . This brings up the Columns dialog box. Delete some of the columns and create new ones—use the minus (−) and plus (+) buttons— to get a feel for this part of the program. Also change some column titles to any description you want. You can change the width, alignment, and font as desired also.

      Another way to change the column width is to simply click and drag the separation line between the column titles. Or, if you just want to change one column, double-click on its heading.

Format the Sight Lines

Sight lines are vertical and horizontal lines that help you visually locate specific information. You can choose which sight lines display and the interval at which they display. You can change sight lines at the Sight Lines dialog box. On the Menu bar, select **Format, Sight Lines** and change the **Vertical Sight Lines** to have a major sight line every one **week** and a minor sight line every **day.**

Format the Bars

At the Bars dialog box, you can choose the bars and endpoints you want to show, and customize their size, style, and color. On the Menu bar, select **Format, Bars** and then enter or remove the check mark on the float bar to make float visible or not visible as desired. You will learn more details about formatting bars later in the chapter.

Format the Screen Colors

You can select colors to emphasize various elements of your layout at the Screen Colors dialog box. On the Menu bar, select **Format, Screen Colors,** select Red, and then click on OK. To get the standard screen color back select P3 Defaults.

Create a New Layout

The overall design of a document is called the layout. The way the design appears on a computer screen is called the screen layout. In P3 you can format your own layout and save the layout specifications to use again, or you can choose from a number of P3 predefined layouts that can be modified to fit your needs. Use the Layout dialog box to create, select, or modify a layout. To save layout specifications, click on **View, Layout, Save As** and title it as you desire—for example, "My favorite layout." Then select that layout by clicking on **View, Layout, Open** or selecting the Layout button 🖳 . The title of the layout you are using is shown at the bottom of the screen in the center box.

Make a new standard bar chart layout that shows only the original duration and the start and finish dates in the columns area. **Format** the **columns** and delete every column and its data except "Original Duration", "Early Start", and "Early Finish". OK the columns and slide the vertical bold line to the edge of the "Early Finish" column and you have your standard bar chart layout. Now save it to a new name by selecting **View, Layout, Save As**, and give it the title of "Standard Bar Chart" and then **Save** it.

To select another layout, click on the Layout button 🖳 and then select the layout desired from the list and **Open** it.

As mentioned earlier in this chapter, the Help buttons are great in P3—most managers use them frequently. Click on Help on the Menu bar and then search for any topic of interest. Also click on the Contents tab and try it out. To close the Help window click on the *X* in the upper right corner of that window. The tutorial is also helpful. There is also a Help button in any dialog box you are working in. Just click on Format, Columns and then select the Help button and read it.

SETTING UP AND PRINTING STANDARD REPORTS

Now that you understand some of the basics of P3, proceed with setting up and then printing the following reports. Each of these reports is to be printed so you can gain experience with the software.

Report 1. Input Check Report

I recommend that you get in the habit of always checking the information you input prior to printing reports. It is confusing and embarrassing to send out reports that are incorrect.

First, we will print a pure logic diagram to check the logic. Select **View, PERT** from the Menu bar. Choose Format, Activity Box Configuration. Select Logic Review-Early Dates. Then click the Modify Template button. In the Name section enter a new name: **Logic Review-Total.** Edit the node or activity box to include all input items. Insert or delete rows, split cells, or delete cells as desired. In this case the input items to check are in these fields: **Activity ID, Original Duration, Description, Superintendent,** and **Subcontractor.** The Modify Template dialog box should look similar to Figure 20.14.

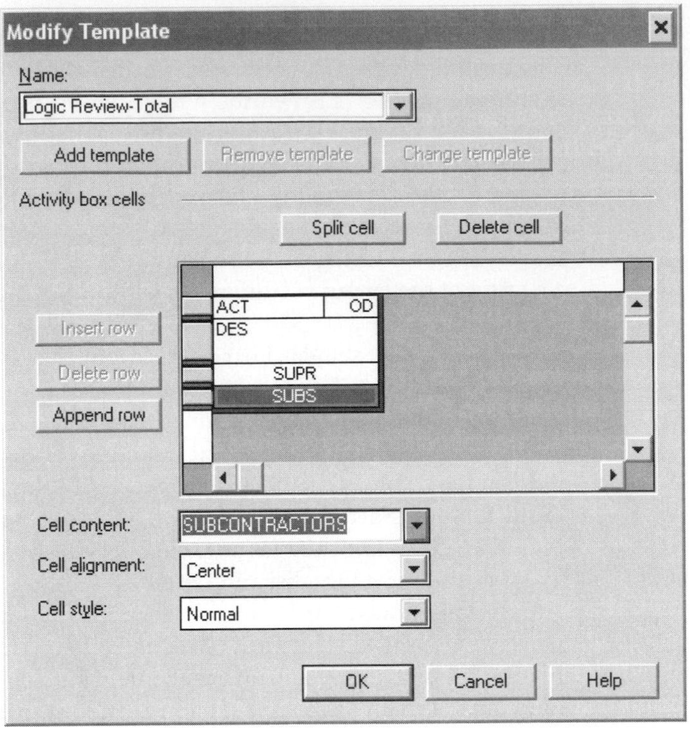

FIGURE 20.14 Use the Modify Template dialog box to change the data in the activity box

Click OK and save the template. You could even move the activity boxes to locations that match the hand drawn schedule if you desire by clicking and dragging the node or activity box.

To make the relationship lines easier to follow, from the Menu line select **Format** then **Relationships** and change the relationships to be **Direct** rather than Separate.

Preview the input check report before printing it. Click **File, Print Preview**, or click on the **Print Preview** button [image]. Then, to change the report to landscape orientation, click on the **Print Setup** button [image] and select **Landscape.** Now, if it looks right, print this report by clicking on the Print button. The report should look similar to Figure 20.15.

If you have input a lot of other information, such as costs and resources, you might want to print a simple tabular report to check that input and use the PERT view report (see Figure 20.11) to check your logic. Consider the following columns: "Activity ID," "Description," "Original Duration," "Calendar," "Superintendent," "Subcontractor," "Predecessors," "Resource," and "Budgeted Cost."

If you have input many lags and want **to check out the type and amount of lags** (start-to-start, finish-to-finish, finish-to-start, and start-to-finish) associated with each activity, it is easiest to do so by selecting **View, Activity Detail,** and then opening the **Predecessors window.** Then scroll down through the activities checking the prede-

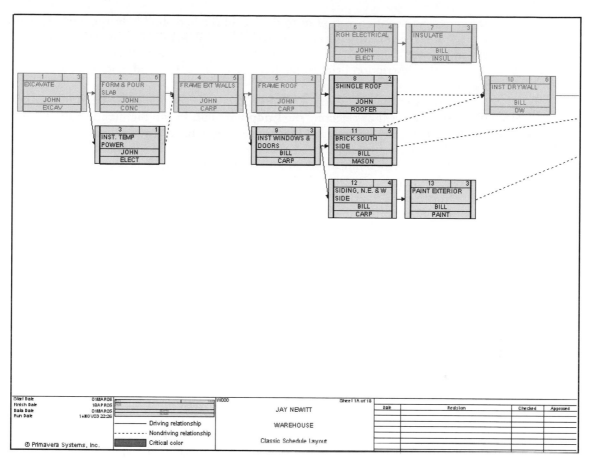

FIGURE 20.15   Logic diagram to check computer input

cessor type and the amount of lag. Having two people do this, one reading the hand-drawn logic diagram and the other the screen, makes this job faster and more accurate.

Report 2. Project Manager's Bar Chart Report

This report will be a rather typical bar chart designed to be used by the project manager who likes to see float. Make sure the activities are listed in chronological or ES, EF sequence or order by clicking on the **Organize** icon and sorting on Early Start and then Early Finish in ascending order.

We desire to show the activity title next to the bars, rather than in the columns to the left. So format the columns to include only the "Activity ID," "Original Duration," and "Superintendent." Align the Activity ID and Duration with the center of the column. Delete the other column data and then click on **Organize Now.**

Format the bars (click on Format, Bars, or select the Format Bars icon on the toolbar) to make the **Early Bar** and the **Float Bar Visible.** Then, to make sure the activity description will print to the left of the bars, highlight the Early Bar and then click on the **Modify button** to open the Modify Bar dialog box. Select the **Label** tab and under "Data" choose "**Activity description.**" Under "Position" select "**Left**" to make the description print to the left of the bar. **OK** it and close the modify dialog box.

If the triangles are showing (endpoints) on the beginning and end of the bars, they can be deleted by selecting the **Endpoints** button and highlighting all start and finish endpoints by clicking and dragging a rubber band around them. Next select a shape that is blank (just after the stars) and OK the Endpoints box and the Bars dialog box. This makes for a more normal-looking bar chart that does not show the triangle start and endpoints.

Now change the **timescale** by selecting **Format, Timescale** or clicking on the portion of the bar chart (yellow, where the dates are) to bring up the Timescale dialog box. Change the Start date to SD −4d and the End date to FD+ 10d. Also change the Minimum time unit to days and then slide the Density button at the top of the dialog box to the right or left, while watching the timescale in the background until the individual days (not just Monday dates) appear in the column headings.

Format the vertical sight lines (**Format, Sight Lines**) to have Major sight lines on the Weeks and Minor sight lines on the Days.

Preview it by clicking on **File, Print Preview** or the Print Preview icon on the toolbar ![icon]. Make sure it is in Landscape orientation (Print Setup icon ![icon]), and it should all fit on one page. If there are no bars showing the timescale may be incorrect. The timescale in Print Preview is not carried over from the Bar chart view. To correct this, click on the **Page Setup** icon and make sure the **Start** date shows SD −4d and the **End** date shows FD+10 days or as desired as you did in the Bar chart view. You can change many options of the report from here, prior to printing the report. When the report looks acceptable, click on the Print icon and it prints exactly as it looks on the Print Preview screen. The report should look similar to Figure 20.16.

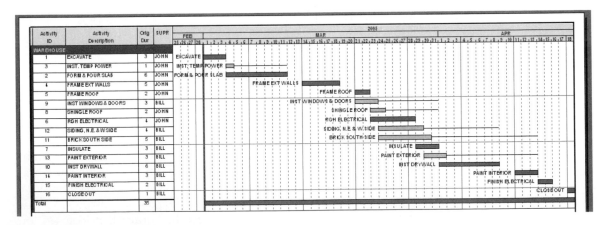

FIGURE 20.16 Project manager's bar chart report showing float

To go back to the Bar chart window click on the Close button.

Save this layout by selecting **View, Layout, Save As;** name the layout Project Manager's Bar Chart. Note at the bottom center of your screen that the name "Project Managers Bar Chart" now appears. The layout has been saved to that name. If you want to use the same layout in the future you can find it by clicking on **View, Layout, Open** or click on the Layouts icon.

Report 3. Subcontractor's Bar Chart Report

We now need a schedule that can be given to all the subcontractors. Make the report an Early Start Daily bar chart of all activities, without showing float. Include column information 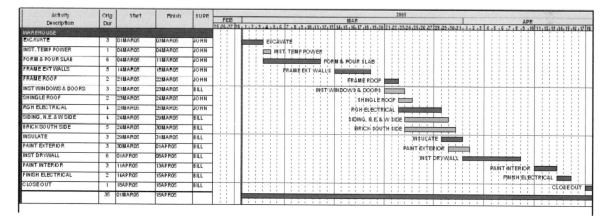 of "Activity Description", "Original Duration", "Early Start", "Early Finish", and "Superintendent". Name the title of the ES column "Start" and the EF column "Finish" by editing the Title in the Columns dialog box.

Preview the printout and make final adjustments prior to printing it. Adjust the timescale to take up the whole page. If you like it, save the layout (View, Layout, Save As) to a new name so that you will always have it and not need to recreate it again. While you are in Print Preview you might also play around with the headings and footings by selecting the Page Setup, tool button or the header or footer tool buttons on the Print Preview toolbar. The report should look similar to Figure 20.17.

Report 4. Subcontractor's Tabular Report

This report will be similar to the last one except it will be printed in portrait orientation and will not include any bars, just the column information.

Format the columns to include "Description", "Duration", "ES" (title ES as "Scheduled Start"), "EF" (title EF as "Scheduled Finish"), "Superintendent", "Actual Start", and "Actual Finish". OK the layout.

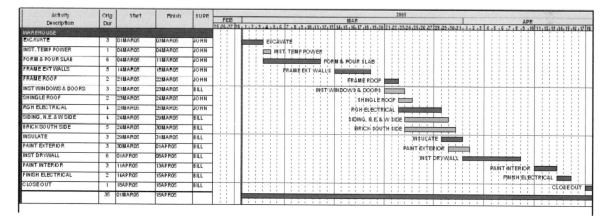

FIGURE 20.17   Subcontractor's bar chart report not showing float

Print preview it and then click on the **Print Setup** tool button and make the page orientation **Portrait** and OK it. Click on the **Page Setup** tool button and **remove the check mark in front of Bars** and OK it. Look at the report. You may want to close the Print Preview screen and go back into the default bar chart part of the program and increase the width of the columns to give the subs more room to write in the actual start and finish dates, and so on. When it looks good, print it. Save the layout to a new name.

Report 5. Owner's Bar Chart Report

To keep the owner from being alarmed if the project goes to the late start dates, make each bar a late start, late finish bar, listed in LS, LF sequence. Don't show any signs of ES, EF or float. Make sense? You may want to review Chapter 12 of this text for additional information on creating bar charts and tabular reports for specific people.

For column information include the "Activity Description", "Duration", "LS", and "LF Dates" (only label the LS and LF dates as "Start Date" and "Finish Date"). To show *Late* on the first line of the column heading and *Start* on the bottom line, enter a | between *Late* and *Start*. The | on typical keyboards is the shift backslash key.

On the Menu bar, click on **Format, Bars** so that the Late bar is visible and everything else is not visible. Close the Bars dialog box and you will notice the activity description is no longer listed next to the bar. To list the description next to the bars, go back into the Bars dialog box and with **Late bar highlighted, Modify it.** Change the label so that the "Data item" column shows the activity description and position it above (Top) of the bar and OK it.

As you look at the screen, notice that all the bars with float have shifted to the right, the LS and LF dates. It is particularly noticeable on the *Inst. Temp. Power* activity.

Also notice that the bars seem to be out of chronological order. **Organize** them to be sorted by **Late Start, Late Finish** order. The final report should look similar to Figure 20.18. Print preview the report and make the format landscape (make sure the bars show). Save the layout and name it something like Owner's Report so you can use it in the future.

Report 6. Critical Activities Only Report

This report will be a bar chart of the critical activities only, in ES, EF sequence.

Click Format, Filter, or select the **Filter icon** on the toolbar. Select the critical activities only, or add a new filter that selects only the critical activities. If you need a new filter, add it and title it **Critical Actys Only.** Under "Select if" right-click and select under "IS" choose Less than; and under "Low value" select 1. Total Float; **OK** it and then Run.

Organize the activities to be in sorted in ES, EF order. The report should look similar to Figure 20.19.

Now you only see the critical activities. Print preview it and print it with the necessary adjustments.

Activity Description	Orig Dur	Start Date	Finish Date	
WAREHOUSE				
EXCAVATE	3	01MAR05	03MAR05	EXCAVATE
FORM & POUR SLAB	6	04MAR05	11MAR05	FORM & POUR SLAB
INST. TEMP POWER	1	11MAR05	11MAR05	INST. TEMP POWER
FRAME EXT WALLS	5	14MAR05	18MAR05	FRAME EXT WALLS
FRAME ROOF	2	21MAR05	22MAR05	FRAME ROOF
RGH ELECTRICAL	4	23MAR05	28MAR05	RGH ELECTRICAL
INSULATE	3	29MAR05	31MAR05	INSULATE
INST WINDOWS & DOORS	3	29MAR05	31MAR05	INST WINDOWS & DOORS
SHINGLE ROOF	2	30MAR05	31MAR05	SHINGLE ROOF
INST DRYWALL	6	01APR05	08APR05	INST DRYWALL
SIDING, N.E. & W SIDE	4	05APR05	08APR05	SIDING, N.E. & W SIDE
BRICK SOUTH SIDE	5	07APR05	13APR05	BRICK SOUTH SIDE
PAINT EXTERIOR	3	11APR05	13APR05	PAINT EXTERIOR
PAINT INTERIOR	3	11APR05	13APR05	PAINT INTERIOR
FINISH ELECTRICAL	2	14APR05	15APR05	FINISH ELECTRICAL
CLOSE OUT	1	18APR05	18APR05	CLOSE
	35	01MAR05	18APR05	

FIGURE 20.18 Bar chart designed for the owner with the late bars showing

Activity Description	Orig Dur	Start Date	Finish Date	
WAREHOUSE				
EXCAVATE	3	01MAR05	03MAR05	EXCAVATE
FORM & POUR SLAB	6	04MAR05	11MAR05	FORM & POUR SLAB
FRAME EXT WALLS	5	14MAR05	18MAR05	FRAME EXT WALLS
FRAME ROOF	2	21MAR05	22MAR05	FRAME ROOF
RGH ELECTRICAL	4	23MAR05	28MAR05	RGH ELECTRICAL
INSULATE	3	29MAR05	31MAR05	INSULATE
INST DRYWALL	6	01APR05	08APR05	INST DRYWALL
PAINT INTERIOR	3	11APR05	13APR05	PAINT INTERIOR
FINISH ELECTRICAL	2	14APR05	15APR05	FINISH ELECTRICAL
CLOSE OUT	1	18APR05	18APR05	CLOSE
	35	01MAR05	18APR05	

FIGURE 20.19 Critical activities only filtered report

Report 7. Separate Bar Chart for Each Superintendent

Now make a separate bar chart for each superintendent that includes his or her activities only. To get all the activities back, remove any filters (**Format, Filter,** and choose the first entry "All Activities"). Format the columns as follows: "Activity ID", "Subs", "Actual Start", and "Actual Finish". Format the bars in their early start position and show float. Have the activity description on top of the bar, the ES date to the left of the bar, and the EF date to the rightmost of the bar. Organize the report by sorting by **ES,**

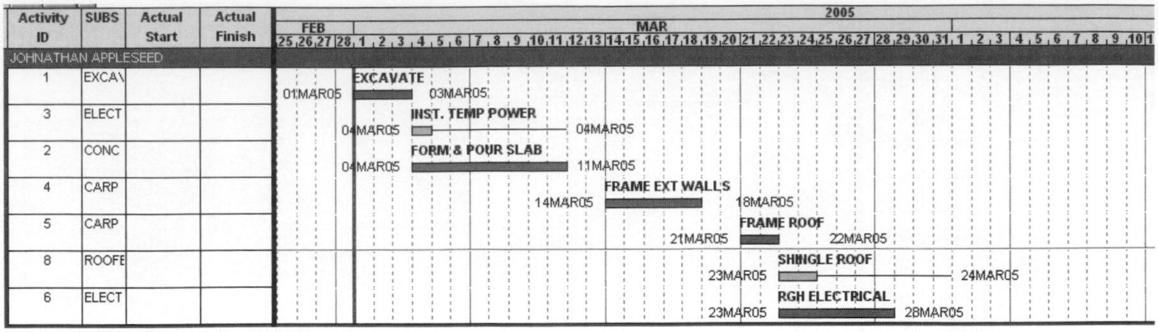

Activity ID	SUBS	Actual Start	Actual Finish	2005

FIGURE 20.20   Superintendent Johnathan Appleseed's bar chart

EF. While organizing, under the "Group by" column select **Superintendent** and **yes** under "New Page". Then print preview it and if it looks OK, print it. In Print Preview, if you want to see all the pages select the View All Pages tool button or, to see additional pages, one at a time, select the down, up, or sideways arrows. The report should be on two separate pages so you can give one to each superintendent. If it looks correct, print it. The report should look similar to Figure 20.20.

Report 8. Tabular Report for a Specific Subcontractor

You just found out you have an electrical subcontractor that can't read a bar chart. Develop a tabular schedule report of column information only (no bars) that shows only the electrical sub's activities. Remember, no signs of float or late dates. Go for it! Choose the subs tabular report layout you created earlier. To select only the electrician's activities, filter for the electrician's activities (**Format, Filter, Plus (+) button**, describe it, "Select if" **Subs**, "Is" Equal to, and "Low value" **Elect** for the electrician's activities only). Then **organize** the report by grouping by subs and then sort by ES, EF. You should see only the three electrical activities with Electrician printed at the top. To get only the tabular information without the bars, while in Print Preview, click on the Page Setup button and remove the check mark next to Bars. The report should look similar to Figure 20.21.

Report 9. Necked Bar Chart for a Subcontractor

The carpentry subcontractor just requested a schedule of his activities only. He wants a bar chart report in chronological order. Can you do it? Go for it! Only this time format the early bar so that the weekends are necked. (In the Format Bars dialog box put a check mark under Neck, and toward the bottom half of the screen put a check mark in *Holidays and Weekends* to allow a necked bar on both of these times. The resulting bar chart should look similar to Figure 20.22.

Time to experiment to review what you have learned. Play around with the bar charts and see what you can do. Have fun doing it. You can see that you can get practically any type of report you want.

FIGURE 20.21   Tabular report for the electrician

Activity Description	Orig Dur	Start	Finish	SUPR
ELECTRICIAN				
INST. TEMP. POWER	1	04MAR05	04MAR05	JOHN
RGH. ELECTRICAL	4	23MAR05	28MAR05	JOHN
FINISH ELECTRICAL	2	14APR05	15APR05	BILL

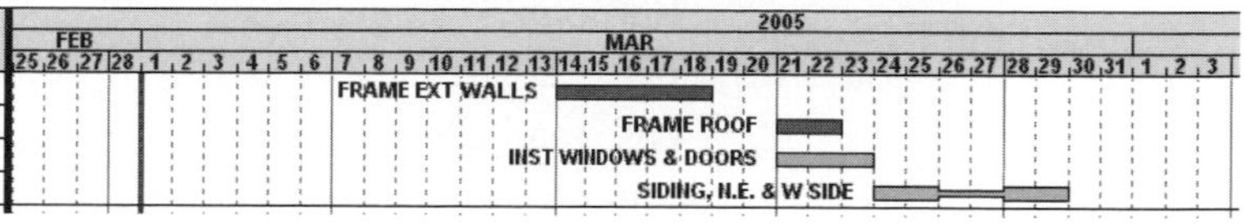

FIGURE 20.22   An example of a bar chart showing the bars necked during non-work times

Report 10. Statusing or Updating the Schedule

Load the schedule to be updated, then complete the following steps:

1. **Copy the file to a new name and version** (Tools, Project Utilities, Copy). On the bottom half of the screen under To, enter the following:

   Project group = enter the new name of the project, 4 characters.

   Project name = leave blank

   Planning unit = Day

   Number/version = 1st Update

   Leave everything else as defaulted and OK it.

   Notice at the top of the screen that you are still in the old schedule. Close the old one and open the new one you just created.

2. **Set the target or baseline schedule.** The target schedule will be used as a benchmark to compare dates, resources, and costs to the current schedule. Before updating the schedule (**1st Update only**) set up the target by clicking on **Tools, Project Utilities, Targets** or select the Target button ⊙ . Under **target 1** select your **original, as-planned schedule** and then OK it.

3. **Format the bars to create a target bar.** Click on Format, Bars (or click on the Format Bars icon 📊 and the plus (+) button to add a new bar choice. Give it a description of Target Bar.

   Select the **Structure** tab

   Position (in the upper right-hand corner) = 2

   Start point = select **Target 1 early start**

   Endpoint = select **Target 1 early finish**

   Bar = Bar Size = 3

   OK it.

Close the Format Bars dialog box and now you see the thinner (size 3) target bar under (position 2) the current bar.

If you desire the **target float** to show (in this case, we do), add another bar choice and title it Target float.

    Position = 2
    Start point = Target 1 EF
    Endpoint = Target 1 LF
    Bar = Dashed line
    OK it and Close it.

You now see total float on the target bar. Pretty nice, huh? You might want to save this layout to a new name, such as Bar Chart with Target.

To create a little more space between the activities format the row height for all activities to around 25, rather than automatically sizing the row height. Your bar chart should look similar to Figure 20.23.

Notice on your screen that the target bar now shows in the ES, EF position, which is good for a target to give to the superintendents to compare actual progress with. If it were a report for the owner, we would put the target bars in their LS, LF position and then if we choose to show the float on the target bar, we would format it to be in front of the bar.

4. **Update the schedule** with actual starts and actual finish dates. Click on the Activity Form button 🖾 in order to show the activity form.

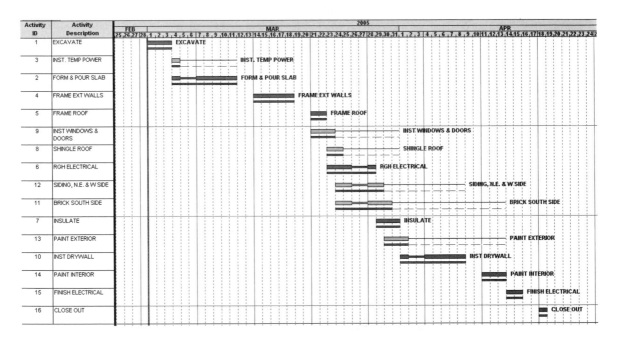

FIGURE 20.23   Bar chart showing the target bars

Highlight the first activity, *Excavate*. Let's show it starting a day late by putting a check mark in the ES box (notice it changes to "AS" for Actual Start). Input the actual start date or select it from the calendar by clicking on the down arrow and selecting the date, which is one work day later than the ES date was. We will show *Excavate* finishing on time by clicking in the EF box (notice it now changes to "AF" for Actual Finish) and we will simply accept the EF date and OK it. Notice the bar for *Excavate* now shows it started one day late and finished on time.

Start *Temp. Power* on time, but finish a little earlier than the LF date (within the float). Start *Slab* on time and finish a work day early. Start *Frame Ext. Walls* on time but enter a remaining duration (*RD*) of eight days (this should cause a delay because the original duration was only five days). Don't put anything in the EF box because the activity has not finished yet, it has only started. It is common to update activities that are in progress by inputting either remaining duration or percent complete, whichever you prefer, and P3 will calculate the other one.

Now calculate (F9 or click on the Schedule button,) the schedule and give it a data date (today's date) of two weeks into the project. Notice the updated activities as compared to the target. The vertical blue line is the data line, which represents today's date. The updated schedule should look similar the Figure 20.24.

Print the updated schedule as report #10.

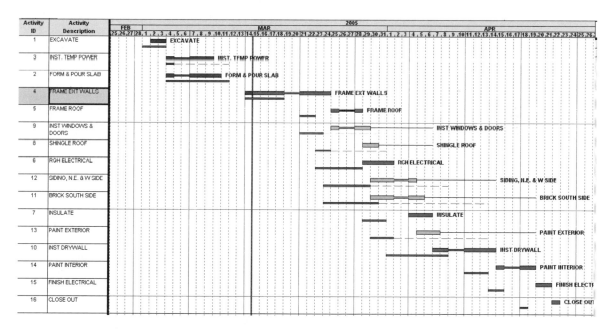

FIGURE 20.24   Updated bar chart showing progress compared to the target

Report 11. Update the Schedule to Finish on the Original Finish Date

Now look at the schedule and determine what you are going to do to finish on the original finish date. Remember, in order to accelerate or crash a schedule, think of all three possibilities: (1) change the **logic** of the critical activities by using lags or allowing some critical activities to be concurrent; (2) change the **durations** of some critical activities; or (3) change the **calendar**—assign some critical activities to work on weekends or holidays. Consider all three options, selecting those which have the least impact on costs, quality, and safety.

Go ahead and make some changes to this schedule so that it finishes on the original finish date and print this report.

For future updates, copy the schedule to be updated to a new name and update the new schedule, saving the old one for historical purposes. Remember, on updates beyond the first, typically you do not make a new target; you just update the completed activities. For more information on when to update, review Chapter 14 of this text.

Report 12. Adding Clip Art, Text, Curtains, Logos, and Drawings

Select the original warehouse as-planned schedule for this exercise. Open the Project Manager's Bar Chart layout. To add clip art select **View, Attachment Tools** to open the attachment configuration dialog box in the upper left-hand corner of the screen. Click on the triangle, circle, and square button to make it active and then click and drag within the bar chart area to show a location for the object to be imbedded.

To embed P3 clip art that comes with P3 make sure the file type is **PMT**. Change the directory to **C:\P3win\P3progs\clipart** or any personal files that contain clip art including bitmap or word metafiles. Put a check mark in the **Preview** box and then select the files you want to import. Browse through all the clip art to find something you want. Check out the clocks, sundial, ships, and so on. When you find something you like, OK it. Now it is in your schedule. Click and drag it to a new location. Click on one of the small square handles and change the clip art size, and so forth.

Any logo, picture, floor plan, or elevation can be scanned or, if it is already in an electronic format, put into the clip art directory. Some graphics from other software applications may need to be imported into Primavera Draw first, then saved as a PMT file to the clip art directory or file folder and then they can be inserted into the schedule. You can also capture clip art from the Internet, such as company logos, and import it into the schedule.

To add text to the schedule, click on the "T" in the Attachment Configuration dialog box. Click and drag the mouse in the location where you want the text to appear. Type in the desired text and change the size, font, color, and so on as desired.

You may want to **add a curtain** to the schedule. A curtain is used, typically with text, to communicate a special time period "or curtain of time" that is important to the project. To create a curtain, click on the lower right-hand button of the Attachment configuration dialog box to activate the curtain and then click on the bar chart where you want the curtain to begin and drag to where you want it to end. You can click and drag that curtain to another location if desired. Figure 20.25 shows an example of an enhanced schedule.

Activity ID	Activity Description	Orig Dur	SUPR
WAREHOUSE			
1	EXCAVATE	3	JOHN
3	INST. TEMP POWER	1	JOHN
2	FORM & POUR SLAB	6	JOHN
4	FRAME EXT WALLS	5	JOHN
5	FRAME ROOF	2	JOHN
9	INST WINDOWS & DOORS	3	BILL
8	SHINGLE ROOF	2	JOHN
6	RGH ELECTRICAL	4	JOHN
12	SIDING, N.E. & W SIDE	4	BILL
11	BRICK SOUTH SIDE	5	BILL
7	INSULATE	3	BILL
13	PAINT EXTERIOR	3	BILL
10	INST DRYWALL	6	BILL
14	PAINT INTERIOR	3	BILL
15	FINISH ELECTRICAL	2	BILL
16	CLOSE OUT	1	BILL
Total		35	

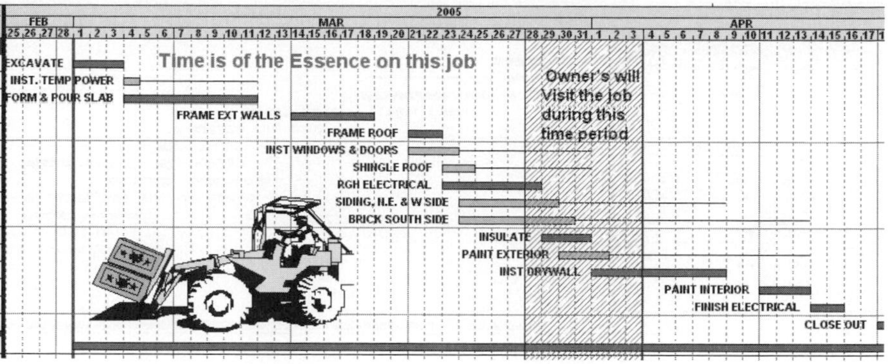

Time is of the Essence on this job

Owner's will Visit the job during this time period

FIGURE 20.25 Schedule with clip art, text, and a curtain

To add a **drawing to** the schedule, select **Insert, Object,** then find and select **Primavera Draw** and OK it. Now draw anything using the pencil, squares, circles, and so on on the toolbar. Change the line width or color using the art pallette. To get your drawing inserted into the schedule close out the drawing program by clicking on the *X* in the upper right corner of the window and then select **Yes** to update it into your schedule. Now your drawing is on your schedule you can move it, change size, and so on. You *can* delete any of these inserts by selecting the pointer tool (arrow) from the attachment configuration dialog box, click on the object to select it, and then press the Delete key.

Report #12 is a schedule of choice with clip art, text, a curtain, and some of your own drawings.

Report 13. Creating a New Project Schedule Based on a Past Project

You have just been awarded a contract to build another warehouse, only this time it will start two months from today. Also, the roof is to be tile which will take seven work days to install and the whole exterior is to be siding, no brick, so siding will take six days instead of four.

1. Open the original warehouse schedule and copy it to a new name. Close the old one and open the new one. Look to the top of the screen and make sure you are in the correct project.
2. Make changes to represent the new project. Change the description of *Shingle Roof* to *Tile Roof* and change the original duration from two days to seven days. Delete the *Brick South Side* activity (highlight the activity and hit the Delete key) and change the duration of *Install Siding* to six days and clean up the description to get rid of the north, east, and west sides.
3. Change the start date. Select **File, Project Overview** from the Menu bar. Change the project start date to two months from today. While in this screen you can change the version and title if desired. If the bars are not visible, recalculate the schedule and they will show up. Remember, anytime

Activity ID	Activity Description	Orig Dur	SUPR					
New Warehouse								
1	EXCAVATE	3	JOHN					
3	INST. TEMP POWER	1	JOHN					
2	FORM & POUR SLAB	6	JOHN					
4	FRAME EXT WALLS	5	JOHN					
5	FRAME ROOF	2	JOHN					
9	INST WINDOWS & DOORS	3	BILL					
8	TILE ROOF	7	JOHN					
6	RGH ELECTRICAL	4	JOHN					
12	INSTALL SIDING	6	BILL					
7	INSULATE	3	BILL					
13	PAINT EXTERIOR	3	BILL					
10	INST DRYWALL	6	BILL					
14	PAINT INTERIOR	3	BILL					
15	FINISH ELECTRICAL	2	BILL					
16	CLOSE OUT	1	BILL					
Total		35						

FIGURE 20.26   New project schedule based on a past project

a change is made that affects the calculations a new forward and backward pass needs to be performed. The schedule for the new project should look similar to Figure 20.26.

You should now have a dual critical path with *Tile Roof* and *Rough Electrical* as both critical. You have your new project already scheduled in three fairly simple steps without needing to redo all that input. It is important to recheck the activities, logic, and durations to make sure this new project schedule correctly represents the way the management team intends on building the project. For more information relating to this, review Chapter 11 of this text.

The layout for this report is the PM's layout created earlier with modifications as you desire.

Report 14. Using Fragnets to Copy Schedules or Parts of Schedules

You have just been awarded the contract to build a large warehouse. The project is divided into three areas, A, B, and C. Each area is very similar to this last warehouse we just scheduled. So, basically, what we want to do is to open the old schedule, copy it to a new name, open the new schedule and then copy and paste the activities to create the three areas. This technique is extremely helpful in scheduling any project with repetitive sequences of activities. Most projects have repetitive strings of activities happening throughout the project. For example, the interior finishes on each floor level are the same. Using this technique, the management team creates an accurate schedule of the first floor and then copies those activities for the remainder floors. Be sure all data points are input to each activity prior to copying. When an activity is copied the duration, costs, predecessors, activity codes, calendar, and so on are all copied as well.

1. Copy the schedule to a new name, preserving the original schedule in case errors are made when duplicating the activities.
2. **Select** the activities that are repetitive, in this case all the activities.
3. Choose the **Copy** button on the toolbar or Edit, Copy. This copies all the selected activities to the clipboard.

4. Choose the **Paste** button or choose Edit, Paste.

5. Put a dot by "Rename activities," then select **Prefix or Suffix** and **OK** it. Put a dot in front of prefix and in the "Additional Characters" box enter an *A* (for area A) and OK it. Paste again and put a prefix of *B* and then again a *C*. This is necessary because each activity ID must be unique; there can't be two activities with the same ID. If you were wanting to add a number to represent a floor or building number, make the prefix a 1 followed by a period (1.) in order to separate the original activity number from the prefix. If the original ID would have had alpha characters for whatever reason we would have added on *A* followed by a period (A.) as a prefix.

6. Notice the schedule is now repeated four times—A, B, C, and the original without a prefix. If all the areas are not grouped together **Organize** the schedule to sort it by activity ID. We do not need the activities without a prefix, so highlight all of them and delete them.

7. Create a **new activity code** (Data, Activity Codes) called "Area" and a description of "Area", with a value of A, and a description of "Area A," and so forth for B and C.

8. Add the *"Area" column* to the layout, so you can assign the proper area to each activity.

9. Assign Area A to the first activity *Excavate* and press the Enter key or click on the Checkmark button. With your mouse pointer on "A" click and drag down through all the A activities, leaving the cursor in the "Area" column. Then paste the A's into all the selected activities by selecting **Edit, Fill Cell.** Do likewise to the B activities and then the C activities. This is an enormous time saver, especially on large projects, to assign the activity codes all at once rather than one activity at a time.

10. Now, to get the activities in ES, EF order and grouped by area **Organize** the schedule. Group it by **Area** and Sort by **ES, EF.** Wow! What a good-looking schedule. If you desire, you can make the bold blue line go across the bars, separating the bar area as well as the column area (Organize, Options, and put a dot in the Bar area group divider as **bands,** rather than lines).

11. You now have the three areas scheduled using fragnets and you didn't have to enter each activity and all the accompanying data three times. However, the three areas are all starting at the same time. We need to decide when each area will start and finish.

12. Because *Tile Roof* is the **critical activity with the longest duration,** use it as the stagging activity and make a start-to-start relationship between the first activity (*Excavate*) of the prior area (A) to the first activity (*Excavate*) in the next area (B) with a start-to-start lag equal to the duration of *Tile Roof,* seven days. Then do this from *Excavate* in area B to *Excavate* in area C and recalculate the schedule.

    Notice all the float in Warehouse A? That is because, as it is currently scheduled, Area A does not need to finish until Area C is finished. If the management team desires to close out each area as soon as possible and not have that much float, put a finish-to-finish relationship with a lag of seven days between *Close Out* in each area. Recalculate the schedule to show the new dates. The schedule should appear similar to Figure 20.27.

Print this report (#14) showing the project organized by the three areas, with other choices as you desire.

This is a very acceptable schedule for the construction of this large warehouse consisting of the three areas. However, another management team may want to crew load the schedule by restraining each activity in each area by its same activity in the preceding area. In other words, *Excavate* could start immediately in Area B after it finishes in Area A. Then after Area B is excavated the crew would like to immediately excavate Area C. In order to schedule the project in this manner each activity would need to be listed as a predecessor to the same activity in the prior area. That would appear to take a lot of time to input, especially if this were a 30-floor office building with each activity scheduled 30 times.

This is really quite easy to do. You don't need to do it now, but remember this hint for future projects. Group the activities by subcontractor, and then by area. If the areas are not to be done in alphabetical or numerical order, change the order in the Ac-

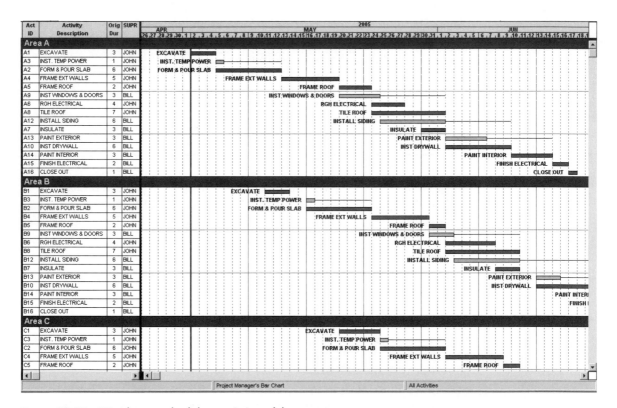

FIGURE 20.27   Warehouse schedule consisting of three areas

tivity Codes dialog box. To create the finish-to-start relationships, simply select all the activities that precede each other, highlighting them, and then select **Edit, Link Activities** or select the Link Activities icon 🖉 from the toolbar. This button may need to be added to the toolbar. This allows you to create detailed and accurate schedules in a very short period of time.

Report 15. Resource Management—Cost Loading the Schedule

To determine and help manage cash flow, we will cost load the original warehouse schedule. First to create a resource-loaded schedule use your original warehouse schedule, open it, and copy it to a new name, such as WR00. We are going to keep this simple by just keeping track of the lump sum costs or value to each activity. (see Figure 20.28.) You could keep a more detailed record of material, labor, equipment, overhead, and so on if you desired. (see the P3 manual or use the Help feature).

1. From the Menu bar select Data and then Resources to open the Resources dialog box. Create a **Resource** called ACTVALUE. Give it a **Description** of Activity Value, **Units** of $. Make sure there is no check mark in Driving.

FIGURE 20.28   Data needed for cost loading and crew loading the schedule

Activity Description	Lump Sum Costs	Crew Size
1 Excavate	$4985	2
2 Form & Pour Slab	2650	5
3 Temp. Power	585	2
4 Frame Ext. Walls	2500	3
5 Frame Roof	3000	5
6 Inst. Windows & Doors	1600	2
7 Rough Electrical	2500	2
8 Insulate	1100	2
9 Shingle Roof	950	3
10 Brick South Side	4000	3
11 Install Siding	3500	2
12 Paint Exterior	700	2
13 Install Drywall	2780	3
14 Paint Interior	800	2
15 Finish Electrical	1800	2
16 Close Out	200	2

Base is the base calendar to use, so we will use calendar 1. We will not limit the number of dollars per activity, so leave the limit (lower left of the dialog box) to 0 and then close the Resources dialog box.

2. Create a layout with the following columns: "Activity ID", "Description", "Duration", "Percent Complete", "Budgeted Cost", units per time period (labeled "Crew Size"), and quantity to complete (labeled "Total Worker Days"). Slide the data line to reveal those columns.

3. In order to input the costs we need to see the Costs window. Select **View, Activity Detail,** and then select the **Costs** window. Highlight the activity you want to cost load, click next to **Resource,** and select the resource **ACTVALUE** you created a minute ago. Now input the **Budgeted Cost** for that activity. You might want to sort the activities (Organize, Sort by) by activity ID because the data are listed that way in Figure 20.28 which makes it easier to enter. Continue entering the **Budgeted Cost** for all the activities. If you make an error in inputting the budgeted costs, zero out all data in the Costs window and start over. Next, in order to see the totals click on **Format, Organize, Group** the activities by **Project, Total at the Bottom,** and you should see a total cost of $33,650. This is the bid amount.

4. To view the Resource Profile on the bottom of the computer screen, click on **View** and select **Resource Profile,** or click on the Resource Profile button on the toolbar 🔳. In the **Resource Profile/Table** dialog box in the lower left of the screen input the following:

   Resources = ACTVALUE and click on Display

   Type = Costs

   Dates = Early

   Time interval = Days (usually it would be weeks or months, but to give you the idea here we will use daily costs)

   Put check marks at Histogram and Curves (we want to see both)

   Format = Bar

   Values = Current Estimate and then Close

You might need to slide the vertical bold line to the left to display more of the bar chart in order to see the resource profile. Also, in order to see daily costs change the timescale of the bar chart to daily. You can click and drag the top of the resource profile window to make it taller.

5. Now the periodic Activity Values (Costs) are shown as a histogram at the bottom of the screen along with cumulative Activity Values (Costs) shown as a progress S-curve. The vertical bars show the daily cash flow with the values to the left of the screen. The values of the progress curve are cumulative costs and are shown to the right of the screen. If you wanted to see the weekly cash flow, change the time interval to weeks. The schedule should look similar to Figure 20.29.

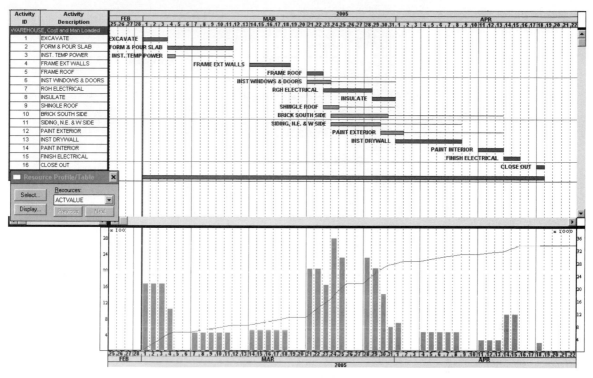

FIGURE 20.29   Warehouse project cash flow histogram and progress S-curve

For more information about resource-loaded schedules, using them as a management tool, and how to interpret the reports review Chapter 15 of this text.

To print report #15, print preview it, select **Page Setup,** and make sure there are check marks next to **Bars** and **Resource/Cost display.** Save this layout if desired.

Report 16. Resource Management—Crew Loading the Schedule

To evaluate and manage the number of workers on the job we need to crew load the schedule. Follow these steps:

1. Add a new resource (Data, Resources) called **Workers** (the number of workers on each activity each day, or crew size). Units are **ea;** give it a description of **Crew Size.**

2. To resource load the schedule you need to see the Resources window. Select **View, Activity Detail,** and then select **Resources.** (Try to remember that costs are entered in the Costs window and resources are entered in the Resources window.) Highlight the activity you want to resource load. Click in the cell to the right of the last resource (in this

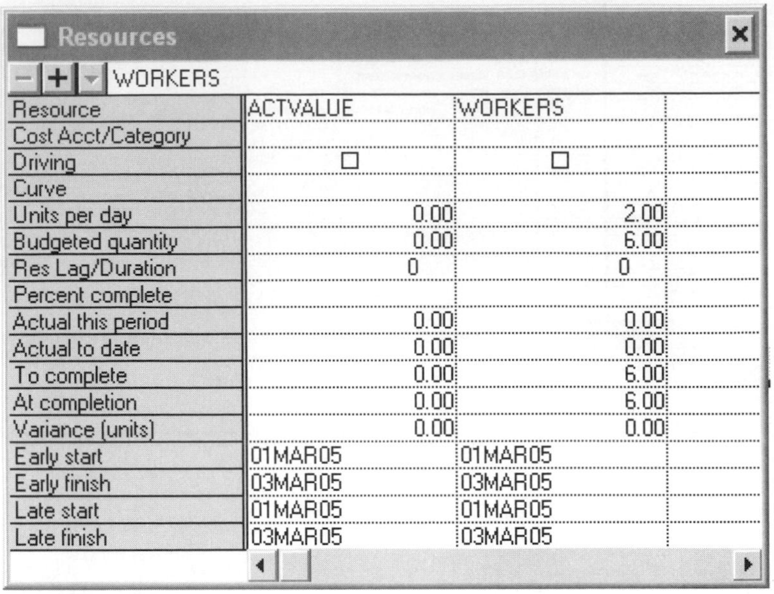

FIGURE 20.30 Resources
window for *Excavate*

Resources			
— + ▾ WORKERS			
Resource	ACTVALUE	WORKERS	
Cost Acct/Category			
Driving	☐	☐	
Curve			
Units per day	0.00	2.00	
Budgeted quantity	0.00	6.00	
Res Lag/Duration	0	0	
Percent complete			
Actual this period	0.00	0.00	
Actual to date	0.00	0.00	
To complete	0.00	6.00	
At completion	0.00	6.00	
Variance (units)	0.00	0.00	
Early start	01MAR05	01MAR05	
Early finish	03MAR05	03MAR05	
Late start	01MAR05	01MAR05	
Late finish	03MAR05	03MAR05	

case ACTVALUE) and select the resource **Workers** you created earlier.
Now input the crew size or number of workers under **Units Per Day.**
The Resources window for *Excavate* should look as shown in
Figure 20.30.

Continue entering the crew size or number of workers assigned, to the
remainder of the activities. You will notice under the column "Total
Worker Days" for each activity is the number of workers or crew size times
the duration of the activity (calculated by P3). When the crew size has been
entered for all the activities your activity table should look similar to
Figure 20.31.

3. To view the Resource Profile on the computer screen, click on **View** and
   select **Resource Profile,** or click on the Resource Profile icon. The
   Resource Profile/Table dialog box pops up in the lower left of the screen.
   Make the following changes:

   Select **Workers** under Resources and then click on Display.

      Type = Units
      Dates = Early
      Activities = All
      Time Interval = Days
      Check marks at Histogram and Curves
      Format = Bar
      Values = Current Estimate

Activity ID	Activity Description	Orig Dur	%	Budgeted Cost	Crew Size	Total Man Days
WAREHOUSE, Cost and Man Loaded						
1	EXCAVATE	3	0	4,985.00	2.00	6.00
2	FORM & POUR SLAB	6	0	2,650.00	5.00	30.00
3	INST. TEMP POWER	1	0	585.00	2.00	2.00
4	FRAME EXT WALLS	5	0	2,500.00	3.00	15.00
5	FRAME ROOF	2	0	3,000.00	5.00	10.00
6	INST WINDOWS & DOORS	3	0	1,600.00	2.00	6.00
7	RGH ELECTRICAL	4	0	2,500.00	2.00	8.00
8	INSULATE	3	0	1,100.00	2.00	6.00
9	SHINGLE ROOF	2	0	950.00	3.00	6.00
10	BRICK SOUTH SIDE	5	0	4,000.00	3.00	15.00
11	SIDING, N.E. & W SIDE	4	0	3,500.00	2.00	8.00
12	PAINT EXTERIOR	3	0	700.00	2.00	6.00
13	INST DRYWALL	6	0	2,780.00	3.00	18.00
14	PAINT INTERIOR	3	0	800.00	2.00	6.00
15	FINISH ELECTRICAL	2	0	1,800.00	2.00	4.00
16	CLOSE OUT	1	0	200.00	2.00	2.00
Total		35	0	33,650.00	42.00	148.00

FIGURE 20.31 Costs and crew size input into P3

4. Now the daily worker loads are shown as a histogram at the bottom of the screen along with cumulative or total number of workers shown as a progress S-curve. Notice from the S-curve that the total number of workerdays is 148. If you add it by hand you get this total. The vertical bars show the numbers of workers on the job daily. The computer screen should look similar to Figure 20.32.

Print report #16 by print previewing it and make sure there is a check mark on Resource/Cost display in the Page Setup dialog box.

When updating a project that is resource loaded you may want to show the Activity Form window, the Costs window, and the Resources window all at once, to the screen, in order to update the start and finish times, costs, and resources used on each activity.

Are you getting the hang of P3 and starting to feel a little confident? You might want to go over this exercise a time or two to keep sharp at it. You have experienced the major portion of the software. There is just one more area you need to get introduced to and that is tabular reports and graphic reports, under Tools on the Menu bar. Before we get into those, play around a little and try to use, from memory, some of your favorite features of P3. If you get confused, look back in this chapter for help and/or use the Help buttons. Go for a break or something and then you will be ready for the final section of this chapter.

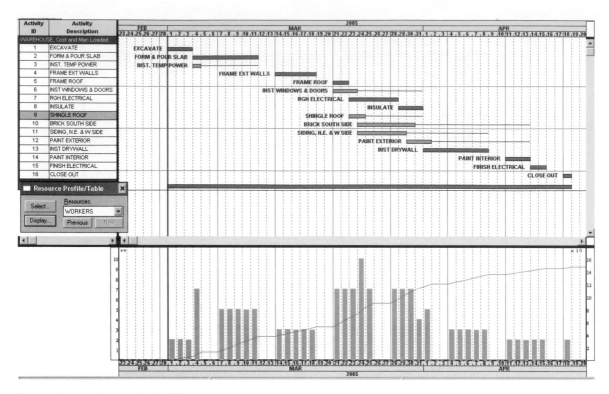

FIGURE 20.32   Worker loaded histogram and progress S-curve

Tabular and Graphic Reports

Tabular and graphic reports are similar to the reports we created earlier under the default bar chart or PERT portion of P3. The advantages of these later reports is that everything is saved in the report specifications, content, filters, colors, and everything else related to the report specification. Once set up they are always the same, whereas the layouts are easy to save over the top of and accidently change without being extremely careful. Also, this portion of P3 has the ability to be set up to print a series of reports consisting of many reports with one setup to the printer. For example, if you print five different reports each Friday, these could be set up as a series and printed all at once, while you do other things. Without this feature you would have to open the layout, filter, check Print Preview and Page Setup, and then print each report independently. You can print the series and the computer and printer do the work while you are out checking the job site (getting donuts). The remainder of this chapter will give you a brief overview of some of these reports. Don't take them too lightly; they are powerful and many heavy users of P3 rely on these as the standards.

The Back Half of P3

You are now going to learn what some call the "back half of P3". It is like a whole new software program. The front half, or default bar chart area that comes up when you load P3, shows the reports as they look on the computer screen, or wysiwyg. They are impressive and fairly easy to use. Back half reports are created an altogether different way. You get to the back half portion from **Tools** on the Menu bar. You create report specifications that are used time and again. A report specification in the back half is possibly more difficult to set up, and some of the reports are not as good looking, but they are not so easy to accidently change as layouts are in the front, default, portion of P3.

Report 17. Tabular Report for the Subcontractors

The first report we are going to use is a tabular report, just columns without the bars. We are going to set up a favorite tabular report for subs. In the prior portion of P3 you cannot select a column that includes log notes—here you can. We are going to enter some log notes for the subcontractor and then create a simple report that communicates to the subcontractor all the information the subcontractor needs to know.

To show the value of this report we are going to enter the following information for the subcontractors. Open the resource-loaded warehouse schedule. To enter log notes, select **View, Activity Detail,** and then **Log**.

Remind the excavator to bring dynamite (highlight the activity *Excavate* and then enter the log notes). If you check the Mask field it will only be shown here; it will not print on any reports. This could be used for private notes concerning the subcontractor, the activity, and so on.

Remind the appropriate subcontractor of the following: Roof shingles are to be autumn brown; concrete slab is to be 6,000 psi; exterior walls are to be framed with 2 × 6 metal studs; siding is to be aluminum and the color is Doeskin; brick is Mocha Brown. Enter a note to "watch the insulation sub, we have reason to think he may be dishonest" and mask that note. Close the Log window.

Select **Tools, Tabular Reports, Report Writer.** Add a new report and give it a title of Subs Report. We won't do anything with the first tab, Arithmetic. Click on the **Content** tab and you see something similar to format columns. Fill it out as follows: First choose the **Data item** and then the rest of the cells are automatically filled in. Then you can change the defaults as desired.

Column 1

Data item = Activity Description (Activity Data, DES, OK)

Field width = 30 (the longest activity title)

Column 2

Data item = Original Duration

Align = Center

Total = Yes

Column 3

> Data item = ES
> Total = No
> Title = "Start" on line 1 and "Date" on line 2

Column 4

> Data item = EF
> Total = No
> Title = "Finish" on line 1 and "Date" on line 2

Column 5

> Data item = Actual Start

Column 6

> Data item = Actual Finish

Column 7

> Data item = Superintendent
> Total = No
> Title = Super

Column 8

> Data item = MEM (Log records)
> Title = Notes
> Field width = 50
> Wrap = Yes

Click on the **Format** tab and skip the page on **SUBS.** Select the **Heading** tab and you see that you have the opportunity to change the heading information. We will go with the defaults here, so don't change anything. On the **Resource Selection** tab we will leave it as defaulted. Select the **Selection** tab and you see a screen similar to the Filter dialog box you used earlier. For this report we don't want to filter for anything.

OK the report specifications and then **Run** it. **View it on screen** and you see that each sub's information is on a separate page ready to hand to, or fax to, or e-mail to that subcontractor. Before you print it (to get out of Primavera Look, click on the upper right *X*; normally there is no need to save changes), to save paper, modify the report specifications, select the Format tab, change the **skip pages** to none and **skip line** on Subs to create a line space rather than a new page between each sub. This report should look similar to Figure 20.33.

JAY NEWITT   PRIMAVERA PROJECT PLANNER

REPORT DATE 15NOV03   RUN NO. 22
                22:40
Subs Report

DESCRIPTION	ORIG DUR	Start Date	Finish Date	ACTUAL START	ACTUAL FINISH	Super	REMARKS
CARPENTER							
FRAME EXT WALLS	5	14MAR05	18MAR05			JOHN	2 x 6 metal studs on ext. walls
FRAME ROOF	2	21MAR05	22MAR05			JOHN	
INST WINDOWS & DOORS	3	21MAR05	23MAR05			BILL	
SIDING, N.E. & W SIDE	4	24MAR05	29MAR05			BILL	Aluminum, Doeskin
CONCRETE SUB							
FORM & POUR SLAB	6	04MAR05	11MAR05			JOHN	Slab is 6,000 psi
DRYWALLER							
INST DRYWALL	6	01APR05	08APR05			BILL	
ELECTRICIAN							
INST. TEMP POWER	1	04MAR05	04MAR05			JOHN	
RGH ELECTRICAL	4	23MAR05	28MAR05			JOHN	
FINISH ELECTRICAL	2	14APR05	15APR05			BILL	
EXCAVATOR							
EXCAVATE	3	01MAR05	03MAR05			JOHN	Bring Dynamite
GENERAL CONTRACTOR							
CLOSE OUT	1	18APR05	18APR05			BILL	
INSULATOR							
INSULATE	3	29MAR05	31MAR05			BILL	
BRICK MASON							
BRICK SOUTH SIDE	5	24MAR05	30MAR05			BILL	Mocha Brown Bricks

FIGURE 20.33   Subcontractor's tabular report

This is a no-frills, no-nonsense report that prints quickly and communicates to the subcontractors the basic information they need to know. The subcontractor can then write in the actual start and finish dates and return the report back to you for updating the schedule. If it looks OK, print it as report #17.

Report 18. Tabular Report for the Owner

Set up this report the same way as for report #17, with the following columns: "Activity Description", "Original Duration", "Supervisor (Super)", "Start Date (LS)", "Finish Date (LF)," with no totals at the bottom. Sort it by late start and then late finish. The report should look similar to Figure 20.34.

JAY NEWITT   PRIMAVERA PROJECT PLANNER

REPORT DATE 15NOV03   RUN NO. 25
              22:51
Owners Report

DESCRIPTION	ORIG DUR	Supervisor	Start Date	Finish Date
EXCAVATE	3	JOHN	01MAR05	03MAR05
FORM & POUR SLAB	6	JOHN	04MAR05	11MAR05
INST. TEMP POWER	1	JOHN	11MAR05	11MAR05
FRAME EXT WALLS	5	JOHN	14MAR05	18MAR05
FRAME ROOF	2	JOHN	21MAR05	22MAR05
RGH ELECTRICAL	4	JOHN	23MAR05	28MAR05
INST WINDOWS & DOORS	3	BILL	29MAR05	31MAR05
INSULATE	3	BILL	29MAR05	31MAR05
SHINGLE ROOF	2	JOHN	30MAR05	31MAR05
INST DRYWALL	6	BILL	01APR05	08APR05
SIDING, N.E. & W SIDE	4	BILL	05APR05	08APR05
BRICK SOUTH SIDE	5	BILL	07APR05	13APR05
PAINT EXTERIOR	3	BILL	11APR05	13APR05
PAINT INTERIOR	3	BILL	11APR05	13APR05
FINISH ELECTRICAL	2	BILL	14APR05	15APR05
CLOSE OUT	1	BILL	18APR05	18APR05

FIGURE 20.34   Owner's tabular report

After printing it, select the *X* to get out of Primavera Look and don't save this specific report.

Report 19. Tabular Report for the Superintendents

Set up this report with the following columns: "Activity ID", "Activity Description", "Original Duration", "Actual Duration", "Early Start", "Early Finish", "Late Start", "Late Finish", and "Total Float"—no totals at the bottom. Format it with a line break between superintendents. Sort by early start and then early finish. The report should look similar to Figure 20.35.

Report 20. Tabular Report of Critical Activities Only for the Project Manager

Set up report #20 with the following columns: "Activity ID", "Activity Description", "Original Duration", "Superintendent", "Early Start", and "Early Finish". Add totals only on durations, sort by early start and then early finish. Filter for the critical activities only. The report should look similar to Figure 20.36.

Report 21. Printing a Series of Reports with One Setup

This report will teach you how to print a series of reports. The series will be the last four reports you create, printed all at one time. Select **Tools, Tabular Reports, Production** and find the RW (Report Writer) reports you just created. Put an *F* for

ACTIVITY ID	DESCRIPTION	ORIG DUR	ACTUAL DUR	EARLY START	EARLY FINISH	LATE START	LATE FINISH	TOTAL FLOAT
JOHNATHAN APPLESEED								
1	EXCAVATE	3	0	01MAR05	03MAR05	01MAR05	03MAR05	0
3	INST. TEMP POWER	1	0	04MAR05	04MAR05	11MAR05	11MAR05	5
2	FORM & POUR SLAB	6	0	04MAR05	11MAR05	04MAR05	11MAR05	0
4	FRAME EXT WALLS	5	0	14MAR05	18MAR05	14MAR05	18MAR05	0
5	FRAME ROOF	2	0	21MAR05	22MAR05	21MAR05	22MAR05	0
9	SHINGLE ROOF	2	0	23MAR05	24MAR05	30MAR05	31MAR05	5
7	RGH ELECTRICAL	4	0	23MAR05	28MAR05	23MAR05	28MAR05	0
WILLIAM TELL								
6	INST WINDOWS & DOORS	3	0	21MAR05	23MAR05	29MAR05	31MAR05	6
11	SIDING, N.E. & W SIDE	4	0	24MAR05	29MAR05	05APR05	08APR05	8
10	BRICK SOUTH SIDE	5	0	24MAR05	30MAR05	07APR05	13APR05	10
8	INSULATE	3	0	29MAR05	31MAR05	29MAR05	31MAR05	0
12	PAINT EXTERIOR	3	0	30MAR05	01APR05	11APR05	13APR05	8
13	INST DRYWALL	6	0	01APR05	08APR05	01APR05	08APR05	0
14	PAINT INTERIOR	3	0	11APR05	13APR05	11APR05	13APR05	0
15	FINISH ELECTRICAL	2	0	14APR05	15APR05	14APR05	15APR05	0
16	CLOSE OUT	1	0	18APR05	18APR05	18APR05	18APR05	0

FIGURE 20.35   Superintendent's tabular report

ACTIVITY ID	DESCRIPTION	ORIG DUR	SUPR	EARLY START	EARLY FINISH
1	EXCAVATE	3	JOHN	01MAR05	03MAR05
2	FORM & POUR SLAB	6	JOHN	04MAR05	11MAR05
4	FRAME EXT WALLS	5	JOHN	14MAR05	18MAR05
5	FRAME ROOF	2	JOHN	21MAR05	22MAR05
7	RGH ELECTRICAL	4	JOHN	23MAR05	28MAR05
8	INSULATE	3	BILL	29MAR05	31MAR05
13	INST DRYWALL	6	BILL	01APR05	08APR05
14	PAINT INTERIOR	3	BILL	11APR05	13APR05
15	FINISH ELECTRICAL	2	BILL	14APR05	15APR05
16	CLOSE OUT	1	BILL	18APR05	18APR05
		35			

FIGURE 20.36   Project manager's tabular report of critical activities only

Friday reports in the "Series" column by each of those reports and close the window. Assume it is Friday afternoon and you want to print your standard Friday reports. Select Tools, Tabular Reports, Production, Run Series, select the *F* series, and OK it. If you viewed them to the screen you can scroll down through them or if to the printer, they should be printing by now. Report #21 is this series printed in one setup.

If you wanted to run a single report the technique would be the same, only you would select the **Run Individual** button and select the report to run. As you can see, once these report specifications are set up they are easy to use.

For interest, look at some of the other reports that come with the software. Look at RW-03 and RW-04. To see some schedule reports (SR-03 and SR-07) select Tools, Tabular Reports, Schedule.

Report 22. Graphic Reports—Timescaled Logic

This is a very popular P3 report (Tools, Graphic Reports, Timescaled Logic). Add a new report and title it "Standard Timescaled Report." Look through all the choices but keep with the defaults and run it. Print it as report #22. It shows activities that share float if you look at it closely. It is a combination bar chart and logic diagram.

Report 23. Cash Flow and Banana Curve

This cash flow report will include an early start and also a late start progress S-curve, or what some managers call a banana curve superimposed over a weekly cash flow histogram. Make sure you are in the warehouse schedule that has the cost information input. From the Menu bar select **Tools, Graphic Reports, Resource and Costs.** Add a new report at whatever number it defaults to. Title it "Cash Flow & Banana Curve". Under the **Resource Selection tab** go with it as defaulted. On the **Content tab,** show data of Cost, Dates as Both, so you get the full banana, both early and late curves. Also check **Both** cumulative and histogram curve so you get them superimposed on each other. On the **Date tab,** change the start date to Start Date − a day or two and the finish date to Finish Date + a day or two. Make the **Timescale** weekly. On the **Format tab,** change major sight lines to monthly and minor sight lines to weekly because you want to see the weekly cash flow. Click on **Titles, Pen, Size, and Selection** as defaulted; you may want to look at them to see if you want changes. **OK** the report specification, **Run** it, and view it on the screen. If it looks good, print it. The first half of P3 gives only the early curve or the late curve, not both. This report should look similar to Figure 20.37.

The blue costs are based on the early start and finish dates and the red costs are based on the late start and finish dates. The actual costs should be within the banana curve. See Chapter 15 for more information on cash flow and banana curves.

Report 24. Bar Chart with a Banana Curve Overlaid

The graphic reports in this portion of P3 are not as impressive or classy as in the first half; however, you can do some things here that cannot be done in the first half. We are going to create a banana curve superimposed over a bar chart. This will be the cre-

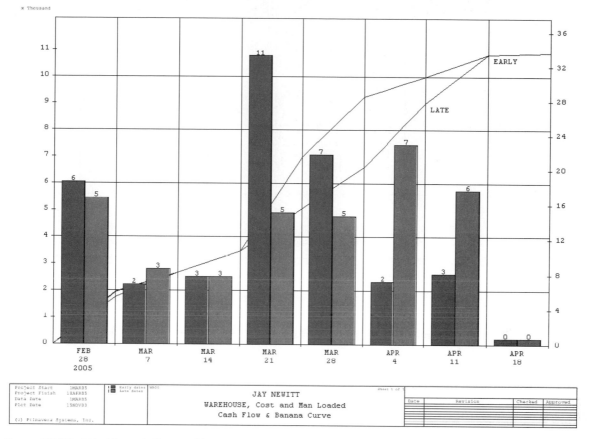

FIGURE 20.37   Weekly cash flow and banana curve

ation of two reports that will be overlaid. First, we will create the banana curve. Select **Tools, Graphic Reports, Resource and Cost** and add a new report specification titled "Banana Curve." On the **Content** tab show **Cost** data, **Both** dates, and the **Cumulative** curve. On the **Date** tab make the Time periods of Start Date **SD −1d,** End Date **FD +1d,** title each **Week,** and timescale each **Week.** On the **Format** tab have vertical sight lines for **Major Month** and **Minor Week. OK** the specification and then **Run** the report. Remember the report ID number RC-??. If it looks OK, close it. The report should look similar to Figure 20.38.

Next, you will create the **bar chart** specification by selecting **Tools, Graphic Reports, Bar,** then add a new specification and title it "Bar Chart with Banana Curve." On the **Activity Data** tab select **Activity Description** only (delete the others) with an Activity title length of **30.** On the **Content** tab show **Both** dates so you see the early bar and the late bar. Where it says **Display graphic RC-** enter the number of the resource

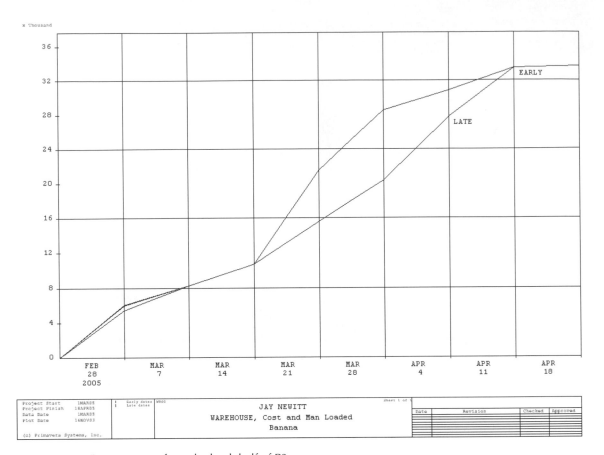

x Thousand

36

32

28

24

20

16

12

8

4

0

	FEB	MAR	MAR	MAR	MAR	APR	APR	APR
	28	7	14	21	28	4	11	18
	2005							

EARLY

LATE

Project Start	1MAR05
Project Finish	18APR05
Data Date	1MAR05
Plot Date	16NOV03
(c) Primavera Systems, Inc.

Early dates
Late dates

JAY NEWITT
WAREHOUSE, Cost and Man Loaded
Banana

Sheet 1 of 1

| Date | Revision | Checked | Approved |

FIGURE 20.38   Banana curve from the back half of P3

and cost report you created a minute ago, probably the last one on the list. On the **Date** tab make the it Start Date **SD −1d**, End Date **FD +1d**, just like you did before, and put a minimum time interval of **Week.** On the **Tailoring** tab put a vertical sight line of **1 week** and **Neck** the bars for periods on inactivity and then **Run** the report. If it looks good, close out of Primavera Look without saving the changes and OK the report specification. Now this report is there for you to constantly use—no more setup time. Run it by selecting it and then select the **Run** button. The combined reports should look similar to Figure 20.39.

This report shows the cumulative planned costs as well as the planned bar chart. If this report were updated you would see the actual costs plotted, hopefully within the banana, and you could create a target to the bar chart so you could compare progress there as well. This report makes it possible to view costs and time in one report. If the costs are outside of the banana you can look at the bars and see which activities are either ahead of or behind schedule. This report is not available in the first half of P3.

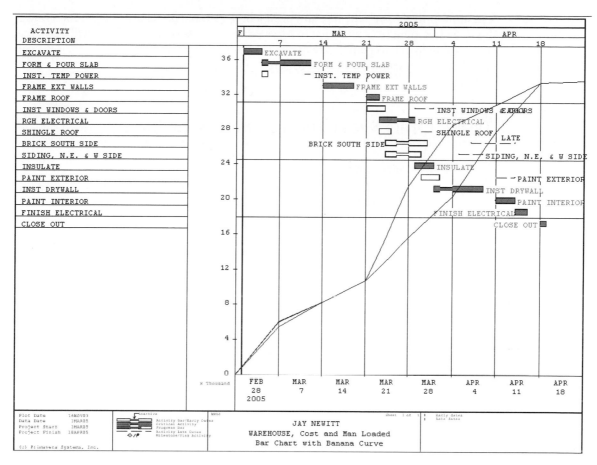

FIGURE 20.39   Combined bar chart and banana curve report

Report 25. Adding a Schedule to a Document

Ah, one last fun thing. Open your word processor while P3 is running and type a short letter concerning something to do with the schedule. Leave the cursor where you would like to import some schedule information. Then get back into P3, click on the Camera button (or Edit, Copy Picture), draw a box (click and drag) around any selected schedule information, including the bars, and then release the mouse button. This copies that information to the clipboard. Get back into your letter and paste that picture from the clipboard. Print this as report #24.

   This concludes your introduction to P3. There is still a lot more to know to be an expert's expert, but this is a good start at knowing how to manage a project with the help of P3. Don't feel you need to know it all at once. Use it by keeping it simple at first, taking it one step at a time. Focus on the part that makes sense to you and if you can input only a basic schedule and print a basic, simple bar chart, that's good enough for now. Learn more as you need it. After using P3 for several months, it will be a great asset and help you to gain better control of your projects and to help you plan, organize, direct, and control in order to safely build quality projects on time and within budget.

TRYING OTHER SHORTCUTS, TECHNIQUES, OR IDEAS

To customize your toolbar, click on *Tools, Options, Toolbar*.

To renumber all the activities; click on *Edit, Select All, Copy, Paste*. Change all activity IDs with **Auto-increment,** starting at whatever and increment by whatever. Select a starting number that is beyond any current activity ID so that there will be no duplicate numbers. If the specifications require the numbering to start at the number 1, recopy and paste the activities again starting at number 1 and delete the old numbered activities.

Link a series of activities with a finish-to-start relationship with zero lag. Drag the mouse over the activity descriptions in the activity columns or select the activities by using the Ctrl key. Choose the series Link button and the identified activities will be linked as FS relationships in the same order as they are listed. This is a fast way to assign predecessors. Just be careful to ensure accuracy. You can also delete relationships this way using the Unlink button.

To delete relationships, click on the relationship line and delete.

What is the difference between dissolve and delete? Dissolve removes the activity or activities selected but connects the predecessors and successors. When using Delete, you need to take care of the relationships (Edit, Dissolve).

To use the summary bars, double-click on the organize band, or use the Summarize button to summarize all at once.

Contact Information

Primavera Systems, Inc.
Three Bala Plaza West
Suite 700
Bala Cynwyd, PA 19004

Phone: (610) 667-8600 or (800) 423-0245
Technical Help: (610) 667-8600 (You will need your serial number; locate it on the P3 diskettes or CDs, or click on Help and About P3.
Fax: (610) 667-7894
E-mail: info@primavera.com
Web address: http://primavera.com

CHAPTER 21

MANAGING PROJECTS USING SURETRAK

INTRODUCTION —
SURETRAK FOR
WINDOWS VERSION 3.0

SureTrak is a very popular project management software program used by a majority of construction-related firms. It is popular with residential as well as commercial and industrial construction. It is a product of Primavera Systems, Inc. Contact information is listed at the end of this chapter.

The software installation requires a Pentium PC or equivalent, 40 MB of hard disk space, 32 MB of RAM, and Windows 95 or later operating system. SureTrak is compatible with projects scheduled with Microsoft Project or Primavera Project Planner (P3).

The following instructions are presented chronologically and are based on *how managers use the software,* rather than explaining every detail and feature of the software in the order the screens appear. These instructions contain examples and assignments that teach how to use the software to communicate and manage the project. There is no claim that these instructions are without error. They are an attempt to help you be successful with SureTrak and to learn it as efficiently as possible. It is not necessary to know everything about any software package in order to be an effective user of it. Stick with the basics and become proficient with the areas that are essentially used and you will find this software to be extremely valuable in helping you control your projects.

As you work through these instructions, make sure you are thinking. Don't allow yourself to get into the mode of just carrying out the instructions without engaging your mind. Make sure what you are doing is logical and makes sense. If you *think* as you do this, you will learn how to use SureTrak. Don't get frustrated if everything doesn't work as you expect. Generally, with computer software, you learn the most when things go wrong. Keep thinking and trying and you will figure it out. These instructions start with significant detailed instructions to help you figure out how to use the software. As you get further into the instructions the detail becomes less. Once you have followed the instructions in detail and accomplished a task, it is assumed you learned that task and from then on the instructions pertaining to that task will be less detailed. So, if later in the chapter you forget how to do a task, go back to the beginning of the chapter to review the details pertaining to that task.

USING THE HELP BUTTONS

The Help buttons are very useful for when you feel lost or confused. There is also a Help feature and tutorial under **Help** on the Menu bar. Each SureTrak window and dialog box also displays a Help button that will provide help directly for that window.

Warehouse
CPM Schedule

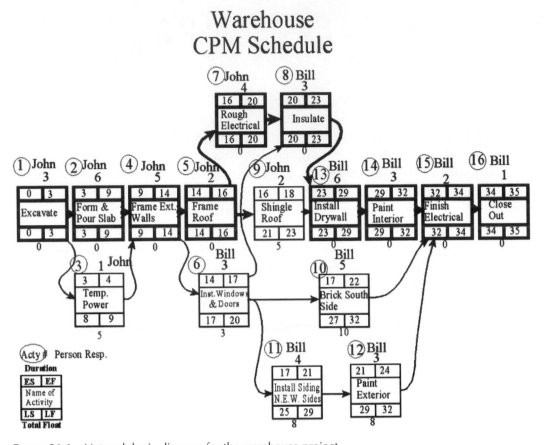

FIGURE 21.1   Network logic diagram for the warehouse project

The schedule shown in Figure 21.1 for the construction of a warehouse will be used to help learn SureTrak. It shows the network logic diagram developed during a meeting with the management team.

The warehouse is to be supervised by two superintendents: Bill and John. John is particularly good at overseeing the earthwork and the structure activities. Bill will be brought in to manage the finishing activities, basically from the insulation to completion. The number in the circle represents the activity ID number. The 35 work days calculated to complete the project is in accordance with the contract provisions.

You are now ready to computerize the schedule.

MAKING A NEW PROJECT FILE

Load SureTrak from the Windows Program Manager. After the program comes up, create a new project file by going to the Menu bar and clicking on **File, New.**

Note: Use the following information to answer the setup questions at the beginning of the project:

Do not use the Enter key as you go from field to field. Use the Tab key, arrow keys, or the mouse. If you make a mistake and use the Enter key before entering all the information, SureTrak assumes you are done with the window you are working in and closes it. To get this project overview screen back, click on **File** on the Menu bar and then choose **Project Overview** to reopen this window.

Current folder	This is where the project will be saved, use the default or Browse to save it to a different folder.
Project name	"Warehouse 00." The *00* represents the first or as-planned schedule. Then, as it is updated, this first schedule will be copied and named Warehouse 01 for the updates through the first month. Warehouse 02 will be used for the updates through the second month, etc. (If you desire to exchange information with P3 users, the project name must be exactly four characters.)
Template	Enter nothing—default.
Type	Make it "SureTrak," if it is a stand-alone project. (If you desire to exchange information with P3 users, choose "Concentric P3.")
Planning Unit	If active, choose "Day."

Don't add the project to a project group (leave the box blank).

Number/Version	"As Planned."
Start date	Enter next Tuesday's date.
Must finish by	Leave blank—enter nothing. If you enter a date the backward pass will be computed based on this date, likely giving either negative or positive float.
Project Title	"Warehouse."
Company Name	Enter your company name.

Click on the **OK** button to accept this information and the computer will now begin creating this project. When you start a new project SureTrak creates approximately 20 files. This software is not like word processing or spreadsheets where you are working in only one file at a time. Keep this in mind as you copy projects and files.

Setting Up the Calendars

Now define calendars by selecting **Define, Calendar** from the Menu bar. If Define is gray and inoperable, hit the Esc (Escape) key. Select the **Standard** tab for the standard calendar. The Calendars dialog box should appear as in Figure 21.2.

First set the **Global Calendar (click on Global Calendar)** and then make the following days as nonwork days or annual holidays as desired: Jan 1 (highlight the day

FIGURE 21.2 Set up the calendar at the Calendars dialog box with the Standard tab selected

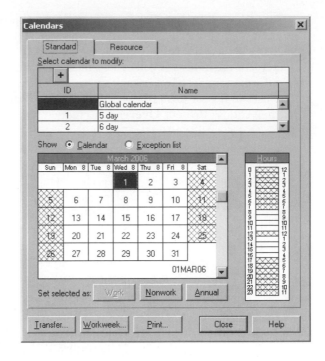

and then click on the "**Annual**" button), July 4, Thanksgiving (4th Thursday in November and click on the "**Nonwork**" button because the date is different each year), and Dec. 25 as an annual holiday. If it is a specific date each year, use the **Annual** button or if it is a different date each year use the **Nonwork** button.

Next, check Calendar #1 (click on ID 1) and name it as your **5 day** calendar by highlighting Normal workweek on the edit line at the top of the window and typing in "5 day." Then click on the check mark to enter it. Next, click on the **Workweek** button and make sure there are no work hours scheduled for Sunday and Saturday (solid *X*'s). Now highlight Calendar #2, the "Seven 24-hr days" calendar, and rename it to **6 day**. Click the **Workweek** button and set up Monday through Saturday as work days from 8–noon and 1–5 by putting a dot in front of the day and clicking on **Work** or **Nonwork** as appropriate (no need to recalculate).

Next, create one more calendar by clicking on the **plus (+)** button ＋ . It will be calendar #3; name it **7 day** calendar and make each day of the week a work day. You are now done with the calendars, so click on the **OK** and **Close** buttons.

You now have a 5-, 6-, and 7-day calendar that can be used for the various trades according to their work schedule and a global calendar that oversees all the individual calendars. You can create many more calendars as needed with additional holidays, and so on. You could have a calendar for the electrician showing he or she works only on Tuesday through Thursday and has the month of July off and then the electrical activities will be allowed to happen only on those days. You have calendars 1–9 and the whole alphabet to use to create calendars.

FIGURE 21.3 Activity Codes dialog box with code values set

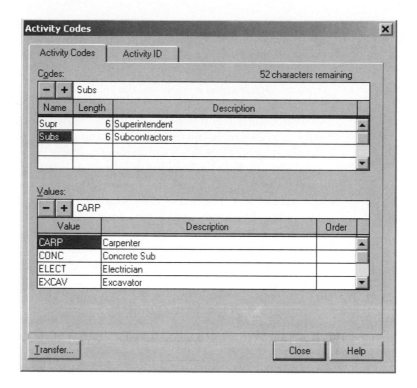

DEFINING ACTIVITY CODES

Next, set up the **Activity Codes (Define, Activity Codes)**. First delete the default codes using the **(minus (−) button, ⎯ Minus key, or Delete key)**. Create the first code as "Supr," with 6 characters in Length and description of "Superintendent." The second code will be "Subs" for the subcontractors and it will be 6 characters in length also, with a description of "Subcontractors." Delete all other activity codes by selecting the minus (−) key.

Now, set the values (click below **Value,** on the bottom half of the screen) for each of the activity codes. To set the values for the superintendents, first highlight **Supr** at the top of the dialog box and then enter the value for the superintendents of Bill and then John. In the "Description" column you can input a full name, such as William Tell or whatever. The Activity Codes dialog box should look similar to Figure 21.3.

For the subcontractors (make sure **Subcontractors** is highlighted above) type in a value and description for each sub needed to complete the project being scheduled. When naming subs, I recommend you use the trade name, rather than real names. That way, when you change subs you won't need to edit this field. For example, use a code title of Elect with a description of Electrician, rather than Rosenbaum Electric. Electricians are not offended if you call them electricians. However, they are offended if you provide a report labeled Rosenbaum Electric and send it to Hanks & Sons Electrical. When you are finished setting up the activity codes and values, close the Activity Codes dialog box.

Note: There are two basic ways to create reports specifically for each subcontractor. One method is to define the subs as an activity code as we are doing here and the other is to define the subs as a resource. The advantage of defining the subs as an activity code is that it is simple to do and understand. The advantage of defining the subs as a resource is you can have the computer automatically level the resources. The disadvantages of that is it is a little more complex because you have to declare the units per hour, the limits, whether or not they are a driving resource, and so on. Plus some managers feel uncomfortable in putting that much trust on the computer to have it automatically level resources. They would rather level the resources by hand, creating resource relationships in the way of predecessors and successors. For the person just learning SureTrak, it is recommended that you start by defining the subs as an activity code. As you get more confident in your scheduling abilities and more sophisticated in your management needs, then you can learn how to set up the subs as resources.

INPUTTING ACTIVITY DATA

You are now ready to input the individual activity data for the schedule. There are three methods used to input the data: (1) the Cells in the rows and columns area (the activity table), (2) the activity form, or (3) the PERT view.

Input Using the Cells in the Rows and Columns (the Activity Table)

Click under the column heading "Activity ID" and enter the **Activity ID** number. Each activity must have a unique number assigned to it. You could use the numbers on the hand-drawn schedule or you could use the default numbers supplied by SureTrak. (If you want SureTrak to automatically enter the activity numbers in sequential order, select **Tools, Options, Defaults** tab and then increase activity ID by 1, or whatever you desire.) Then enter the activity **Description** or task name and the **Original Duration** in the appropriate cells.

To input the Calendar, Superintendent, and Subcontractors you created a few minutes ago, format the activity table to include those columns.

From the Menu bar select **Format, Columns,** and insert "Calendar," "Superintendent," "Subcontractors" and "Predecessors" as column headings in the location of choice. The Columns dialog box should look similar to Figure 21.4.

Now click and slide the vertical bold line separating the column information from the bar chart area to the right to expose those new columns as shown in Figure 21.5.

Now that the columns needed are available you can input the Activity ID, Description, and Duration in the appropriate cells. The "Calendar," "Superintendent," and "Subcontractor" can be selected and entered by clicking in the appropriate cell and then from the input edit line, above the column headings, click on the down arrow to

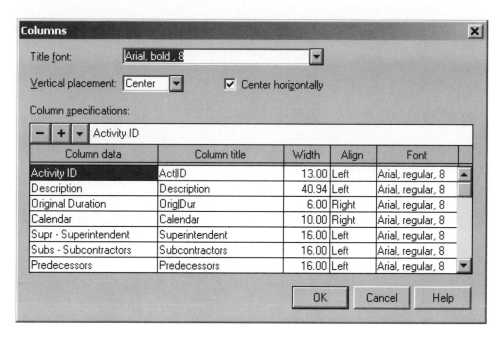

FIGURE 21.4   Columns dialog box showing added column data

Act ID	Description	Orig Dur	Calendar	Superintendent	Subcontractors	Predecessors

FIGURE 21.5

select the proper data. For example, to select the calendar to an activity click in the proper cell, click on the edit line, and then click on the down arrow and select the proper calendar. Repeat this procedure of clicking in the cell, then click in the input edit line, click the down arrow, and select the superintendent, the subcontractor, and any other activity codes you desire. The "predecessor" column cannot be used to input the predecessors for the activity. It will only list the predecessors as you input them as described below. Repeat this for the first five activities.

ASSIGN PREDECESSORS.   Once the activities are entered you will assign the Predecessors by opening the Predecessors window. Do this by selecting **View** from the Menu bar, choose **Activity Detail,** and then **Predecessors** to open the Predecessors window.

Slide the window out of the way by clicking and dragging the window heading. Now you can enter the predecessors to each activity. Do this by clicking under the

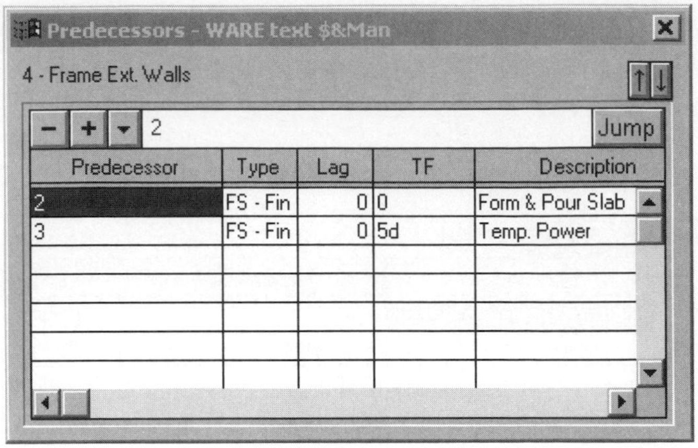

FIGURE 21.6   Predecessors window for *Frame Ext. Walls*

"Predecessor" heading and enter the activity number of each predecessor. You do not need to enter the description, which shows up automatically; just enter the activity number. Notice the Predecessors window in Figure 21.6.

The current activity is #4 *Frame Ext. Walls* and the predecessors are #2 and #3. Also notice, in the bar chart area, how the bars now move to their proper location, after the predecessor has been assigned, depending on which activities precede them. The computer is automatically doing the forward and backward pass and showing the activity bars according to those calculations.

Continue doing the same steps for each activity entered and make sure each is correct. If there are lags, they can also be entered in the Predecessors window. The **Type** of lag (FS, SS, FF, and FS) and the amount of **Lag** is entered in the appropriate cells. The **TF** (total float is not entered; it is calculated). When finished, close the Predecessors window.

Input Using the Activity Form

The activity form will be used to input the next five activities. From the Menu bar, select **View** and **Activity Form.** Or, from the toolbar select 🔲 the Activity Form icon. You now see the activity form at the bottom of the screen as shown in Figure 21.7.

Create a new activity by clicking the cell (in the top half of the screen) in the **Description** column under the last activity you input above. Notice the activity **ID** is automatically entered in the activity form at the bottom of the screen. If it is not correct, correct it. Now, all the input is done in the activity form. Input the **Description, Duration, Calendar,** then click on the **More** button to reveal more of the activity form in order to input the proper activity codes of the **Superintendent** and **Subcontractor** for that activity. To input these activity codes, click on the appropriate cell and then the down arrow to select the correct activity code. To assign the predecessors from the Activity Form window, select the **Details** button and then **Predecessors** and the Predecessors window appears for you to assign predecessors, just as before.

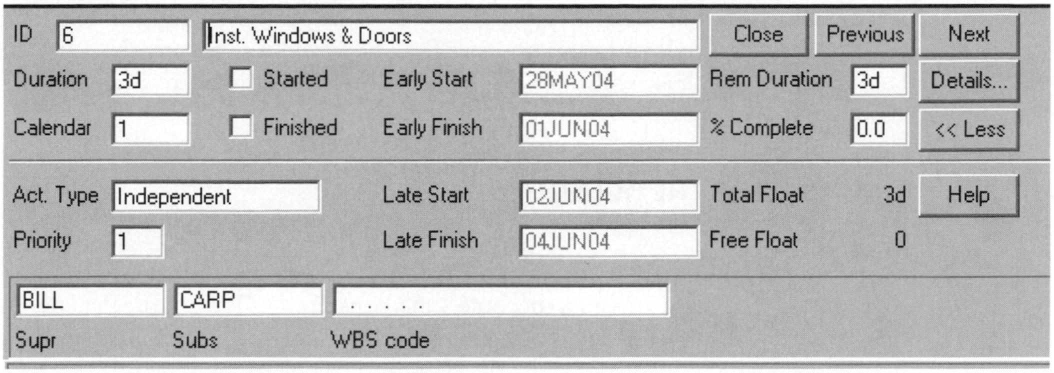

ID	6	Inst. Windows & Doors	Close	Previous	Next

Duration 3d ☐ Started Early Start 28MAY04 Rem Duration 3d Details...

Calendar 1 ☐ Finished Early Finish 01JUN04 % Complete 0.0 << Less

Act. Type Independent Late Start 02JUN04 Total Float 3d Help

Priority 1 Late Finish 04JUN04 Free Float 0

BILL CARP . . . . .

Supr Subs WBS code

FIGURE 21.7   The activity from for *Inst. Windows & Doors*

Note: Each window (Activity Form, Predecessors, etc.) can be on the screen at one time. Click and drag on the window heading to position the window on the screen where you desire it. You can also click and drag on the window borders to size the window as desired. Some schedulers prefer to input the project using the activity form with the Predecessors window also open, inputting everything for one activity at once.

Input Using the PERT View

The PERT view will be used to input the final six activities. From the Menu bar select **View** and then **PERT,** or select the PERT icon ⊞ from the toolbar.

You now see the PERT view which is very similar to the hand-drawn logic diagram. You can click and drag the activity boxes to very nearly match the hand-drawn logic diagram. This makes it easy to input the final activities. Click and drag the activity boxes to match the hand-drawn schedule. To create room at the top of the screen, select all the activities by clicking and dragging a box around all the activities together and then drag them to a lower location on the screen.

To create a new activity, simply move your pointer to the area of the screen where you want the new activity box to be located and double-click. The activity box appears where you clicked and the activity form appears at the bottom of the screen. Input the information in the activity form just as before.

To create the predecessors, simply click from the end of the predecessor box to the beginning of the successor box. To create a finish-to-start relationship, be careful to drag from the end of the predecessor to the beginning of the successor. If you click on the beginning of the predecessor to the beginning of the successor you will create a start-to-start relationship. Of course, a click on the end of the predecessor to the end of the successor will create a finish-to-finish relationship. The relationships can be deleted or edited by clicking directly on the relationship line.

You can change the format of the activity boxes, the relationship lines, and other options by selecting **Format** and whatever is desired in the PERT view. Play around a little in the PERT view to better familiarize yourself with the options available.

This method of input is very desirable for small projects. You can eliminate the need to draw the logic diagram on paper first; however, it is not nearly as useable for large projects. With several hundreds of activities, it is difficult to drag and find the successor activity to connect the relationships.

CALCULATING THE SCHEDULE

SureTrak defaults to automatically calculate the schedule as information is entered. With large schedules, this may become time consuming. The auto calculate feature may be turned off by selecting **Tools** from the Menu bar and then **Schedule** and turning off automatic schedule calculation. Then, to calculate the schedule, click on the Schedule Now icon 🕐 or press the F9 key. If you turn off auto calculate you need to remember to recalculate the schedule to see the effect of any and all changes.

CHECKING THE NUMBER OF DAYS TO COMPLETE

It's a good idea to check the number of work days the schedule has calculated at this time to compare with the hand-drawn schedule (see Figure 21.8). You can do this from the Menu bar by selecting **Format, Organize** or clicking on the Organize icon 🖼.

In the Organize dialog box under **Group by,** right-click and choose **Project.** Then under **Total** choose **Bottom.** This will total the columns and show the results at the bottom of the column. Click **Ok.**

Go to the last activity, slide the vertical bold line to the right to expose the duration column, and note the total number of work days listed at the bottom of the "Duration" column. For the warehouse project, it should be 35 days. If you have completed the forward pass by hand, this total duration should match your calculations. If it does not show 35 days you have missed an activity, entered a duration incorrectly, or not correctly identified the proper predecessors to each activity. Check those three items with the hand-drawn logic diagram and the total duration should now be 35 days.

Note: Remember to save the project occasionally. If the power went off right now or your computer has a problem, your input is lost. Select **File, Save** from the Menu bar once in a while to save what you have created.

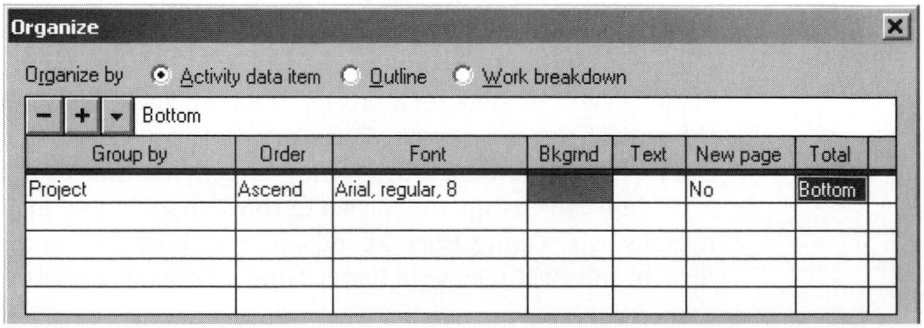

FIGURE 21.8 The Organize dialog box showing how to get the total project duration on the report

Group by	Order	Font	Bkgrnd	Text	New page	Total
Project	Ascend	Arial, regular, 8			No	Bottom

Overview of Formatting

To give you an idea of what the software will help you do, we will now briefly discuss formatting the columns, organizing the schedule, formatting the bars, changing the timescale, formatting the sight lines, and filtering for specific activities.

Format the Columns

To change the columns of information to the left of the bar chart, slide the bold vertical line to the right of the screen, exposing more of the columnar information and less of the bar chart. Double-click in the column heading area (or from the Menu bar, select **Format** and then **Columns**) to bring up the Format Columns dialog box. Delete some of the columns and create new ones (use the minus [−] and plus [+] buttons) to get a feel for this part of the program. Also change some column titles to any description you want. For example, you may want the data to be the early start date, but show a column title of "Start Date." You can change the width, alignment, and font as desired also. To move a column, while in the Format Columns dialog box, hold down the Control key and click and drag up or down to the location desired.

Another way to change the width of a column, while in the bar chart view, is to simply click and drag the separation line between column titles. Use that technique to adjust the width of a few columns to not show so much "white" or wasted space.

Organize the Schedule

You will now notice that the bars show the proper start and finish dates on the screen, but may be a little mixed up as far as the order they appear in. To list the activities in chronological or Early Start, Early Finish order, organize the schedule, click on **Format,** then **Organize,** or use the Organize icon ▦ . Then change **Sort by** (bottom right of the window) to Early Start and then Early Finish, rather than Activity ID. See Figure 21.9.

To do this, click on the cell, then right-click, and choose **Early Start**. Repeat this procedure to put **Early Finish** in the second row. This will sort the activities by early start. If more than one activity has the same start date, the next criteria will be early finish. Click **OK** and see how great the bar chart looks! It is in true chronological order of early start and early finish. Also notice the noncritical (green) and the critical (red) activities.

Format the Bars

The height, color, shape, start points, end points, fill pattern, showing or not showing float, and showing the bars in their early position or late position are a few of the attributes that can be changed with the bars. To format the bars, click on the Format Bars icon ▦ or choose **Format, Bars,** or right-click in any area of the window and select **Format, Bars.**

From the Format Bars dialog box, the data items are selected. An example of the data items that could be selected are shown in Figure 21.10.

If, for a specific report, you did not want to show float, you would uncheck the "Visible" box in the Total float bar row. If you do not like the looks of the little triangles at the beginning or end of the bars, make the Early start point and Early finish

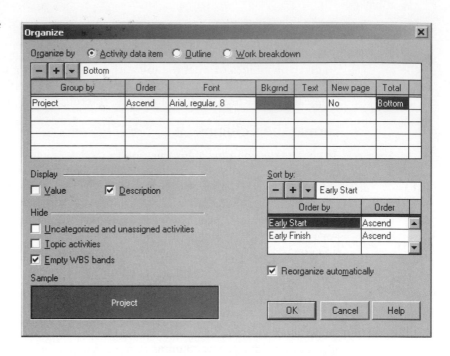

FIGURE 21.9 Organize the project to be ordered by Early Start and Early Finish

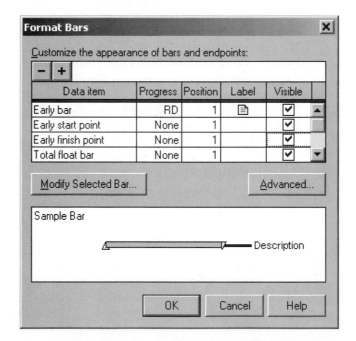

FIGURE 21.10 Format the bars at the Format Bars dialog box

point not visible by removing the check marks. Other bar formatting items can be found by pressing the Modify Selected Bar button or the Advanced button. We will use these buttons later for some of the reports.

Change the Date/Timescale on Bar Charts

Slide the bold vertical line to the left of the screen, exposing only the Activity ID and the Description. Now move the mouse pointer to the top two lines (Year and Month Lines) of timescale or heading at the top of the bar chart and double-click (or from the Menu bar select **Format, Timescale**). Change the Begin date to SD − 1d and the End date to FD + 10d. Make the Minimum time increment to a **Day,** then **OK** it. Notice how long the bars are now. If you want to change the scale to a smaller scale, move the mouse to the days line (the bottom line on the timescale) and then click and drag the timescale left or right to the density you desire.

Change the Sight Lines on the Bar Charts

This is similar to formatting or changing the timescale. Move the mouse pointer to the colored dates or heading area at the top of the bar chart, to the top two lines (Year and Month Lines). Double-click to bring up the **Timescale** dialog box. Or, another way to bring up the Timescale dialog box is, from the Menu bar, select **Format, Sight Lines.** Now that the **Timescale** dialog box is showing, select the **Sight Lines tab.** Put a **Vertical Major** sight line every one week and a **Minor** sight line every one day. Notice how much easier it is to read the bar chart with these changes.

Filter

You can filter for the critical activities only by selecting the Filter button [icon] or **Format, Filter** and then click on the plus (+) button to make a new filter. Give it a four-character ID that will communicate in the future, such as CRIT, with a description as desired, such as, "Critical Activities Only." Then click on the **Modify** button and on Level 1, **Select if,** choose **Total Float; Is,** choose **Less or equal to;** and a **Low value** of **0.** Click on **OK** and apply it by clicking on the **Apply** button.

To get all the activities back, filter again and choose **All Activities. Apply** the filter and all the activities appear back on the screen.

Using the same steps, filter for the activities that belong to the electricians by selecting the Filter button. Then make a new filter, name, and describe it as desired, Modify it to Select if **Subcontractor** is equal to **Electrician.** Press **OK** and **Apply** it. Now you should see only the activities you have assigned to the electrician.

To continue to learn more about SureTrak, filter again to get all the activities back.

CREATE AND SAVE A LAYOUT

The overall design of a document is called the layout. The way the design appears on a computer screen is called the screen layout. In SureTrak the layout includes the formatting of the columns, timescale, bars, sight lines, row height, screen colors, and grouping and sorting of activities. The way the project is filtered is not part of the layout. If you save the project, the layout is also saved and includes these changes the next time you use it.

SureTrak comes with many layouts, some of which you may want to delete as you become more familiar with the program. You can use the layouts that come with Sure-Trak, overwrite any original layout by changing it and saving your changes, or you can save your changes to a new layout, adding it to the list of available layouts.

To make a new layout, click on the Layouts icon 🖼 or, from the Menu bar select **View, Layouts.** The layout you are using is highlighted with brackets around it. Either highlight it or pick another layout on which you want to base the new one. To create the new layout, click on the plus (+) button and enter a **Name** and **Description** as desired.

After inputting a name and description, click on the **Format Selected Layout** button Format Selected Layout ▾ . Next, select **Columns** and format the layout to include the columns as desired. Press **OK** for the columns. To format other options of the layout, select the **Format Selected Layout** button again and **Organize** the layout as desired to include the way the schedule is **Grouped** and **Ordered.** Select the **Format Selected Layout** button again and format the **Bars** as desired. Select the **Format Selected Layout** button again and format the **Timescale** and **Sight Lines** as desired. When you are finished with the formats, click on **Apply** to see that layout.

If you want to change the layout you can reformat it as desired and then save it by clicking on the Save Layout button 🖼 or **File, Save.** If you are asked if you want to save the old layout, select No or the old one will be the same as the new one.

PRINT REPORTS

To print the schedule in this layout first preview it. Click on the Print Preview button 🔍. To change the print setup for headings, footings, landscape or portrait orientation, and so on while in print preview, select **File, Page Setup** or select the Page Setup button 🖨. If the report looks correct and you want to print it, click on the Print button 🖨. To return to the bar chart screen, click on the Format Bars icon ▤ on the upper left of the screen.

Next, you will apply what you have learned above by creating some reports for managing the warehouse project schedule you have entered.

SETTING UP AND PRINTING STANDARD REPORTS

Now that you have an idea of what SureTrak will do, we will proceed with creating standard reports. For the first few reports there is quite a lot of detailed instructions. Then as the instructions continue, it is assumed you have learned the earlier techniques and so there are fewer details given.

Report 1. Input Check Report

It is very easy to make errors while inputting information relating to the schedule. Selecting the wrong predecessor, typing a wrong duration, or assigning inaccurate activity codes would result in a schedule with incorrect information. If that bogus schedule gets distributed to all the parties involved and then is found incorrect, it is not easy to get rid of all the incorrect copies. Even if a corrected schedule is provided with instructions to destroy the old one, it seems the old one keeps coming up and confuses the team members.

To avoid this, get in the habit of always checking the information you input, prior to printing and distributing the reports. The following report is designed to check the information you have input. So that this layout will always be available to select, rather than recreating it each time you want to use it, **create a new layout.** To do this, click on the Layouts icon 🖼 , (or **View, Layouts**) and click on the plus (+) button. Give it a name of **"Input"** and a description of **"To check information entered."** Then **Apply** that layout.

Next, press on the **Format Selected Layout** button, select **Columns,** and set up the desired columns to check all information entered into the computer to make sure it was entered without errors. For the warehouse project, we want the following columns: "Activity ID", "Description", "Original Duration", "Calendar", "Superintendent", "Subcontractors", and "Predecessors". **OK** that layout.

This is an excellent layout to use to check the keyboard input to each activity. Notice the activity *Frame Ext. Walls* has a duration of 5 days, calendar 1 is assigned to it, the superintendent is John, the subcontractor is the carpenters, and it has two predecessors, Activity 2 and 3 (*Form & Pour Slab* and *Temp. Power*). Check the rest of the activities and their corresponding data.

You could also check the input data using the PERT view and create an activity box that contains all the necessary input data to check. In addition, you can format the relationship lines to display the lag and the amount of lag.

Another popular way to see the predecessors, including their lags, is to group the schedule by successors. This lists the successors with their predecessors under the activity. To do this, select **Format, Organize** or the Organize button 🖬 and change the **Group by** to **Successor** then add the columns **Relationship Type** and **Relationship Lag.** Slide the bold vertical line separating the columns and the bar chart area to expose the column information desired. Or, you could also resize the columns to the width desired by clicking and dragging the line separating the column headings.

To print this information, first print preview it. Click on the Print Preview button 🔍. For this report we are interested in only the column information, not the bars. To get rid of the bars, while in print preview, select **File, Page Setup** or the Page Setup icon 📄, change the **Show Bars** to **No,** in the "Visible" column and click **OK.** If the report looks correct and you want to print it, click on the Print icon 🖨. To return to the bar chart screen, click on the Bar Chart button 🖳 in the upper left of the screen.

Report 2. Project Manager's Bar Chart Report

This report will be a rather typical bar chart designed to be used by the project manager.

To make a new layout, click on **View, Layouts** or use the Layouts icon ▦ , select the plus (+) button, and then give the layout the name of PM's Bar and a description of Project Manager's Bar Chart, or as you desire. Select the **Format Selected Layout** button and then **Columns.** Format the columns to include only the "Activity ID," "Description," "Original Duration," and "Superintendent." Delete the other column data and press **OK.** Select the **Format Selected Layout** button again and then **Organize.** We want to have the activities listed in chronological or ES, EF sequence or order. To do this, **Order by** and select **Early Start** as the first sort and then select **Early Finish** as the second sort.

Select the **Format Selected Layout** button again and then **Bars** in order to format the bars as desired for the project managers. Show the float bar by putting a check mark in the "**Visible**" column across from **Total float bar.** Also, if you want to remove the start and finish triangles on the bar, to make the bar look a little more normal, remove the check mark in the "**Visible**" column across from **Early start point** and **Early finish point.**

Select the **Format Selected Layout** button again and then **Timescale** and **Sight Lines** and change the **Begin date** to **SD − 1d** and the **End date** to **FD + 10d.** This starts the timescale on the top of the bar chart 1 day before the project starts and continues the timescale to 10 days after the project finishes. While in this window also change the **Minimum time increment** to a **day.** Next, drag the **Density** scale to the right, to increase the timescale spacing. As you slide the Density scale, you can see the timescale move in the background on your bar chart. While in the Timescale dialog box select the **Sight Lines tab** and change the **Vertical Major site line** to **one Week** and **Minor site line** to **one day.** Click **OK** and now you see a nice-looking bar chart for the project manager, showing float and with sight lines, which helps the bar chart communicate accurate start and finish dates.

If you want to change the layout you can reformat it as desired and then save it by clicking on the Save Layout icon ▦ or **File, Save.**

To make sure the report is the way you want it and eliminate wasted paper, it is a good idea to preview the report before printing it. This can be done by clicking on **File, Print Preview** or by selecting the Print Preview icon ▧. You can change many options of the report from here, prior to printing the report. When the report looks acceptable, click on the Print icon 🖨 and it prints exactly as it looks on the print preview screen.

To go back to the project window click on the Bar Chart icon ▤ in the upper left corner of the screen.

Report 3. Superintendent's Bar Chart Report

This bar chart will be very similar to the project manager's bar chart, with the exception that it will be organized by the two superintendents, showing their activities grouped together. The bars will still show float and be sorted in ES, EF order.

To make this quick change, first make sure you are in the project manager's layout you created above. Then organize the schedule by selecting **Format, Organize** or choose the Organize icon and under **Group by,** select **Superintendent.** Then under **New page** select **Yes,** which will create a page break between the superintendents. To make the divider between the groups more pronounced **Format, Sight Lines** and for **Group divider** select **Band.**

You can summarize the superintendents' schedules to one bar by double-clicking on the organize band by each superintendent's name (the band between the superintendent activities) and it will show one bar for that superintendent. You can double-click on it again and it expands back to show the detail.

Print preview the report and you see a separate page for each superintendent.

If you want to save this layout for future use, select **View, Layouts** or the **Layout** icon 🖼 and then the plus (+) button and enter an appropriate name such as **SuprBar** (you are limited to eight characters) and a description of **Superintendent's Bar Chart.** Then **Apply** the layout and respond **NO** to **Save changes** to the project manager's layout or you will have changed the project manager's layout to be exactly the same as the superintendent's layout.

Now you have experienced two methods of making and saving layouts: (1) **View, Layouts,** give it a name and description and use the Format Selected Layout button `Format Selected Layout ▾` to make changes to the layout; or (2) make the format changes to the screen in any existing layout and then **View, Layouts,** give it a name and description, **Apply** it and **DO NOT save changes** to the previous layout. To see how you can move back and forth in the layouts **View Layouts,** and select the project manager's layout and then reselect the superintendent's layout. You can see those layouts will always be there for your use. You don't need to reformat everything in order to get the report you want.

Report 4. Subcontractor's Bar Chart Report

We now need a schedule we can give to all the subcontractors. This bar chart will be very similar to the superintendent's bar chart except it will not show float. The columns to be included for the subcontractors are: "Activity Description", "Original Duration", "Early Start", "Early Finish", and "Superintendent". Name the title of the ES column "Start" and the EF column "Finish." Organize the schedule in ES, EF order and group it by subcontractor with a new page between each sub. Show the early bar without float. Make the timescale and time line as desired, as long as the schedule communicates. Save the layout so you can use it again.

See if you can create that schedule based on the above information only. If you need additional help, follow the hints below or review the prior reports or layout information.

To make a new layout, **View, Layout,** plus (+) button, and give it a name and description. Then select the **Format Selected Layout** button and **Columns** to insert the columns listed above. Next, select the **Format Selected Layout** button again and **Organize** it so that it is **Grouped by Subcontractor** with a page break (New page = Yes) between subs and is ordered by ES and EF. Then, continue selecting the **Format Selected Layout** button to format the **Bars** to make the **Early bar,** "Visible" and the **Total float bar, Not Visible.** Do not show the start and end points on the bars. Next, format the **Timescale,** and finally the **Sight Lines** as desired. **Apply** the layout and check it out. Make changes if necessary and if changes are made resave the layout by selecting the **Save Layout** icon.

Print preview the report to make sure there is a page break between the subcontractors.

You might also play around with the headings and footings while in print preview.

Report 5. Subcontractor's Tabular Report

This report will be similar to the last one except it will include only column information (no bars) and it will be printed in portrait rather than landscape orientation. In addition, it will include a log text line to remind the subs of important information. Experienced schedulers use this type of report as their favorite to simply communicate information to all parties involved in the project. It does not have the flair of flashy graphics or dazzling diagrams, but it does communicate who does what, when, and where. It is a simple report that you can easily attach to e-mail, put on the Web, or download to a Palm Pilot or other PDA to give everyone the information they need to know.

To create a new layout, give it a unique name and description that communicates. The **Columns** to be included are: "Activity Description", "Original Duration", "Early Start", "Early Finish", "Superintendent", and "Log Text 1". Name the title of the ES column "**Start,**" the EF column "**Finish,**" and the Log Text 1 column "**Notes.**" Delete all other columns. **Organize** the schedule in **ES, EF order** and **Group by Subcontractor** with a **New page** between each sub. Set up the pages (**File, Page Setup**) to make the **Columns** "Visible" and the bars to **No,** not visible. While in Page Setup have the report printed in **Portrait** orientation rather than landscape.

Slide the bold vertical line over to uncover the *"Notes" column* and add the following notes: Remind the excavator to bring dynamite, roof shingles are to be autumn brown, concrete slab is to be 6,000 psi, exterior walls are to be framed with 2×6 metal studs, siding is doeskin color—aluminum, and the brick is mocha brown.

Preview it in Print Preview and, if it looks good, print it. If you make any changes to the layout remember to save the layout by selecting the Save Layout icon 🖼 .

Report 6. Owner's Bar Chart Report

This will be a standard bar chart designed for the owner of the project. To keep the owner from being alarmed if some of the activities start later than the early start date, but within the float (therefore, not delaying the project) the report will show the late bar, rather than the early bar. This will be the major change in the report.

Format, Bars so the **Late bar** is visible and everything else is not visible. **OK** that layout and you will notice the activity description is no longer listed next to the bar. To get the activity description next to the bars, get back into format bars, select **Late bar,** click under **Label,** then add **Description** as a Data item and position it to the **Right** of the bar.

As you look at the screen, notice that all the bars with float have been shifted to the right, their LS and LF dates. It is particularly noticeable on the *Temp. Power* activity. Also notice the bars seem to be out of chronological order. **Organize** the schedule so the activities will be in **Late Start, Late Finish** order. Also, while you are organizing the schedule, **Group** the activities by **Project** with the total number of work days at the bottom of the duration column so the owner can see the total number of work days scheduled.

The columns of interest to the owner are: "Description", "Duration", "Superintendent" (in case the owner has a question for one of the superintendents), "Late Start" (labeled "Start Date"), *"Late Finish"* (labeled "Finish Date"), *"Actual Start"*, and *"Actual Finish"*. If you want the "Start Date" column heading to show Start on the top line and Date on the bottom line, put the pipe symbol (on most keyboards the pipe symbol is the shift, backward slash key) between Start and Finish so it looks like this: Start|Date. You could do the same for the Finish Date.

Just for variety, change the color scheme to "Southwest" **(Format, Screen Colors,** and select **Southwest).**

Print preview the schedule and make the orientation landscape. Save the layout and name the report for the owners so you can use it in the future. As you save it, remember to not save the prior layout or the prior layout will be changed to look like this owner layout.

Note: Showing the late bar for the owner is not trying to deceive the owner. It is just to keep an owner who is not an expert in the use of CPM scheduling to think an activity is late when it happens after the ES date, but within the float. If an owner has expertise in using CPM, you may want to provide that owner with the disk of all the scheduling information.

Report 7. Critical Activities Only Report

This report will be a bar chart of the critical activities only, ordered by ES, EF. Make a new layout and name it "ESEF" with a description of Chronological Order. Organize it so that the activities are ordered by Early Start and then Early Finish. Format the columns to provide information as desired. Filter by selecting **Format, Filter** or the Filter icon ▼ and select the critical filter you set up earlier. If the critical path filter is not there, create it by clicking on the plus (+) button to make a new filter. Give it a four-character ID that will communicate in the future, such as "CRIT" with a description as desired, such as "Critical Activities Only." Then click on the **Modify** button and on Level 1, **Select if** and choose **Total Float; Is,** choose **Less or equal to;** and a **Low value** of **0.** Click on **OK** and **Apply** it. Now you see only the critical activities on the computer screen. To get all the activities back, filter for all activities.

Report 8. Making Standard Reports

You have already learned how to make a layout that can be used continually. However, the problem with layouts is the layout does not include the filter or the way you want the page to be set up. Therefore, in order to create reports that include the layout, filter, and page setup, SureTrak has a report function. It is accessed by selecting **Tools, Reports** from the Menu bar.

We will make a new report that will always filter for the critical activities only, listing them in chronological order. Make this new report, at the Reports dialog box

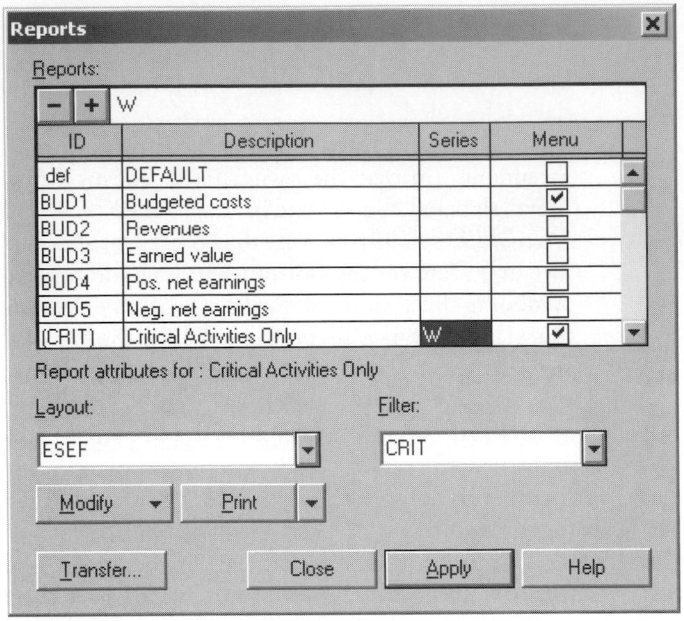

FIGURE 21.11 Select the
layout and filter for report
in the Reports dialog box

(Figure 21.11). Selecting **Tools, Reports,** and click on the plus (+) button and give
it an **ID** of **CRIT** (you are limited to four characters) and a **Description** of **Critical
Activities Only.**

As shown in Figure 21.11, the Layout option shows ESEF and the Filter option
shows CRIT which you created earlier. The "Series" column is used if you want this
report to be included into a series of several reports that could be printed at once. In
the example (Figure 21.11) a *W* is shown to make this report one of the reports you
will want to print each week. The "Menu" box is checked if you want this report to be
included on the menu of frequently printed reports. If you want to change the page
setup to format the headers, footers, orientation, margins, showing the bars or just the
columns, and so on, select the **Modify** button and then **Page Setup.**

Now, to test the report, select **Tools, Run Report** and then select the **Critical
Activities Only** report you just created from the drop-down menu (if you did not put
a check mark under "menu", it would not be listed); then click **OK** to print it. It is not
a bad idea to clean up the reports menu by removing the check marks under the "Menu"
column for all except the reports you frequently print. Any report can be printed,
whether on the report menu or not, by selecting **Tools, Reports, Apply** and then
printing the report. The report menu is a shortcut to quickly print popular reports.

Report 9. Printing a Series of Reports with One Setup

Make the project manager's bar chart layout, the superintendent's bar chart layout, and
the subcontractor's tabular report layout (which you created earlier), along with the
prior critical activities report, to all be included in a series of reports to be printed weekly.

You will need to do the following for each of the reports: Select **Tools, Reports** and then the plus (+) button to create a new report. Select the appropriate **Layout** and **Filter** (filter will typically be **All Activities**). If you need to change the page setup, as you will for the subcontractor's tabular report (no bars shown), select the **Modify** button and then **Page Setup.** Assign each of the reports to be part of the weekly (*W*) report series. Then, to print this series, select **Tools, Run Report Series** and select **W.** All four of the reports are now printing.

You can see how simple the printing of reports can be as you become proficient with CPM and this software.

Time to practice what you have learned. You might create and use a layout called Junk, so that you will not mess up a good layout. Review what you have learned in these first nine layouts and reports. Experiment with the bar charts and PERT view and see what you can do. Practice formatting columns, organizing the activities, formatting to show different bars (early, late, float), changing the sight lines, adjusting the timescale, creating standard reports that are included or not included on the report menu, and creating some report series. You will realize that you can create basically any type of report you can imagine.

Following are a couple of practice reports:

A. You just found out you have an electrical subcontractor that can't read a bar chart. Develop a tabular schedule report showing the electrician's activities only. Remember, no signs of float, or late dates. Choose the subcontractor's tabular report layout. To select the electricians activities use the following: (Format, Filter, plus (+) button, name and describe it, Modify button, Select if Subs, is Equal to ELECT).

B. A bar chart for the carpenter. The carpentry subcontractor just requested a schedule of his activities only. He wants a bar chart report in chronological order. Can you do it? Go for it!

C. Filter for the electrician's activities that are critical. The item to watch for on this one is to make sure you have selected the button on the Filter dialog box that shows level one must meet **all** of the following criteria. If the **any** button is selected the filter will give you the critical activities **and** the electrical activities.

D. Another filter to try out, is having the software ask which subcontractor you want to filter for. Create a new filter with **Subcontractor** is **Equal to,** check the **Ask me** box and then **Apply** the filter.

Report 10. Adding Logos, Clip Art, Curtains, and Text to Enhance the Schedule

Company logos and/or clip art can enhance a schedule to be used in a proposal for construction services. The appropriate use of clip art can make a schedule look impressive and professional. Common items to add to the schedule are the footprint or floor plan of a building, an elevation, a rendering, or a photograph. Of course, whatever is to be added must be in electronic format.

From the Menu bar, select **Insert, Object/Picture; Browse** the C:\stwin\ clipart directory and change **Files of type** to **all files,** select a file, **Open,** and **OK** it. Now, that particular graphic shows on the schedule. Click and drag it to any location and make it any size you desire.

Some graphics from other software applications may need to be imported or copied and pasted into Primavera Draw first. Then it should be saved as a PMT file to the Clip Art directory or file folder, allowing it to be inserted into the schedule.

If Primavera Draw is not loaded on your computer, you can copy it from the Sure-Trak CD in the Support\Prmdraw folder. In this folder there are four files that begin with Prm characters. Copy these four files to the SureTrak folder on your computer and then create a shortcut to the Prmdraw.exe file. Now you can run the Primavera Draw program.

DOWNLOADING LOGOS FROM THE INTERNET.   First, go to the desired Internet site, right-click on the logo or item to be copied, and select **Save Picture as.** At the top of the **Save Picture** dialog box in the **Save in** space, browse to the location you want to save the picture to, such as C:\stwin\clipart. Next give it a **File name** of choice, save it as a **Bitmap** type of file, and select **Save.** Now get back into SureTrak, select **Insert, Object/Picture,** and **Browse** to find the file you just named and saved and **OK** it. You now see the picture, logo, and so on you downloaded from the Internet in the upper left corner of your bar chart area where you can click and drag it to any location or size it as desired.

SHOWING A CURTAIN.   You can show a curtain of available time when an activity or series of activities should happen. Select **Insert, Curtain,** and choose a **Duration** for the length of time the curtain is to show, a **Border color,** a **Fill color,** a **Fill pattern,** and **OK** it. The curtain is displayed on the left edge of the bar chart schedule where you can click and drag it to the desired dates.

ADDING TEXT TO THE SCHEDULE.   This is done similar to clip art or curtains. Select **Insert, Text,** enter the text, select the **Font, Text color,** and so forth and **OK** it. That text now appears in the top left corner of the bar chart where you can click and drag it to the location of choice. Print report #10 as any selected schedule with some enhancements on it.

Now that you have basic skills with inputting a schedule into SureTrak, creating layouts and basic reports, and enhancing the schedule, it is time to learn how to use the schedule for managing the project. The first step is to learn how to update the schedule.

Report 11. Updating the Schedule

Load the schedule to be updated (most likely it is already opened).

    A. *Save the Project to a New Name and Version.* Preserve the as-planned schedule so that you will have the project team's original thinking saved. To do this select **File, Save As** and give the project a new **Name,** such as

Warehouse 01, **Number/Version,** such as 1st Update and **Title,** such as Warehouse 1st Update. This creates new schedule files that will be used to update the project for the first month. At the beginning of the second month you could save the schedule again, to another new name, to update through the second month, and so on. This gives a historical record of what happened on the project throughout the project's life. The original project files will now be used as a historical copy, whereas the new project files will continue to be updated with the current status of the project.

B. *Create a Target or Baseline Schedule.* Before making the first update **(1st update only)** Select **Define, Target Dates,** and Assign **Early** or **Late** dates as target dates. Some managers prefer early dates so they can compare the updated schedule with the earliest possible dates of the target schedule. Other managers prefer the late dates as the target, so they can see the latest possible dates that an activity can take place. Then, if an activity starts or finishes later than the early dates, yet within float, the activity will not appear late.

This baseline or target schedule will be used for the rest of the job, enabling the project team to compare the current schedule with the target schedule. If, during the course of the project, you have significant changes that require a new target schedule, you can reset the target. However, if you do this, the original as-planned schedule is no longer the target schedule and you will not see the comparison of the current with the old target. This is one of the differences in SureTrak and Primavera Project Planner (P3). With P3 you can change the target several times and then still compare the current schedule with any previous schedule. With SureTrak, once a new target is set, the old one is no longer available.

C. *Format the Bars to Make the Target Bar Visible.* To do this, put a check mark in the "Visible" column across from **Target bar.** Format the rest of the report as desired.

D. *Organize Manually.* To keep the activities from jumping around as you update, select **Format, Organize** and remove the check mark in the box to the left of **Reorganize automatically** toward the bottom right of the dialog box. Without doing that, as you update the schedule, with some activities starting earlier or later than planned, the activities would automatically reorganize themselves in the new ES, EF positions and move up and down on the screen. Most schedulers find that annoying. Now, as the activities are updated they stay in their same position or sort. From this point on, you will need to remember that for the schedule to reorganize in a new grouping, sort, or order you must force reorganizing by selecting **Format, Reorganize Now**.

E. *Set the Data Date.* The data date represents today's date. If the project has not been updated, the data date is the project start date. In SureTrak the data date is always in the morning. To update a project through Friday night, make the data date Saturday morning. For this exercise, set the data

Act ID	Description	Orig Dur	
			FEB / MAR timeline: 28 01 02 03 04 05 06 07 08 09 10 11 12 13 14 15 16 17 18 19 20 21 22 23 24 25 26
Warehouse			
1	Excavate	3d	Excavate
3	Temp. Power	1d	Temp. Power
2	Form & Pour Slab	6d	Form & Pour Slab
4	Frame Ext. Walls	5d	Frame Ext. Walls
5	Frame Roof	2d	Frame Roof
6	Inst. Windows & Doors	3d	
9	Shingle Roof	2d	
7	Rough Electrical	4d	
11	Install Siding NEW Sides	4d	
10	Brick South Side	5d	

FIGURE 21.12   Setting the data date

date to be about three weeks beyond the project start date. (Do not update activities beyond three weeks because you will update them later by the use of e-mail.) The easiest way to set the data date is to move the mouse pointer over the data date line (red vertical line on the bar chart) until it turns to a double arrow with *DD* on it. Click and drag the data date through the time period you want to update and those activities will be highlighted or spotlighted. The position where the new black line remains is the new data date. The computer screen should look similar to Figure 21.12.

F. *Update the Schedule.* Right-click anywhere on the screen and select **Update Activity** or select **Tools** and **Update Activity** to make the update dialog box appear. Highlight the first activity to update. Change **Early Start** to **Actual Start** and input the actual start date of the activity or click on the down arrow to bring up a calendar. Then double-click on the actual start date. Now change **Early Finish** to **Actual Finish** and select the activity's actual finish date.

Continue updating all activities that have started and/or finished up through the current date (in this case three weeks) into the schedule. Make some activities early and some late. If an activity has started, but not finished, update the **Percent complete** or **Remaining duration.** You will notice that percent complete and remaining duration are linked together. You input only one and the other automatically calculates. If you would rather input both, and unlink percent complete and remaining duration, select **Tools, Options**, the **Resource tab** and remove the check mark in front of **Link remaining duration and schedule percent complete.** To advance to the next activity, click on the arrow button in the top right corner of the update dialog box.

If an activity is interrupted after it starts, you can **Suspend** and **Resume** an activity while in the update screen.

When finished updating, recalculate the schedule by clicking on the **Schedule Now** icon ⊙ on the toolbar or hit the F9 key. This causes SureTrak to do a new forward and backward pass in order to update the schedule. You now see all the future activities adjusted to their new start and finish dates based on the updated schedule. You can also see the difference in the target schedule and the current schedule.

Remember that typically, for updates beyond the first, you do not make a new target. You simply change the data date and then update the completed activities. Many experienced schedulers update daily, dealing only with old activities that have finished or new activities that have started. Daily updates take only a few minutes. The end of the month updates require not only start and finish dates but also percent complete or days remaining, in order to receive payment on percent complete of the total project. Print the updated schedule as report #11.

Report 12. Creating a New Schedule Based on an Old Schedule

You have just been awarded a contract to build another warehouse—only this time it will start two months from today. Also, the roof is to be a tile roof system that will require seven work days to install and the entire exterior is to be siding, no brick. Therefore, siding will take six days instead of four.

A. Open the original warehouse schedule and save it **(File, Save As)** to a new name, such as New Warehouse.

B. Make changes to represent the new project. Change the description of "Shingle Roof" to "Tile Roof" and change the original duration from two days to seven days. Delete the *Brick South Side* activity (highlight the activity and hit the Delete key) and change the duration of *Install Siding* to six days and clean up the description. (*Note:* Use caution when deleting activities because other activities may lose their predecessor-successor relationships, which may need to be reassigned.)

C. Change the start date by selecting **File** and then **Project Overview** from the Menu bar. Now change the **Project start** date to two months from today. While in this screen, you can also change the version and title if desired.

D. Check the input changes and recalculate the schedule. You should now have a dual critical path showing *Tile Roof* with zero days of total float.

E. Print reports.

Report 13. Using Fragnets to Copy Schedules or Parts of Schedules

Many projects include sequences of activities that are repetitive. These repetitive sequences are called "network fragments" or "fragnets." Copy and Paste can be used to greatly decrease the time required in inputting these repetitive activities.

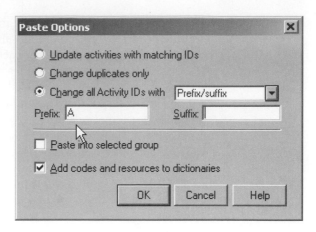

FIGURE 21.13 The Paste Options dialog box is used to put a prefix in front of the activity ID number

For example, you have just been awarded the contract to build a large warehouse complex. The project is divided into three warehouses: A, B, and C. Each warehouse is similar to the original warehouse we scheduled. So, basically we want to **Open** the Original Warehouse project, **Save it** to a new name such as Warehouse Complex, and then copy and paste the activities to create the three warehouses.

This is a 10-step process as follows:

1. Select the activities to be copied. In this case select all **(Edit, Select All)** the activities in the schedule. Make sure all predecessors, durations, activity codes, and so on are properly assigned to the activities before you copy them, because all information tied to the activity is copied with the activity and you will not need to reenter all that information.

2. Select the **Copy Activity** button ▣ or **Edit, Copy Activity**. This copies all the selected activities to the clipboard.

3. Select the **Paste Activity** icon ▣ or choose **Edit, Paste Activity.** The **Paste Options** dialog box appears similar to Figure 21.13.

    Put a dot in the "Change all Activity ID's with," then select **Prefix/Suffix** and in the "Prefix" box, enter an *A* (for building A), and **OK** it. Select the **Paste Activity** tool again (the activities are already copied to the clip board) and assign a **Prefix** of *B*. Repeat this for building C.

4. Now you have duplicates of each activity. **Organize** the schedule to **Order by, Activity ID** in order to get the activities of each building grouped or sorted together.

5. Create a new activity code by selecting **Define, Activity Codes** named "Bldg" with a length of one and a **Description** of "Building." Next, create a **Value** of "A," with a **Description** of "Building A," and so forth for B and C. The Activity Codes dialog box will look similar to Figure 21.14.

6. Add the "Building" column to the layout so you can assign the proper building to each activity.

FIGURE 21.14 Use the Activity Codes dialog box to create the Building activity code

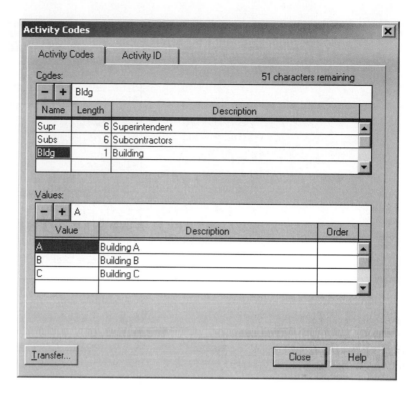

7. Under the "Building" column, Assign Building **A** to activity ID "A1"—
   Excavate. Next, highlight the **A** you just assigned and then select **Edit,
   Copy Cell** (not copy activity). Then, under the "Building" column, select
   all the activities you want to assign an *A* to (all activity ID's with a prefix of
   A). Next, select **Edit, Paste Cell** and an *A* is assigned to all the activities
   belonging to building A in one move. This can be an enormous time saver,
   rather than assigning the building to each activity independently. The
   "Building" column should have the *A*'s assigned as shown in Figure 21.15.

8. Repeat this procedure of **Copy Cell** and **Paste Cell** to assign Building "B"
   to each of the B activities and Building "C" to each of the C activities.

9. **Delete** the original activities without the ID prefix of *A*, *B*, or *C*. You don't
   need them anymore.

10. **Organize** the schedule and **Group** it by **Building** and **Sort** it by **ES, EF.**

You now have the three buildings scheduled using fragnets and you didn't have
to enter each activity three times. Notice, however, the three buildings are each starting at the same time. We need to decide when each building will start and finish and
schedule them that way. There are three different ways of accomplishing this.

The first method is to look for the **critical activity with the longest duration.**
In this case the *Form & Pour Slab* and the *Install Drywall* activities with a duration of six

FIGURE 21.15 Assign Building A to all the activities belonging to that building

Act ID	Description	Orig Dur	Building
A1	Excavate	3	A
A10	Brick South Side	5	A
A11	Install Siding NEW Sides	4	A
A12	Paint Exterior	3	A
A13	Install Drywall	6	A
A14	Paint Interior	3	A
A15	Finish Electrical	2	A
A16	Close Out	1	A
A2	Form & Pour Slab	6	A
A3	Temp. Power	1	A
A4	Frame Ext. Walls	5	A
A5	Frame Roof	2	A
A6	Inst. Windows & Doors	3	A
A7	Rough Electrical	4	A
A8	Insulate	3	A
A9	Shingle Roof	2	A

days each. We will use the longest critical duration as the amount of lag in a start-to-start relationship between the *Excavate* activity in Building A and the *Excavate* activity in Building B. Then do the same between Excavate in Building B and C. Use the Predecessors window **(View, Activity Detail, Predecessor)** to do this. Highlight the activity and assign the **Predecessor,** with a **Type** of Lag of **Start-to-Start** and a **Lag** of six days. If you want to eliminate the extra float in each building, assign a **Finish-to-Finish Lag** of six days to the last activity in each building as well.

The second method to offset the start and finish of each building is with date constraints. Highlight the activity to be constrained, right-click, and choose **Activity Detail, Constraints**. Put a **Mandatory Start** Constraint on the first activity in each building and a **Mandatory Finish** Constraint on finish date of each building. This forces these activities to happen on these days, in spite of the schedule logic. You may want to show both the Constraints window and the Dates window at the same time to aid you to do this.

The third method is to restrain each activity, in each building by assigning the same activity in the preceding building as a predecessor. Excavate the first area, then excavate the second area, and finally excavate the third area. Repeated with each activity in each building. That will ensure that no single crew will be working in two places at one time. Also, a delay by a crew will show the real effects down line in the project. This can be accomplished by highlighting the activities to be linked and then using the Link Activities button ⬚ or **Edit, Link Activities.** Another way to create predecessors is to highlight the activities to be linked in a finish-to-start predecessor relationship, and then click on the Link Activities button. Either of the above three methods could be the best, depending on the way the management team wants to schedule the work.

Report 14. Resource Management—Cost Loading the Schedule

To create a resource-loaded schedule, use the original warehouse schedule, **Open** it, and **Save** it to a new name, such as Warehouse Resource.

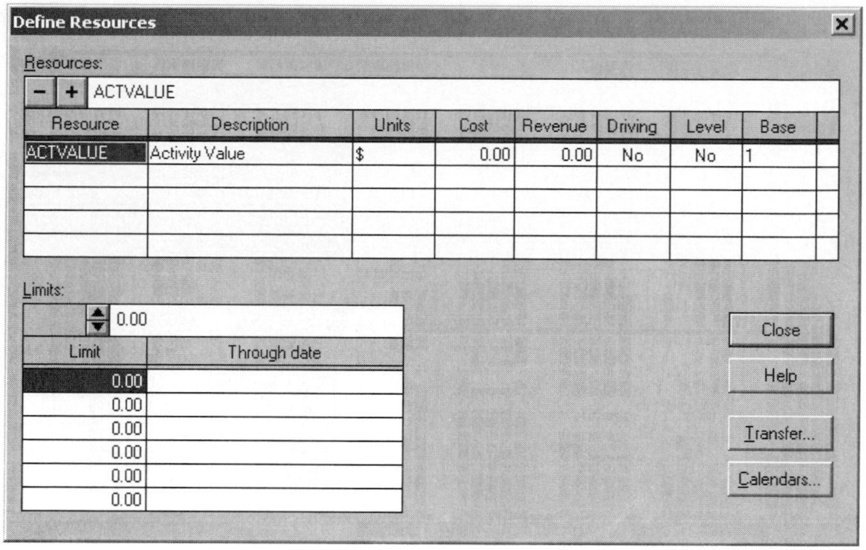

FIGURE 21.16 Define Resources dialog box

The purpose in cost loading the schedule is to determine and help manage cash flow. We are going to keep this simple by keeping track of only the lump sum costs or value to each activity. You could keep a more detailed record of costs to include material, labor, equipment, overhead, and so on (see Chapter 15 for more information).

The following outlines a six-step process for cost loading a schedule:

1. Create a resource by selecting **Define, Resources** called "ACTVALUE." Give it a **Description** of "Activity Value," **Units** of "$", "0" **Cost,** "0" **Revenue,** and make sure **Driving** is **No** and **Level** is **No.** We do not want the schedule to automatically level the resources, nor do we want the schedule to be resource driven, rather than duration driven. The Define Resources dialog box should appear as in Figure 21.16.

   Base is the base calendar to use, so we will use calendar **1.** We will not limit the number of dollars per hour; therefore, set the **Limit** (lower left of dialog box) at "0" and then close the dialog box.

2. Create a layout with the following columns: "Activity ID," "Description," "Percent Complete," "Budgeted Cost," "Actual Cost to Date," "Cost to Complete," "Cost at Completion," "Cost Variance," "Percent Expended," and "Earned Value Cost". Slide the data line to reveal those columns. Save the layout to a desired name, such as, Resource Layout.

3. Select **View, Activity Detail,** and open the **Costs** Window. Highlight the activity you want to cost load. Click under **Resource 1** and select the resource **ACTVALUE** you created earlier. Now input the cost **At completion** for that activity.

FIGURE 21.17   Costs window for the *Excavate* activity

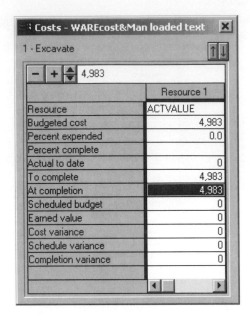

Figure 21.17 is how the Costs window should look for the activity *Excavate*. You may want to sort the activities **(Organize, Sort by)** by activity **ID** because the data is listed by activity number on the following table. That will make it a little easier to enter.

Figure 21.18 is a table of each activity and its associated value.

Continue selecting the resource **ACTVALUE** and entering the cost **At completion** for all the activities. To move down the list of activities, click on the down arrow button in the top right corner of the Costs window. When all the costs have been input the total on the bottom of the **Budgeted Costs** column should be $33,642. **(Organize, Group by Project,** and **Total at the Bottom).**

4. Now that each activity is cost loaded, resort the activities in early start, early finish order. This will give you the cash flow based on the early dates.

5. To view the Resource Profile at the bottom of the computer screen, click on **View** and select **Resource Profile,** or click on the Resource Profile icon 📊. Then choose **ACTVALUE** in the bottom left of the Resource Profile window. Next, press the **Format . . .** button and select the **Display** tab. In the **Display** box, select **Budget, Calculate Total** and show the **timescale** with **Day intervals** in order to get daily cash flow. (Normally you would probably want monthly intervals, but for this little project we will choose daily intervals.) Select the **Profile** tab and **Show the histogram** as **Bars, Side by side** and also **Show the total cumulative curve** and **OK** the window.

FIGURE 21.18 Information needed to cost load the warehouse project

Activity Description	Activity Value
1 Excavate	$4,983
2 Form & Pour Slab	$2,652
3 Temp. Power	$585
4 Frame Ext. Walls	$2,500
5 Frame Roof	$3,000
6 Inst. Windows & Doors	$1,599
7 Rough Electrical	$2,500
8 Insulate	$1,098
9 Shingle Roof	$950
10 Brick South Side	$4,000
11 Install Siding	$3,500
12 Paint Exterior	$699
13 Install Drywall	$2,778
14 Paint Interior	$798
15 Finish Electrical	$1,800
16 Close Out	$200
Total	$33,642

You may need to slide the vertical bold line separating the columns from the bars to the left to display more of the bar chart in order to see the cash flow histogram. Also, if you want to see daily costs, change the timescale of the bar chart to show each day. The cash-loaded schedule should look similar to Figure 21.19.

The vertical bars in Figure 21.19 show the daily cash flow with the values on the left side, which you notice is multiplied by 100. The cumulative activity value is shown as a progress S-curve with the values on the right side, which you notice is multiplied by 1,000. If you want to see the weekly cash flow, format the resource profile to a weekly interval. For most major projects you would probably want to see the costs on a monthly scale. Save the layout if desired (File, Save).

6. To print the report, **Print Preview** it, then select **Page Setup** and check to make sure the bars are visible. Then click on the **Resource Profile/Table** tab and put a check mark in front of **Print Resource Profile** and **Print**

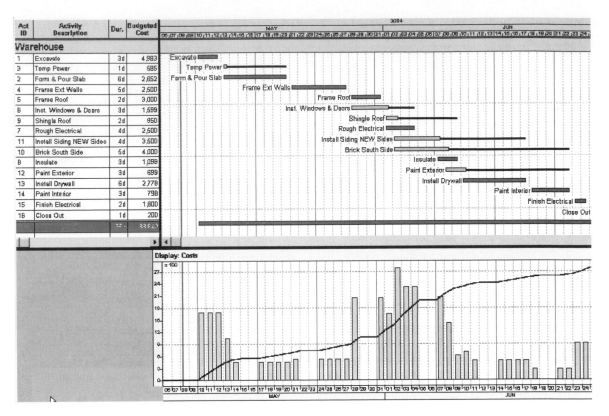

FIGURE 21.19   Cash-loaded schedule for the warehouse project

Resource Table. Change the **Resource displayed in profile/table** to **ACTVALUE** and **OK** the setup. You may have to select the down arrow in the Print Preview window to see the cash flow histogram on the next page. If you want it at the bottom of the bar chart, as shown previous, in the Print Preview window, select **Page Setup,** then **Resource Profile/Table** tab, and set the **Profile height** to 1.5 inches. It should fit at the bottom of the bar chart.

When updating a project that is cost loaded, you may want to show the Update Window and the Costs Window at the same time. This will allow you to update the start and finish times and costs related to each activity at the same time. Update a few of the activities of the warehouse project with some activities costing more, some less, and some right on. Evaluate the costs and see if they make sense to you. Make sure you have organized the activities by project and show totals at the bottom of each column.

Report 15. Resource Management—Labor Loading the Schedule

The purpose of labor loading the schedule is to determine and help manage the number of labor hours per day on the project. You could use the float in the schedule to balance or level the number of daily labor hours on the project. To do this, it is necessary to know the crew size or number of people assigned to each activity.

Labor loading the project is a six step process:

1. Create a new Resource by selecting **Define, Resources** called **"LABORHRS"** (you are limited to 8 characters in this cell). Give the resource a **Description** of "Total Labor Hours," **Units** of "ea.," "0" **Cost,** "0" **Revenue,** and check to make sure **Driving** is **No.** We want the schedule to be duration driven rather than resource driven. Mark **Level** as **Yes** so you can have the computer level the resource if you desire. **Base** is the base calendar to use, so we will use calendar **1.** We will not limit the number of units per hour; therefore, put the **Limit** (lower left of window) to "0" and then close the Define Resources dialog box.

2. Format the columns to include the **Units per Hour** and the **Quantity at Completion** columns.

3. Select **View, Activity Detail,** and open the **Resources** window. Highlight the activity you want to labor load. Click under **Resource 2** and select the resource **LABORHRS** you created earlier. Now input the crew size (Units per hour) for each activity as listed on Table 21.20. The labor hours at completion as calculated by SureTrak will be that activity's crew size, times the activity's duration, times 8 hours per day. You may want to sort the activities **(Organize, Sort by)** by activity **ID** because the data is listed by activity number in Figure 21.20.

   Continue to select each activity and select the resource **LABORHRS** from the Resources window and enter the crew size (Units per hour). Notice SureTrak totals the labor hours for that activity at the bottom of the Resources window. To move down the list of activities, click on the down arrow button in the top right corner of the Resources window. When the crew size for each activity has been input, the total at the bottom of the **Quantity at Completion** column **(Organize, Group by Project, and Total at the Bottom)** should be "1,048" labor hours for the warehouse project.

4. Now that all the activities are labor loaded, re-sort the activities to be in **Early Start, Early Finish** order. This will give you the cash flow based on the early dates.

5. To view the Resource Profile at the bottom of the computer screen, click on **View** and select **Resource Profile** or click on the Resource Profile icon . Then choose **LABORHRS** in the bottom left of the resource profile window.

FIGURE 21.20 Information needed to labor load the warehouse schedule

Activity Description	Crew Size
1 Excavate	1
2 Form & Pour Slab	2
3 Temp. Power	1
4 Frame Ext. Walls	3
5 Frame Roof	4
6 Inst. Windows & Doors	2
7 Rough Electrical	2
8 Insulate	3
9 Shingle Roof	3
10 Brick South Side	4
11 Install Siding	2
12 Paint Exterior	2
13 Install Drywall	3
14 Paint Interior	2
15 Finish Electrical	2
16 Close Out	1
Total Labor Hours	1048

Next, press the **Format . . .** button and select the **Display** tab. In the **Display** box, select **Quantity, Calculate Total** and show the **timescale** with **Day intervals** in order to get the number of labor hours per day on the project. Select the **Profile** tab and **Show the histogram** as **Bars, Side by side,** check the cumulative curve box if you want to see the progress S curve and the then **OK** the window.

You may need to slide the vertical bold line separating the columns from the bars to the left to display more of the bar chart in order to see the resource histogram. The labor loaded schedule should look similar to Figure 21.21.

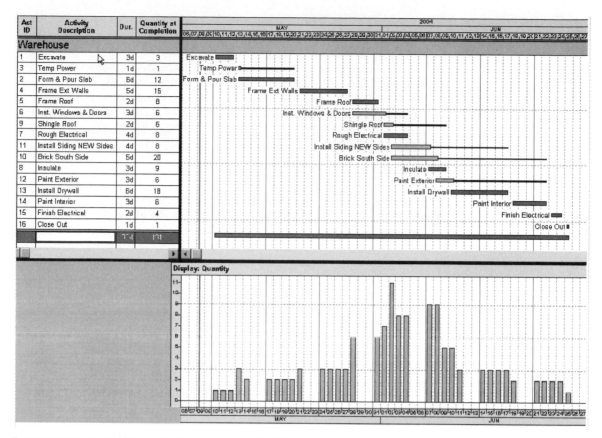

FIGURE 21.21   Partial view of a labor loaded schedule of the warehouse project

If you click on any of the vertical bars it will show the number of labor hours for that day. If you right click on the progress S cumulative curve it will display the total labor hours up through that date.

If you prefer to show the actual number, rather than the histogram click on **Format . . .** on the bottom of the resource histogram screen and select the **Table** tab. If the date table shows asterisks you may have to slide the timescale to make the columns a little larger for the data to show on the screen. If you wanted to know the number of workers on the project each day you would need to divide that number by 8 if you are working 8 hours per day. If you wanted to level out the labor hours you could make *Install Siding* a predecessor to *Brick South Side*. That, of course, would eliminate some of the float in those activities, but it would level the number of daily labor hours on the project without delaying the completion date.

6. To print the report, **Print Preview** it, then select **Page Setup** and check to make sure the bars are visible. Then click on the **Resource Profile/Table** tab and put a check mark in front of **Print Resource Profile** and/or **Table** as desired. Change the **Resource displayed in profile/table** to **LABORHRS** and **OK** the setup. You may have to select the down arrow in the Print Preview window to see the resource histogram on the next page. If you want the histogram at the bottom of the bar chart, as shown previous, in the Print Preview window, select **Page Setup,** then **Resource Profile/Table** tab, and set the **Profile height** to 1.5 inches and it should fit at the bottom of the bar chart.

When updating a project that is labor loaded, you may want to show the Update window and the Resources window at the same time. This will allow you to update the start and finish dates and resources related to each activity concurrently.

BACKING UP A SCHEDULE

To make a copy of a schedule to a diskette for backup purposes or to share the schedule with other SureTrak users, the easiest way is to back up the project and then give it to the other users by either disk or e-mail. The reason to use backup rather than just copying the files is there are approximately 26 files associated with each project. If you manually copy each file, you may overlook one file and render the backup useless. If you are e-mailing the project, 26 attachments may be overwhelming. A backed-up, compressed project is only one file. Also, backing up a compressed project reduces the file size, allowing a large project schedule fit on a diskette.

To back up a project, select **Tools, Project Utilities, Backup**. You then need to select which project to back up and set the location to back up the file to. The default location is the same folder as the projects folder. Give the project a name and put a check mark in the **Include shared layouts** box, if you want to keep the layouts with the project. Also add a check mark to **Compress** the schedule. Then select **Backup** to make it happen. The file name extension assigned to the backup file is .stx. Be aware that the backed-up file needs to be restored prior to being able to open the project files. The restore instructions are below.

RESTORING A SCHEDULE

Project Restore allows the user to decompress and open a backed-up file from Sure-Trak. To restore a project, select **Tools, Project Utilities, Restore**. The **From** folder defaults to the projects folder. If the project to be restored is not in this folder, you need to **Browse** to the folder containing the backed-up file.

The **To** folder is where the project will be placed. It defaults to the projects folder. If this location is not where you would like it to be, **Browse** to the folder where you would like the project to reside. Typically include the shared layouts. Then, select **Restore** to make it happen. If that does not work you may need to use Explore to change the name of the file to be restored with an .exe suffix and then double-click on that file within Explore.

E-MAILING A SCHEDULE

Overview

SureTrak can send and receive updated project information to other SureTrak users. This is accomplished by e-mailing *status sheets*. For this portion of the exercise, you will send a status sheet to another user, then they will update it and e-mail it back to you. Use the schedule that was previously updated. The file name was Warehouse 01 with a project name of Warehouse Update, or whatever you named it. Save this project as Warehouse Update Email or as desired.

Mail Setup

To e-mail the project schedule, you first need to make sure the computer is set up properly. Select **File**, **Mail**, **Setup**, and then select the **Advanced** button. To use the e-mail features of SureTrak, the e-mail server needs to be either a MAPI or VIM type of server. Check with your network administrator to be sure you have the correct type of setup. If you do not use either of these types of e-mail servers, of if you want to bypass SureTrak's mail capabilities and send the status sheets with conventional e-mail as attached files, place a check mark in both Bypass boxes and use standard e-mail attachments. For this exercise, place a **check mark in both Bypass boxes.**

    Standard status sheets offer a standardized method for updating activity information by always sending the same activity information, you determine only how progress is collected, either **With Percent Complete** or **With Remaining Duration.** The **Standard** status sheet always sends the activity ID and description, early start and finish dates, actual start and finish dates, and either remaining duration or percent complete.

    Mark the **Bypass Mail System to Send Mail** to bypass SureTrak's mail system. You will then save a file (to a specified drive and folder) that can be attached to an e-mail. Mark **Bypass Mail System to Open Sent Mail** bypass SureTrak's mail system and open a saved e-mail attachment.

    If you bypass the mail system, you may want to create two folders near the project folder. Name these directories INBOX and OUTBOX. This will help you keep track of where the attachments are for your e-mail program.

E-Mailing Updates to SureTrak Users

CUSTOM STATUS SHEETS.   SureTrak matches activities in the mail message and the project by activity ID. If an activity in the mail message has the same ID as an activity in the current project, the information in the mail message replaces its existing information. If an activity in the mail message has an ID that does not exist in the current project, the activity is added to the project. If an activity exists in the project but not in the mail message, it is unaffected by the mail merge.

Sending an Update Request

To e-mail a Status Update sheet to another SureTrak user, select **File, Mail, Send**. This will send the update request for the project that is currently opened. Typically you would want to update only selected activities for the next month or so. In this case with this small schedule, select all activities and **OK** it.

Now, set the date you would like the other person to update his or her schedule through. For this exercise, make it two weeks later than the last update and then press **OK**.

With the Bypass box selected from the **Mail, Setup**, you are now asked where to save the Update Status sheet. If you created the **OUTBOX** folder, you may want to save the file there. You may want to add the date to the end of the file name. This will help you keep track of which attachment is the current attachment for the project. Then to send it, use your regular e-mail and include this file as an attachment. The suffix to the file name will be .prd, which identifies the file as a Primavera mail file. If you did not select the Bypass boxes, SureTrak would automatically send this e-mail.

Receiving an Update Request

Once you receive an e-mail with the update request attachment, the attachment needs to be saved to a folder. A good location for this folder would be in a folder named "Inbox," near the Projects folder.

Next, if you have bypassed the mail system, in order to receive the requested update, select **File, Mail, Receive**. Navigate to the folder that contains the saved attached file.

Now, select the current file that is requested to be updated (the extension of this file should be .prd). The user is now asked if it is OK to merge the update request file with the project located on the computer. Items to consider before pressing **OK** are:

1. SureTrak matches activities in the mail message and the project by activity ID. If an activity in the mail message has the same ID as an activity in the current project, the information in the mail message replaces its existing information.
2. If an activity in the mail message has an ID that does not exist in the current project, the activity is added to the project.
3. If an activity exists in the project but not in the mail message, it is unaffected by the mail merge.

If you are agreeable to the three items above, **Select the project to be updated** and press **OK.** If not, press cancel.

A Received Mail window opens, allowing you to enter updated information for each activity. If there is resource date to be updated, be sure to select the **Resource Data** circle to update the resource information as well.

When you are finished updating the schedule, select **File, Mail, Send**. The update can now be sent back to the original person requesting the update.

CREATING WEB REPORTS

Creating a report that can be viewed on the Internet is relatively easy. Keep in mind that the reports generated from the Web Reports options are, essentially, graphical pictures that cannot be modified or updated by the person receiving the report.

First, in the Print Preview window, make the printout look as you desire.

Select **File, Save as Web Page**. The default folder where the report is stored is in the SureTrak folder in a subfolder named Web Reports.

Now give the Web page a file name. (Some Web servers do not allow spaces in the file name. Remember this as you are creating the file name.)

Select the **Target image Size**—typically, 1024 × 768 is good size. The file format of JPG is in most cases the best selection.

SureTrak creates two files for each page of the report. The first page is an HTML page allowing the person viewing the schedule to navigate between the pages of the report. The second file is a JPG file which contains the actual graphics of the page.

If you wanted to e-mail these reports instead of posting them on a Web page, that would work as well.

SHARING NOTES WITH PROJECT GROUPS

With many companies, projects affect, and are affected by, other projects. They may share resources where one project's activities may depend on completion of another project's activities. Upper management may want to see consolidated reports that show the status of all projects together for companywide decision making. With project groups, you can plan, schedule, control, update, and manage interrelated projects separately and together.

To take advantage of the project groups feature, use the following guidelines:

1. Create the project group that will be the "**container**" for all the member projects and then you can add the member projects to that group. From the Menu bar choose **File, New,** and give the project a name with four characters max. For the **Type** of project select **Project Groups** and fill out the rest of the New Project dialog box as desired.

2. In this container project set up the **Base Calendar, Activity Codes,** and **Values, Resource Dictionary, Resource Calendars,** and **WBS Codes**

that will be used on all the project group members. You may want to assign an activity code that corresponds to each project—project #, Building #, House # or such—to allow you to organize the group schedule as you may wish. The individual projects will all use these same codes, although, the individual projects may add to these codes as well. **Close the container project.**

3. Create the new project, **File, New. Name it** with **four** characters, Choose **Project Groups** for the **Type** of project. Put a check mark in the **"Add this new project to a project group"** box. Select the group and give the new project a **two-character ID;** the first character must be a letter, the second can be alpha or numeric. This ID becomes the first two activity ID characters for each activity in the project. **OK** the New Project dialog box.

   If you are adding an existing project to the project group, use the Project Group Wizard. Close all open projects. Choose **Tools, Wizards, Project Group Wizard** and follow the Wizard's help.

4. As you create the new project schedule you will notice the first two characters of the ID make up the two-letter code you chose earlier. You can change the remaining characters of the Activity ID as you desire.

5. **Assign the appropriate activity codes** (such as building #) using copy cell and paste cell.

6. Now, if you want to see the group of schedules, open the group schedule and you have all projects under that group.

ADDING CONSTRAINTS

Constraints are used to make sure an activity meets a deadline or must happen before or after a certain date. You are constraining, or restricting, an activity to a specified date. The most commonly used constraints are deadlines, or no-later-than constraints, and potential delays, or no-earlier-than constraints. They can be attached to either the start or finish of an activity. For example, you can put a deadline on the start or finish of an activity (it must start or finish no later than the date you specify) or a potential delay (it can start or finish no earlier than the date you specify).

Typically, an experienced scheduler would enter the project into the computer without constraints first and examine the project purely on CPM logic. Then add constraints, one at a time—watching to see how each one affects the entire schedule. Remember that constraints override the CPM logic. If a mandatory start constraint is put on an activity, that activity will start on that date regardless of the CPM logic, regardless of whether or not the predecessors are finished. Or if the project is ahead of schedule, the constrained activity will not automatically adjust to the possible new early date.

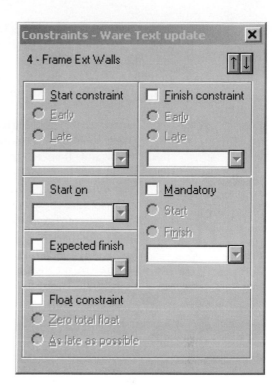

FIGURE 21.22 Constraints
window

To constrain an activity, first select the activity you desire to constrain and then use the Constraints window by right-clicking, selecting **Activity Detail**, and then selecting **Constraints** (see Figure 21.22). **Then specify the constraint type and date.** Another method used to constrain activities is, with the mouse, move the arrow near the start of the bar you desire to constrain. Press the Ctrl key and continue to move the mouse until a hammer and nail appears with arrows on each side. Then press the left mouse button and drag the activity to its desired constrained start.

SureTrak offers two kinds of constraints: (1) date constraints, which override schedule logic because you attach, or "nail," an activity to a specific date (on, before, or after that date); and (2) float constraints, which work with schedule logic to schedule an activity as soon or as late as possible.

Date constraints are most often used for deadlines and delivery dates. They affect not just the constrained activity, but also its predecessors and successors (and by extension the entire project). Therefore, they should be used sparingly. Using too many constraints diminishes the value of using critical path method, because activities that are constrained cannot be as freely rescheduled when other parts of the project are rescheduled.

Start constraints specify that an activity can start no earlier than, or no later than, a specified date. For example, if an activity cannot begin until the delivery of a piece of equipment on a particular date, make that date an early start constraint. The activity can start on or after that date, as calculated according to the logic of the schedule, but not before. If an activity must start by a certain date, attach a late start constraint (choose **Late**).

Finish constraints are used to specify that it must finish no earlier than, or no later than, a specified date. For example, if an activity must finish by a certain date, attach a late finish constraint. If an activity can start at any time but cannot finish until a particular date, perhaps after a scheduled customer inspection, attach an early finish constraint.

Mandatory constraints constrain an activity to establish a definite date for its start or finish. Use these constraints with caution; they control activity dates whether or not they are consistent with schedule logic. Therefore, an activity with a mandatory constraint could be scheduled before its predecessor.

Start-on constraints are equivalent of applying both a start-no-earlier-than and start-no-later-than constraint to an activity. It sets the early and late start dates equal to the specified date, but protects schedule logic (unlike the mandatory start constraint), so the activity can have positive or negative float.

Expected finish constraints force the duration of an activity to depend on its scheduled finish date, attach an expected finish constraint and the computer will calculate the duration for the activity from its early start date to the expected finish date you specify here. If the activity is under way, the computer will calculate its remaining duration as the difference between the data date and the expected finish date. Because it is calculated, the software will display the duration with an asterisk.

Float constraints affect the scheduling of an activity; but, unlike date constraints do not override schedule logic. Mark float constraint to establish the constraint, then choose the type of float constraint.

Zero total float causes an activity to be scheduled as soon as possible. Choose **Zero Total Float** to set the late dates for an activity equal to its early dates. It then has zero total float. The activity will be scheduled to occur on the first dates it can occur and it will appear critical.

As late as possible is used to set the dates of an activity so that the activity is scheduled as late as possible without delaying the early start date of its earliest successor. This eliminates any free float on the constrained activity. This constraint is commonly used for payments and deliveries.

TRYING OTHER SHORTCUTS, TECHNIQUES, OR IDEAS

Customize your toolbar—**Tools, Customize, Toolbar**—to put the tool icons on the toolbar that you frequently use.

Use **Copy Cell** and **Paste Cell** to assign activity codes to several activities at once.

To renumber all the activities, Edit, select all, Cut, Paste. Change all activity IDs with **Auto-increment,** starting at whatever number and increment by whatever number. Choose a starting number that is greater than any currently existing activity number in the project. Remember, no two activities can have the same ID number. If you desire to have the activities renumbered starting at the number 1, copy and paste again starting at 1, using numbers less than the previous copy. Then delete the activities with IDs that will not be used.

Link a series of activities by dragging the mouse over the activity descriptions in the activity columns or select the activities by using the Ctrl key. Choose the Link Activities icon 🖉 and the identified activities will be linked as FS relationships in the same order as they are listed. This is a fast way to assign predecessors. Just be careful to ensure accuracy. You can also delete relationships this way using the Unlink Activities icon 🖉. These icons can be put on the toolbar.

Deleting relationships by clicking on the relationship line and deleting. Or, use the Predecessors window.

When you **Dissolve** (Edit, Dissolve), you remove the activity selected but the software still connects the predecessors and successors. When you **Delete,** the predecessor and successor relationships are deleted as well.

To import all or part of the schedule showing on the computer screen into a word processor, from the Menu bar select **Edit, Copy Picture.** Drag a box around the area of the screen you want to take the picture of. Then open your word processor and paste the copied picture where you desire. This could be done in a spreadsheet program as well.

The Shift key turns the pointer into a tack icon to update AS, AF dates. This also brings up the Update window.

If something odd is happening with your computer—like no print preview—try **Ctrl, Shift, Reorganize Now** icon all at once. This repacks the data base.

To get a second resource column to appear: **Organize, Group by, Resource.**

If you want a resource histogram and progress S-curve based on late dates: Make a target based on late dates and then use BCWS which calculates based on the target. If the target is showing late dates this will produce a late start, late finish histogram and S-curve. You can't get both early and late S-curves at the same time with SureTrak.

To show both $ and Mandays: Open Resource Profile; choose LS Costs, press Ctrl key and Mandays (doesn't show on screen) and then you need to print preview it. In Print Preview, select Page Setup and make the Resource Profile equal to yes. For Resource, use the Ctrl key again to select both resources.

Contact Information

Primavera Systems, Inc.
Three Bala Plaza West
Suite 700
Bala Cynwyd, PA 19004

Technical help phone: (610) 667–7100
Fax: (610) 667–0652
Technical help hours: 8:00 A.M. – 8 P.M. EST M–F; 9:00 A.M. – 2:00 P.M. Sat
E-mail: Sttech@Primavera.com
Web address: http://Primavera.com

CHAPTER 22

MANAGING PROJECTS USING MICROSOFT PROJECT

INTRODUCTION—
MICROSOFT
PROJECT 2003

Microsoft Project 2003 is an extremely popular project management program used by all types of project managers. It is a product of Microsoft Corporation. Contact information is listed at the end of this chapter.

Microsoft Project 2003 requires a Pentium PC with a 233 MHz or higher processor; Pentium III is recommended. The recommended memory is 128 MB or more of RAM. Hard-disk space of 130 MB is suggested (hard disk usage will vary depending on configuration; custom installation choices may require more or less hard-disk space). The required display is a Super VGA (800 × 600) or higher resolution monitor. The program requires Microsoft Windows 2000 with Service Pack 3 or later, or Microsoft Windows XP or later operating system.

The following instructions are presented chronologically and are based on *how managers use the software,* rather than explaining every detail and feature of the software, in the order the screens appear. These instructions contain examples and assignments that teach how to use the software to communicate and manage the project. It is not necessary to know everything about any software package in order to be an effective user of it. Stick with the basics and become proficient with the areas that are essentially used and you will find this software to be extremely valuable in helping you control your projects.

As you work through these instructions, make sure you are thinking. Don't allow yourself to get into the mode of just carrying out the instructions without engaging your mind. Make sure what you are doing is logical and makes sense. If you *think* as you do this, you will learn how to use MS Project. Don't get frustrated if everything doesn't work as you expect. Generally, with computer software, you learn the most when things go wrong. Keep thinking and trying and you will figure it out. These instructions start with significant detailed instructions to help you figure out how to use the software. As you get further into the instructions the detail becomes less. Once you have followed the instructions in detail and accomplished a task, it is assumed you learned that task and from then on the instructions pertaining to that task will be less detailed. So, if later in the chapter you forget how to do a task, go back to the beginning of the chapter to review the details pertaining that task.

USING THE HELP BUTTONS

The Help buttons are very useful for when you feel lost or confused. There is also a Help feature and tutorial under **Help** on the Menu bar. Each MS Project window also displays a Help button that will provide help directly for that window.

You will use the warehouse project in Figure 22.1 to help learn how to manage projects with the use of Microsoft Project. You will input this project and then generate some management reports to communicate the schedule to all team members. The subcontractors are as noted in italics above each activity in the schedule.

Figure 22.1 is the network logic diagram developed during a meeting with the management team. The 35 work days calculated to complete the project is in accordance with the contract provisions.

You are now ready to computerize the schedule.

Start MS Project from the desktop by clicking on the MSProject 2003 icon, or click on the **Start** button in the lower left corner of the screen and then select **Programs, Microsoft Project.**

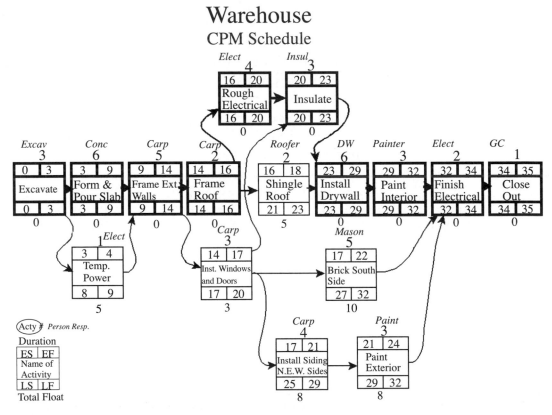

FIGURE 22.1 Network logic diagram for the warehouse project

Check to see if the default toolbars have been selected. From the Menu bar select **View**, then **Toolbars** and make sure the **Standard, Formatting**, and **Project Guide** toolbars have been selected. At the top of the screen you see the **Menu bar** (first line), the **Standard toolbar** below it at the left, the **Formatting toolbar** to the right half of the standard toolbar, and the **Project Guide** on the third line. Another toolbar you will be using is the **View bar**. To see the **View bar** (a vertical bar), to the left of the screen select **View, View bar**. Close down the extra Help information at the sides of the screen to allow more room for your schedule information. The screen should look very similar to Figure 22.2.

MS Project is programmed with many macros or wizards to help create schedules, layouts, formatting options, reports, and so on. This chapter teaches how to do these things without the help of the wizards in most instances. If you rely on the wizards it is

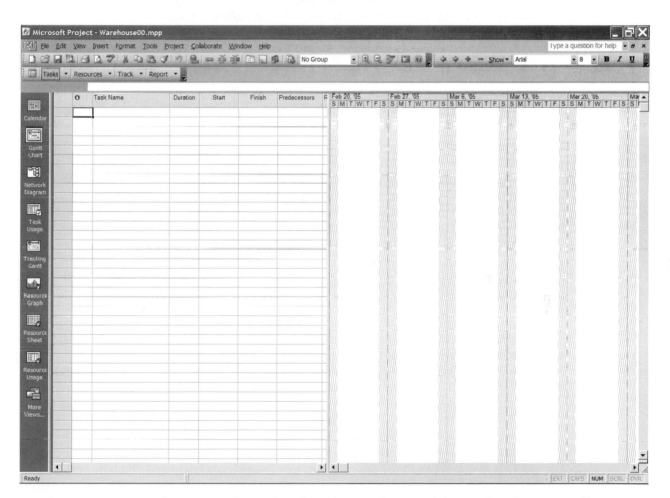

FIGURE 22.2   Microsoft Project window with toolbars shown at the top and the View bar shown vertically at the left

easier to accomplish many tasks; however, it is more difficult to edit those changes. Learning the software with less reliance on the wizards is a little more difficult but gives you more control over the software.

STARTING A NEW PROJECT

To create and name the file, from the Menu bar select **File, Save As,** and enter the **File name (Project name)** as you desire in the proper folder. It is recommended that you add a couple of zeros to the end of this file name to represent the original schedule. Then as you update this file, save it as the same name with a 01, 02, and so forth appended to the name. That way you have a paper trail if you need it in the future. For example, Warehouse00 is the as-planned schedule; then the project is copied to the name Warehouse01 for updating through the first month. Then it is copied to Warehouse02 for updating through the second month, and so on. The extension of .mpp is automatically added to identify the file as a microsoft project file. You can see the name of the file or schedule you are in at the top left corner of your computer screen.

   To set a start date, from the Menu bar select **Project, Project Information,** enter a **Start date,** and **OK** it. Typically a start date is all that is entered, allowing the software to determine the finish date based on the forward pass. If a finish date is entered the backward pass is calculated from the date entered, which may cause positive or negative float on all activities.

   To title the project, from the Menu bar select **File,** expand the window by clicking on the two arrows at the bottom of the window, select **Properties, Summary,** and then fill out the window. You may want to use the **Project Title** as the name of the project or customer's name and the **Subject** as the version of the schedule such as, As Planned or First Update, and so on. Identify yourself as the **Author and Manager.** Fill out the rest of the form as desired and **OK** it.

SETTING UP THE CALENDARS

Setting up the calendars, from the Menu bar select **Tools, Change Working Time.** With the Standard Calendar chosen, change the typical holidays to nonwork days by selecting the date and clicking on the dot next to **Nonworking time.** Do this for all holidays throughout the planned duration of the project. Next, you will create a new calendar for the activities you want to schedule to work six days a week (working on Saturday). Select **New** at the bottom of the window. Give it a title of **6 Day Work Week,** make it a copy of the Standard calendar, and **OK** it. To change all Saturdays to work, click on **Sat** in the column heading to highlight all Saturdays and then select **Nondefault working time.** Repeat this process to make another new calendar called **7 Day Work Week** showing all Saturdays and Sundays as work days. Double-check to see that all Saturdays and Sundays are scheduled as work days.

   You are now ready to input the activity information. There are two primary methods of inputting activities into Microsoft Project: (1) Using the Network Diagram view, and (2) using the Gantt Chart view. You will experience both methods and then you can choose your favorite.

Entering Tasks from the Network Diagram View

To learn the program you will first enter all the activities of the warehouse project using the Network Diagram view. From the View bar (the vertical bar to the left of your screen) select **Network Diagram.** (If the View bar is not showing, select **View** and put a check mark by View bar). To input the first activity, from the Menu bar, select **Insert** and **New Task.** You will notice the task box is bigger than we need at this point.

To make the box smaller, in order to see more of the schedule on the computer screen and make it easier to create the schedule, **Format** the **Box Styles** and make a new template. Select **More Templates**, **New,** and give it a **Template name** of **Input Net** or whatever. Next, select **Cell Layout** and make it two rows and one column, **100% of standard size,** and **OK** it. Then under **Choose Cells** click in the top cell, click on the selection button, and select **Duration.** In the lower cell select **Name**, then **limit cell text** to three lines and **OK** it.

To make this new box the default, from the Menu bar select **Format, Box Styles** again, making sure **Critical** is selected as the **Style settings.** For the **Data template** choose the **Input Net** template you just created; then, under **Border shape** select the smaller rectangle and **OK** it. Next, under **Style settings** select **Noncritical** and select the same Data template and Box shape. You are now ready to click and drag new boxes to create the schedule. From this experience you see that you can make the box many shapes and include any information desired from the data base. Enter the duration and activity name by looking at the hand-drawn logic diagram created by your team.

A new activity or task is made by moving the mouse to the center of the existing task box and dragging a line to the location of the next box. Then enter the duration and name of the new task. If the activity duration is 1 day, you should enter a 1-day duration rather than allowing the default of 1? Duration. The "?" duration is used if the duration is not known and is only a rough estimate. Continue in this manner until several tasks and their relationships have been entered.

A dual relationship is created by simply dragging from the predecessor tasks to the successor tasks. **To delete a relationship,** double-click on the relationship line to be deleted and click on the Delete button. **To delete an activity,** click on that activity and press the Delete key.

Microsoft Project defaults to automatically place the activity boxes where it wants. To give you control of this select **Format Layout**, then click next to **Allow manual box positioning.** While still in this window, to make it easier to see the relationships and compress the schedule a little, change the row and column spacing each to **30** and change the **Link style** to **Straight.**

Now you can click on the border line of the box (where your cursor turns into the four-way arrows) and drag the box to a new location; play around here a little. Most managers prefer to put the boxes where they desire in order to organize and control the look of the network diagram. Continue inputting the remainder of the warehouse

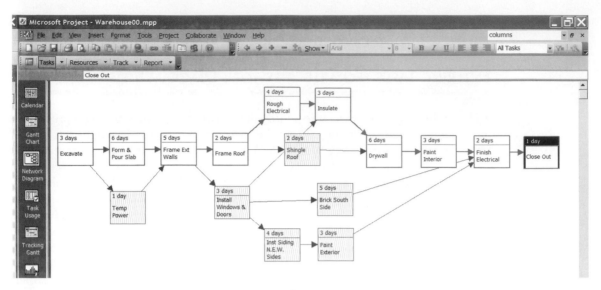

FIGURE 22.3   Warehouse input into MS Project using the network diagram

activities, placing the activity boxes as desired. Figure 22.3 shows the network logic diagram looking very similar to the hand-drawn logic diagram.

The placement of the activity boxes does not need to look exactly like Figure 22.3, but the logic should be the same with the arrows showing the same predecessors and successors. The durations should also be the same.

It's not a bad idea to **save your work** now by selecting from the Menu bar **File, Save.** Then if the power goes out or you experience some difficulty with your computer you will have already saved your input to the disk. The program can be changed to automatically save every few minutes. Many project managers do not like to have the schedule automatically saved because it is common to use the computer to play "what-if games" to analyze different management scenarios and then, after playing around a little, saving the best one. If the program auto saves during one of these times a schedule may be lost or ruined.

ENTERING TASKS FROM THE GANTT CHART VIEW

Create another new project and enter the activities using the Gantt Chart view this time. Do this by selecting **Gantt Chart** from the View Bar on the left of the screen. The prior first four steps still need to be done before inputting activity data: naming the file, selecting the start date, giving the project a title, and setting up the calendars. Enter the **Task Name** and **Duration** in the appropriate cells. After entering the Name and Duration you will assign the predecessors. By the way, everything done in one view is saved to the database and therefore also shows in every other view.

LINKING TASKS

There are four popular ways **to create predecessors or link tasks in the Gantt Chart view.**

1. *Highlight the tasks to be linked.* Highlight the tasks in the **order** they are to be linked using the Ctrl key and then **select the Link Tasks** button to link them in a finish-to-start relationship without lag. If you desire to use a lag, double-click on the relationship line and fill out the window.

2. *Click and Drag.* Click on the center of the predecessor bar and drag to the center of the successor bar. Be extra careful with this method because you can also click on the bars to change the durations and create date constraints. It is easy to make a mistake without knowing it.

3. *Use the Task Information Dialog box.* Highlight a task by double-clicking on it which opens the **Task Information Dialog box**. Select the **Predecessors tab,** and list the immediate predecessor to each task and define that relationship with the proper amount of lag. This latter method is a little more time consuming, but some managers think it is more accurate. If you number the tasks on the hand-drawn schedule and then enter them in order, the numbering is less confusing. You have to watch the activity numbers in Microsoft Project because the software will change the numbers as you insert new activities.

4. *Use the Predecessors Column.* Another method to enter the predecessors is to use the **Predecessors** column (slide the vertical black line dividing the column information area of the screen from the bar chart area, to the right to expose the Predecessors column) and then simply list the predecessors by activity number with a comma between each predecessor. If you number the tasks on the hand-drawn schedule and then enter them in order, the numbering is less confusing. That way you do not need to look up the activity number on the screen.

To move a task in Gantt Chart view or reposition it (be careful here because it may remove the task relationships if they have already been input), highlight the **task #** and then use **cut and paste** to move it to a new location. Or, click and drag the activity to the new location. If you want to preserve the relationships when manually moving tasks go to **Tools, Options, Schedule** tab, and clear the **Autolink inserted or moved tasks** check box. A better way to get the tasks in the order you desire is by sorting the tasks as will be discussed later.

To **insert a new task** in the Gantt Chart view, highlight the task you want the new task inserted above and then select **Insert** from the Menu bar and a new task will be created above the highlighted task.

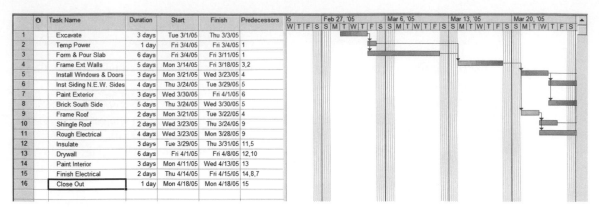

	●	Task Name	Duration	Start	Finish	Predecessors
1		Excavate	3 days	Tue 3/1/05	Thu 3/3/05	
2		Temp Power	1 day	Fri 3/4/05	Fri 3/4/05	1
3		Form & Pour Slab	6 days	Fri 3/4/05	Fri 3/11/05	1
4		Frame Ext Walls	5 days	Mon 3/14/05	Fri 3/18/05	3,2
5		Install Windows & Doors	3 days	Mon 3/21/05	Wed 3/23/05	4
6		Inst Siding N.E.W. Sides	4 days	Thu 3/24/05	Tue 3/29/05	5
7		Paint Exterior	3 days	Wed 3/30/05	Fri 4/1/05	6
8		Brick South Side	5 days	Thu 3/24/05	Wed 3/30/05	5
9		Frame Roof	2 days	Mon 3/21/05	Tue 3/22/05	4
10		Shingle Roof	2 days	Wed 3/23/05	Thu 3/24/05	9
11		Rough Electrical	4 days	Wed 3/23/05	Mon 3/28/05	9
12		Insulate	3 days	Tue 3/29/05	Thu 3/31/05	11,5
13		Drywall	6 days	Fri 4/1/05	Fri 4/8/05	12,10
14		Paint Interior	3 days	Mon 4/11/05	Wed 4/13/05	13
15		Finish Electrical	2 days	Thu 4/14/05	Fri 4/15/05	14,8,7
16		Close Out	1 day	Mon 4/18/05	Mon 4/18/05	15

FIGURE 22.4   Activities input using the Gantt Chart view

CREATING LAGS

To create lags, double-click the relationship arrow on the Gantt or PERT chart and select the lag type and amount. Or, use the Task Information dialog box by double-clicking on the task and selecting the **Predecessors tab**.

Finish inputting the activities, durations, and predecessors of the warehouse using the Gantt Chart view. The Gantt Chart view with the activities input should look similar to Figure 22.4.

FORMATTING COLUMNS

To insert new columns, highlight the column heading to the right of where you want to insert the new column and then click on **Insert, Column** and fill out the Column Definition window. Choose the **Field Name** you desire from the data base, give it a **title** that communicates, and typically select the **Best Fit** button to format the width of the column. To delete a column highlight the heading with the **right mouse** button and select **Hide Column.** To insert a column to the far right you need to insert columns and then delete or hide the last column.

ASSIGNING RESOURCES

To assign resources such as subcontractors, highlight the task and then select the **assign Resources** button, [icon] **select or enter the name of the sub or other resource,** and **assign** the resource to that task. Typical resources would be the person responsible, subcontractor, supplier, and so on. For the warehouse schedule the resource is the subcontractors. All the subcontractors can be created at once by clicking on the **Assign Resources** button [icon] and entering the names of the subcontractors in the **Resource**

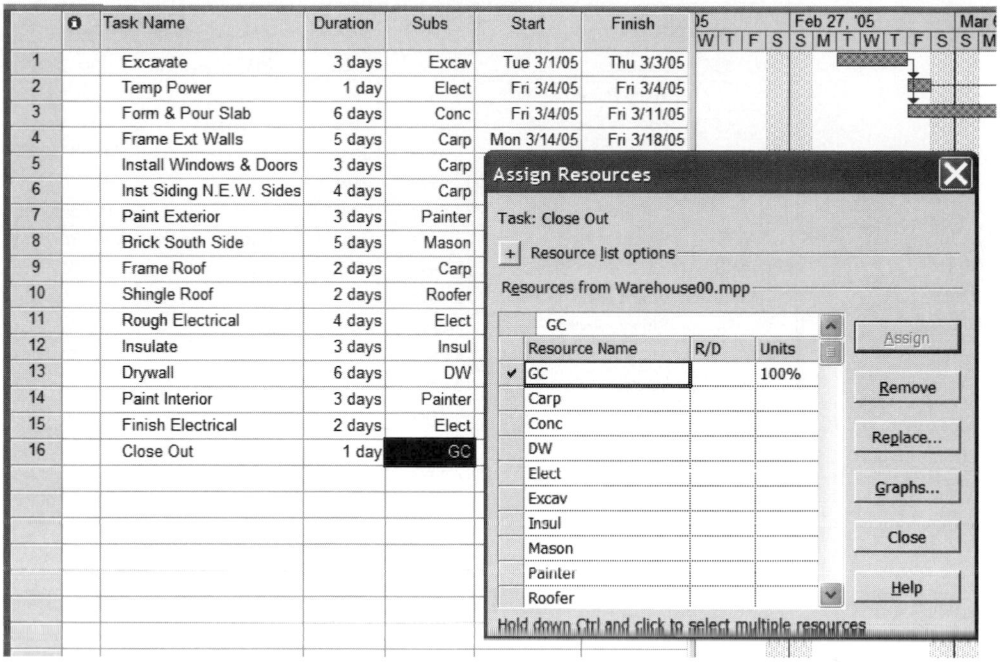

	❶	Task Name	Duration	Subs	Start	Finish
1		Excavate	3 days	Excav	Tue 3/1/05	Thu 3/3/05
2		Temp Power	1 day	Elect	Fri 3/4/05	Fri 3/4/05
3		Form & Pour Slab	6 days	Conc	Fri 3/4/05	Fri 3/11/05
4		Frame Ext Walls	5 days	Carp	Mon 3/14/05	Fri 3/18/05
5		Install Windows & Doors	3 days	Carp		
6		Inst Siding N.E.W. Sides	4 days	Carp		
7		Paint Exterior	3 days	Painter		
8		Brick South Side	5 days	Mason		
9		Frame Roof	2 days	Carp		
10		Shingle Roof	2 days	Roofer		
11		Rough Electrical	4 days	Elect		
12		Insulate	3 days	Insul		
13		Drywall	6 days	DW		
14		Paint Interior	3 days	Painter		
15		Finish Electrical	2 days	Elect		
16		Close Out	1 day	GC		

Assign Resources

Task: Close Out

[+] Resource list options

Resources from Warehouse00.mpp

	GC		
	Resource Name	R/D	Units
✓	GC		100%
	Carp		
	Conc		
	DW		
	Elect		
	Excav		
	Insul		
	Mason		
	Painter		
	Roofer		

Assign
Remove
Replace...
Graphs...
Close
Help

Hold down Ctrl and click to select multiple resources

FIGURE 22.5   Gantt Chart view with resources entered

Name column. Then you can select the activity and assign the resource to the proper activity.

Or, another way to assign resources would be to insert the **column** "Resource Names" and title it Subs or whatever the resource is, and then enter or select the sub in this column. Try it both ways and assign the appropriate subcontractor to each activity in the warehouse project.

To assign resources (or anything else) to several activities at once you can use the Ctrl key to select several tasks and then make the assignments all at once. Or, you can assign it once to one cell and then click on the fill handle and drag it through all the activities (see Figure 22.5).

ADDING NOTES TO ACTIVITIES

To make a note relating to a task, resource, or subcontractor, highlight the task and then from the toolbar select the **Task Notes** button ▣. This is a good way to communicate to the subcontractors the specifics relating to the task, such as paint colors, plumbing fixtures, brick type, and so on.

This could also be done by creating a **column** for "Notes," or you could create a column **Text1, Text 2,** and so forth, giving the column any title you want that communicates the purpose of those notes (Figure 22.6). Many managers prefer the column

	ℹ	**Task Name**	**Duration**	**Subs**	**Notes**	**Start**	**Finish**
1	📝	Excavate	3 days	Excav	Bring Dynamite	Tue 3/1/05	Thu 3/3/05
2		Temp Power	1 day	Elect		Fri 3/4/05	Fri 3/4/05
3	📝	Form & Pour Slab	6 days	Conc	7,000 psi	Fri 3/4/05	Fri 3/11/05
4		Frame Ext Walls	5 days	Carp		Mon 3/14/05	Fri 3/18/05
5		Install Windows & Doors	3 days	Carp		Mon 3/21/05	Wed 3/23/05
6		Inst Siding N.E.W. Sides	4 days	Carp		Thu 3/24/05	Tue 3/29/05
7	📝	Paint Exterior	3 days	Painter	Doeskin Brown	Wed 3/30/05	Fri 4/1/05
8	📝	Brick South Side	5 days	Mason	Mocha Brown	Thu 3/24/05	Wed 3/30/05
9		Frame Roof	2 days	Carp		Mon 3/21/05	Tue 3/22/05
10		Shingle Roof	2 days	Roofer		Wed 3/23/05	Thu 3/24/05
11		Rough Electrical	4 days	Elect		Wed 3/23/05	Mon 3/28/05
12		Insulate	3 days	Insul		Tue 3/29/05	Thu 3/31/05
13		Drywall	6 days	DW		Fri 4/1/05	Fri 4/8/05
14	📝	Paint Interior	3 days	Painter	Whisper White	Mon 4/11/05	Wed 4/13/05
15		Finish Electrical	2 days	Elect		Thu 4/14/05	Fri 4/15/05
16		Close Out	1 day	GC		Mon 4/18/05	Mon 4/18/05

FIGURE 22.6 Gantt Chart view with "Notes" column added

method over the task note method. Add the following notes for the subcontractors building the warehouse: Remind the **Excavator** to bring dynamite, the **Concrete** subcontractor that the slab is 7,000 psi concrete, the **Painter** that the interior paint is Whisper White and the exterior paint is Doeskin Brown, and the **Brick Mason** that the brick is Mocha Brown.

SORTING THE TASKS

To sort or change the order in which the tasks are listed, from the Menu bar select **Project, Sort,** and then select the desired sort. The most common sort is by start date. You can create a custom sort on any items in the database by selecting **Project, Sort, Sort by** and filling out the dialog box. Another popular sort is to get the activities in chronological order by sorting by early start and then early finish. See Figure 22.7.

Notice in Figure 22.7 the activities are in early start order and if two activities start on the same day, the one that is listed first has the earliest finish date. Notice the *Temp. Power* activity, along with the *Frame Roof* activity, and the *Install Siding* activity.

GROUPING DATA ITEMS TOGETHER

To group anything from the database together, such as subcontractors, from the Menu bar select **Project, Group By,** then select the desired grouping. To group the subcontractors activities together, group by **Resource Names.** If the grouping is not

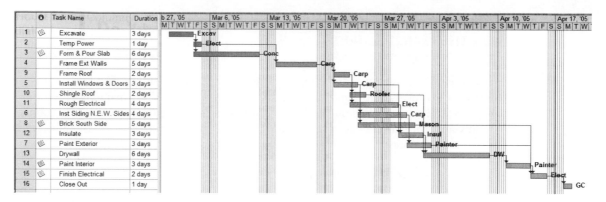

FIGURE 22.7   Warehouse activities sorted by early start and then early finish

listed select **More Groups, New, Name it** "Subcontractors," select **Resource Names,** and then **Apply** it. Now you see the warehouse activities grouped under each subcontractor.

To select other groupings, notice the center of the toolbar line where it currently shows **Subcontractors.** Click on the down arrow to the right and group the activities by Critical. Now you see the noncritical and critical activities grouped together. Group it by **No Group** to get it back to normal.

FILTERING FOR SPECIFIC TASKS OR INFORMATION

From the Menu bar select **Project, Filtered for,** and then select the desired filter. For example, If you want to see the critical activities only, select **Critical.** If you only want to see the carpenter's activities only select **Project, Filtered for, More Filters, New,** name it Carpenter's Activities, **Field Name** select Resource Names, **Test** select equals, **Value** select Carp, **OK,** and **Apply** it. Now the only activities that show are the carpenter's activities. If you want this filter on the pull-down menu, place a check mark in the **Show in Menu** square as you edit or create the filter and from this time forth that filter will be on the menu. It can be accessed by clicking on **Project, Filtered for,** and selecting it.

If you want a more convenient way to filter select **Tools, Customize, Toolbars, Options tab,** and put a check mark next to **Show Standard and Formatting toolbars on two rows.** Notice the bottom toolbar has some additional tools. To the left of the Auto Filter button ▼= it shows the name of the current filter. Select the down arrow and the filter menu opens for you to select the filter of choice. Or, an even easier method to filter on any column heading is to click on the Auto Filter button ▼= which makes the column headings able to filter. Then simply click on the Resource name (Subs) column heading, select carpenter, and it filters for the carpenter's activities only. To turn off the Auto Filter capabilities click on the Auto Filter tool again.

SHOWING OR NOT SHOWING THE RELATIONSHIP ARROWS ON THE GANTT CHART

The relationship arrows can be either shown or not shown on the Gantt chart by selecting **Format, Layout,** and showing the lines as desired. Many managers prefer not to show the relationships on the Gantt chart because many times they are difficult to follow and, therefore, cause a miss communication of the predecessors. If you want to show the relationships, consider the network diagram.

To Change the Bar Styles in the Gantt Chart

If you want to change the bar styles (for example, to show the **critical activities in red**), from the toolbar select the **Gantt Chart Wizard** and follow the instructions. Put a dot next to **Critical path** and select other choices as desired.

To Show the Float Bar on the Gantt Chart

If you want to show the float bar, use the **Gantt Chart Wizard** again (Figure 22.8). Choose the **Custom Gantt Chart** option on the second screen, **Next, Yes** to show critical activities and other choices as desired until it asks **What kind of additional Gantt bars do you want to display?** Choose **Total slack** and then other items as desired.

Your screen should show the total float similar to Figure 22.8. Other choices may be different depending on how you have selected groups, filters, columns, and sorts.

To Add the Task Name or Notes to the Bars

In the Gantt chart, first select all tasks by clicking in the square in the top left of the column headings and then from the Menu bar select **Format, Bar, Bar Text Tab** and you can add many field information items to the bars. A common format is to have the **Name** of the task to the **left** of the bar and the **Resource names** to the **right** as shown in Figure 22.9.

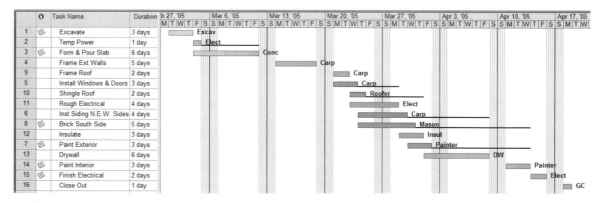

FIGURE 22.8   Gantt chart showing float

To Change the Timescale

In the Gantt chart, right-click in the timescale heading area or from the Menu bar select **Format Timescale.** To see calendar dates, rather than week days, on the **Bottom Tier** tab change the **Label** to **1, 2, . . .** and **OK** it.

To Format the Gridlines

First, select all activities by clicking in the upper left cell in the Gantt Chart View, then select **Format, Gridlines, Gantt Rows** and put the gridlines at an interval of 2 or whatever and choose the type of line (dots are common). To format the columns select **Middle Tier Columns,** Normal black solid line. Next select **Bottom Tier Columns,** Normal, Gray, dotted line. The bar chart portion of the screen should show the gridlines similar to Figure 22.10.

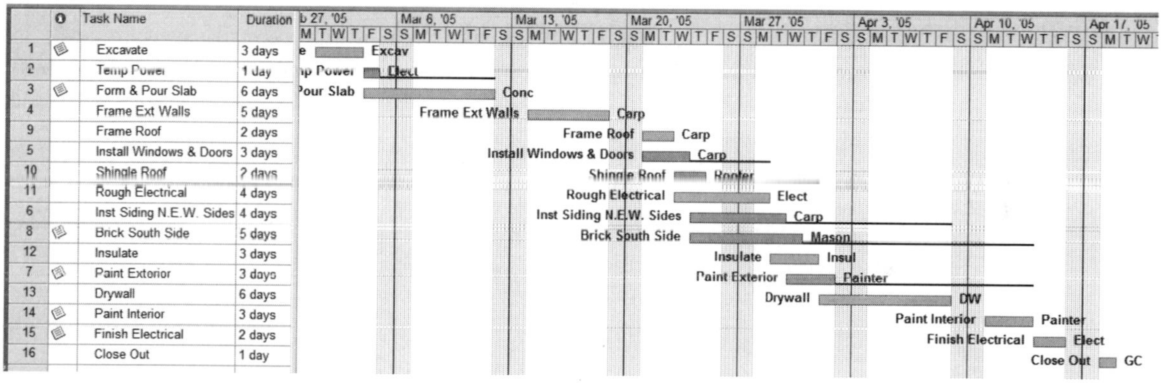

FIGURE 22.9 Bars with the task name to the left and the subcontractor to the right

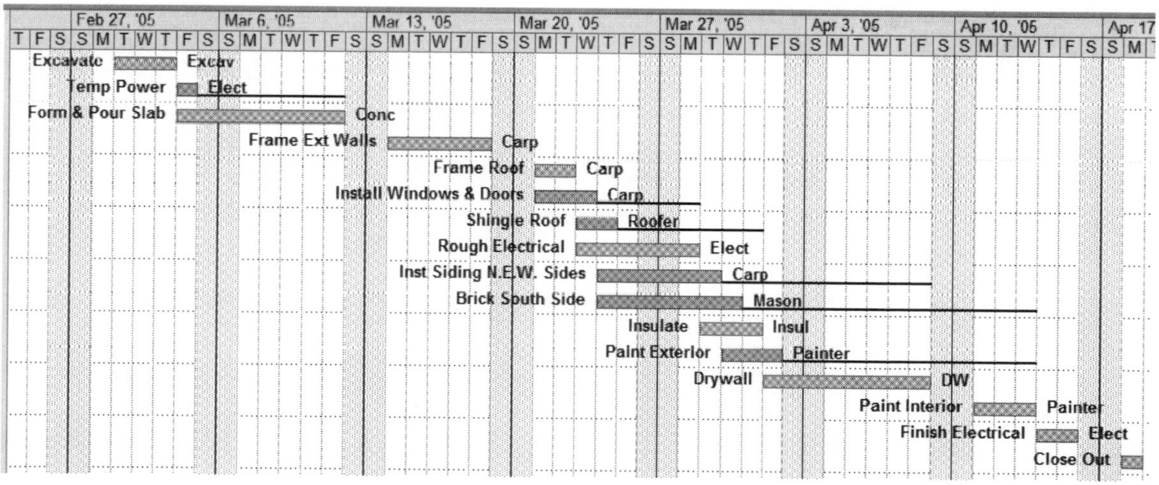

FIGURE 22.10 Bar chart with gridlines showing

CREATING SUMMARY ACTIVITIES

A summary activity is made up of subtasks and summarizes those subtasks. On the bar chart it is one bar whose duration is dependent upon the activities it summarizes. To create an activity that summarizes other activities, create the summary activity first by inserting it above the first activity to be summarized. On the warehouse schedule insert a new activity and name it "Warehouse." Don't give it a duration. Highlight the tasks you want to indent (all the tasks of the warehouse) and then click on the right arrow, located at the left of the Formatting toolbar, to indent the selected activities. Notice the minus (−) button key to the left of the summary activity **Warehouse,** click on it, and the activities under the summary activity are rolled into the one bar. Use the plus (+) or minus (−) buttons to expand or summarize the activities as desired. A bar chart with the activities indented, showing warehouse as a summary activity, is shown in Figure 22.11.

Notice in Figure 22.11 the duration for the summary activity warehouse is 35 days. This duration was not entered. This duration is the duration of the activities summarized under *Warehouse.* If you have done the forward pass by hand, this duration should match the hand-calculated duration.

To experience additional examples of summarized activities let's make two more summary activities for the warehouse: an **Exterior Phase** and an **Interior Phase.** Insert the summary activities in the proper location and then further indent their respective activities. Your schedule should look similar to Figure 22.12

To summarize everything, highlight all activities by clicking in the square in the upper left corner of the columns and then select the minus (−) button. **To open all**

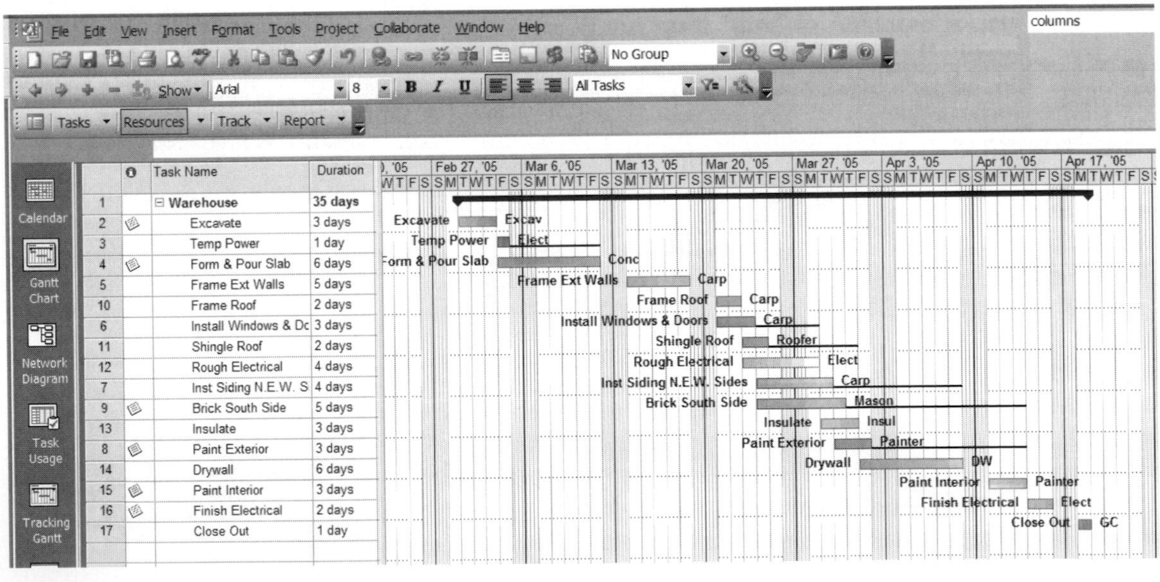

FIGURE 22.11   Warehouse shown as a summary activity

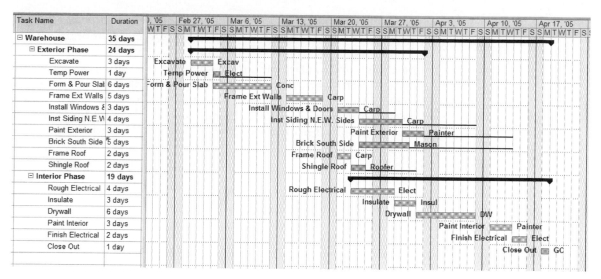

Task Name	Duration	), '05	Feb 27, '05	Mar 6, '05	Mar 13, '05	Mar 20, '05	Mar 27, '05	Apr 3, '05	Apr 10, '05	Apr 17, '05
⊟ **Warehouse**	**35 days**									
⊟ **Exterior Phase**	**24 days**									
Excavate	3 days	Excavate ▨▨ Excav								
Temp Power	1 day	Temp Power ▨ Elect								
Form & Pour Slab	6 days	Form & Pour Slab ▨▨▨ Conc								
Frame Ext Walls	5 days	Frame Ext Walls ▨▨▨ Carp								
Install Windows &	3 days	Install Windows & Doors ▨▨▨ Carp								
Inst Siding N.E.W	4 days	Inst Siding N.E.W. Sides ▨▨▨ Carp								
Paint Exterior	3 days	Paint Exterior ▨▨▨ Painter								
Brick South Side	5 days	Brick South Side ▨▨▨ Mason								
Frame Roof	2 days	Frame Roof ▨▨ Carp								
Shingle Roof	2 days	Shingle Roof ▨▨ Roofer								
⊟ **Interior Phase**	**19 days**									
Rough Electrical	4 days	Rough Electrical ▨▨▨ Elect								
Insulate	3 days	Insulate ▨▨ Insul								
Drywall	6 days	Drywall ▨▨▨ DW								
Paint Interior	3 days	Paint Interior ▨▨ Painter								
Finish Electrical	2 days	Finish Electrical ▨▨ Elect								
Close Out	1 day	Close Out ▨ GC								

FIGURE 22.12   Warehouse with an exterior phase and an interior phase

Task Name	Duration	), '05	Feb 27, '05	Mar 6, '05	Mar 13, '05	Mar 20, '05	Mar 27, '05	Apr 3, '05	Apr 10, '05	Apr 17, '05
⊟ **Warehouse**	**35 days**									
⊞ **Exterior Phase**	**24 days**									
⊞ **Interior Phase**	**19 days**									

FIGURE 22.13   Summarized at level 2

activities select the **Show** button on the Formatting toolbar and then the + + **All Sub-tasks** button. Experiment with the **Show** button to see what the different outline levels do to the schedule. Also experiment with the plus (+) and minus (−) buttons to the left of the activity name to see how you can open and close summary activities. Figure 22.13 shows the schedule at outline level 2 under the **Show** button.

PRINTING REPORTS

Even though the software is basically wysiwyg (what you see is what you get) it is a good idea to print preview your reports by clicking on the **Print Preview button** (the button to the right of the printer, a piece of paper with a magnifying glass). You can see how many pages are included in the report by clicking on the arrowheads or selecting the multiple page button. You can change the orientation from portrait to landscape, margins, headers, footers, and so on in Print Preview **Page Setup,** or you can select **File, Page Setup** from the Menu bar. **To select a different printer,** select **File, Print,** and then the Print dialog box opens where you can change the printer.

To print just the column information without the bar chart graphics, slide the vertical line separating the columns from the bars to the extreme right of the screen. Now in Print Preview 🔍 you see only column information.

To create a page break, place the cursor where you want the page break and from the Menu bar select **Insert, Page Break.** The page break location shows as a dashed line. **To delete a page break,** in the Task Name or Resource Name field, select the task or resource with which the page break is associated. Select Insert and remove page break. **To delete all manual page breaks,** select all the tasks in your view by clicking any column heading. On the Insert menu, click Remove All Page Breaks. This will work unless the page breaks are inserted on grouped activities, wherein the page breaks must be manually deleted.

SETTING UP AND PRINTING STANDARD REPORTS

Now that you are familiar with the basics of MS Project it is time to apply the skills you have gained to develop some basic reports. You may need to review the basics occasionally in order to complete the following reports.

To make this exercise a review of everything learned to this point, input again the warehouse project data from the beginning. This warehouse is to be built in Spanish Fork, Utah, therefore, name it SFWarehouse or as desired. Remember to create the project, set up the calendars, and do other tasks. The only summary activity to create is one that summarizes the whole project.

Report 1. Input Check Report

I recommend that you form a habit of always double-checking the information you input into the computer prior to printing reports. It is confusing and embarrassing to send out several reports that are incorrect. Think of all the information that was input in order to create the report. The warehouse project required the following input: **Task Name, Duration, Predecessors, Resource Names (Subs),** and **Notes.** Format the columns to match that data. Compare the input data with the hand-drawn network logic diagram to make sure all data is correct. This is sometimes easier and more accurate if done by two people—one reads the computer report while the other reads the hand-drawn network logic diagram.

Report 2. Project Manager's Bar Chart Report

This report will be a rather typical bar chart designed to be used by the project manager who likes to see float. Make sure the activities are sorted by start date. Show the activity name to the left of the bars, as well as in the activity table. So, format the columns to include the "Activity Name," "Duration," and "Subcontractor." Make the Activity Name and the Subs aligned to the left of the column, the Duration aligned to the center of the column. Delete the other columns. Format the bars (Gantt Chart Wizard, Custom Gantt) so that the critical activities are red, the total float shows, and the relationship arrows do not show.

Format the timescale to show calendar dates rather than week days. Format the gridlines to show a vertical line for each day and a horizontal line every four activities.

Preview it by clicking on **File, Print Preview** or the Print Preview button . Make sure it is in landscape orientation (Page Setup), where you can also force the report to fit to one page wide and one page tall. When the report looks acceptable, click on the Print button and it prints exactly as it looks on the Print Preview screen. The report should look similar to Figure 22.14.

To get back to the bar chart window, click on the **Close** button.

That is a lot of formatting work to be done for each report. This layout or view, as it is called in MS Project, can be saved so you do not need to go through all that formatting again. Rather, you can just select that view.

Creating your own favorite views, first create the Table, Group, and Filter if they are not already created. The difference between a table and a view is that the view includes the table, the group, and the filter, each of which must be created prior to creating the view. The table is the rows and columns of information to the left of the

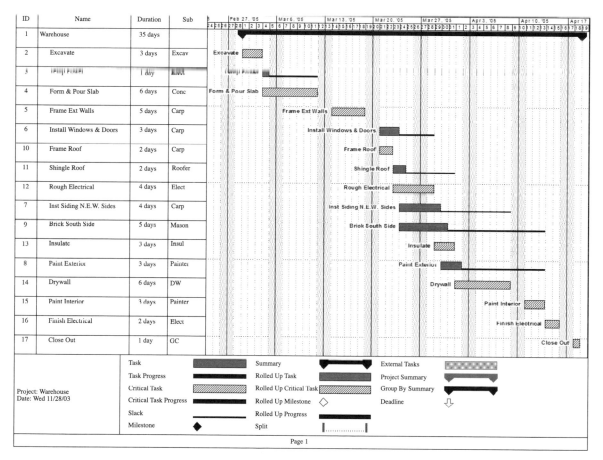

FIGURE 22.14 Project manager's bar chart

typical bar chart. The group is the manner in which you want the information grouped. The filter is which activities you want in or out of the report. The view combines the table, group, and filter together. Once a view has been created it can be shown on the View bar.

To create a new table select **View, Table, More Tables, New,** name it "Project Manager's," and list the column headings of choice under **Field Name** (ID, Name, Duration, and Resource Names). **Align** the **Data** as desired and select the appropriate **Width** and **Title. OK** it and **Apply** it. This report will not be grouping activities or filtering, so you are now ready to create the view.

To create a new view select **View** (click on the down arrows to increase the window offerings) **More Views, New, Single, Name it** "PM's Bar chart," and then select the desired **Table** (Project Manager's), **Group** (No Group), and **Filter** (All Tasks). If you put a check mark by **Menu,** the view will show up on the View menu that typically shows on the left of the computer screen. **OK** the view and **Apply** it. You may still need to use the **Gantt Chart Wizard** to get the bars looking as you wish, but now you have this view always available. The completed view should look similar to Figure 22.15.

Notice the cursor in Figure 22.15 is pointed at the PM's Bar Chart view, which is on the View bar because it was formatted to show on the menu. The views and tables are saved to the schedule, not the computer.

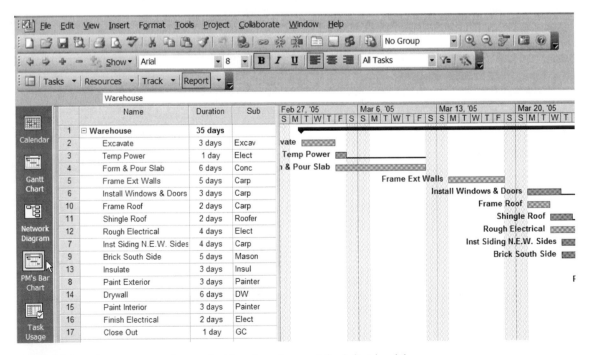

FIGURE 22.15   Create a new view at the View bar shown at the left side of the screen

This process of creating new views can save enormous time once you have learned enough about MS Project and CPM scheduling to know what you want for your favorite views and reports. Don't forget this concept. The remainder of this chapter will not consist of creating views for each report. After completing the chapter exercises you should consider what you want in standard reports and views and then create the few views that you will learn to rely on.

Report 3. Converting the Schedule to a Calendar View

Select the Calendar view from the top of the View bar at the left of the computer screen. You now see the schedule as shown in Figure 22.16.

The Calendar view is a favorite report for some project managers. However, if there are a lot of concurrent activities, they may not fit on the calendar and it creates a problem.

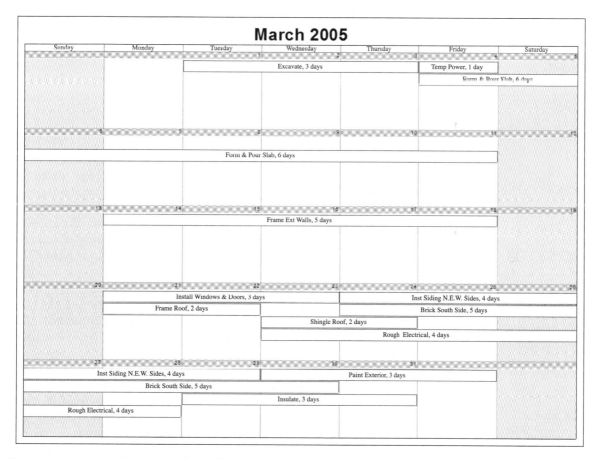

Figure 22.16   Calendar view of the warehouse schedule

	Name	Durati	Sul	Early Sta	Early Fini
1	⊟ Warehouse	35 day		Tue 3/1/05	Mon 4/18/05
3	Temp Power	1 day	Elect	Fri 3/4/05	Fri 3/4/05
12	Rough Electrical	4 days	Elect	Wed 3/23/05	Mon 3/28/05
16	Finish Electrical	2 days	Elect	Thu 4/14/05	Fri 4/15/05

FIGURE 22.17   Electrician's bar chart schedule

Report 4. Subcontractor's Bar Chart Report

This will be a bar chart designed for the individual subcontractor. The columns will be "ID," "Activity Name," "Duration," "Resource Name (Sub)," "Early Start," and "Early Finish." The bars will not show float, critical activities, or relationship lines. The bars will have the **Activity Name** to the **Left** of the bar. The schedule is to be **Sorted** by **Start** date. The activities will be **Filtered** by the **Subcontractors** and printed so that each subcontractor will see only his or her activities. The filtering is easy if you select the **Auto Filter** button which make it possible to filter on every column heading. Click on the selection button in the "Sub" column heading and then print each filtered subcontractor's activities. Figure 22.17 is the bar chart for the electrician. To turn off Auto Filter click on the Auto Filter button again. To get all the activities back select the **All Tasks** filter.

Report 5. Owner's Bar Chart Report

This will be a bar chart designed for the project owner. The columns will be "ID," "Activity Name," and "Duration." The bars will not show float, critical activities, or relationship lines. The bars will be in their late start and finish positions (scheduled **As Late As Possible**) and will have the **Activity Name** to the **Left** of the bar. The schedule is to be **Sorted** by **Finish** date.

The difficulty with this report specification is to get the bars in their **As Late As Possible** position. To do this, select all the activities by clicking in the top left cell and then selecting the **Task Information** button 🗒 . Or, another way to get to the Task Information window is to select **Project, Task Information.** In the Multiple Task Information window select the **Advanced** tab and then next to **Constraint type** select **As Late As Possible.** Because all the activities are highlighted, this moves all the bars with float to their late start and finish dates. Now the schedule looks out of order, so sort it by late start dates. This is done by selecting **Project, Sort, Sort by,** select **Late Start**, and then clicking on the **Sort** button. The completed schedule for the owner should look very similar to Figure 22.19.

Look carefully at Figure 22.19 and notice how the activities with float have now shifted to their late start and finish positions. Particularly noticeable is Temp. Power, Inst. Siding, and Paint Exterior. Compare those dates with prior schedules. This late bar display allows the owner to focus on the pessimistic dates and not get alarmed if an activity does not start as early as possible and yet finishes within its float, therefore, not causing a potential delay to the project. For more information on how to use bar charts see Chapter 12 of this text.

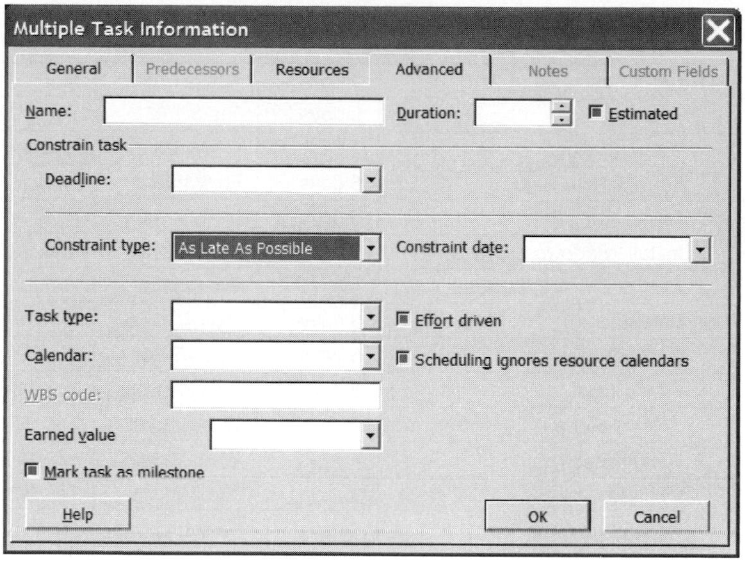

FIGURE 22.18 Use the Multiple Task Information dialog box to make all the bars show in their late position

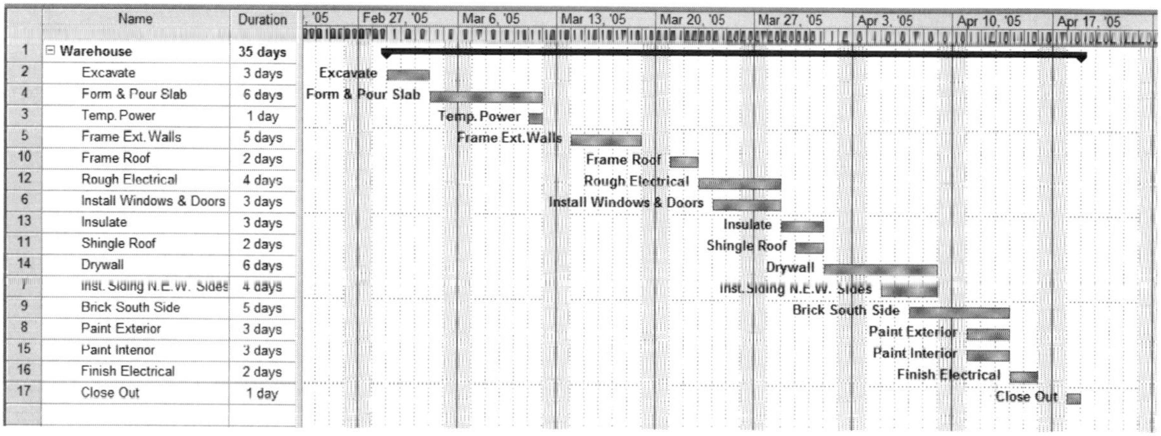

FIGURE 22.19 Bar chart for the owner showing the bars in their late positions

To get the bars back to their early positions all the above needs to be reversed, showing all the bars in their **As Early As Possible** position.

Report 6. Owner's Tabular Report

Because the bar chart for the owner is a not convenient to create with MS Project, a popular report for the owner is a tabular report or what some project managers call an activity table. The report consists of rows and columns of cells without any bars; in other words, the table information to the left of the bar chart in MS Project. The columns for this report will be "ID," "Activity Name," "Duration," "Late Start" data

ID	Name	Duration	Planned Start	Planned Finish	Actual Start	Actual Finish
1	**Warehouse**	**35 days**	**Tue 3/1/05**	**Mon 4/18/05**	**NA**	**NA**
2	Excavate	3 days	Tue 3/1/05	Thu 3/3/05	NA	NA
3	Temp. Power	1 day	Fri 3/11/05	Fri 3/11/05	NA	NA
4	Form & Pour Slab	6 days	Fri 3/4/05	Fri 3/11/05	NA	NA
5	Frame Ext. Walls	5 days	Mon 3/14/05	Fri 3/18/05	NA	NA
6	Install Windows & Doors	3 days	Thu 3/24/05	Mon 3/28/05	NA	NA
7	Inst. Siding N.E.W. Sides	4 days	Tue 4/5/05	Fri 4/8/05	NA	NA
8	Paint Exterior	3 days	Mon 4/11/05	Wed 4/13/05	NA	NA
9	Brick South Side	5 days	Thu 4/7/05	Wed 4/13/05	NA	NA
10	Frame Roof	2 days	Mon 3/21/05	Tue 3/22/05	NA	NA
11	Shingle Roof	2 days	Wed 3/30/05	Thu 3/31/05	NA	NA
12	Rough Electrical	4 days	Wed 3/23/05	Mon 3/28/05	NA	NA
13	Insulate	3 days	Tue 3/29/05	Thu 3/31/05	NA	NA
14	Drywall	6 days	Fri 4/1/05	Fri 4/8/05	NA	NA
15	Paint Interior	3 days	Mon 4/11/05	Wed 4/13/05	NA	NA
16	Finish Electrical	2 days	Thu 4/14/05	Fri 4/15/05	NA	NA
17	Close Out	1 day	Mon 4/18/05	Mon 4/18/05	NA	NA

FIGURE 22.20   Owner's tabular report

titled "Planned Start," **"Late Finish Data"** titled "Planned Finish," **"Actual Start,"** and **"Actual Finish."** Align the data as desired and make the column width as desired. This again allows the owner to focus on the late dates, thus not becoming alarmed if some of the activities start and finish within their float. For more information on tabular reports and how to use them review Chapter 12 of this textbook.

To print just the column information without the bar chart graphics, slide the vertical line separating the columns from the bars to the extreme right of the screen. Now in Print Preview (magnifying glass tool button to the right of the printer) you only see the table information without the bars as shown in Figure 22.20. As the schedule is updated the actual dates will appear in their proper cells.

Report 7. Subcontractor's Tabular Report

The columns for this report will be "ID," "Activity Name," "Resource Names (Subs)," "Duration," "Remaining Duration," "Duration Variance," "Early Start," "Early Finish," "Actual Start," "% Complete," "Actual Finish." The report would be AutoFiltered and then printed for each individual subcontractor. The carpenter's tabular report would appear similar to Figure 22.21.

Tabular reports are an extremely popular option for experienced project managers. They are not fancy, but they do communicate very effectively who is to do what, when, and where.

	Name	Sub	Duration	Remaining Duration	Duration Variance	Early Start	Early Finish	Actual Start	Physical % Complete	Actual Finish
5	Frame Ext. Walls	Carp	5 days	5 days	5 days	Mon 3/14/05	Fri 3/18/05	NA	0%	NA
6	Install Windows & Doors	Carp	3 days	3 days	3 days	Mon 3/21/05	Wed 3/23/05	NA	0%	NA
7	Inst. Siding N.E.W. Sides	Carp	4 days	4 days	4 days	Thu 3/24/05	Tue 3/29/05	NA	0%	NA
10	Frame Roof	Carp	2 days	2 days	2 days	Mon 3/21/05	Tue 3/22/05	NA	0%	NA

FIGURE 22.21 Carpenter's tabular report

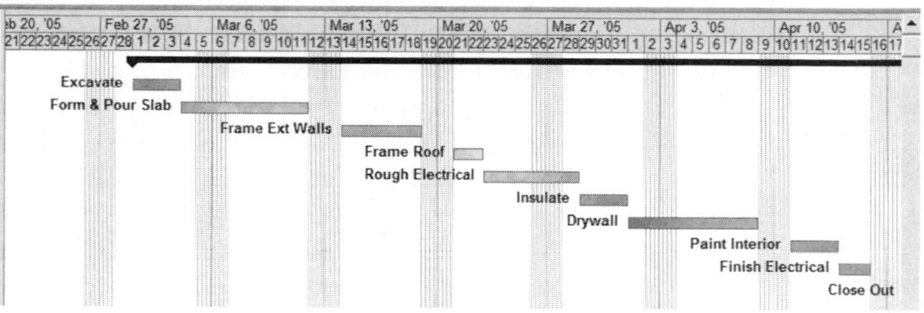

FIGURE 22.22 Critical activities only report

Report 8. Critical Activities Only Report

For this report you can choose the type of bar chart you want and what columns of data you will include. However, only the critical activities can be included. Filter for the critical activities. The report should resemble Figure 22.22.

Now that you are familiar with the basic input and reporting capabilities of MS Project it is time to learn how to update the schedule with the actual start and actual finish information.

Report 9. Updating the Schedule

Follow these basic steps to update the schedule:

1. **Save it to a new name, File, Save As,** leaving the original as-planned schedule for historical purposes. For the warehouse project save it as "Warehouse01."

2. **Set a baseline** schedule to compare the baseline or target schedule with the current schedule by selecting **Tools, Tracking, Save Baseline.** This basically takes a picture of your schedule at this time, enabling you to compare the future to this baseline. Notice the baseline does not yet show. The get the baseline bars to appear on the screen the bars need to be formatted to show the baseline.

3. **Format the bars** to show the baseline by using the **Gantt Chart Wizard**. Use the following steps within the wizard: (A.) Open the wizard by clicking on the Gantt Chart Wizard button ; (B.) Custom Gantt Chart;

(C.) Critical displayed differently—Yes; (D.) Next; (E.) Next; (F.) Next, (G.) Next; (H.) Baseline & Slack; (I.) Custom Task information; (J.) select name to right of the bar; (K.) Next; (L.) Next; (M.) No links or as desired; (N.) Format It and Exit the Wizard. Now you see the target bars on top of the current bars.

4. **Insert columns** to assist in updating. Format the columns to include the following: "ID," "Indicators," "Task Name," "Duration," "Baseline Start," "Baseline Finish," "Actual Start," "Actual Finish," and "% Complete." Align data to the left or as desired.

5. **Show the Status Date Line** (Today's Date) by selecting **Tools, Tracking, Progress Lines**, and normally you would put a check mark by **Always Display** and then select **Current Date.** However, for this project select the **Status Date** in order to fool the program into thinking a future date is today. You are going to update the schedule on the day that *Frame Roof* should have been completed by (note that date). Select **Project, Project Information**, then enter that date as the **Status Date.** This fools the program into thinking that that date is today. Again, normally you simply choose the **Current Date** which will be the date of the update. The schedule should now look similar to Figure 22.23.

The red line shows how far the activities are behind due to not being updated. Where the red line goes vertically straight is today's date.

6. **Update the scheduled tasks. You do not update summary tasks, you only update tasks. The summary dates are derived from the tasks under them.** To update the tasks, in the **Task Name** field, select the task you want to update. Click on **Tools, Tracking,** and then **Update Tasks.** In the Update Tasks dialog box enter the **Actual Start** and **Actual Finish**

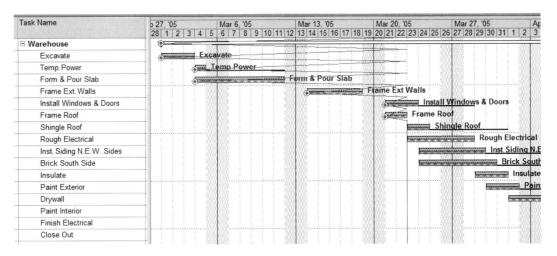

FIGURE 22.23   Status date lines

dates. Or, if an activity has started but not finished enter the Actual Start and the % Complete or Remaining duration. An easier method to input the actual dates that many managers use, is to show the appropriate columns, as we have here, and simply enter the **Actual Start** and **Actual Finish** dates or **% Complete** in the proper cells.

Update the warehouse project as follows: *Excavate* started a work day late and finished on the original finish date. *Temp. Power* started two work days late and finished a day prior to the late finish date, where the float bar ends. After updating these two activities, notice under the **Indicators** column there are check marks indicating those activities have been updated. Continue updating: *Form & Pour Slab* started a day late and finished two days late. Now you see the remainder activities calculated to finish two days late based on that delay. *Frame Ext. Walls* started two days late due to the previous delay and is 60% complete. Your updated schedule should look similar to Figure 22.24.

Notice in Figure 22.24 the total Warehouse is 27% complete. Also notice the backward status date line shows the project is behind two additional days. When the status line goes backward, such as in the *Frame Ext. Walls* activity, that indicates additional delays. Notice the current bar for *Frame Ext. Walls* shows the bar 60% complete. To move the uncompleted portion of that bar to start tomorrow, click and drag it to that location as shown in Figure 22.25.

Now as you compare the baseline schedule with the current schedule you see you are a total of four work days behind. Note the summary bar shows those four days as well. Print this updated schedule as report #9.

For quick updating, if a number of tasks started and finished on time, you can set the actual start and actual finish information for all of those tasks at once. In the **Task Name** field, hold down Ctrl and click the tasks that started and finished on time. On the **Tools** menu, point to **Tracking**, and then click **Update Project**. Click **Update work as complete through,** type or select a date, and then under **For,** click **Selected tasks.**

	0	Task Name	Duration	Baseline Start	Baseline Finish	Actual Start	Actual Finish	% Complete
1		☐ Warehouse	36 days	Tue 3/1/05	Mon 4/18/05	Wed 3/2/05	NA	27%
2	✓ ✎	Excavate	2 days	Tue 3/1/05	Thu 3/3/05	Wed 3/2/05	Thu 3/3/05	100%
3	✓	Temp. Power	3 days	Fri 3/4/05	Fri 3/4/05	Tue 3/8/05	Thu 3/10/05	100%
4	✓ ✎	Form & Pour Slab	7 days	Fri 3/4/05	Fri 3/11/05	Mon 3/7/05	Tue 3/15/05	100%
5		Frame Ext. Walls	5 days	Mon 3/14/05	Fri 3/18/05	Wed 3/16/05	NA	60%
6		Install Windows & Doors	3 days	Mon 3/21/05	Wed 3/23/05	NA	NA	0%
10		Frame Roof	2 days	Mon 3/21/05	Tue 3/22/05	NA	NA	0%
11		Shingle Roof	2 days	Wed 3/23/05	Thu 3/24/05	NA	NA	0%
12		Rough Electrical	4 days	Wed 3/23/05	Mon 3/28/05	NA	NA	0%
7		Inst. Siding N.E.W. Sides	4 days	Thu 3/24/05	Tue 3/29/05	NA	NA	0%
9	✎	Brick South Side	5 days	Thu 3/24/05	Wed 3/30/05	NA	NA	0%
13		Insulate	3 days	Tue 3/29/05	Thu 3/31/05	NA	NA	0%
8	✎	Paint Exterior	3 days	Wed 3/30/05	Fri 4/1/05	NA	NA	0%
14		Drywall	6 days	Fri 4/1/05	Fri 4/8/05	NA	NA	0%
15	✎	Paint Interior	3 days	Mon 4/11/05	Wed 4/13/05	NA	NA	0%
16		Finish Electrical	2 days	Thu 4/14/05	Fri 4/15/05	NA	NA	0%
17		Close Out	1 day	Mon 4/18/05	Mon 4/18/05	NA	NA	0%

FIGURE 22.24 Partially updated schedule

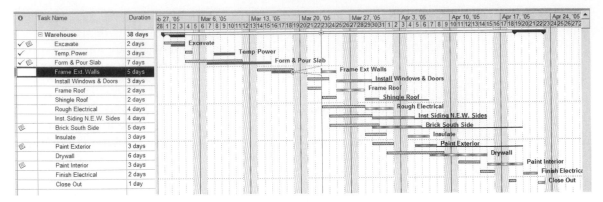

FIGURE 22.25   Schedule adjusted for activities that are behind schedule

Report 10. Adjust the Schedule to Finish on the Original Finish Date

If this were a large schedule of hundreds or thousands of activities, the first thing you would do is filter for the critical activities only. So, to learn proper procedures, filter the warehouse project schedule for the critical activities only. There are three techniques to consider when compressing a schedule: (1) change the calendar to allow critical activities to take place on the weekend; (2) change the duration of critical activities; or (3) change the logic to allow critical activities to happen concurrently or overlapped with lags. Pick the technique that would have the least impact on cost, quality, and safety. Because this schedule is four days behind we will use all three techniques. Pick an activity that is scheduled through the weekend and change the calendar to allow working on Saturday. Double-click the activity name to bring up the **Task Information** window. Change the calendar to use the 6 day work week calendar, put a check mark in the **Scheduling ignores resource calendars,** and **OK** it. That reduces the number of days behind the baseline to three days.

Change the duration of two critical activities by one day each. This saves another two days so that you are only one day behind. Finally, change the relationship between **Close Out** and **Finish Electrical** to have a **Finish-to-Finish** Lag of "0," forcing the two activities to finish on the same day. This is also done in the **Task Information** window. Double-click on the activity **Close Out,** select the **Predecessors** tab, and change the relationship to **Type and Lag.** Now you are back to finishing on the same day as the baseline schedule. To get all the activities back, filter for **All Tasks.** The schedule should now look similar to Figure 22.26.

Your schedule will be different depending on which activities you chose to accelerate. However, it should show completing on the original completion date.

Report 11. Scheduling Repetitive Activities

You are scheduling the interior finishes for a three-floor office building. The network logic diagram for one-floor level has been developed by the management team and is shown in Figure 22.27.

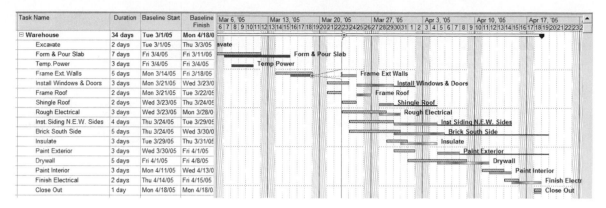

Task Name	Duration	Baseline Start	Baseline Finish
⊟ Warehouse	34 days	Tue 3/1/05	Mon 4/18/0
Excavate	2 days	Tue 3/1/05	Thu 3/3/05
Form & Pour Slab	7 days	Fri 3/4/05	Fri 3/11/05
Temp. Power	3 days	Fri 3/4/05	Fri 3/4/05
Frame Ext. Walls	5 days	Mon 3/14/05	Fri 3/18/05
Install Windows & Doors	3 days	Mon 3/21/05	Wed 3/23/0
Frame Roof	2 days	Mon 3/21/05	Tue 3/22/05
Shingle Roof	2 days	Wed 3/23/05	Thu 3/24/05
Rough Electrical	3 days	Wed 3/23/05	Mon 3/28/0
Inst. Siding N.E.W. Sides	4 days	Thu 3/24/05	Tue 3/29/05
Brick South Side	5 days	Thu 3/24/05	Wed 3/30/0
Insulate	3 days	Tue 3/29/05	Thu 3/31/05
Paint Exterior	3 days	Wed 3/30/05	Fri 4/1/05
Drywall	5 days	Fri 4/1/05	Fri 4/8/05
Paint Interior	3 days	Mon 4/11/05	Wed 4/13/0
Finish Electrical	2 days	Thu 4/14/05	Fri 4/15/05
Close Out	1 day	Mon 4/18/05	Mon 4/18/0

FIGURE 22.26 The warehouse schedule adjusted to finish on the original finish date

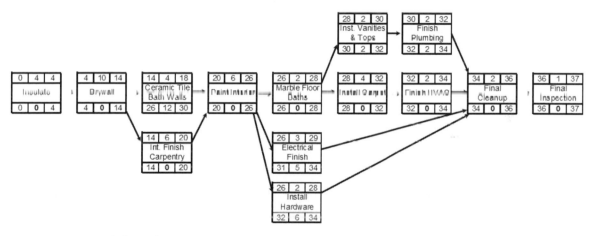

FIGURE 22.27 Hand-drawn logic diagram of the first floor level of an office building

Input the schedule in Figure 22.27 as a new schedule into MS Project.

The network logic diagram as input into MS Project should look similar to Figure 22.28, depending on how you format the activity boxes.

The Gantt bar chart should look similar to Figure 22.29.

If you have not already done so, create the first floor level summary activity as in Figure 22.29. Input the subcontractors required for each activity and your bar chart should look similar to the bar chart in Figure 22.29, depending on how you have the bars formatted and which columns you have chosen to show. For instructional purposes format your columns and bars to match Figure 22.29. Choose the beginning date to be whatever date you wish.

To create the second-floor level click on the Activity **ID** number of the *1st Floor Level* summary activity and **Copy** that summary activity. Move your cursor to just below the last activity and click on the **Paste** button. Correct the name of the second summary activity to *2nd Floor Level.* Outdent the *2nd Floor Level* to be equal to the

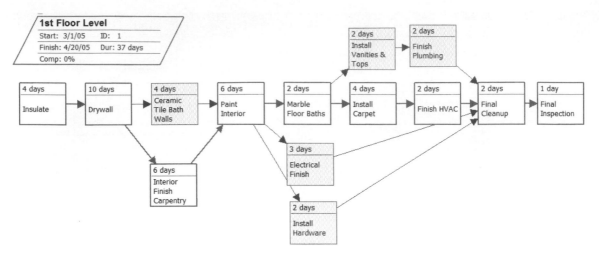

FIGURE 22.28   Logic diagram of the first-floor level input into MS Project

	❶	Task Name	Duration	Subs	Predecessors
1		⊟ 1st Floor Level	37 days		
2		Insulate	4 days	Insul	
3		Drywall	10 days	DW	2
5		Ceramic Tile Bath W:	4 days	Cer Tile	3
4		Interior Finish Carpen	6 days	Carp	3
6		Paint Interior	6 days	Painter	5,4
7		Marble Floor Baths	2 days	Marble	6
9		Install Hardware	2 days	HDWR	6
8		Electrical Finish	3 days	Elect	6
11		Install Vanities & Top	2 days	Cabinet	7
10		Install Carpet	4 days	Carpet	7
13		Finish Plumbing	2 days	Plumber	11
12		Finish HVAC	2 days	HVAC	10
14		Final Cleanup	2 days	Cleaning	12,8,9,13
15		Final Inspection	1 day	F. Inspect	14

FIGURE 22.29   Gantt bar chart of the first-floor level input into MS Project

1st Floor Level. Click below the last activity on the *2nd Floor Level* and paste again to create the *3rd Floor Level.* Now all three-floor levels have been input into the computer in a very short period of time. Your schedule should look similar to Figure 22.30.

Notice that as you copied the activities by clicking in the "ID" column you copied all the data tied to those activities as well—the durations, subs, and predecessors. The only problem with the schedule in Figure 22.30 is that work on all three floor levels is happening at the same time. This would be OK if you have sufficient tradespeople to manage all three floors concurrently. However, that is not typically the situation. You only have one crew. There are at least two ways to solve this problem; read through both of them before deciding which one to use.

One way to schedule this project would be to look for the critical task with the longest duration and use that duration as a staging activity for the project. In other words, *Drywall* is the critical activity with the longest duration (10 days), so you could

#	ⓘ	Task Name	Duration	Subs	Predecessors
1		☐ 1st Floor Level	37 days		
2		Insulate	4 days	Insul	
3		Drywall	10 days	DW	2
5		Ceramic Tile Bath W:	4 days	Cer Tile	3
4		Interior Finish Carpen	6 days	Carp	3
6		Paint Interior	6 days	Painter	5,4
7		Marble Floor Baths	2 days	Marble	6
9		Install Hardware	2 days	HDWR	6
8		Electrical Finish	3 days	Elect	6
11		Install Vanities & Top	2 days	Cabinet	7
10		Install Carpet	4 days	Carpet	7
13		Finish Plumbing	2 days	Plumber	11
12		Finish HVAC	2 days	HVAC	10
14		Final Cleanup	2 days	Cleaning	12,8,9,13
15		Final Inspection	1 day	F. Inspect	14
16		☐ 2nd Floor Level	37 days		
17		Insulate	4 days	Insul	
18		Drywall	10 days	DW	17
19		Interior Finish Carpen	6 days	Carp	18
20		Ceramic Tile Bath W:	4 days	Cer Tile	18
21		Paint Interior	6 days	Painter	19,20
22		Marble Floor Baths	2 days	Marble	21
23		Electrical Finish	3 days	Elect	21
24		Install Hardware	2 days	HDWR	21
25		Install Carpet	4 days	Carpet	22
26		Install Vanities & Top	2 days	Cabinet	22
27		Finish HVAC	2 days	HVAC	25
28		Finish Plumbing	2 days	Plumber	26
29		Final Cleanup	2 days	Cleaning	23,24,27,28
30		Final Inspection	1 day	F. Inspect	29
31		☐ 3rd Floor Level	37 days		
32		Insulate	4 days	Insul	
33		Drywall	10 days	DW	32
34		Interior Finish Carpen	6 days	Carp	33
35		Ceramic Tile Bath W:	4 days	Cer Tile	33
36		Paint Interior	6 days	Painter	34,35

FIGURE 22.30 Schedule of all three-floor levels

put a start-to-start lag of 10 days between the start of *Insulate* on the first floor to *Insulate* on the second floor and so forth to the third floor. This could be done easily in the Network Diagram view. You would also probably put a finish-to-finish lag of 10 days between the final inspections of each floor level as well to eliminate excessive float showing. This would give you an acceptable schedule for this project.

Another way to solve the problem of having each crew working in three places at once is to crew load the project. Make *Insulate* on the first floor a predecessor to *Insulate* on the second floor, and *Insulate* on the second floor a predecessor to *Insulate* on the third floor. This would be done with each activity and would ensure that no crew would be working in two places at once. However, it would require a lot of time inputting all those relationships. An extremely valuable technique to solve this problem is to first **Group** the activities by **Sub.** This is done by clicking on **Project, Group by, More Groups,** and then selecting **Subcontractors** or **Resource Names** depending on how you have it set up. You may need to create a new group by reviewing prior steps in this chapter. After the schedule is grouped by subcontractors your screen looks similar to Figure 22.31.

Now that it is grouped by subcontractors, even though the subcontractors are in alphabetical order, all you need to do is highlight the activities each sub is responsible for and then click on the **Link Tasks** button on the toolbar (see Figure 22.32). Notice the arrow pointing to the Link Tasks button.

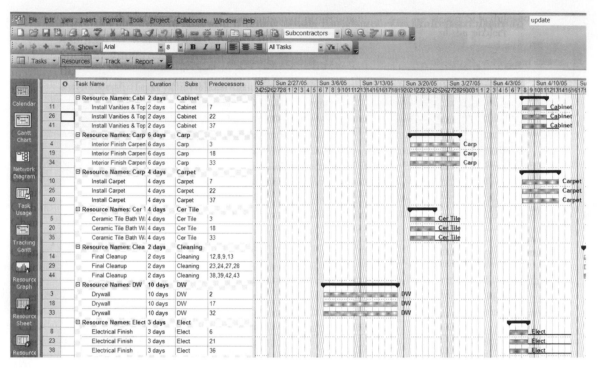

FIGURE 22.31   Schedule grouped by subcontractors

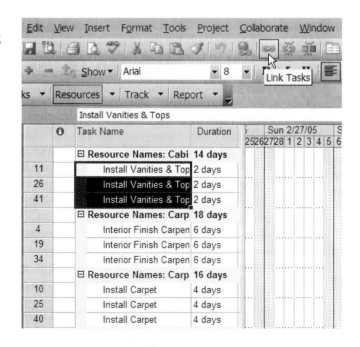

FIGURE 22.32   Link grouped tasks by selecting the Link Tasks button on the Standard toolbar

Continue linking the tasks for each crew. You are now assured that no single crew will be working in two places at the same time and the whole building is properly scheduled. This would not have taken much longer if it were a 15-floor office building. Remove the grouping by clicking on **Project, Group by,** and selecting **No Group.** The schedule, which now looks like Figure 22.33, is an accurate method of scheduling the project—it shows a true critical path throughout the project.

If you wanted to eliminate some of the float and close out each level as it is completed, you could use a finish-to-finish relationship of five days between the final inspections, or a date constraint to constrain the final inspection of each floor level.

These exercises have provided you with some valuable experience with MS Project. Refer to this chapter in order to improve your ability to manage projects. This gives you a good beginning. It is certainly not all there is to know about using MS Project to manage projects, but even if you know only how to input the project and create a few very basic reports it will help you to control your projects, rather than allowing them to control you. Don't feel you need to know everything, all at once. When you use MS Project, keep it simple at first, taking it one step at a time. Learn more as you need to. Focus on the parts that makes sense to you. After several months it will be a

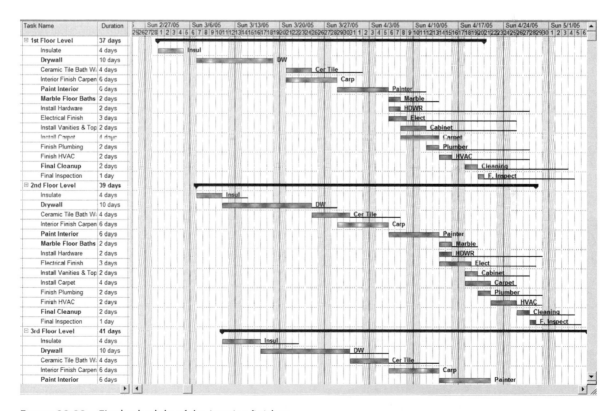

Figure 22.33 Final schedule of the interior finishes

great asset to help you to plan, organize, direct, and control in order to build quality projects on time, within budget, and in a safe work environment.

The projects created and worked on in this chapter are contained on the CD accompanying this text. Consult them if it is helpful.

TRYING OTHER SHORTCUTS, TECHNIQUES, OR IDEAS

Scheduling multiple projects with Microsoft Project is powerful. Start by creating a schedule of each separate project with appropriate start dates. Then create a new project that is basically just a new file and save it as whatever name you desire **(File, Save As).** Then, from the Menu bar select **Insert** and then **Project** and select the first project to insert. Continue inserting projects into that file until all the projects you are now managing are listed in this new project. You can then view them all together, update them, print multiproject reports, and let the computer help you to manage all the projects you are responsible for. Then, to see which project the subcontractor is to work on insert a "Text 1" column and title it "Project" or whatever and assign the activities of each project to that column. Then, if you group the multiprojects by subcontractors you can see which project the subcontractor is to be working on.

Creating date constraints bring up the Task Information window by double-clicking on a task name and then select the **Advanced tab** where you can constrain the task to start or finish on a specific date or no earlier than or no later than a specific date. The default is to start as soon as possible. Be careful when doing this because it overrides the CPM logic established in the network diagram. Use it only as necessary; date constraints do not make up for using bad logic and then just constraining a task in order to get it to happen when you want. Date constraints are typically used because of outside influences, such as activities that cannot start earlier than May 15 due to typical weather conditions, landscaping, or asphalt paving, for example. See Chapter 18 for more information on date constraints.

Saving a schedule as a template select **File, Save As,** give it a name as desired, next to **Save as type** select **Template,** and it will be saved as an MPT file which designates it as a template where MPP files are regular Microsoft Project files. Then, as you use the template MS Project makes you save it to as an MPP file, keeping the template without changes. To change the template, make the changes and then save it as a template file.

Saving a new task or changing a duration to an existing baseline highlight the selected task or tasks and then select **Tools, Tracking, Save Baseline,** and click in the **Selected Tasks** check box. If you had selected an entire schedule rather than just the new added or changed task, you would have reset the plan for the entire schedule and lost the original baseline.

Automatically saving to or opening from a specific folder, click on Tools, Options, and Save, and then change the projects folder as desired.

Contact Information

Microsoft Corporation
One Microsoft Way
Redmond, WA 98052-6399

Phone: (425) 882-8080
Fax: (425) 706-7329
Web address: microsoft.com

CHAPTER 23

MANAGING PROJECTS USING P3F/C

Introduction—Primavera Project Planner for the Enterprise for Construction

Using the Help Buttons

Making a New Project File

Setting Up the Calendars

Defining Activity Codes

Inputting Activity Data

Input Using the New Activity Wizard

Input Using the Activity Table

Input Using the Activity Network

Making a Copy of the Project Schedule

Calculating the Schedule

Organizing the Schedule

Sort Activities

Group Activities

Checking the Number of Days to Complete

Filtering Activities

Formatting Bar Charts

    Change the Date/Timescale

    Change the Columns

    Format the Bars

    Create a New Layout

Setting Up and Printing Standard Reports

    Report 1. Input Check Report

    Report 2. Project Manager's Bar Chart Report

    Report 3. Superintendent's Bar Chart Report

    Report 4. Subcontractor's Bar Chart Report

        Creating Page Breaks   Adding Notes

    Report 5. Owner's Bar Chart Report

    Report 6. Subcontractor's Tabular Report for the Next Three Weeks

    Report 7. Owner's Tabular Report—Using Layouts

    Report 8. Owner's Tabular Report—Using the Report Wizard

    Report 9. Critical Activities Only Report

    Report 10. Tabular Report for a Specific Subcontractor

    Report 11. Printing a Batch of Reports

    Report 12. Statusing or Updating the Schedule

    Report 13. Update the Schedule to Finish on the Original Finish Date

    Report 14. Adding a Curtain or Text

    Report 15. Creating a New Schedule Based on an Old Schedule

    Report 16. Using Fragnets to Copy Schedules or Parts of Schedules

INTRODUCTION— PRIMAVERA PROJECT PLANNER FOR THE ENTERPRISE FOR CONSTRUCTION

P3e/c is a product suite designed to support the project management needs of organizations that manage large numbers of projects at one time. According to the P3e/c *Project Manager's Reference Manual,* P3e/c is designed for large businesses that have hundreds, or even thousands, of projects under way at one time. These businesses have limited resources that must be shared throughout all these projects. P3e/c is designed to provide the reporting and managing capability of all these people in differing roles and responsibilities. Enterprise project management provides comprehensive information on all projects in an organization, from executive-level summaries to detailed plans by project. Individuals across all levels of the company can analyze, record, and communicate reliable information and make timely, informed decisions that support their corporate mission. P3e/c is a product of Primavera Systems, Inc. Contact information is listed at the end of this chapter.

The major difference between P3 and P3e/c is that with P3, individual projects are managed separately by one or more project managers, each with their own set of codes, resources, calendars, reports, and so on. P3e/c changes the focus from a single-user environment to a multiuser, role-based environment. This provides the opportunity for upper management to evaluate thousands of projects in a single database, enabling management to review all the projects and resources within the organization. Individual project managers also can review just the data that is relevant to them.

P3e/c contains the following components: Project Manager, Methodology Manager, Portfolio Analyst, Progress Reporter, Primavision, Mobile Manager, and Software Development Kit. This chapter focuses on the portion of P3e/c that is designed for the project manager. From this point on it will be referred to as "Project Manager."

The following instructions are presented chronologically and are based on *how managers use the software,* rather than explaining every detail in the order the screens appear and feature of the software. These instructions contain examples and assignments that teach how to use the software to communicate and manage the project. However, these instructions are not foolproof and do not guarantee success. They are simply a guide to help you learn the basics of this dynamic program. If you find an error in the instructions, find a way around it. Keep in mind that with project management software it is not necessary to know everything in order to be an effective user. These instructions cover only the basics of Project Manager. Learn these basics so you can start scheduling now, and then as you become proficient with scheduling you can learn additional details as you find a need for them.

As you work through these instructions, make sure you are thinking. Don't allow yourself to get into the mode of just carrying out the instructions without engaging your mind to make sure what you are doing is logical and makes sense. If you *think* as you do this, you will learn how to use Project Manager. Don't get frustrated if everything doesn't work as you expect. Generally, with computer software, you learn the most when things go wrong. Keep thinking and trying and you will figure it out. Once you have followed the instructions in detail and accomplished a task, it is assumed you learned that task and from then on the instructions pertaining to that task will be less detailed. So, if later in the chapter you forget the details on how to do a task, go back to the beginning of the chapter to review the details pertaining to that task.

USING THE HELP BUTTONS

The Help buttons are very useful for when you feel lost or confused. There is also a Help feature and a tutorial under **Help** on the Menu bar. Each P3e/c window also displays a Help button that will provide help directly for that window. The schedules used in the tutorial are included on the CD accompanying this text. They are contained in the P3e/c folder. The schedules must be imported by selecting File, Import, and following the prompts of the Import Wizard. The layouts must also be imported by selecting View, Layouts, Open, Import, and then selecting the layouts contained on the CD in the P3e/c folder. These schedules are not necessary; they are only included as reference material.

The schedule shown in Figure 23.1 for the construction of a warehouse will be used to help learn Project Manager. This is a warehouse you will be constructing for the State of Utah. Figure 23.1 is the network logic diagram developed during a meeting with the management team.

The warehouse is to be supervised by two superintendents: Bill and John. John is particularly good at overseeing the earthwork and the structure activities. Bill will be brought in to manage the finishing activities, basically from the insulation to completion. The number in the circle represents the activity ID number. The 35 work days calculated to complete the project is in accordance with the contract provisions.

You are now ready to computerize the schedule.

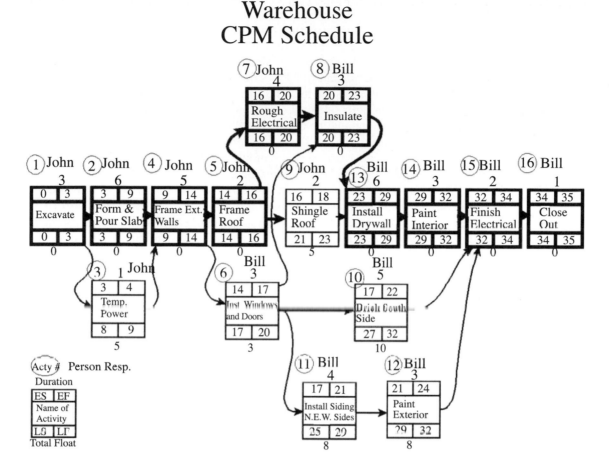

FIGURE 23.1 Network logic diagram for the warehouse project

MAKING A NEW PROJECT FILE

To load Project Planner, click on the **Start** button at the bottom left corner of the computer screen, select **Programs, Primavera P3ec for Construction,** and **Project Manager.** A user name and password is required in order for the program to boot. On a new installation the default Login name is "admin" and the default Password is also "admin." Or, check with your company's computer specialist for your user name and password.

Now that Project Manager is loaded, to make it easier to learn the program, turn on all the toolbars by selecting from the Menu bar **View, Toolbars,** and put a check mark by all the toolbars. You may need to repeat View, Toolbars several times to get checks by each available toolbar.

Before you create a new project you need to create a new Enterprise Project Structure (EPS) for the new project to belong to and you need to add yourself to the Organizational Breakdown Structure (OBS). This project is for the State of Utah, so we want to create the Utah EPS. To make a new EPS, select **Enterprise** from the Menu bar. Then select **Enterprise Project Structure.** Click on the **Add** button and enter the **EPS ID** of **Utah** and an **EPS Name** of **State of Utah.** The new EPS is listed under an existing EPS; to slide it to the left to make it a top-level EPS, select the left arrow button on the right side of the window, above the Help button. This slides the new EPS to the left, making it a top-level EPS. Now close the window.

To add yourself to the OBS, select **Enterprise, OBS,** highlight **Construction** to add yourself to the construction group or any other area where you belong, and then click on the **Add** button and enter your name.

To create a new project under this EPS, from the Menu bar, select **File, New.** In the **Select EPS** box click on the button to the right and select the **Utah** EPS you created above. Then select **Next.** Give it a **Project ID** of Warehouse00. Some managers use these last two numbers (00) to identify the update number. The first or as-planned schedule would be Warehouse00. Then, as the project is updated, this first schedule will be copied and named Warehouse01 for the updates through the first month. Warehouse02 will be used for the updates through the second month, and so on. This provides an audit trail that will help analyze the project should that need arise in the future. Input a **Project Name** as desired, such as **Warehouse, as planned.** Input the **Planned Start** date of the project. If a **Must Finish By** date is entered the backward pass will be calculated from that date creating either negative or positive float. Most managers prefer not to input anything in this box, allowing the project to finish as determined by the forward pass. For the **Responsible Manager** select yourself from the Organizational Breakdown you created earlier. **Rate Type** is as defaulted. Do not run the Project Architect for now. The new project is now created. Select the **Finish** button. **To open** this project highlight it, right-click, and select **Open Project.**

SETTING UP THE CALENDARS

Before you input activities and activity data you should set up the general parameters of the schedule, namely the calendars and the activity codes. First, set up the calendars for Project Manager to use. You can establish an unlimited number of calendars to match the requirements of each activity. For the warehouse project you will need a default five-day work week, six-day work week, and a seven-day work week calendar. You set up the calendars by selecting **Enterprise** and then **Calendars** on the Menu bar. Make sure there is a dot by the **Global** calendar. Also make sure there is a check mark for the **Standard 5-Day Workweek** calendar. This calendar will now be the default calendar. It needs to have the holidays declared so that Project Manager will not allow activities to happen on the holidays. To declare the holidays select the **Modify** button. Then select the following dates and make them **Nonwork** days: Jan 1, Memorial Day (last Monday in May), July 4, Labor Day (1st Monday in September), Thanksgiving (4th Thursday in November), December 25. Then **OK** the global calendar. This global calendar will override the project calendars. Therefore, the holiday dates entered into the global calendar will also be scheduled as nonwork days in the project calendars.

Set up the project calendars by putting a dot by **Project** in the Calendar dialog box. Then check the **Add** button and select the **Standard 5-Day Workweek** calendar you declared the holidays on previously to copy from. Give the new calendar a name of **6-Day.** This calendar will be used for the activities that will work on Saturday. **Modify** this new calendar, select **Workweek**, and make sure it is scheduled to work eight hours per day on every day except Sunday. **OK** it. **Add** another project calendar, copied again from the **Standard 5-day Workweek** calendar, name it **7-Day, Modify** it to work eight hours a day, all seven days, and **OK** it. Close the Calendar dialog box.

DEFINING ACTIVITY CODES

This chapter is using Project Manager in a stand-alone project mode. In an effort to keep it simple for the beginning stages we will be using the activity codes functions to schedule the superintendents and the subcontractors. As Project Manager is used in the enterprise mode the superintendents and the subcontractors would be used as resources, rather than activity codes.

Set up the **Activity Codes** by selecting from the Menu bar **Enterprise, Activity Codes** and put a dot to the left of **Project.** Click on the **Modify** button and add the first activity code of **Superintendent** and **Close** the window. Now that the superintendent has been created, **Add** the **Code Value** of John (Code Values are limited to seven characters) with a **Description** of John Wayne. Add the **Code Value** of Bill with a **Description** of William Tell. Figure 23.2 shows how the activity codes for the superintendents should look.

Next, set up the activity codes for the subcontractors. **Modify, Add, Subcontractors,** and then enter all the **Code Values** and **Descriptions** of each subcontractor needed to construct the warehouse. When naming subcontractors some project managers recommend the trade name, rather than given names. That way when you change

FIGURE 23.2 Activity codes for the superintendents

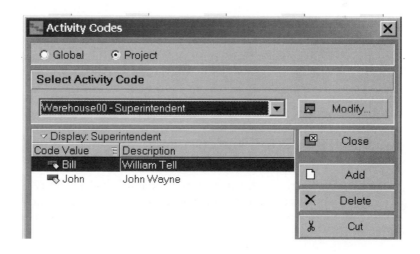

FIGURE 23.3 Activity
codes for subcontractors

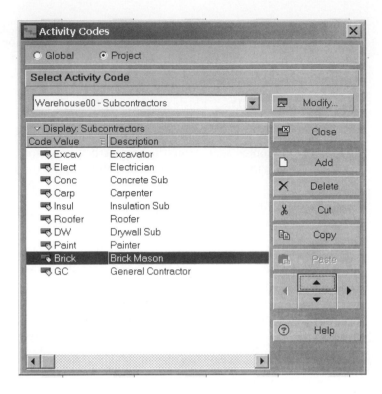

subs you won't need to edit this field; for example, you might use code title of Elect with a description of Electrician, rather than Mountain Electric. Then if you choose another electrical subcontractor this activity code will not need to be edited. The activity codes for the subcontractors should look similar to Figure 23.3. They do not need to be in the same order, just as long as they are all there.

This is all the activity codes needed for now, so close the Activity Codes dialog box.

Now that you have the basic parameters of the schedule—the calendar and the activity codes defined—it is time to enter the activity data. But before doing so, in order to have the activity ID number added automatically, set the activity ID to be inserted by increments of 1. Do this by selecting from the Menu bar **Enterprise, Projects** and then make sure the activity details show at the bottom of the screen by selecting **View, Show on Bottom, Project Details.** Change **Auto-numbering Defaults** as follows: Activity ID Suffix = 1, Increment = 1, and put a check mark in Increment Activity ID based on selected activity. To get back to the project activities click on **Project** and then **Activities.**

INPUTTING ACTIVITY DATA

You are now ready to input the individual activities of the schedule. There are three primary methods to enter activity data: (1) using the New Activity Wizard, (2) using the Activity Table, and (3) using the Activity Network.

FIGURE 23.4 Columns
dialog box

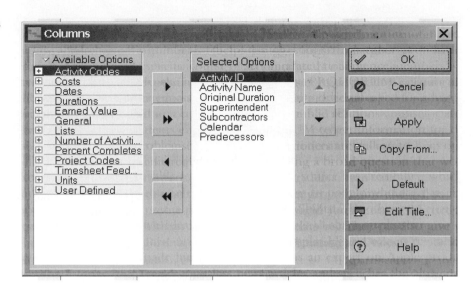

Input Using the New Activity Wizard

To make sure the New Activity Wizard is turned on, choose **Edit, User Preferences, Assistance tab,** mark the **Use New Activity Wizard** checkbox. To turn off the New Activity Wizard remove the check mark.

To add a new activity select the Add button **+** at the upper right side of the screen. Follow the instructions of the New Activity Wizard. Enter **Activity ID** as shown on the hand-drawn schedule, **Activity Name, Next** (at this point if you do not know what to enter, use the default and select Next), **Duration, Assign Predecessors** (don't assign successors), **Assign Activity Codes** for the **Project,** and **Finish.** Continue repeating this process for the first five activities. Then use the Activity Table for the next five activities.

Input Using the Activity Table

The Activity Table is the rows and columns of information to the left of the screen, left of the bar chart area. First, turn off the New Activity Wizard by following the prior directions. In order to use the Activity Table it is necessary to show the columns of information to be added. Select **View, Columns** or use the Columns button 🗐 and then use the arrow keys to make the **Selected Options** show the following columns: "Activity ID", "Activity Name", "Original Duration", "Superintendent", "Subcontractors", "Calendar", and "Predecessors". The Columns dialog box is shown in Figure 23.4.

The column headings that you entered appear in the Activity Table area. You may need to position the mouse over the bold vertical line separating the activity columns from the bar chart area until the cursor turns into two vertical lines, then click and drag the line to the right to expose the additional columns.

To insert a new activity, select the activity immediately above where you want to add a new activity and then use the **Insert key** on your keyboard or click on the **Add button +**. Input the Activity ID, Activity Name, Original Duration, Superintendent,

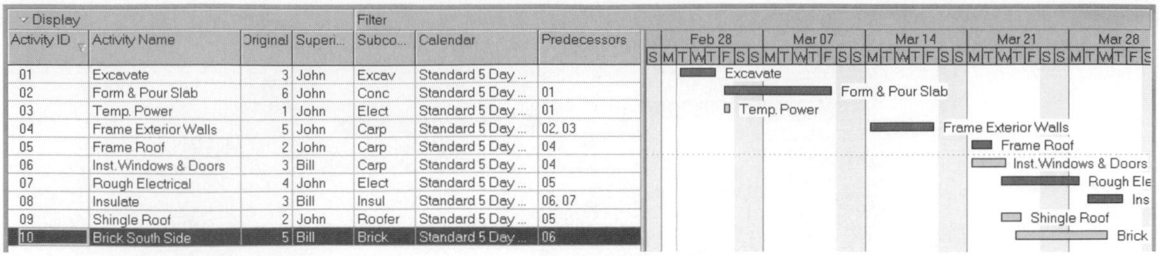

FIGURE 23.5 Appropriate columns, schedule calculated, and activities in ID order

Subcontractor, Calendar, and Predecessors data. The Superintendent, Subcontractor, Calendar (make sure you display the proper calendar, either Project or Global), and Predecessors are selected by double-clicking in the cell and then selecting the appropriate data. To assign lags—start-to-finish, start-to-start, or finish-to-finish relationships—you need to view the relationships at the bottom of the screen. Do this by selecting **View, Show on Bottom, Activity Details**, and then select the **Relationships tab.** Continue to input through activity #10 using this method. After inputting the first 10 activities press the **F9 key** or select the **Schedule Button** ⚙ to have Project Manager perform the calculations by doing the forward and backward passes. The bars have now moved to their appropriate positions. To get the bars **sorted according to Activity ID**, click on the "Activity ID" column heading to put them in the forward or reverse order. This will work with all activity column headings. Your schedule should now look very similar to Figure 23.5.

Input Using the Activity Network

To use the Activity Network select the Activity Network button ⊞ᗡ. This shows the schedule in the Network Logic Diagram view. Click on the Zoom In or Zoom Out button to make the Activity Network logic diagram large enough to read. To make the activity boxes easier to read select **View, Activity Network, Activity Network Options,** and then select the **Activity Name** for a **Template.** Choose the **Activity Network Layout tab** and **Organize Along the Top. OK** it.

You can click and drag the activity boxes to look very similar to the hand-drawn logic diagram. If it looks like the hand-drawn network, it will be easier to input the remaining activities. To create more space at the top of the screen select all the activities by dragging a rubber band around all the activities (or, use the mouse and the Ctrl key) and then drag all the activities to the lower portion of the screen. To deselect all the activities, click anywhere on the screen except on an activity.

To insert an activity in the Network Logic Diagram view select the Add button ✚ or use the Insert key. The activity is inserted at the beginning of the logic diagram and must be moved to the proper location. To create the relationships, move the cursor near the end of the predecessor until the cursor turns into an arrow, then click and drag to the beginning of the successor. It is a little inconvenient to add all the activity data while in the Network Logic Diagram view, therefore many managers simply input the activity ID number, name, and the relationships in the Network Logic Diagram view and then change to the Bar chart view to input the rest of the data in the appropriate rows and columns. The New Activity Wizard could be turned back on and used to input the activity data or the activity details could be shown at the bottom in the Network Logic Diagram view **(View, Show at Bottom, Activity Detail)** and used to input the activity data. It is necessary to calculate the schedule again by pressing the **F9** key or the **Schedule** button. Now you see the critical activities in red and the noncritical activities in green.

While in the Network Logic Diagram view, some other popular options are to show the detailed logic just before and after any activity at the bottom of the screen. Do this by selecting **View, Show on Bottom, Trace Logic.** Now as you select any activity in the top portion of the screen the details of the logic for that activity are shown in the bottom portion of the screen. This is very handy for large projects.

Another popular option is to change the information in the activity box. Do this by selecting **View, Activity Network, Activity Network Options**, and then select the **Activity Box Template tab** and the Activity Box template of choice. You can change the data displayed in the activity box by selecting the **Box Template** button at the bottom of the screen and then adding additional data.

To get back into the Bar chart view click on the **Gantt Chart** button ![icon].

Note: There is no File, Save or File, Save As option. Project Manager automatically saves all changes to the disk. Keep this in mind if you want to just experiment with a schedule. First, copy and paste it to a new name so that you don't mess up the original schedule.

MAKING A COPY OF THE PROJECT SCHEDULE

Select **Enterprise, Projects**, then select the project you want to copy. Click on **Copy** on the Command bar. Select the position in the EPS where you want to copy the project to. Click on **Paste** in the command bar. In the **Copy Project Options dialog box**, mark the check box next to each type of information you want to copy and OK it. The new project ID and name can be changed as desired. If both projects are open, go to Enterprise and close the one not desired.

You do not need to exit P3e/c now, but when you are ready, do it properly.

1. Click on the *X* in the upper right corner to properly exit P3e/c.
2. Then close Windows by clicking on the Start button at the bottom left corner of the screen and choose Shut Down. After Windows shuts down you can turn off the computer. If you do not exit Windows properly, files remain open which may fragment some of the files and cause problems in the future.

CALCULATING THE SCHEDULE

Anytime you change a duration, relationship, or calendar the schedule needs to be recalculated by forcing a new forward and backward pass. To have Project Manager do the calculations either use the F9 key or select the Schedule button ![icon] from the

FIGURE 23.6   Sort window

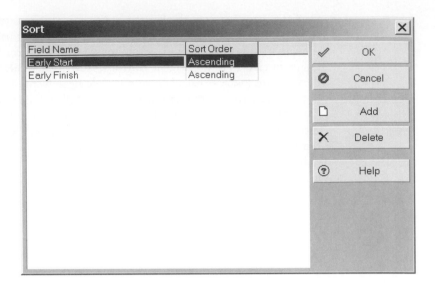

toolbar. The **Data Date** is the start date of the schedule or the date of the update. If you want a report from the calculations, put a check mark in the **Log to file** box. Then click on the Schedule button. Reselect the Schedule button and click on the View Log button to see the report. One of the main items to check on this log report is how many activities are without predecessors (should be only the first activity) and how many activities are without successors (should be only the last activity). This report also identifies the critical activities and states how many critical activities there are, and gives the total number of activities in the schedule.

ORGANIZING THE SCHEDULE

Sort Activities

You will now notice the bars show the proper start and finish dates, but activities may not be listed in the proper order. To make them appear in chronological order or early start, early finish order, the schedule needs to be sorted. Click on **View, Group and Sort** or, click on the Group and Sort button ▣ , then click on the **Sort** button. Under "Field Name" select **Early Start,** then click on the **Add** button and select **Early Finish** listed under Early Start, both in ascending order.

Figure 23.6 shows how the Early Start, Early Finish Sort dialog box is set up. With this sort the computer will look first for the earliest start date to list those activities first. If two activities have the same early start date, the computer will then look to the early finish date to see which activity to list next. You might want to slide the vertical line sep-

Activity ID	Activity Name	Original	Feb 28	Mar 07	Mar 14	Mar 21	Mar 28	Apr 04	Apr 11	Apr 18
01	Excavate	3								
03	Temp. Power	1								
02	Form & Pour Slab	6								
04	Frame Exterior Walls	5								
05	Frame Roof	2								
06	Inst. Windows & Doors	3								
09	Shingle Roof	2								
07	Rough Electrical	4								
11	Install Siding N.E.W. Si...	4								
10	Brick South Side	5								
08	Insulate	3								
12	Paint Exterior	3								
13	Install Drywall	6								
14	Paint Interior	3								
15	Finish Electrical	2								
16	Close Out	1								

FIGURE 23.7   Activities sorted in ES, EF order

arating the activity column information to the left to expose more bar chart area. The activities now appear in chronological or early start, early finish order as in Figure 23.7.

Notice in Figure 23.7 how good looking the bar chart is! It is sorted in true chronological order of early start and early finish sequence. The two activities *Temp. Power* and *Form & Pour Slab* have the same start date, but *Temp. Power* has the earliest finish date so it is listed first. It is the same with *Frame Roof* and *Inst. Windows & Doors*, and so on.

In Project Manager this sort can be overridden quickly by **clicking** on a **column heading**. For example, click on the column heading "Activity ID" and the activities are sorted by ID number. Another click will put the activities in reverse activity ID order. If you click on the "Superintendent" column heading the activities are sorted in order of the superintendents. Format the columns to show the "Early Start" column using the Columns button ▦ . As you click on the "Early Start" column the activities are listed in order of their early start, but the second sort level is not early finish. It appears the second sort level must be total float because the activities with the same start date appear to be sorted according to the amount of float they have.

Clicking on the column heading is an easier method of sorting than going to the **Group and Sort** button and then setting up the sort parameters. However, clicking on the column headings does not provide the multiple levels of sorts that are available through the Group and Sort option.

Group Activities

Project Manager has the ability to group like activities together and to show the number of work days in the grouping. For example, you might want to know how many work days a project is scheduled to take. If you have done the forward pass by hand you already know how many days the project should take. It would be nice to verify that the project has been input correctly and that the computer agrees on the number days required to complete the project.

CHECKING THE NUMBER OF DAYS TO COMPLETE

To do this, click on the **Group and Sort** button ▣ and under **Group By** select **Project** and **OK** it. Notice the name of the project appears at the top of the schedule and notice in the "Original Duration" column that the total number of work days appears. For the warehouse project this should be 35 work days. If it is incorrect check the computer input on the durations and the predecessors. Compare the data input with the hand-drawn network logic diagram. Make sure the predecessors are all finish-to-start relationships with zero lag. Do this by showing the Predecessor Activity Detail at the bottom of the screen. (**View, Show on Bottom, Activity Details**, and click on the **Relationships tab.**) It is not necessary to check both predecessors and successors. If you check all predecessors, or vice versa, the successors should by OK as well. Make sure you double-check the relationship type and amount of lag. It is easy to make errors in inputting the predecessors.

To further understand what grouping will do, group the project by the superintendents. Click on the **Group and Sort** button and underneath **Group By**, under **Project** select **Superintendent** and OK it. Now you see the project grouped by project and then grouped by the two superintendents. Because John is on the project for the first part of the schedule you may want to make sure his activities are listed first. To do this, check your activity codes by clicking on **Enterprise, Activity Codes,** and make sure John is listed first by clicking on John and then the **up arrow** moves him above Bill. Then **Close** the Activity Code dialog box. Your schedule should look similar to Figure 23.8.

Notice in Figure 23.8 that John's activities are grouped together in ES, EF order and then Bill's (William Tell's) activities are also grouped together in chronological order. Also notice the project will take 35 days to complete, whereas Bill will be on the job 21 days and John will be on the job for 20 days.

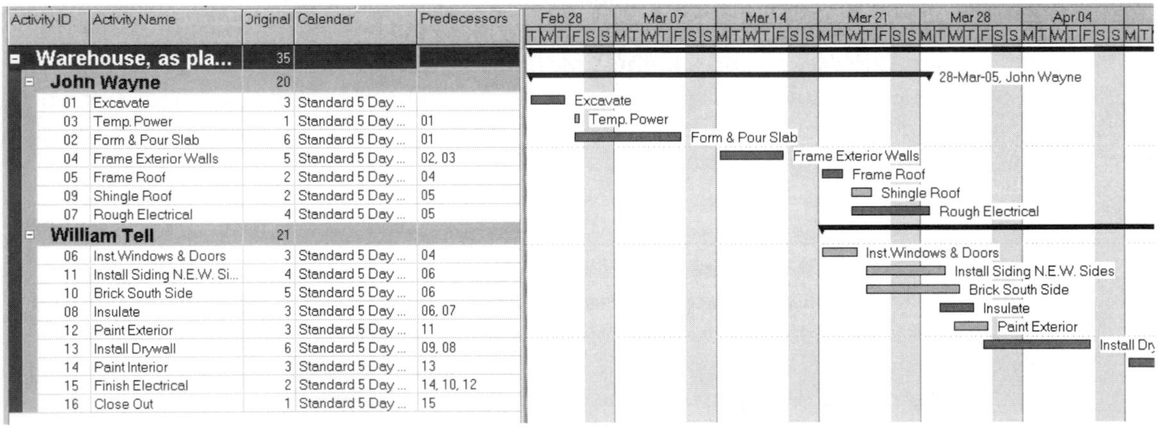

FIGURE 23.8   Activities grouped by superintendent

FILTERING ACTIVITIES

Prior to filtering, make the bar chart a little more normal looking by removing the grouped by superintendent option (**Group and Sort** button and then **delete** the **superintendent**). Filtering is an extremely beneficial capability of project management software. By filtering you are able to look at just the activities or portion of the schedule you desire. In this case you want to look at the critical activities only. Even if there were thousands of activities in the schedule this filter would show you just the critical activities. To filter for the **Critical Activities Only** click on the **Filters** button and select the **Critical** filter by putting a check mark next to that filter; **OK** it. You may need to slide the right side of the Filters dialog box over a bit to see the check boxes. Now you see only the critical activities.

To get all the activities back, **Filter** again and put a check mark next to **All Activities** (All Activities is always at the top). **OK** it and all the activities appear again.

To filter for the activities that John is responsible for, select the **Filters** button and you don't see a filter for John's activities only, so you need to create it. Do this by moving to the bottom of the existing filters, where it says **User Defined**, and clicking on **New.** Input a filter name that makes sense to you, such as **John's Activities**. Under "Parameter" select **Superintendent**; under "Is" select **Equals;** and under "Value" select **John** and **OK** it. So now it will filter for superintendent that is equal to John. You see only the seven activities that John is responsible for. If you want to see only the critical activities John is responsible for put a check mark in both Critical and John's Activities and OK it. Now you only see John's activities that are critical. For some strange reason filtering slides the columns portion of the screen to the extreme right. You may need to slide the scroll bar below the columns area back to the left to see the activity names.

The above filter specified both or all conditions. What if you wanted the activities that were either critical or belonged to John? Select Filters, put a check mark by Critical, and another check mark by John's activities, just as before, only this time notice the little dots at the top of the Filters dialog box where the dot is in **All selected filters**; change that and put the dot in **Any selected filter**. This makes the filter select any of the checked items. If the condition meets critical or John, either conditions. Where the first application was if the condition meets critical and John, both conditions. With **Any selected filter** marked you now see all the activities that are either critical or belong to John.

FORMATTING BAR CHARTS

Change the Date/Timescale

Slide the bold vertical line to the left of the screen, exposing only the activity ID and the activity name. Now, move the cursor to the bottom row of the timescale, the week day line, and click and drag the timescale to expand or compress the timescale. If you click and drag on the top line, the weeks line, the whole timescale or bar chart area moves the same as if you slide the horizontal scroll bar at the bottom of the bar chart area.

The timescale defaults to a week/day format, with weeks on the top line of the timescale and days on the bottom line. That can be changed to another format, such as month/week where the months will be on the top row and the weeks on the bottom row. To do this click on **View, Timescale**, or click on the **Timescale button**. Change the **Date Interval** to be **Month/Week** and **OK** it. Now you see the months on the top line and the weeks on the bottom. Click on the Timescale button ▦ again and notice the **PS** in the **Timescale Start** area. The *PS* stands for **Earliest Project Start**. As a schedule is updated you may want to change this to **CD**, the **Current Date**. Then the timescale will start on the current date. For a future project the PS is the best choice.

Change the Columns

The columns of information to the left of the bar chart in the Activity Table can contain any information desired from the database. Slide the bold vertical line further to the right of the screen, exposing more of the columnar information and less of the bar chart. To change the columns, click on **View, Columns**, or click on the **Columns button** ▥. This brings up the Columns dialog box. The center dialog box shows the current selected columns. The columns are moved from **Available Options** to **Selected Options** using the arrow keys between the two windows. Change some of the columns to get a feel for this part of the program. The position of the columns can be changed using the up and down arrows or you can click and drag the columns to a new location. You can also **Edit the Title** of the columns—for example, it you wanted to shorten the name of the Original Duration to Org. Dur. or, even OD. Your edited title appears in the column heading. As you edit the column title you can also **Align** the information **Left, Center,** or **Right.**

Figure 23.9 shows the Columns dialog box, the Edit Column Title dialog box, and how those columns appear in the Activity Table to the left of the bar chart.

The column width can be adjusted in the edit window width box of the Edit Column Title dialog box or simply by clicking on the divider line between columns in the heading area and drag the line to make the column wider or narrower in order to show the desired information without wasting space.

Format the Bars

The bars can be formatted to show or not show float, to show the early bar or the late bar, to show or not show the baseline or target bar, and so on. This is accomplished by clicking on **View** and then **Bars** or selecting the **Bars button** ▤. To learn how to do this, you will make a bar chart for the project manager showing float. Do this by putting a **check mark** next to the **Float Bar** and then **OK** it. Now you see the float bar on the screen, but the activity name is on top of the float bar making it difficult to read. Change this by clicking on the **Bars** button again, selecting or highlighting the **Current Bar**, and then selecting the **Bar Labels tab** and changing the **Activity Name** to be in a **Position** to the **Left** of the bar. **OK** it. Now the activity name is to the left of the bars, thus not interfering with the float bar, as shown in Figure 23.10. You will learn more about changing the bars as you complete the remainder of this chapter.

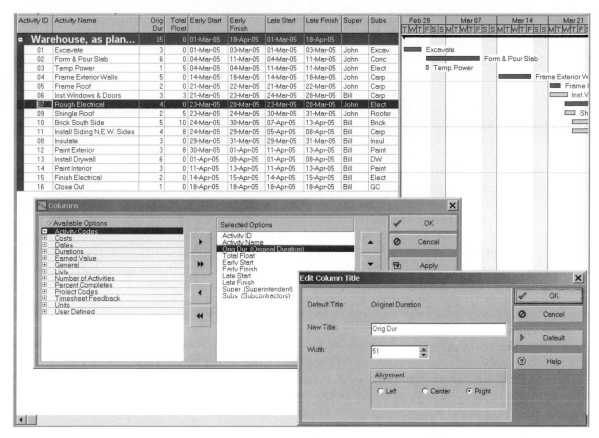

Activity ID	Activity Name	Orig Dur	Total Float	Early Start	Early Finish	Late Start	Late Finish	Super	Subs
▣	Warehouse, as plan...	35	0	01-Mar-05	18-Apr-05	01-Mar-05	18-Apr-05		
01	Excavate	3	0	01-Mar-05	03-Mar-05	01-Mar-05	03-Mar-05	John	Excav
02	Form & Pour Slab	6	0	04-Mar-05	11-Mar-05	04-Mar-05	11-Mar-05	John	Conc
03	Temp. Power	1	5	04-Mar-05	04-Mar-05	11-Mar-05	11-Mar-05	John	Elect
04	Frame Exterior Walls	5	0	14-Mar-05	18-Mar-05	14-Mar-05	18-Mar-05	John	Carp
05	Frame Roof	2	0	21-Mar-05	22-Mar-05	21-Mar-05	22-Mar-05	John	Carp
06	Inst.Windows & Doors	3	3	21-Mar-05	23-Mar-05	24-Mar-05	28-Mar-05	Bill	Carp
07	Rough Electrical	4	0	23-Mar-05	28-Mar-05	23-Mar-05	28-Mar-05	John	Elect
09	Shingle Roof	2	5	23-Mar-05	24-Mar-05	30-Mar-05	31-Mar-05	John	Roofer
10	Brick South Side	5	10	24-Mar-05	30-Mar-05	07-Apr-05	13-Apr-05	Bill	Brick
11	Install Siding N.E.W. Sides	4	8	24-Mar-05	29-Mar-05	05-Apr-05	08-Apr-05	Bill	Carp
08	Insulate	3	0	29-Mar-05	31-Mar-05	29-Mar-05	31-Mar-05	Bill	Insul
12	Paint Exterior	3	8	30-Mar-05	01-Apr-05	11-Apr-05	13-Apr-05	Bill	Paint
13	Install Drywall	6	0	01-Apr-05	08-Apr-05	01-Apr-05	08-Apr-05	Bill	DW
14	Paint Interior	3	0	11-Apr-05	13-Apr-05	11-Apr-05	13-Apr-05	Bill	Paint
15	Finish Electrical	2	0	14-Apr-05	15-Apr-05	14-Apr-05	15-Apr-05	Bill	Elect
16	Close Out	1	0	18-Apr-05	18-Apr-05	18-Apr-05	18-Apr-05	Bill	GC

Columns

Available Options:
- ▣ Activity Codes
- ⊞ Costs
- ⊞ Dates
- ⊞ Durations
- ⊞ Earned Value
- ⊞ General
- ⊞ Lists
- ⊞ Number of Activities
- ⊞ Percent Completes
- ⊞ Project Codes
- ⊞ Timesheet Feedback
- ⊞ Units
- ⊞ User Defined

Selected Options:
Activity ID
Activity Name
Orig Dur (Original Duration)
Total Float
Early Start
Early Finish
Late Start
Late Finish
Super (Superintendent)
Subs (Subcontractors)

[OK] [Cancel] [Apply]

Edit Column Title

Default Title: Original Duration

New Title: Orig Dur

Width: 51

Alignment: ○ Left ○ Center ● Right

[OK] [Cancel] [Default] [Help]

FIGURE 23.9 Activity table and bar chart, Columns dialog box, and Edit Column Title dialog box

Activity ID	Activity Name	Orig Dur
▣	Warehouse, as plan...	35
01	Excavate	3
03	Temp. Power	1
02	Form & Pour Slab	6
04	Frame Exterior Walls	5
05	Frame Roof	2
06	Inst.Windows & Doors	3
09	Shingle Roof	2
07	Rough Electrical	4
11	Install Siding N.E.W. Sides	4
10	Brick South Side	5
08	Insulate	3
12	Paint Exterior	3
13	Install Drywall	6
14	Paint Interior	3
15	Finish Electrical	2
16	Close Out	1

FIGURE 23.10 Bar Chart showing float, with activity names left of the bars

Create a New Layout

The way the screen looks is called the screen layout. It includes the selected columns, the way the activities are grouped and sorted, the format of the bars, and the timescale. To save a layout, format it the way you want it on the screen first, then click on the **View, Layout, Save As, Name** the layout as you desire, and click on the **Save** button. That layout is now available anytime you want it by simply clicking on **View, Layout, Open,** selecting that layout, and opening it. To know which layout is currently active look at the top left of the screen, above the Activity ID and Activity Name, and you will see the title of the current layout.

As you can see, layouts are a very valuable tool. From this point on as you create your favorite screen for the owner, superintendents, architect, subcontractors, executive officer, and so on, you can save each of them as a layout and then just open that layout rather than needing to reformat everything for each particular end use.

As discussed in the previous chapters, the Help buttons are great in Project Manager. Use them whenever you have a question. Now that you have some knowledge and experience with Project Manager, click on Help on the Menu bar and then search for any topic of interest. Help is also available in most dialog boxes. If you click on Help in an individual dialog box you are given help for that specific dialog box. Try it out; click on the **Columns button** and then click on **Help** in the Columns dialog box. This gives you help specific to the Columns dialog box.

SETTING UP AND PRINTING STANDARD REPORTS

Now that you have an idea of what Program Manager will do and a basic introduction of how to do it, you will apply that basic understanding and those skills to create some standard layouts and reports. Project Manager comes with many reports already created. To view them, click on **Tools** on the Menu bar and then click on **Reports,** and **Reports** again. If you want to preview a standard report, highlight the report, click on **Run Report**, and then choose **Print Preview** and click **OK.** To get back to the schedule and the activities click on **Project** and then **Activities**, or click on the Back button. You can print any layout by bringing that layout to the screen, selecting **File, Print Preview** to make sure it looks like you think it should and then if you like it, select the **Print** icon.

The main difference in printing a layout and creating and printing reports is that standard reports are basically Activity Table reports rather than graphic reports such as bar charts or networks. One of the problems with layouts is that it is easy to accidently change a layout without realizing you changed it, whereas *reports take deliberate actions to chang the specifications.* Another advantage of the reports function is you can create a batch of reports that are standard reports printed weekly or monthly and they will all print with one command, rather than needing to open each layout and printing each report individually.

In order for you to learn how to make your own reports, instead of just selecting standard reports, you will first make a new group for your reports to reside in. To do this click on **Tools, Reports, Report Groups,** and then click on the **Add** button.

Type in your name plus "Reports," for example, "Jay's Reports." This will give you an area to keep all your reports in. Then, using the arrow buttons at the bottom right of the screen, move your report group to the top so you can always find it quickly.

Report 1. Input Check Report

It is always advisable to check the information input prior to printing any reports. Therefore, the first report to print is something that will allow you to check all data that has been input. It is confusing and embarrassing to send out reports that are incorrect. Once incorrect information is out there it is difficult to get rid of it. You can correct the schedule and send out an amended schedule, but the wrong one keeps showing up and the corrected one never seems to get to the people needing it. It is extremely easy to make keyboarding errors when inputting data into the schedule. Also, prior to printing reports it is a good idea to review Chapter 11, "Reviewing and Analyzing the Schedule."

To check the data that has been input, set up the Activity Table to include columns that show all information input. For the warehouse project you need the following columns: "Activity ID", "Activity Name", "Original Duration", "Calendar", "Superintendent", "Subcontractors", and "Predecessors". If you cannot remember how to create those columns, review that information earlier in this chapter. If resource or cost data are input, create the columns to check these out as well. It would probably make it easier to check the input if the activities are sorted by early start and then early finish. If you want to save that layout for future use, click on **View, Layout, Save As** and name it "Input Layout" or whatever. To print the layout select **File, Print Preview**. If you like the way it looks select the **Print button** 🖨 to print it. The Activity Table (rows and columns) portion of that report should look similar to Figure 23.11.

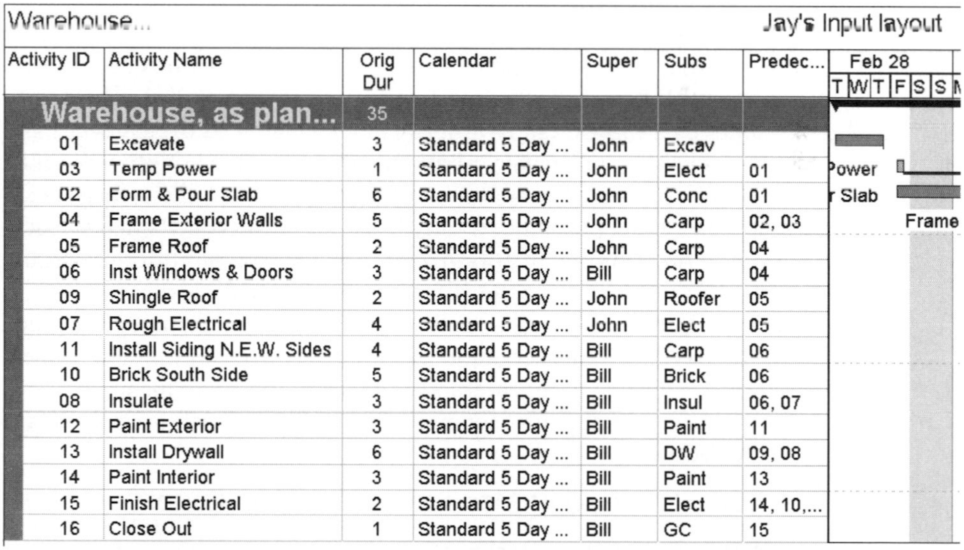

Activity ID	Activity Name	Orig Dur	Calendar	Super	Subs	Predec...	Feb 28 T W T F S S M
	Warehouse, as plan...	35					
01	Excavate	3	Standard 5 Day ...	John	Excav		
03	Temp Power	1	Standard 5 Day ...	John	Elect	01	Power
02	Form & Pour Slab	6	Standard 5 Day ...	John	Conc	01	r Slab
04	Frame Exterior Walls	5	Standard 5 Day ...	John	Carp	02, 03	Frame
05	Frame Roof	2	Standard 5 Day ...	John	Carp	04	
06	Inst Windows & Doors	3	Standard 5 Day ...	Bill	Carp	04	
09	Shingle Roof	2	Standard 5 Day ...	John	Roofer	05	
07	Rough Electrical	4	Standard 5 Day ...	John	Elect	05	
11	Install Siding N.E.W. Sides	4	Standard 5 Day ...	Bill	Carp	06	
10	Brick South Side	5	Standard 5 Day ...	Bill	Brick	06	
08	Insulate	3	Standard 5 Day ...	Bill	Insul	06, 07	
12	Paint Exterior	3	Standard 5 Day ...	Bill	Paint	11	
13	Install Drywall	6	Standard 5 Day ...	Bill	DW	09, 08	
14	Paint Interior	3	Standard 5 Day ...	Bill	Paint	13	
15	Finish Electrical	2	Standard 5 Day ...	Bill	Elect	14, 10,...	
16	Close Out	1	Standard 5 Day ...	Bill	GC	15	

Warehouse...   Jay's Input layout

Figure 23.11 Activity table used to check the data input into the computer

Now, with the hand-drawn schedule also in front of you, check all the data that have been input. This task is somewhat easier if it is done with two people, one reading from the hand-drawn network, while the other is checking the computer screen or printed report. Be sure and check all data pertaining to each activity. The only data that cannot be checked in the Activity Table with the appropriate columns are the relationship type (FS, SS, FF, SF) and the amount of lag. This seems awkward and maybe future updates will correct this shortcoming. Those items must be checked by creating a special report or on screen by viewing the **Activity Details** at the bottom of the screen **(View, Show on Bottom, Activity Details, Relationships tab)**. The **Activities Details tabs** can be modified by selecting **View, Bottom Layout Options**, and then selecting the tabs desired to be displayed.

To create a report that shows the relationships and the amount of lag, click on **Tools, Reports,** select your report group created earlier, click on **Add**, and then the Report Wizard automatically opens to assist you in the creation of the report. Click **Next.** When asked to select **subject area**, select **Activity Relationships** and click on **Next.** In the **Fields** dialog box click on Fields, **open General**, and list the following as **Selected Options: Relationship Type, Predecessor ID, Predecessor Name, and Lag, OK,** and **Next.** In the Group and Sort dialog box click on **Group By Successor** with no sorting. Grouping the report by successors will list the successor and then the predecessors with their relationships and lags under them. Click on **No filters** and **No Column Sizing, Name** the report **Activity Relationships & Lags**, run the report and then print preview it. Figure 23.12 shows how the report should look. If it looks right, **Save** the report and click on **Finish.** This report will now always be there in order to check the relationships and lags.

To get back into the project activities click on **Project** and then **Activities.** It would be nice if all this input data could be checked on one report, but that does not seem possible with the current version.

Another method to check the relationships (however, not the amount of lag) is to print the Network Logic Diagram view. The activity box could be changed to show the activity ID, activity name, original duration, superintendent, and subcontractors or other data of interest. Do this by first changing to the Network Logic Diagram view, then clicking on **View, Activity Network, Activity Network Options, Activity Box Template, Box Template**, and **Add**. The cells in the activity box can be split in half to take only a portion of a line. For example, if you wanted the activity ID in the left of the first line and the original duration on the right of the first line, make the width of both of those 50 percent as shown in Figure 23.13.

There are several options for checking the data that you input into the computer. After trying all the techniques mentioned above you will determine which method you prefer and stick to that method. The main thing is to make sure your data has been input into the computer accurately or it will haunt you for the remainder of the project life cycle.

Report 2. Project Manager's Bar Chart Report

This report will be a rather typical bar chart designed to be used by the project manager. Sometimes it is best to design the report by hand first. This helps you to think

FIGURE 23.12   Report to
check relationship types
and the amount of lag

Activity Relationships & Lags

Successor Relatio Type	Predecesso ID	Predecessor Name	Lag
Form & Pour Slab			
FS	01	Excavate	0
Temp Power			
FS	01	Excavate	0
Frame Exterior Walls			
FS	02	Form & Pour Slab	0
FS	03	Temp Power	0
Frame Roof			
FS	04	Frame Exterior Walls	0
Inst Windows & Doors			
FS	04	Frame Exterior Walls	0
Rough Electrical			
FS	05	Frame Roof	0
Insulate			
FS	06	Inst Windows & Doors	0
FS	07	Rough Electrical	0
Shingle Roof			
FS	05	Frame Roof	0
Brick South Side			
FS	06	Inst Windows & Doors	0
Install Siding N.E.W. Sides			
FS	06	Inst Windows & Doors	0
Paint Exterior			
FS	11	Install Siding N.E.W. Sides	0
Install Drywall			
FS	09	Shingle Roof	0
FS	08	Insulate	0
Paint Interior			
FS	13	Install Drywall	0
Finish Electrical			
FS	14	Paint Interior	0
FS	10	Brick South Side	0
FS	12	Paint Exterior	0
Close Out			
FS	15	Finish Electrical	0

375

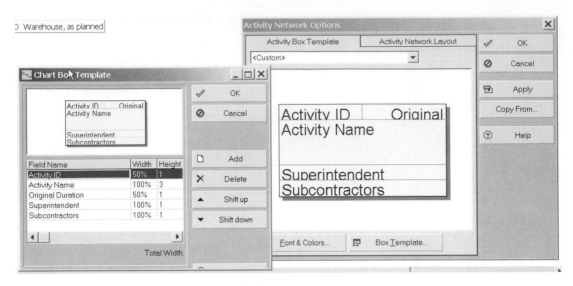

FIGURE 23.13 Using the Chart Box Template dialog box on the left to create the activity Box Template to the right

about what columns of information you want to include, how you want to format the bars, and any other information you may want to include on the report without overloading the project manager with unnecessary information, as was discussed in Chapter 19. This report also uses the recommendations from Chapter 12 about making bar charts for the specific person receiving the report.

A typical project manager's report would contain the following columns: "Activity ID", "Activity Name", "Original Duration", "Early Start", "Early Finish", and "Total Float". Have the bars located in their early position (rather than late position) with total float showing. Include the Superintendent's name to the left of the bars. Sort the activities in early start order.

See if you can set up that report without additional help. If you need additional help see the instructions below.

To format the columns click on the **Columns button** 🏢 . Select the columns as listed above. If the float bar is not showing click on the **Bars button** 🗐 and make sure there is a check mark in front of **Float Bar.** If the activity name is not to the left of the bar, click on the **Bars button,** highlight the **Current Bar**, click on the **Bar Label tab,** and then put the superintendent's name to the left. **Sort** the activities in **Early Start** order by clicking on the "Early Start" column heading. Save that layout (**View, Layout, Save As**) as "Project Manager's Bar layout" so it will always be there for you to use. To print this report click on **File, Print Preview**, and if it looks correct select the Print button to print it. The printed report should look similar to Figure 23.14

Your printed report may be slightly different due to varying dates. However, the columns, activities, durations, and the order of the activities should be the same. This is an appropriate bar chart report for the project manager.

Activity ID	Activity Name	Orig Dur	Early Start	Early Finish	Total Float	Feb 28	Mar 07	Mar 14	Mar 21	Mar 28	Apr 04	Apr 11
	Warehouse, as pla...	**35**	**01-Mar-05**	**18-Apr-05**	**0**							
01	Excavate	3	01-Mar-05	03-Mar-05	0	John						
02	Form & Pour Slab	6	04-Mar-05	11-Mar-05	0	John						
03	Temp. Power	1	04-Mar-05	04-Mar-05	5	John						
04	Frame Exterior Walls	5	14-Mar-05	18-Mar-05	0		John					
05	Frame Roof	2	21-Mar-05	22-Mar-05	0			John				
06	Inst. Windows & Doors	3	21-Mar-05	23-Mar-05	3			Bill				
07	Rough Electrical	4	23-Mar-05	28-Mar-05	0			John				
09	Shingle Roof	2	23-Mar-05	24-Mar-05	5			John				
10	Brick South Side	5	24-Mar-05	30-Mar-05	10			Bill				
11	Install Siding N.E.W. Sides	4	24-Mar-05	29-Mar-05	8			Bill				
08	Insulate	3	29-Mar-05	31-Mar-05	0				Bill			
12	Paint Exterior	3	30-Mar-05	01-Apr-05	8				Bill			
13	Install Drywall	6	01-Apr-05	08-Apr-05	0				Bill			
14	Paint Interior	3	11-Apr-05	13-Apr-05	0					Bill		
15	Finish Electrical	2	14-Apr-05	15-Apr-05	0						Bill	
16	Close Out	1	18-Apr-05	18-Apr-05	0							Bill

FIGURE 23.14 Bar chart report for the project manager

If you desire a report to be printed in portrait rather than landscape orientation; with different margins, headers, footers; or adjusted to a certain number of pages, from **Print Preview**, click on the **Page Setup button**, or select **File, Page Setup** and make the adjustments needed.

Report 3. Superintendent's Bar Chart Report

This report will be a standard bar chart for the superintendent's use. The assumption is that the superintendent knows how to read CPM schedules, is familiar with the different types of float, and knows that float is generally shared with other activities. Therefore, the superintendent wants a schedule similar to the project manager's with the float showing, except he or she wants their individual activities grouped together and the activity names to the left of the bars. Try to make the changes. If in doubt, check the information below.

Group (Group and Sort tool button) the activities by **Superintendent** and **Sort** by **Early Start**. To get the activity name to the left of the bars, click on the **Bars button**, highlight the Current Bar, click on the Bar Labels tab, and change it so the **Activity Name** is to the left of the bar. Now that you have created the layout the way you want it, save it (View, Layout, Save As) to a name such as "Superintendents Bar Chart." Print the report. It should look similar to Figure 23.15.

Report 4. Subcontractor's Bar Chart Report

This report will be a bar chart designed for the individual subcontractor. It will be similar to the superintendent's bar chart except there will be no float shown in columns or on the bars. The report will be grouped by the subcontractors so that all their activities will be listed together and each subcontractor's activities are to be printed on separate pages. Try it out; if you have questions see below.

Click on the Columns button and unselect the "Total Float" column. Click on the Bars tool button and remove and the check mark by the Float Bar and the check

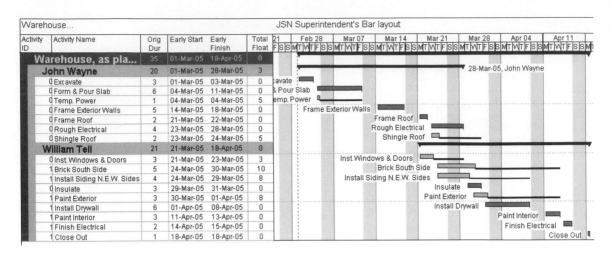

	Warehouse...			JSN Superintendent's Bar layout									
Activity ID	Activity Name	Orig Dur	Early Start	Early Finish	Total Float								
	Warehouse, as pla...	35	01-Mar-05	18-Apr-05	0								
	John Wayne	20	01-Mar-05	28-Mar-05	3							28-Mar-05, John Wayne	
0	Excavate	3	01-Mar-05	03-Mar-05	0								
0	Form & Pour Slab	6	04-Mar-05	11-Mar-05	0								
0	Temp. Power	1	04-Mar-05	04-Mar-05	5								
0	Frame Exterior Walls	5	14-Mar-05	18-Mar-05	0			Frame Exterior Walls					
0	Frame Roof	2	21-Mar-05	22-Mar-05	0				Frame Roof				
0	Rough Electrical	4	23-Mar-05	28-Mar-05	0				Rough Electrical				
0	Shingle Roof	2	23-Mar-05	24-Mar-05	5				Shingle Roof				
	William Tell	21	21-Mar-05	18-Apr-05	0								
0	Inst. Windows & Doors	3	21-Mar-05	23-Mar-05	3			Inst.Windows & Doors					
1	Brick South Side	5	24-Mar-05	30-Mar-05	10				Brick South Side				
1	Install Siding N.E.W. Sides	4	24-Mar-05	29-Mar-05	8				Install Siding N.E.W. Sides				
0	Insulate	3	29-Mar-05	31-Mar-05	0					Insulate			
1	Paint Exterior	3	30-Mar-05	01-Apr-05	8					Paint Exterior			
1	Install Drywall	6	01-Apr-05	08-Apr-05	0					Install Drywall			
1	Paint Interior	3	11-Apr-05	13-Apr-05	0							Paint Interior	
1	Finish Electrical	2	14-Apr-05	15-Apr-05	0							Finish Electrical	
1	Close Out	1	18-Apr-05	18-Apr-05	0								Close Out

FIGURE 23.15   Typical bar chart for the superintendent

	Warehouse...			JSN Subcontractor's Bar Chart								
Activity ID	Activity Name	Orig Dur	Early Start	Early Finish								
	Electrician	31	04-Mar-05	15-Apr-05								
03	Temp. Power	1	04-Mar-05	04-Mar-05	Temp. Power							
07	Rough Electrical	4	23-Mar-05	28-Mar-05				Rough Electrical				
15	Finish Electrical	2	14-Apr-05	15-Apr-05							Finish Electrical	

FIGURE 23.16   Bar chart for the electrician

mark by the Summary Bar, just to simplify the report. Click on the Group and Sort tool button and group the activities by Subcontractor and Sort by Early Start. Save the layout and name it "Subcontractor's Bar Chart." When you print preview it you will notice all the subcontractors' activities are printed on one page.

CREATING PAGE BREAKS.   While in Print Preview, select the **Page Setup button**, then the **Options tab** and put a check mark by **Break Page Every Group** and **OK** it. This way you are able to create individual reports (pages) for each subcontractor but using one printer setup. You could have done this by filtering for each subcontractor and printing the report for that sub, then repeating the filtering and printing process for all subcontractors. Figure 23.16 shows how the report for the electrician should look.

ADDING NOTES.   Another common addition to the reports for the subcontractors would be to **add a "Notes" column** with detailed information for the subcontractor. For example, you may want to remind the subcontractors of the following:

Brick mason—the bricks are Mocha Brown
Carpenter—the exterior studs are 2 × 6

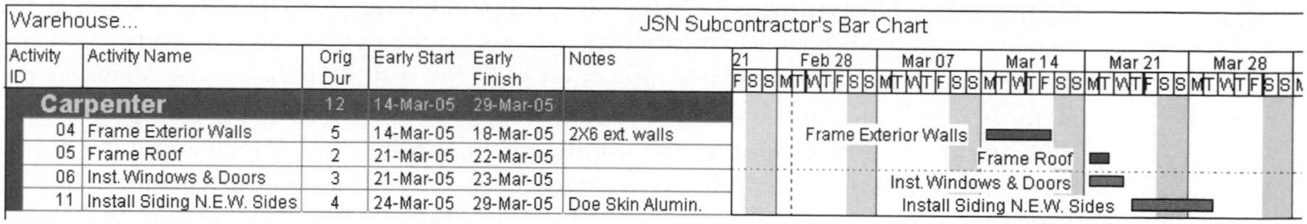

FIGURE 23.17   Carpenter's bar chart with "notes" column added

Siding is Doeskin aluminum

Concrete sub—the slab is to be 6,000 psi

Drywall sub—all the drywall is to be 5/8" thick

Electrician—the service is 250 amp

Painter—the interior paint is Whisper White and the exterior is Tahoe Brown

Remember, the purpose of the schedule is to force detailed thinking and then communicate that thinking and planning to all involved in the process. Anything you can do to improve communications, in simple ways, will pay off. Let the schedule reports assist you in doing that.

To add notes to the schedule, a simple method is to add a "Notes" column. Click on the **Columns** button. Then under **User Defined** select **user text1**, highlight user text1, and then Click on **Edit the Title** to be "**Notes**." The resulting report for the carpenter subcontractor would be similar to Figure 23.17.

Report 5. Owner's Bar Chart Report

This will be a typical bar chart designed for the owner. The columns are to be "Activity Name", "Original Duration", late start (titled "Start Date"), and late finish (titled "Finish Date"). You don't need to show all the activities to the owner. We would like to select the following activities that the owner is particularly interested in, such as *Excavate, Frame Ext. Walls, Shingle Roof, Brick South Side, Paint Exterior and Interior,* and *Close Out.* The bars are to have the activity name to the right of the bars. Also, the bars are to be in their late start position so the owner focuses on the late dates and then, as activities are done on the early dates, the owner will be pleasantly surprised. Or, at least if some of the activities are done on the late dates, the owner will not become over-alarmed. No float is to show.

This one is tough, but give it a try and then see below for additional help as necessary. Set up the columns. Remember to select the late start and late finish columns and to name those columns "Start Date" and "Finish Date". To get the selected activities, you need to set up an activity code for the owner by clicking on **Enterprise, Activity Codes.** Put a dot to the left of **Project. Add** a new activity code that has a **Code Value** of Owner and a **Description** of Owner's Interest. Click on the **Modify** button and add the activity code **Owner**, and then **Close** the dialog box, **Add** the **Code Value** of

Owner with a **Description** of Owner's Interest and **Close** the dialog box. Now that the owner activity code has been created you can assign the owner's activity code to the activities the owner is particularly interested in. This is done by selecting View on the menu bar and selecting **Activity Detail** of **Codes** at the **Bottom** of the screen. Then click on the **Activity Codes** button on the extreme right of the screen and put a dot by **Project**. Highlight the activity you want to assign the code to and then double-click on **Owner** in the Assign Activity Codes dialog box. Highlight the next activity and assign owner again, and so on. When Owner has been assigned to all the activities the owner has a particular interest in, **Filter** for the Owner's activities by selecting the **Filter button**. Go down to **User Defined**, click on **New,** and give it a Name of "Owner". Then under "Parameter" select Owner; "Is" select Equals; and "Value" select Owner. OK it. Now you have only those activities the owner is interested in, showing on the screen.

To get the late bar to show format the bars by clicking on the **Bars button**. Remove the check marks by all the existing bars. Click on the **Add** button and name it **Late Bar**, make the **Timescale Late Bar**, make the **Filter Normal**, and the **color orange** so it is different than the other bars. Click on the **Bar Label tab**, have the **Activity Name** to the **Right** of the bar, and **OK** it. Now the bars seem to be all mixed up, so sort them in early start order by clicking on the "Start Date" column (which is really late start) heading or Group and Sort to late start.

That was a lot of work formatting the layout for the owner, so you might want to save this layout as an owner's bar chart. Print preview the layout and, if it looks good, print it. Figure 23.18 shows approximately what this report should look like.

Notice in Figure 23.18 that the activity *Temp. Power* has moved to its late start and finish position. The same is true with all the activities with float. This focuses the owner's attention on the late dates and then, as some of the activities are finished earlier, the project manager looks really good. It is not meant to deceive the owner; the purpose is to keep the owner, who may not fully understand CPM, to not be alarmed

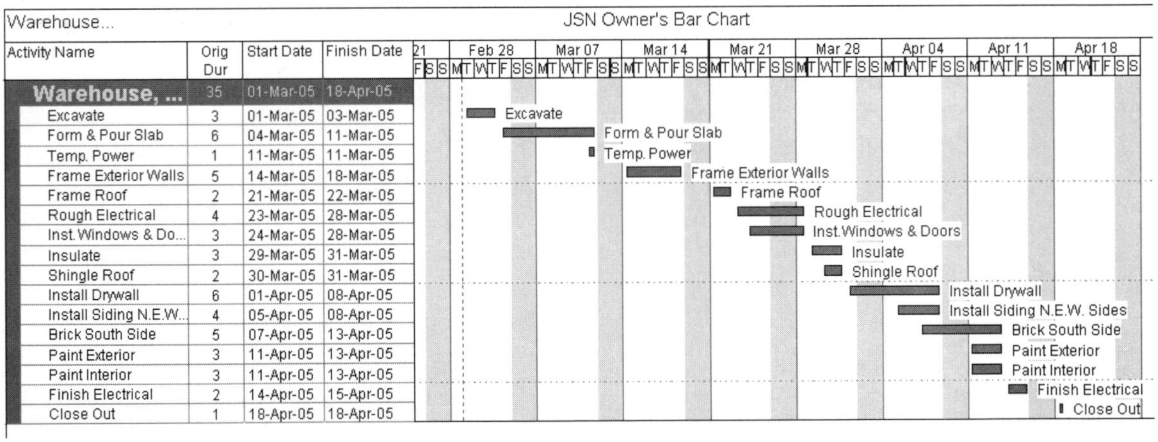

Activity Name	Orig Dur	Start Date	Finish Date
Warehouse, ...	35	01-Mar-05	18-Apr-05
Excavate	3	01-Mar-05	03-Mar-05
Form & Pour Slab	6	04-Mar-05	11-Mar-05
Temp. Power	1	11-Mar-05	11-Mar-05
Frame Exterior Walls	5	14-Mar-05	18-Mar-05
Frame Roof	2	21-Mar-05	22-Mar-05
Rough Electrical	4	23-Mar-05	28-Mar-05
Inst. Windows & Do...	3	24-Mar-05	28-Mar-05
Insulate	3	29-Mar-05	31-Mar-05
Shingle Roof	2	30-Mar-05	31-Mar-05
Install Drywall	6	01-Apr-05	08-Apr-05
Install Siding N.E.W...	4	05-Apr-05	08-Apr-05
Brick South Side	5	07-Apr-05	13-Apr-05
Paint Exterior	3	11-Apr-05	13-Apr-05
Paint Interior	3	11-Apr-05	13-Apr-05
Finish Electrical	2	14-Apr-05	15-Apr-05
Close Out	1	18-Apr-05	18-Apr-05

FIGURE 23.18 Owner's bar chart

if some of the activities are done later than their early dates but still within float. When dealing with an owner who understands CPM scheduling techniques, the owner's report would be created in a different manner.

Report 6. Subcontractor's Tabular Report for the Next Three Weeks

This report is basically the Activity Table (rows and columns of information without bars). This report is designed to show updated schedule information for a project in progress. Click on **View, Layout, Save As** and give it a name of **Subs Tabular Layout**. To make it a report of tabular information or what Project Manager calls an Activity Table, click on the Activity Table button 🔲 . Note the layout now contains only tabular information in the cells of rows and columns—there are no bars. Format the report with the following columns: "Activity ID", "Activity Name", "Original Duration", "Remaining Duration", "Variance Duration", "Early Start", "Early Finish", "Actual Start", "Physical % Complete", "Actual Finish", and "Activity Status". **Group** the activities by the subcontractors, and **Sort** in ES, EF. Create a new **filter** and name it "3 Week Look ahead." Filter for any of the following: "Where" **Start**; "Is" Within range of DD; and "DD" + 3W. **Add** another condition Or Physical % Complete is within range of 1% and 99 %. This last line will ensure the report includes all activities that are currently under progress. Select the new filter by putting a **check mark next to it** and **OK** it. Now you see only the activities that will start in the next three weeks or are currently under progress.

     Print preview the report **(File, Print Preview)** and click on the **Page Setup button** to print the report in **Landscape**. Then, to get a **page break** between each group of subcontractors, select the **Options tab** and put a check mark at **Break Page Every Group**. OK it and you are ready to print the report to give to each of the subcontractors. This report could be used as a turnaround report where the subs input the actual start, actual finish, and percent complete and turn it back at the end of the reporting period to be used to update the schedule. The report for the *Excavate* activity should look similar to Figure 23.19.

Report 7. Owner's Tabular Report—Using Layouts

You will create this report first as a layout and then again in report #8 as a report using the Report Wizard to learn the differences in the two methods. Save a new layout as Owner's Tabular Layout. This report will be using the Activity Table only, rather than the bar chart portion of the screen. So click on the **Activity Table button** and then format the columns to include the following column headings: "Activity Name",

Warehouse...				JSN Subs Tabular Layout					01-Nov-	14:47
Activity ID	Activity Name	Orig Dur	Remaining Duration	Variance - Duration	Early Start	Early Finish	Actual Start	Physical % Complete	Actual Finish	Activity Status
Excavator		3	3	0	01-Mar-05	03-Mar-05				
01	Excavate	3	3	0	01-Mar-05	03-Mar-05		0%		Not Started

FIGURE 23.19 The excavator's tabular report

Warehouse...			JSN Owner's Tabular Layout			01-Nov-03 14:45	
Activity Name	Orig Dur	Physical % Complete	Start Date	Finish Date	Actual Start	Actual Finish	
Warehouse, ...	35		01-Mar-05	18-Apr-05			
Excavate	3	0%	01-Mar-05	03-Mar-05			
Form & Pour Slab	6	0%	04-Mar-05	11-Mar-05			
Temp. Power	1	0%	11-Mar-05	11-Mar-05			
Frame Exterior Walls	5	0%	14-Mar-05	18-Mar-05			
Frame Roof	2	0%	21-Mar-05	22-Mar-05			
Rough Electrical	4	0%	23-Mar-05	28-Mar-05			
Inst. Windows & Do...	3	0%	24-Mar-05	28-Mar-05			
Insulate	3	0%	29-Mar-05	31-Mar-05			
Shingle Roof	2	0%	30-Mar-05	31-Mar-05			
Install Drywall	6	0%	01-Apr-05	08-Apr-05			
Install Siding N.E.W...	4	0%	05-Apr-05	08-Apr-05			
Brick South Side	5	0%	07-Apr-05	13-Apr-05			
Paint Exterior	3	0%	11-Apr-05	13-Apr-05			
Paint Interior	3	0%	11-Apr-05	13-Apr-05			
Finish Electrical	2	0%	14-Apr-05	15-Apr-05			
Close Out	1	0%	18-Apr-05	18-Apr-05			

FIGURE 23.20   Owner's tabular report—using layouts

"Original Duration", "Physical % Complete", late start (title it "Start Date"), late finish (named it "Finish Date"), "Actual Start", and "Actual Finish". **Group** the activities by **Project** and **Sort** them by **Late Start** and **Late Finish**. This way the owner is again focusing on the late dates and then, when at least some of the activities are done on earlier dates, the project will be looking good. If you showed the early dates and then some of the activities were done on the late dates, owners who do not have a good understanding of CPM would possibly overreact.

There is no need of filters on this report, so it is ready to print preview. The report should look similar to Figure 23.20.

Report 8. Owner's Tabular Report—Using the Report Wizard

To make a report using the Report Wizard, Click on **Tools, Reports, Reports**. Highlight your Report Group made earlier, then click on the **Add button** and follow the Report Wizard's help for a new report. It will be an **Activities Report**, with the following **fields** (columns): "Activity Name", "Original Duration", "Physical % Complete", late start (title it "Start Date"), late finish (name it "Finish Date"), "Actual Start", and "Actual Finish". **OK** the fields and click on **Next**. **Group** the activities by **Project** and **Sort** them by **Late Start** and then **Late Finish**. There are no filters; go with the defaults on the column sizes unless you desire to adjust them a little. Title the report "Owner's Tabular Report." **Run** the report and **Print Preview** it. It should look similar to Figure 23.21.

If the report looks OK, click on the **Next** button, **Save** the report, and you are finished. Examine the two reports. Are they both in late start order? Now, as you want to print this report again you do not need to open layouts, just select **Tools, Reports,**

Owner's Tabular Report

Project Activity Name	Original Duration	Physical % Complete	Start Date	Finish Date	Actual Start	Actual Finish
Warehouse00 Warehouse, as planned						
Excavate	3	0%	01-Mar-05	03-Mar-05		
Form & Pour Slab	6	0%	04-Mar-05	11-Mar-05		
Temp. Power	1	0%	11-Mar-05	11-Mar-05		
Frame Exterior Walls	5	0%	14-Mar-05	18-Mar-05		
Frame Roof	2	0%	21-Mar-05	22-Mar-05		
Rough Electrical	4	0%	23-Mar-05	28-Mar-05		
Inst. Windows & Doors	3	0%	24-Mar-05	28-Mar-05		
Insulate	3	0%	29-Mar-05	31-Mar-05		
Shingle Roof	2	0%	30-Mar-05	31-Mar-05		
Install Drywall	6	0%	01-Apr-05	08-Apr-05		
Install Siding N.E.W.	4	0%	05-Apr-05	08-Apr-05		
Brick South Side	5	0%	07-Apr-05	13-Apr-05		
Paint Exterior	3	0%	11-Apr-05	13-Apr-05		
Paint Interior	3	0%	11-Apr-05	13-Apr-05		
Finish Electrical	2	0%	14-Apr-05	15-Apr-05		
Close Out	1	0%	18-Apr-05	18-Apr-05		
Subtotal	35		01-Mar-05	18-Apr-05		

FIGURE 23.21   Owner's tabular report—using the Report Wizard

Reports, highlight the report, and click on **Run Report** at the right of the screen. It either prints or you can print preview it. Try it.

If you want to edit a report created with the Report Wizard, first highlight the specific report, select the wizard again, and follow the directions. To get from Reports back into the Activities, click on Project, Activities.

Report 9. Critical Activities Only Report

This report will to be a tabular report of the critical activities only, in ES, EF sequence. Create it using the Report Wizard. **Columns** desired are "Activity ID", "Activity Name", "Calendar", "Original Duration", "Total Float", "Early Start", and "Early Finish". Show the total number of work days on the report and sort the activities by ES and then EF. Try it, if you have problems see below.

The filter to get critical activities only is, if total float is less than 1. To get the total number of work days, either group it by project or in the Group dialog box put a check mark in the Show Grand Totals box. The report should look similar to Figure 23.22.

Report 10. Tabular Report for a Specific Subcontractor

You just found out you have an electrical subcontractor that has difficulties reading a bar chart. Using the Report Wizard, create a tabular report that shows only the electrician's activities. Remember, no signs of float or late dates. Choose the columns that you desire; however, for a minor challenge have the durations centered in the column. You should see only the three electrical activities. The report should look similar to Figure 23.23.

Critical Activities Only

Activity ID	Activity Name	Calendar	Original Duration	Total Float	Early Start	Early Finish
01	Excavate	Standard 5 Day Workweek	3	0	01-Mar-05	03-Mar-05
02	Form & Pour Slab	Standard 5 Day Workweek	6	0	04-Mar-05	11-Mar-05
04	Frame Exterior Walls	Standard 5 Day Workweek	5	0	14-Mar-05	18-Mar-05
05	Frame Roof	Standard 5 Day Workweek	2	0	21-Mar-05	22-Mar-05
07	Rough Electrical	Standard 5 Day Workweek	4	0	23-Mar-05	28-Mar-05
08	Insulate	Standard 5 Day Workweek	3	0	29-Mar-05	31-Mar-05
13	Install Drywall	Standard 5 Day Workweek	6	0	01-Apr-05	08-Apr-05
14	Paint Interior	Standard 5 Day Workweek	3	0	11-Apr-05	13-Apr-05
15	Finish Electrical	Standard 5 Day Workweek	2	0	14-Apr-05	15-Apr-05
16	Close Out	Standard 5 Day Workweek	1	0	18-Apr-05	18-Apr-05
Total			**35**	**0**	**01-Mar-05**	**18-Apr-05**

FIGURE 23.22   Critical activities only report

Activity Name	Original Duration	Early Start	Early Finish	Superintendent
Temp. Power	1	04-Mar-05	04-Mar-05	John
Rough Electrical	4	23-Mar-05	28-Mar-05	John
Finish Electrical	2	14-Apr-05	15-Apr-05	Bill

FIGURE 23.23   Electrician's tabular report

Report 11. Printing a Batch of Reports

This will teach you how to create a batch of reports that can be run with one setup. You are going to use the last three reports. Click on **Tools, Reports, Batch Reports**. **Add** a new batch report and name it "Try Out Batch Reports." Then, in the bottom of the Global Batch Reports dialog box click on **Assign** and select those last three reports—Owner's Tabular Report, Critical Activities Only, and the Electrician's Tabular Report. The Global Batch Reports dialog box should look similar to Figure 23.24.

If the selections in the Global Batch Reports dialog box look correct, Close it.

Now click on the **Run Batch** button at the right side of the computer window, select the new "Try Out Batch Reports," **OK** it, and then print the reports. This is a very powerful feature. You could create batches of your weekly, monthly, and quarterly

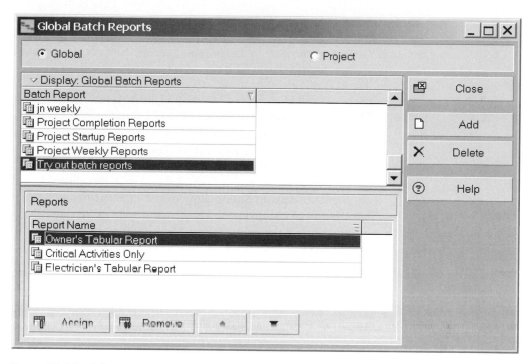

Figure 23.24 Select reports to print as a batch at the Global Batch Reports dialog box

reports and then print them with one setup. The only problem is that it apparently will not work for bar charts or other graphical reports. Maybe that will be corrected in future versions of Project Manager.

Now that you are familiar with the basic input and reporting capabilities of Project Manager it is time to learn how to update the schedule with the actual start and actual finish data.

Report 12. Statusing or Updating the Schedule

Open the project to be updated (Enterprise, Projects, right-click on the desired project, click on Open). It is a good idea to copy the project prior to updating it so that you always have a copy of the as-planned schedule.

1. *Make a new copy of the project* by selecting **Enterprise** from the Menu bar, then **Projects**. Choose the project you want to copy then select **Copy** from the command bar on the right side of the screen and then **Paste**. In the **Copy Project Options** dialog box mark the check box next to each type of information you want to copy. Notice the new project is listed with a dash 1 to the right of the Project ID. Change the **Project Name** to "Warehouse, 1st Update." To open this project, select it, right-click on it, and then click on **Open**. If the new project is showing on the screen under the old project (both showing at once on the screen), select Enterprise,

select the new project, right-click, and then open it. Now as you look at the top of the screen you see you are in the new copied project to be updated.

2. *Change user preferences* in order to have the bars correctly show the actual start and finish dates. This needs to be done only on the original update. The software defaults to show finish dates at 12:00 a.m. rather than that evening. This is corrected by going to **Edit, User Preferences**, select the **Dates tab**, and then put a dot next to **12 hour**.

3. *Create the target or baseline schedule.* The baseline schedule will be used as a benchmark to compare dates, resources, and costs to the current schedule. Before updating the schedule **(1st Update Only)** create the baseline by clicking on **Project** on the Menu bar and then **Baselines**. Click on **Add** and put a dot next to **Save a copy of the current project as a new baseline** and **OK** it. If you put a dot next to "Convert another project to a new baseline of the current project" you will no longer have access to the original project (unless you restore a baseline; see Help menu). You now see that a baseline schedule has been created under the schedule to be updated as shown in Figure 23.25. Put a check mark in the **Primary Baseline** box and as a **Baseline Type** select **Initial Plan**.

4. *Format the bars to show the baseline bar.* In order to show the schedule in a typical layout, open the project manager's layout created earlier (View, Layout, Open, and select the Project Manager's Bar Layout). To show the baseline bar click on the **Bars button** and put a check mark next to **Primary Baseline**. Then with Primary Baseline highlighted, select the second **Bar Style** from the top (this makes the baseline more prominent than the default), leave the color yellow or as desired, and OK it. Now your bar chart looks similar to Figure 23.26.

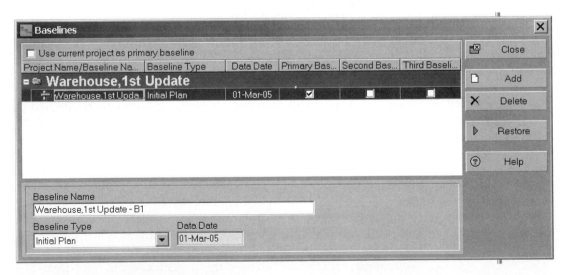

FIGURE 23.25 Baselines dialog box

Figure 23.26 shows the baseline bars (yellow thin bar) directly under the current bars. As you update the schedule, you will see the baseline remain constant and the updated bar move so you can compare performance with the as-planned schedule.

5. *Update the schedule* with actual start and actual finish dates. There are two common methods used to do this: (1) create the columns in the Activity Table area to the left of the bar chart and then update in the activity table, or (2) open the Activity Details window at the bottom of the screen and update within the activity details. You will use both methods and then choose the one you prefer. Using the first method, update with the use of the Activity Table. Add the actual start, actual finish, and physical percent complete columns to the Activity Table. To input the actual dates, double-click the **Actual Start** cell for *Excavate*, click on the selection button, and select the actual start date. Check at the bottom of the calendar and make sure the **Hour** dialog box shows **08 AM**. Show *Excavate* starting a day late by looking at the early start date and selecting a calendar date one work day later and double-click on that date. For the actual finish, let's say it finished on the original early finish date. So double-click in the **Actual Finish** cell, click on the selection window, make sure it shows **Hour** at 04 PM, and then double-click on the correct calendar date (the early finish date). Notice the *Excavate* bar shows it starting one day late and finishing on time. If the new bar is at the bottom of the schedule sort it by Actual Start (click on the "Actual Start" column heading) and it will move back to the appropriate place.

Note on hours: With construction activities it is typical to schedule by the full day. If an activity could be done in a few hours, it is still typically given a duration of a day.

Activity ID	Activity Name	Orig Dur
■	**Warehouse, 1st Up...**	05
01	Excavate	3
02	Form & Pour Slab	6
03	Temp. Power	1
04	Frame Exterior Walls	5
05	Frame Roof	2
06	Inst. Windows & Doors	3
07	Rough Electrical	4
09	Shingle Roof	2
10	Brick South Side	5
11	Install Siding N.E.W. Sides	4
08	Insulate	3
12	Paint Exterior	3
13	Install Drywall	6
14	Paint Interior	3
15	Finish Electrical	2
16	Close Out	1

Figure 23.26   Bar chart with baseline bar showing under current bar

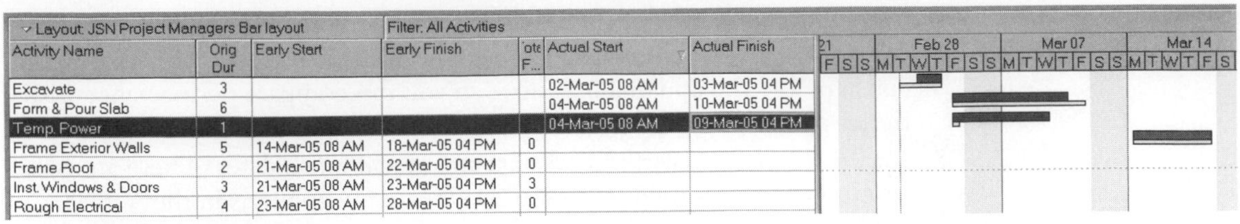

Activity Name	Orig Dur	Early Start	Early Finish	Tota F...	Actual Start	Actual Finish
Excavate	3				02-Mar-05 08 AM	03-Mar-05 04 PM
Form & Pour Slab	6				04-Mar-05 08 AM	10-Mar-05 04 PM
Temp. Power	1				04-Mar-05 08 AM	09-Mar-05 04 PM
Frame Exterior Walls	5	14-Mar-05 08 AM	18-Mar-05 04 PM	0		
Frame Roof	2	21-Mar-05 08 AM	22-Mar-05 04 PM	0		
Inst. Windows & Doors	3	21-Mar-05 08 AM	23-Mar-05 04 PM	3		
Rough Electrical	4	23-Mar-05 08 AM	28-Mar-05 04 PM	0		

FIGURE 23.27 Partially updated bar chart

It is tough to get a subcontractor for a specific day let alone at a specific hour. If you start scheduling by the precise hour an activity is started or finished and you show an activity finishing at 1:00 p.m., the remainder activities will show a start and 1:00 p.m. and go to 1:00 p.m. on their finish day. So, a one-day duration would show a bar two days long. To avoid this show all activities starting at 8:00 a.m. and finishing at 4:00 p.m., unless you are truly scheduling the whole project by the hour and you have that much control.

Update the *Form & Pour Slab* activity to start on time and finish a day early. Remember to check the hour for starting and finishing.

Update *Temp. Power* to start on time but finish a little earlier than the LF date (within the float time).

Now the bar chart should look similar to Figure 23.27.

You will now use the second method of updating, using the Activities Detail window at the bottom of the screen. Click on the **Activities Detail** button and then click on the **Status tab**. Highlight the next activity, *Frame Exterior Walls*, and start it a day late and finish a day late by putting a check mark in the **Started** box and change the start date to one day late. As you do that Project Manager changes the finish date to maintain the same duration, which in this case is desired, so just put a check mark in the Finished box and the finish date has automatically been adjusted.

Update *Frame Roof* to also start and finish a day late. Recalculate the schedule to force a new forward and backward pass by pressing the F9 key and input the current date as the end of the day that the *Frame Roof* activity finished. On a real project these dates would be more automatic. Then click on the Schedule button. The bar chart should now look similar to Figure23.28.

A close examination of Figure 23.28 shows the project is one day behind schedule. The vertical blue dotted line is the data line, which represents today's date.

That's all there is to updating the schedule. If an activity is started but not finished you would input the start date and the percent complete without entering a finish date. For future monthly updates, copy the schedule to be updated to a new name and update the new schedule, saving the old one for historical purposes. Remember that on updates beyond the first, typically you do not make a new target, just update the completed activities. For additional information on updating and how often to update, see Chapter 14 of this text.

Print the updated schedule as report #12. The printed report should look similar to Figure 23.29.

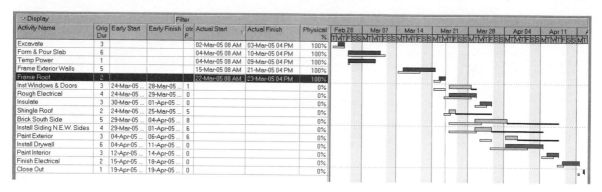

FIGURE 23.28   Updated bar chart showing actual dates compared with baseline dates

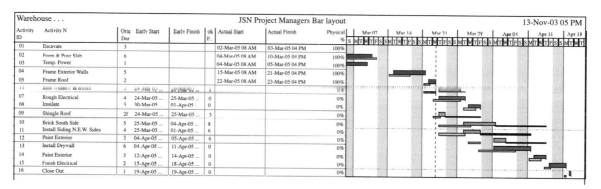

FIGURE 23.29   Printout of updated schedule

Report 13. Update the Schedule to Finish on the Original Finish Date

Examine the schedule and determine what can be done to finish on the original finish date and make those changes. Print the report. Remember, in order to accelerate or crash a schedule, consider the three following options: (1) change the logic by using lags or changing predecessors to allow critical activities to overlap, (2) shorten the durations of critical activities, and (3) have critical activities work on weekends or holidays by assigning a different calendar. Consider all three options and select the option that has least impact on cost, quality, and safety.

Report 14. Adding a Curtain or Text

A curtain is used to communicate that something special is to happen to the project during a certain period or curtain of time. To add a curtain select **View, Attachments, Curtain**. Input the curtain start and finish dates and OK it. Now you see the curtain on the screen. You can click and drag on the curtain edges and change the time of the curtain.

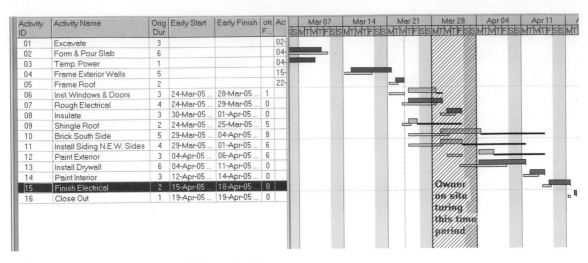

Activity ID	Activity Name	Orig Dur	Early Start	Early Finish	ote F...	Ac
01	Excavate	3				02-
02	Form & Pour Slab	6				04-
03	Temp. Power	1				04-
04	Frame Exterior Walls	5				15-
05	Frame Roof	2				22-
06	Inst. Windows & Doors	3	24-Mar-05 ...	28-Mar-05 ...	1	
07	Rough Electrical	4	24-Mar-05 ...	29-Mar-05 ...	0	
08	Insulate	3	30-Mar-05 ...	01-Apr-05 ...	0	
09	Shingle Roof	2	24-Mar-05 ...	25-Mar-05 ...	5	
10	Brick South Side	5	29-Mar-05 ...	04-Apr-05 ...	8	
11	Install Siding N.E.W. Sides	4	29-Mar-05 ...	01-Apr-05 ...	6	
12	Paint Exterior	3	04-Apr-05 ...	06-Apr-05 ...	6	
13	Install Drywall	6	04-Apr-05 ...	11-Apr-05 ...	0	
14	Paint Interior	3	12-Apr-05 ...	14-Apr-05 ...	0	
15	Finish Electrical	2	15-Apr-05 ...	18-Apr-05 ...	0	
16	Close Out	1	19-Apr-05 ...	19-Apr-05 ...	0	

FIGURE 23.30   Curtain and text added to schedule

Text can be added to the schedule to bring attention to some item of the schedule or to communicate additional information about the project. To add text select **View, Attachments, Text** and input the desired text, font, font size, and color. Figure 23.30 is an example of a curtain and text added to the schedule. Add a curtain and some text to your schedule.

Report 15. Creating a New Schedule Based on an Old Schedule

You have just been awarded a contract to build another warehouse, only this time it will start two months from today. Also, the roof is to be tile which will take seven workdays to install and the whole exterior is to be siding, no brick; siding will take six days instead of four.

1. Open the original warehouse schedule and copy and paste it to a new name (**Enterprise, Projects,** select the original as-planned warehouse), click on **Copy, Paste,** select options, change the **Project ID** to "New Warehouse," and change the **Project Name** to "as planned." Click on the **Dates tab** in the Project Details at the bottom of the screen and change the planned start date. To open the new warehouse select it, right-click, and open it. Do a new forward and backward pass by pressing the F9 key.

2. Make changes to represent the new project. Change the description of *Shingle Roof* to *Tile Roof* and change the original duration from two days to seven days. Delete the *Brick South Side* activity (highlight the activity and hit the Delete key) and change the duration of *Inst. Siding N.E.W. Sides* to six days and clean up the description to eliminate the three sides.

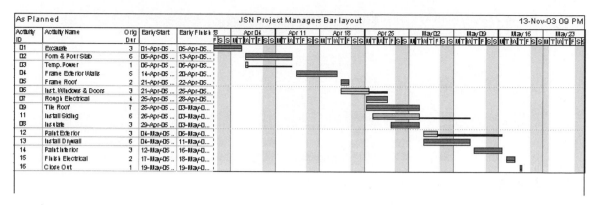

Activity ID	Activity Name	Orig Dur	Early Start	Early Finish
01	Excavate	3	01-Apr-05	05-Apr-05
02	Form & Pour Slab	6	06-Apr-05	13-Apr-05
03	Temp. Power	1	06-Apr-05	06-Apr-05
04	Frame Exterior Walls	5	14-Apr-05	20-Apr-05
05	Frame Roof	2	21-Apr-05	22-Apr-05
06	Inst. Windows & Doors	3	21-Apr-05	25-Apr-05
07	Rough Electrical	4	25-Apr-05	28-Apr-05
09	Tile Roof	7	25-Apr-05	03-May-0...
11	Install Siding	6	26-Apr-05	03-May-0...
08	Insulate	3	29-Apr-05	03-May-0...
12	Paint Exterior	3	04-May-05	06-May-0...
13	Install Drywall	6	04-May-05	11-May-0...
14	Paint Interior	3	12-May-05	16-May-0...
15	Finish Electrical	2	17-May-05	18-May-0...
16	Close Out	1	19-May-05	19-May-0...

FIGURE 23.31   New warehouse schedule

3. Check the input changes and recalculate the schedule. You should now have a dual critical path with *Tile Roof* and *Rough Electrical* as both critical. In three simple steps you have your new project already scheduled.

4. Print reports. Print a bar chart for the project manager. Use the PM's layout created earlier with modifications as desired. The printed bar chart should look similar to Figure 23.31.

Report 16. Using Fragnets to Copy Schedules or Parts of Schedules

You have just been awarded the contract to build a large warehouse. The project is divided into three areas, A, B, and C. Each area is similar to the last warehouse you just scheduled, so basically what you want to do is open the old schedule, copy it to a new name such as "Big Warehouse," open the new one, and then copy and paste the activities to create the three areas.

1. Create a **new activity code** for the project named **Area** with code values of **A, B, and C**. Click on **Enterprise, Activity Codes, Modify, Add "Area," Close**. Then **Add, Code Value "A"** with a **Description of "Area A"** and repeat the same for Areas B and C. The Activity Codes dialog box should look similar to Figure 23.32.

2. Add "Area" as a column in the activity table.

3. **Select** all the activities of the fragnet—in this case all the activities—and click on **Copy** and **Paste**. Select all information to be copied. While the activities just copied are still highlighted, assign the Area activity code by clicking on the **Activity Codes button**, put a dot by Project, and double-click on Area A. Paste again and assign Area B; Paste again and assign Area C.

4. Group the activities by area. Then highlight and delete the activities that have no area assigned. Your schedule should look similar to Figure 23.33.

FIGURE 23.32 Activity
Codes dialog box

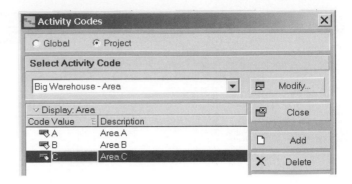

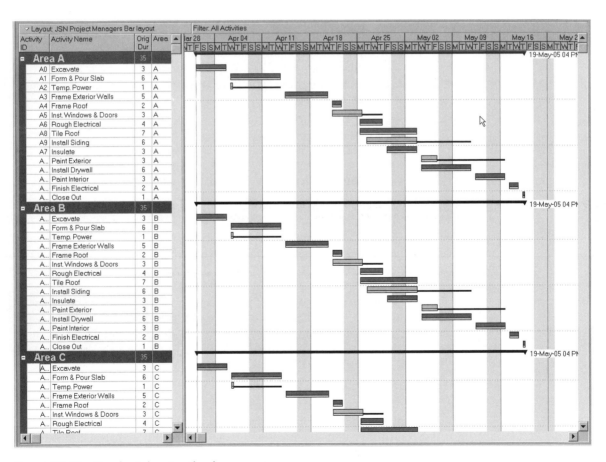

FIGURE 23.33 Bar chart showing the three areas

Now you have the three warehouse areas created and you didn't have to enter each activity and the data attached (durations, predecessors, etc.) to those activities three times. However, the three areas are all starting at the same time. You need to decide when each area will start and finish unless you have sufficient resources to build all three concurrently.

5. Because *Tile Roof* is the **critical activity with the longest duration**, use it as the stagging activity and make a start-to-start relationship between the first activity *(Excavate)* of the prior area (A) to the first activity *(Excavate)* in the next area (B) with a start-to-start lag equal to the duration of *Tile Roof*, seven days. Then do this from *Excavate* in Area B to *Excavate* in Area C. An accurate way to do this is to change to the **Activity Network view** by selecting the Activity Network button ⊞ . Next, **Group** the activities by area and use the **Ctrl key** to select all three areas. Click and drag from the start of the *Excavate* activity in Area A to the *Excavate* activity in Area B. Then do the same from Area B to C. Double-click on those new relationship lines and put in a **lag of seven days**. The network logic diagram should now look similar to Figure 23.34. Go back to the **Bar chart view** and reschedule the project (F9). You now see the three areas offset by the seven days as shown in Figure 23.35.

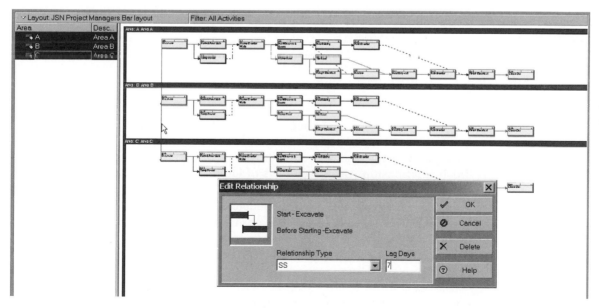

FIGURE 23.34 Network logic diagram showing the three areas

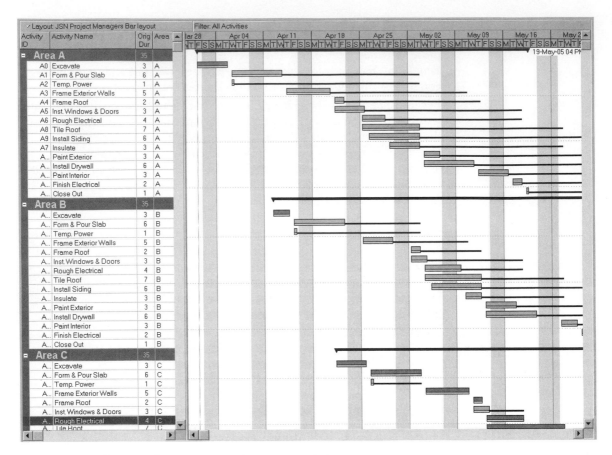

FIGURE 23.35   Three warehouse areas starting seven work days apart

Notice in Figure 23.35 the large amounts of float. That large amount of float may be realistic; however, you may want to punch out and finish each area as early as possible and get rid of the float. If you want to get rid of the float in each area put a **finish-to-finish relationship with seven days of lag** between **Close Out** in each area the same way you did the start-to-start relationships. Of course, after creating those relationships you need to recalculate the schedule. If you want the relationship arrows to show in the bar chart, turn on the relationship arrows by selecting the Relationship Lines button. Now the three areas look similar to Figure 23.36.

Print this report (#16) showing the project organized by the three areas, with other choices as you desire.

It is really better to crew load the schedule by restraining each activity, in each area by its same activity in the preceding area. This way, a delay by a crew will show the real effects down line in the project. This isn't that tough to do if you group the activities by subcontractor, select like crews with the Ctrl key, and use the Link tool (Edit,

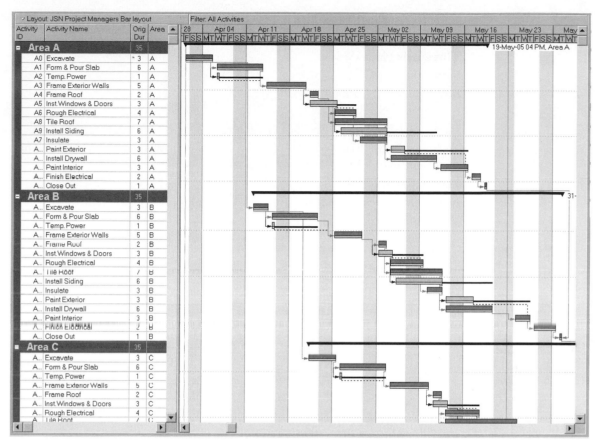

FIGURE 23.36   Three warehouse areas with less float

Link Activities) to create FS relationships between like crews. You do not need to do this right now, but remember this hint for future projects where it is desirous to crew load the project showing a crew going from one area of the project to another area. This ensures that a single crew will not be scheduled to be in two areas at the same time.

This gives you a good introduction to P3e/c Project Manager. There is still a lot more to know, but if you have developed the skills discussed in this chapter, they will be a great asset to help you control the project rather than letting the project control you. Don't feel you need to know everything, all at once. Use Project Manager by keeping it simple at first, taking one step at a time. Focus on the part that makes sense to you and if you can only input a basic schedule and print a basic, simple bar chart, that's good enough for a beginning. Learn more as you need it. As you keep with it for several months it will be a great asset to help you to plan, organize, direct, and control in order to safely build quality projects on time and within budget.

Contact Information

Primavera Systems, Inc.
Three Bala Plaza West
Suite 700
Bala Cynwyd, PA 19004

Phone: (610) 667-8600 or (800) 423-0245

Technical Help: (610) 667-8600 (You will need your serial number; locate it on the diskettes or CDs, or click on Help and About P3e/c

Fax: (610) 667-7894

E-mail: info@primavera.com

Web address: http://primavera.com

INDEX